HOW TO GET A JOB IN DALLAS/ FORT WORTH

THOMAS M. CAMDEN
RICHARD S. CITRIN, PH.D.

THE INSIDER'S GUIDE SERIES

Surrey Books
CHICAGO

HOW TO GET A JOB IN DALLAS/FORT WORTH

Published by Surrey Books, Inc., 230 E. Ohio St., Suite 120, Chicago, IL 60611. Telephone: (312) 751-7330.

This book is manufactured in the United States of America.
5th Edition. 1 2 3 4 5

Library of Congress Cataloging-in-Publication data:
Camden, Thomas M., 1938-
      How to get a job in Dallas/Fort Worth / Camden, Citrin. — 5th ed.
      420p. cm.
      Prepared by Thomas M. Camden and Richard S. Citrin.
      Citrin's name appears first on the 4th edition.
      Includes bibliographical references and index.
      ISBN 0-940625-78-4 (pbk.) : $15.95
      1. Job hunting—Texas—Dallas. 2. Job hunting—Texas—Fort Worth. 3. Job vacancies—Texas—Dallas. 4. Job vacancies—Texas—Fort Worth. 5. Professions—Texas—Dallas. 6. Professions—Texas—Fort Worth. 7. Occupations—Texas—Dallas. 8. Occupations—Texas—Fort Worth. 9. Dallas (Tex.)—Industries—Directories. 10. Fort Worth (Tex.)—Industries—Directories. I. Citrin, Richard. II. Title.
HF5382.75.U62T42 1994   93-46591
650.14'09764'2812—dc20   CIP

AVAILABLE TITLES IN THIS SERIES — $15.95

(*Pacific Rim* and *Europe* $17.95)

How To Get a Job in Atlanta by Thomas M. Camden, Diane C. Thomas, and Bill Osher, Ph.D.

How To Get a Job in Greater Boston by Thomas M. Camden and Paul S. Tanklefsky.

How To Get a Job in Chicago by Thomas M. Camden and Susan Schwartz.

How To Get a Job in Dallas/Fort Worth by Thomas M. Camden and Richard S. Citrin, Ph.D.

How To Get a Job in Europe by Robert Sanborn, Ed.D.

How To Get a Job in Houston by Thomas M. Camden and Robert Sanborn, Ed.D.

How To Get a Job in The New York Metropolitan Area by Thomas M. Camden and Joan Mark.

How To Get a Job in the Pacific Rim by Robert Sanborn, Ed.D., and Anderson Brandao.

How To Get a Job in The San Francisco Bay Area by Thomas M. Camden and Donald A. Casella, Ph.D.

How To Get a Job in Seattle/Portland by Thomas M. Camden and Robert W. Thirsk, Ed.D.

How To Get a Job in Southern California by Thomas M. Camden and Jonathan Palmer.

How To Get a Job in Washington, DC, by Thomas M. Camden and Kathy Strawser.

Single copies may be ordered directly from the publisher. Send check or money order for book price plus $3.50 for first book and $1.50 for each additional book to cover insurance, shipping, and handling to Surrey Books at the above address. For quantity discounts, please contact the publisher.

Editorial production by Bookcrafters, Inc., Chicago.
Cover design by Hughes Design, Chicago.
Typesetting by On Track Graphics, Chicago.
"How To Get a Job Series" is distributed to the trade by Publishers Group West.

Acknowledgments

The authors would like to thank the following people for their help: Publisher Susan Schwartz; Managing Editor Gene DeRoin; Editorial Assistant Michael Stoeger; Researcher Nancy Myers; and Art Director Sally Hughes. Special appreciation goes to Project Coordinator Rob Rainey who provided new and useful insights into this revision. Nancy Bishop edited previous editions of this book and her efforts facilitated our work. Thanks also are due to Sheila Collins for her loyal support.

Note to Our Readers

We, the authors and editors, have made every effort to supply you with the most useful, up-to-date information available to help you find the job you want. Each name, address, and phone number has been verified by our staff of fact checkers. But offices move and people change jobs, so we urge you to call before you write, and write before you visit. And if you think we ought to include information on companies, organizations, or people that we've missed, please let us know.

The publisher, authors, and editors make no guarantee that the employers listed in this book have jobs available.

JOB HUNTING?
THESE BOOKS, COVERING 10 MAJOR MARKETS PLUS EUROPE & THE PACIFIC RIM, CAN HELP.

HOW...
to get the job you want: Each book gives you more than 1,500 major employers, numbers to call, and people to contact.

WHERE...
to get the job you want: How to research the local job market and meet the people who hire.

PLUS...
how to use: Local networks and professional organizations; advice on employment services; how to sell yourself in the interview; writing power resumes and cover letters; hundreds of names and numbers, many available nowhere else!

FOR EASIER ORDERING CALL 1-800-326-4430

Please send the following at $15.95 each ("PACIFIC RIM" and "EUROPE" $17.95)

___HOW TO GET A JOB IN ATLANTA
___HOW TO GET A JOB IN BOSTON
___HOW TO GET A JOB IN CHICAGO
___HOW TO GET A JOB IN DALLAS/FORT WORTH
___HOW TO GET A JOB IN EUROPE
___HOW TO GET A JOB IN HOUSTON
___HOW TO GET A JOB IN NEW YORK
___HOW TO GET A JOB IN THE PACIFIC RIM
___HOW TO GET A JOB IN SAN FRANCISCO
___HOW TO GET A JOB IN SEATTLE/PORTLAND
___HOW TO GET A JOB IN SOUTHERN CALIFORNIA
___HOW TO GET A JOB IN WASHINGTON, D.C.

Name_____
Address_____
City_____State _____Zip_____
Enclosed is my check/money order for $_____
AmEx/Visa/MasterCard #_____ Exp Date _____
Signature_____

Send check or money order, and include $3.00 for first book and $1.50 for each additional book to cover insurance, shipping and handling to:
Surrey Books, 230 E. Ohio St., Suite 120, Chicago, IL 60611
Or call toll-free: 1-800-326-4430
Allow 4–6 weeks for delivery. Satisfaction guaranteed or your money back.

CONTENTS

v

3 Writing a Resume That Works

Page 33

The resume—what it is, what it can and cannot do for you. The basics of a good resume. Useful resume formats. Books on resume writing. Pros and cons of hiring someone else to write your resume. Firms that prepare resumes: what they cost, how to evaluate them. Sample resumes. How to write cover letters with samples.

4 Researching the Dallas/ Fort Worth Job Market

Page 53

The importance of doing your homework. The local library business section, the best friend a job hunter ever had. Locations and phone numbers of local libraries. How to conduct a computer job search. The Big Four directories and how they can help you. Dozens of other directories that might come in handy. Dallas/Fort Worth area newspapers and how to use them. Pros and cons of answering want ads. Business magazines. Job-hunt-related publications. Trade and special interest magazines—how to use them. Listing of trade magazines with editorial offices in the Dallas/Fort Worth area. General interest magazines and newspapers. Telephone job banks.

5 Developing a Strategy: The ABCs of Networking

Page 79

The importance of having a job-search strategy. How long will it take to find a job? Tried and true advice about nurturing your ego. Establishing a job-hunting schedule. Networking—the key to a successful job search. The exploratory interview. Developing professional contacts. How to keep yourself organized. How to identify and contact hiring authorities. Scenarios for landing an interview. Books on job-hunting strategy. A unique list of selected Dallas/Fort Worth area networks, professional organizations, trade groups, clubs, and societies, with descriptions, contacts, and phone numbers. Informal networking at favorite watering holes of various professions. Network groups for women.

6 Using Professional Employment Services
Page 116

Employment agencies—what they can and cannot do for you, how they charge, where to check up on them. Listing of Dallas/Fort Worth employment agencies and their specialties. Career consultants; some words to the wise and questions to ask before retaining one. Executive search firms—how they operate, pros and cons; selected list. Social service and government employment agencies.

7 How To Succeed In an Interview
Page 132

Formal and informal interviews and how to prepare for them. Mastering the five-minute resume. The interview as a sales presentation. Steps to a successful interview. What interviewers look for. Handling the interview. Making sure you get your own questions answered. What to do following the interview. Books on interviewing. How to use your references.

8 What To Do If Money Gets Tight
Page 143

Reviewing your assets and liabilites. Pros and cons of part-time and temporary work. List of selected sources for part-time work. Books on part-time and flexible employment. If you need further help: government assistance and social service agencies. How to use the Texas Employment Commission. How to sign up for unemployment benefits. Additional sources of help, providing everything from money management counseling to emergency food and clothing.

9 Where To Turn If Your Confidence Wilts
Page 155

How to deal with being fired. Recognizing stress signals. Guidelines for seeking professional counseling or therapy. Selected counseling centers and institutions that offer therapy and support—costs and programs. Career transition issues.

How To Get the Most from This Book

So you want to get a job in the Dallas/Fort Worth area? Well, you've picked up the right book. Whether you're a recent graduate, new in town, or an old hand at the great Texas Job Search; whether or not you're currently employed; even if you're not fully convinced that you are employable—this book is crammed with helpful information.

It contains the combined wisdom of two top professionals: Dr. Richard Citrin, a psychologist and career development specialist who has been practicing in Dallas/Fort Worth for over 10 years, and Tom Camden, a personnel professional who currently heads the nationally known consulting firm of Camden and Associates.

Tom contributes expert advice on both basic and advanced job-search techniques, from how to write a resume to suggestions for racking up extra points in an employment interview. Richard shares his knowledge of Dallas/Fort Worth's employment scene, developed through his years as a psychologist at Texas Christian University as well as his contacts with the scores of career hunters and job changers he has helped over the years at the IATREIA Institute.

Whether you're looking for a job in the city or the suburbs, his extensive listings will save you hours of research time.

Dozens of other metro-area insiders have contributed tips, warnings, jokes, and observations in candid, behind-the-scenes interviews. We've done our level best to pack more useful information between these covers than you'll find anywhere else.

We would love to guarantee that this book is the only resource you will need to find the job of your dreams, but we are not miracle workers. This is a handbook, not a Bible. There's just no getting around the fact that finding work takes work. You are the only person who can land the job you want.

What we can do—and, we certainly hope, have done—is to make the work of job hunting in Dallas/Fort Worth easier and more enjoyable for you. We have racked our brains, and those of many others, to provide you with the most extensive collection of local resources in print.

To get the most from this book, first browse through the Table of Contents. Acquaint yourself with each chapter's major features, see what appeals to you, and turn to the sections that interest you the most.

It may not be necessary or useful for you to read this book from cover to cover. If you're currently employed, for example, you can probably skip Chapter 8—"What To Do If Money Gets Tight." If you have no interest in using a professional employment service, you'll only need to browse through Chapter 6.

There are certain parts of this book, however, that no one should overlook. One of them is Chapter 4—"Researching the Dallas/Fort Worth Job Market." Unless you're a professional librarian, we'd bet money that you won't be able to read this chapter without discovering at least a few resources that you never knew existed. We've tried to make it as easy as possible for you to get the inside information that can put you over the top in an employment interview.

Chapter 5 is another Don't Miss—especially our unique listing of organizations that you should know about to develop your network of professional contacts. We strongly suggest that you read Chapter 7, even if you think you already know all about how to handle an interview. And then, of course, there's Chapter 11—listings of the Dallas/Fort Worth area's top 1,500 employers of white-collar workers.

There's another thing you should know about in order to get the most from this book. Every chapter, even the ones you don't think you need to read, contains at least one helpful hint or insider interview that is set off from the main text. Take some time to browse through them. They contain valuable nuggets of information and many tips that you won't find anywhere else.

Keep in mind that no one book can do it all for you. While we've touched on the basic tasks of any job search—self-analysis, developing a resume, researching the job market, figuring out a strategy, generating leads, interviewing, and selecting the right job—we don't have space to go into great detail on each and every one of them. What we have done is to supply suggestions for further reading. Smart users of this book will follow those suggestions when they need to know more about a particular subject.

Dallas/Fort Worth in the Mid-1990s

What's the economic outlook for the metropolitan area over the next decade? We would love to be able to look into our crystal ball and tell you exactly what jobs have the most promising future, but it's not that easy.

As the population of the Dallas-Fort Worth Metroplex expands to over four million people in 1994, the economy appears to be stable and growing in a way that provides a bright and promising future to all who live here. Employment expanded at around 2-3% in 1993, and the area added close to 40,000 new jobs during the year.

The manufacturing sector continues to provide a rich source of employment for the area, especially in the telecommunications business. Despite cutbacks in military spending, manufacturing is expected to grow at a modest rate. As with other parts of the nation, the service sector is the fastest growing employment area with a rate of 3-4%. In the Dallas-Fort Worth area, a growing employment picture is occurring in both the utility and transportation sectors.

Dallas/Fort Worth is still one of the top choices for corporate relocators. Articles in business publications such as *Fortune* magazine and *Investor's Business Daily* reported that Dallas is considered the top U.S. business city, with over 2,000 new companies having made Dallas their home. A look on the map will tell you why. By making a quick drive to the centrally located Dallas/Fort Worth International Airport, you can board a plane and be anywhere in the U.S. in a matter of three hours or less.

Companies such as J.C. Penney, GTE Corp., and Fujitsu have relocated their national headquarters to the area, citing these other advantages: the area's central time zone, inexpensive office space, moderately priced housing, and favorable tax rates. J.C. Penney Chairman William Howell said, "When you start putting 1,400 pins on a map and six major catalog distribution centers, it makes your mind focus on the reality that the logical place to be with today's modern communication and transportation is somewhere in the center."

According to the Greater Dallas Chamber of Commerce's Dallas Partnership Group, Dallas, the eighth most populous city in the U.S., ranks fourth in the number of industrial and service companies located there. The Dallas/Fort Worth Metroplex is the ninth largest in the country. Thirty-one Fortune 500 companies call the Metroplex home, with twenty-six of them residing in Dallas County.

North Dallas' high-tech corridor, sometimes referred to as the "Telecom Corridor," represents a major structural change in the city's economy. Over 500 companies are located in this North Dallas area. Despite some setbacks, the defense industry remains strong in North Texas, with many area companies holding major contracts. The biggest government contract holder is Texas Instruments, with Lockheed, Bell Helicopter, E-Systems, and Rockwell International also receiving substantial government business.

Fort Worth is home to a strong base of entrepreneurial spirit. It was recently named the best city in the country to start a business. Despite facing the challenges of cutbacks in the defense industry at Lockheed and the realignment of Carswell Air Force Base, Fort

Worth is well on the way to realigning its economic position. Fort Worth as a city offers stable neighborhoods, a solid working class population, a network of parks with total acreage second only to Chicago, and it was recently named an All-American City. By the way, rush hour traffic is rare in Fort Worth.

While there are still many inherent differences between buttoned-down, cosmopolitan Dallas and Fort Worth, which still bills itself as the "Place Where the West Begins," Fort Worth has many industrial as well as cultural attractions, with three of Texas' top art museums, a ballet company, opera, and symphony. Downtown's Sundance Square, developed by the Bass Family, has created a national model for revitalizing downtowns and is attracting commercial, retail, and residential investors to see this unique blend of Western "can do."

Fort Worth's largest employers are American Airlines, Lockheed, Delta Airlines, and of course Tandy Corporation, the parent company of Radio Shack and the "INCREDIBLE UNIVERSE" super electronics stores. Fort Worth's economic base is a diversified blend of aerospace, high-tech research and development, corporate management, manufacturing, and commercial activities.

The Fort Worth metropolitan area is ranked tenth among cities in manufacturing job growth. It has drawn such major businesses as Burlington-Northern, Motorola, and the United States Department of Treasury Currency Plant. Future growth is expected to be buoyed by the Alliance Airport located in North Fort Worth, the nation's first industrial airport, which is expected to generate 5,000 jobs in the next couple of decades.

Many of the area's suburban cities have become more than bedroom communities. They've become employment centers for many major companies. Arlington led the way in the 1950s by attracting General Motors. The drive to broaden the business base in suburban cities has continued on a grand scale with Las Colinas, a mini-downtown built near D/FW Airport, which is home to Kimberly-Clark, Exxon Corp., GTE Corp., and the Dallas Communications Complex.

The Metroport cities of Haslet, Roanoke, Keller, Southwest-Westlake, Grapevine, and Colleyville have become attractive places for major companies. IBM moved many employees from Las Colinas to a 900-acre office and retail park in Westlake/Southlake. Northeast Tarrant County is considered an economic hot spot because of its proximity to D/FW and Alliance airports.

Are there downsides to the economic situation in Dallas-Fort Worth? Of course, there are. No one can project when business may go sour or when a company may lose a big contract. Far and away, however, the greatest strength in this region of the country is the people who live here. North Texans are honest, hard working, and firmly committed to providing the best quality of life possible for their families.

Need Help Finding Your Way Around the Dallas/Fort Worth Area?

Keep in mind that most Dallas/Fort Worth residents depend on their cars to get around the 1,748-square-mile metropolitan area. And there's a good reason why. Public transportation is available and has improved, but in some areas, especially the suburbs, service is slow and limited.

If you plan to be in the area for several days, your best bet is to rent a car. Automobile rental companies are available in and around the Dallas/Fort Worth International Airport and Love Field.

Dallas has beefed up its DART scheduled bus service in recent years. If you're downtown, however, don't think you're seeing things if a blue bus painted to look like a bunny pulls up. In fact, you might also see a red kangaroo bus or a green frog bus. It's one of the Hop-A-Buses that makes frequent runs around major hotels and businesses. Call **(214) 979-1111** to find out bus routes and when and where the bus is scheduled to run. The schedule varies during weekdays and on weekends.

Depending on the route, bus service in the Dallas area is available from 5:45 a.m. to midnight Monday through Sunday, although the buses run less frequently on Sunday. You'll have a much easier time catching a bus during peak weekday business hours than on weekends or in the evening. And be sure to allow plenty of time to get from one destination to another.

If you live in a suburban area not served by a bus route, you can call **(214) 742-2688** 24 hours in advance and a van will pick you up and take you to the nearest terminal. The charge is $1.75 each way.

For Fort Worth-area bus service, call The "T," **(817) 871-6200**, which operates from 4:47 a.m. to 12:10 a.m. Monday through Saturday and from 8:00 a.m. to 7:30 p.m. Sunday. An airport shuttle service is provided. Pickups are made at major downtown hotels, and a park-and-ride service, Airporter, is located at 1000 Weatherford St.

Other airport shuttle services include the Super Shuttle, which provides door-to-door service: call **(817) 329-2000.**

Major taxi companies include Taxi Dallas (214) 823-3950, State Taxicab Co. (214) 371-0777, Republic Taxi (214) 631-5544, Richardson Cab Company (214) 235-3500, American Cab Co. (817) 332-1919, and Yellow Checker Cab (817) 534-5555.

Chambers of Commerce

Most major chambers of commerce have published material that is especially helpful to newcomers or anyone who wants to be better informed about the Dallas/Fort Worth area. These brochures and maps are available free or for a nominal charge and provide much of what you want to know about area businesses, city services, transportation, public schools, utilities, and entertainment.

If you have a question that is not answered in one of the publications, ask one of the Chamber's representatives. The two largest chambers in the area are:

Greater Dallas Chamber
Newcomers Information Department
1201 Elm St., Suite 2000
Dallas, TX 75270
(214) 746-6700 or 746-6600
For an orientation to Dallas, check out the newcomer's packet. It includes a Dallas Housing/New Resident Guide, a Dallas street map, Greater Dallas Business Guide, Newcomers and Relocation Journal, and other materials for a $14.91 fee that covers postage and handling. The Chamber also helps entrepreneurs with a source book called "How to Start a Business in the City of Dallas." This book costs $19.24, including postage and handling. Ask the Chamber for its list of other resource materials that can be picked up at the main office downtown or mailed. Booklets are available on everything from the top 100 companies to foreign-owned companies in the Dallas/Fort Worth area.

Fort Worth Chamber of Commerce
777 Taylor St., Suite 900
Fort Worth, TX 76102
(817) 336-2491
Ask for the free newcomer's packet, which includes a booklet and map to help you find out more about Fort Worth. You can pick up this information at the downtown office or request that it be mailed to you free of charge. If you want information about starting a business or have questions about existing companies, check with the Economic Development Department. The Chamber's information department publishes many helpful booklets and guides, including *Major Employers Directory*, and informative material on major employers and manufacturers.

OTHER CHAMBERS OF COMMERCE

Addison Chamber of Commerce: (214) 416-6600
Allen Chamber of Commerce: (214) 727-5585
Arlington Chamber of Commerce: (817) 275-2613
Balch Springs Chamber of Commerce: (214) 557-0988
Benbrook Area Chamber of Commerce: (817) 249-4451
Burleson Area Chamber of Commerce: (817) 295-6121
Carrolton Chamber of Commerce: (214) 416-6000
Cedar Hill Chamber of Commerce: (214) 291-7817
Colleyville Area Chamber of Commerce: (817) 488-7148
The Colony Chamber of Commerce: (214) 625-4916
Coppell Chamber of Commerce: (214) 393-2828
Crowley Chamber of Commerce: (817) 297-4211
Dallas Black Chamber of Commerce: (214) 421-5200
Dallas Hispanic Chamber of Commerce: (214) 637-2420
Decatur Chamber of Commerce: (817) 627-3107 (previously Southwest
   Wise Chamber of Commerce)
Denton Chamber of Commerce: (817) 382-9693
DeSoto Chamber of Commerce: (214) 224-3565
Duncanville Chamber of Commerce: (214) 298-6128
East Dallas Chamber of Commerce: (214) 368-6000
Everman Chamber of Commerce: (817) 293-3957
Farmer's Branch Chamber of Commerce: (214) 416-6600
Forest Hill Chamber of Commerce: (817) 535-7057
Fort Worth Hispanic Chamber of Commerce: (817) 625-5411 (Minority
   Procurement Program: (817) 625-4331)
Fort Worth Jaycees: (817) 336-0696

Fort Worth Metro. Black Chamber of Commerce: (817) 531-8510
French American Chamber of Commerce: (214) 821-7475
Garland Chamber of Commerce: (214) 272-7551
Grand Prairie Chamber of Commerce: (214) 264-1558
Grapevine Chamber of Commerce: Metro (817) 481-1522
Hurst-Euless-Bedford Chamber of Commerce: (817) 283-1521 (metro: (817) 267-5111)
Hutchins Chamber of Commerce: (214) 225-8850
Irving Chamber of Commerce: (214) 252-8484
Keller Chamber of Commerce: (817) 431-2169
Kennedale Chamber of Commerce: (817) 483-6794
Lakewood Chamber of Commerce: (214) 827-8921
Lake Worth Area Chamber of Commerce: (817) 237-0060
Lancaster Chamber of Commerce: (214) 227-2579
Mansfield Chamber of Commerce: (817) 473-0507
Mesquite Chamber of Commerce: (214) 285-0211
Metrocrest Chamber of Commerce: (214) 416-6600 (Includes Northwest Dallas)
North Dallas Chamber of Commerce: (214) 368-6485
Northeast Tarrant County Chamber of Commerce: (817) 281-9376
Oak Cliff Chamber of Commerce: (214) 943-4567
Plano Chamber of Commerce: (214) 424-7547
Red Oak Chamber of Commerce: (214) 617-0906
Richardson Chamber of Commerce: (214) 234-4141
Roanoke Chamber of Commerce: (817) 491-1222
Rockwall Chamber of Commerce: (214) 771-5733
Saginaw Chamber of Commerce: (817) 232-0500
Seagoville Chamber of Commerce: (214) 287-5184
Southeast Dallas Chamber of Commerce: (214) 398-9590
Southlake Chamber of Commerce: Metro (817) 481-8200
White Settlement Chamber of Commerce: (817) 246-1121

What If Your Company Transfers You

Imagine how lost and confused most people feel when their company first transfers them to the Dallas/Fort Worth area. They take a look at the two major cities and dozens of suburbs and wonder: Where's the best place to live? Where should I enroll my kids in school? And what about job prospects for my spouse?

Anyone who has experienced the nightmare of moving from one house to another can imagine the dread that fills those facing major relocation from one part of the country to another. But if they're moving to Dallas/Fort Worth they're lucky, because **The Relocation Center** is available to help the transition. With Relocation Centers in Las Colinas, Fort Worth, and Richardson, the independently owned enterprise, founded thirteen years ago by Larry Powers has become a valued ally of corporations anxious to make employee relocation a happy experience. The Center is located in The Central Tower at Williams Square, 5215 N. O'Connor Blvd., Suite 1750, Irving, Texas.

Visitors entering The Center are met with striking photos that depict the type of lifestyles available in the Dallas/Fort Worth area and soothing colors that open up a relaxed environment. Trained relocation consultants are available to counsel with families to determine the type of housing in which they are interested, as well as the location, information about schools, and needs such as special education and more.

Because housing is a primary need, The Center provides extensive information on all the options available. Families can easily find what homes, apartments, townhouses, or condominiums are available in the area as well as their cost. A media library provides access to local newspapers and lifestyle magazines and is equipped with tables and telephones for convenience.

The Center also assists transferee spouses who are beginning a job search. They can browse through employment guides, including this one, and watch a videotape on how to conduct a successful job hunt. For individual career counseling, The Relocation Center refers people to career counselors and consultants in the Dallas/Fort Worth area.

The Center provides a free education guide that lists basic information about area school districts, such as the tax rate, student/teacher ratio, talented and gifted program, special education services, and teacher pay scale. The Center also provides information about the National Child Care Association Services that provides referrals to day-care centers and offers suggestions on how to evaluate them.

To make an appointment for the free service, contact The Relocation Center at these locations: Dallas, (800) 477-3131 or (214) 869-3131. In Fort Worth call (800) 299-3131 or (817) 332-3131, and in Richardson call (800) 256-3131 or (214) 497-9191.

Establishing an Objective: How To Discover What You Want to Do

One of the most common mistakes job seekers make is not establishing an objective before beginning the job search. Practically everyone wants a job that provides personal satisfaction, growth, good salary and benefits, prestige, and a desirable location. But unless you have a more specific idea of the kind of work you want, you probably won't find it. You wouldn't take off on your big annual vacation without a clear destination in mind. As David Campbell puts it, "If you don't know where you're headed, you'll probably wind up somewhere else."

Many of our readers already have a clear objective in mind. You may want a job as a systems analyst, paralegal, sales manager, or any of a thousand other occupations. The *Dictionary of Occupational Titles,* available at your public library, lists 25,000 jobs! If you know what you're looking for, you're to be commended because establishing an objective is a necessary first step in any successful job search.

Discovering Your Aptitudes

The world of work requires you to have an understanding of the degree to which you desire to work with people, data, or things as well as an appreciation for the aptitudes you possess. Each job requires a certain degree of aptitude or skill in order to do the work successfully. Knowledge of your particular aptitudes is essential if you are going to find real satisfaction in your chosen career. An aptitude battery can be administered by either a career counselor or the guidance department of an area college. The typical aptitudes assessed are:

Intelligence—the ability to think critically, to reason logically and analytically, to understand complex and abstract ideas. This is essential to the successful mastery of any job. The more demanding the job or career, the higher the intelligence level required.

Verbal—the ability to understand and use language effectively in both writing and speaking. Required of individuals who aspire to careers where persuasion, interaction, and communication with others is important.

Numerical—the ability to understand and use advanced mathematical concepts and operations. Especially important in career fields such as engineering, accounting, and finance.

Spatial—the ability to visualize forms and objects clearly in your "mind's eye" without actually seeing them in real life, to be able to "see" the inside of an object, flip it around, open it up all in your mind's eye. A critical ability for architects, engineers, physical scientists, construction workers, surgeons, and dentists.

Form Perception—the ability to spot quickly and easily pertinent details or information in objects, pictures, charts, or graphs.

Clerical Perception—the ability to spot quickly and easily pertinent details or information in written or printed materials.

Motor Coordination—the ability to coordinate your eyes, hands, and fingers quickly and accurately to perform a function or task. Important in careers like music, skilled crafts, jewelry, and electronic repair, and assembly work.

Finger Dexterity—the ability to move your fingers quickly and accurately to perform some function or task.

Manual Dexterity—the ability to move your hands quickly and accurately to perform a function or task.

Mechanical Reasoning—the ability to understand mechanical principles and applications related to skilled crafts and trades.

Getting Involved

No matter what you decide to pursue, there will be some degree of involvement with other people, and therefore it is important for you to determine to what extent you want to interact with others on the job—high, medium, or low people involvement.

High People Involvement—A high involvement level means you prefer to be very much involved with people in your day to day activities at work. This could mean being in a position of authority where you are responsible for the work of others. You might be in a teaching position, possibly a counselor or in sales.

Moderate People Involvement—A moderate level of people involvement means you are interested in working with people on a regular basis as part of your job but not to the extent as indicated above. This might mean working as an assistant to a professional or manager and helping them solve their problems.

Low People Involvement—At this level of involvement, you would prefer only a minimal degree of contact with people as a regular aspect of your job.

To some extent all jobs require a certain amount of dealing with things such as tools, machinery, typewriters, computers, copy machines, and telephones. To what extent—low, medium, or high—do you desire to work with things and use your hands to manipulate things on the job?

Low Involvement with Things—This would mean you have little desire to use your hands and work with tools or machinery in your occupation.

Moderate Involvement with Things—At this level of involvement, you would not mind using some equipment or tools to perform your job as long as it did not represent a major aspect of your day to day activity.

High Involvement with Things—A high level of involvement indicates that you prefer your job to center around the use of your hands and/or tools and machinery in your daily activity.

Every occupation requires some degree of data handling and manipulation. Determine to what extent you want to work with data—high, medium, or low involvement.

High Data Involvement—This would mean that you prefer to be extensively involved in analyzing and interpreting information and data on a regular basis.

Medium Data Involvement—This level of involvement indicates a willingness to compile and use data and information in your work, but you would prefer not to be involved in higher levels of analysis.

Low Data Involvement—At this level you would prefer to have little involvement in the collection and use of data in your work environment.

Do a Self-Appraisal

Even if you have an objective, you can benefit from a thorough self-appraisal. What follows is a list of highly personal questions designed to provide you with insights you may never have considered and to help you answer the Big Question, "What do I want to do."

To get the most from this exercise, you must write out your answers. Writing out your responses to these questions forces you to consider carefully the kind of person you are and what values and priorities you hold. You can always change your priorities later, but by putting them down on paper, you have a great beginning. Give yourself the benefit of responding to these questions over several days or a week-long time period. By allowing yourself time to complete the exercise, you won't feel rushed and will give your career and job search the attention it deserves. By the way, by carefully

11

completing this exercise, you will find that you've made a great start on your resume!—a subject we'll discuss in more detail in the next chapter.

When you've completed the exercise, consider sharing your responses with a trusted friend, loved one, or a mentor. Ask these people to listen to your answers and not to criticize your responses. After you've shared your responses, ask them to respond to the questions as they see you, and tape record their answers. Although we think we know ourselves, we seldom have the objectivity to see ourselves clearly. By obtaining "friendly feedback," we can begin to evaluate our history and ourselves.

Remember to take your time—maybe just answering one question a day—but do so in an honest and forthright manner. And, of course, there are no right or wrong answers.

Questions About Me

1. What is my personality like? Am I outgoing, prefer being with people or more of a loner? How well disciplined am I? Am I quick tempered or easygoing? Am I self-motivated or do I need to be jump-started? How sensitive am I to other people's needs?
2. What kind of problem solver am I? Do I tend to take a conventional, practical approach to problems, or am I more of an imaginative, experimental type person? Am I a leader or a follower? Do I feel challenged by problems, or do I prefer more routine activities that tend to keep life easy and regular?
3. Do I prefer working with people, data, or things, and to what extent—low, moderate, or high.
4. What is my philosophy of life? And how does work enter into my philosophy?
5. How important is it for me to be in charge of the work of other people?
6. What are my most important life achievements to date?
7. Where do I want to live and work? (choose a part of the country, or world, and when you've selected an area, identify how far you want to live from your work place)
8. What role does money play in my value system? What is the minimum amount of money I want to make from work? What is the maximum I'd like to make?
9. Is my career the center of my life or just a part of it? Where does my family fit in? How does my career impact them?
10. What are my main interests?
11. What do I enjoy most in life?
12. What displeases me most?
13. To what extent do I like working with my hands and using various tools or operating equipment?

Questions About Your Job

1. Beginning with your most recent employment and then working back toward school graduation, describe in detail each job you had. Include your title, company, responsibilities, salary, achievements and successes, failures, and reason for leaving. (If you're

a recent college graduate and have little or no career-related work experience, you may find it helpful to consider your collegiate experience.)

2. How would you change anything in your job history if you could?
3. In your career thus far, what responsibilities have you enjoyed most and least? Why?
4. What kind of job do you think would be a perfect match for your talents and interests?
5. What responsibilities do you want to avoid?
6. How hard are you really prepared to work?
7. If you want the top job in your field, are you prepared to pay the price?
8. What have your subordinates thought about you as a boss? As a person?
9. What have your superiors thought about you as an employee? As a person?
10. Can your work make you happier? Should it?
11. If you have been fired from any job, what was the reason?
12. How long do you want to work before retirement?

Your answers to these highly personal questions should help you to see more clearly who you are, what you want, what your gifts are, and what you realistically have to offer. They should also reveal what you don't want and what you can't do. It's important to evaluate any objective you're considering in light of your answers to these questions. If a prospective employer knew nothing about you except your answers to these questions, would he think your career objective was realistic?

People who are entering the job market for the first time, those who have been working for one company for many years, and those who are considering a career change need more help in determining their objectives. If you're still in college, be sure to take advantage of the free counseling and career planning services that are available on most campuses. Vocational analysis, also known as career planning or life planning, is much too broad a subject to try to cover here. But we can refer you to some excellent books.

CAREER STRATEGY BOOKS

Baldwin, Eleanor. *300 Ways to Get a Better Job*. Holbrook, MA: Bob Adams, Inc., 1991.

Ball, Ben. *Manage Your Career: A Self Help Guide to Career Choice/ Change*. Oakland, CA: Beckman Publishers, 1989.

Bastress, Frances. *Relocating Spouse's Guide to Employment,* 3rd ed. Chevy Chase, MD: Woodley Publications, 1989.

Baxter, Rogene, and Marcelle Brashear. *Do It Yourself Career Kit: A Career Planning Tool*. Maraga, CA: Bridgewater Press, 1990.

Beatty, Richard H. *The Complete Job Search Book*. New York: John Wiley & Sons, 1988.

Boldt, Lawrence. *Zen and the Art of Making a Living*. New York: Penguin Books, 1993.

Bolles, Richard N. *The Three Boxes of Life and How to Get Out of Them*. Berkeley, CA: Ten Speed Press, 1983.

Bolles, Richard N. *What Color Is Your Parachute?* Berkeley, CA: Ten Speed Press, 1994. The Bible for job hunters and career changers, this book is revised every year but is so full of career-hunting details that it can be overwhelming for the person in need of quick practical information. Of particular usefulness is the companion booklet, "The Quick Job Hunt Map," which takes the reader through a more practical series of exercises for career hunting and job changing.

Camden, Thomas M. *The Job Hunter's Final Exam.* Chicago: Surrey Books, 1990.

Ciabattari, Jane. *Winning Moves: How to Come Out Ahead in a Corporate Shakeout.* New York: Rawson Associates, 1988.

Dubin, Judith A., and Melonie R. Keveles. *Fired for Success.* New York: Warner Books, 1990.

Harkavy, Michael. *One Hundred One Careers: A Guide to the Fastest Growing Opportunities.* New York: John Wiley & Sons, 1990.

Hirsch, Arlene S. *Careers Checklists.* Lincolnwood, IL: National Textbook, 1990.

Jackson, Tom. *Guerrilla Tactics in the Job Market.* New York: Bantam Books, 1991. Filled with unconventional but effective suggestions.

Kastre, M., N. Rodriguez-Kastre, and A. Edwards. *The Minority Career Guide.* Princeton, NJ: Peterson's Guides, 1993.

Kennedy, Joyce Lane, and Darryl Laramore. *Joyce Lane Kennedy's Career Book.* Lincolnwood: VGM Career Horizons, 1993.

Kleiman, Carol. *The 100 Best Jobs for the 1990s & Beyond.* Chicago: Dearborn Financial Publishing, 1992.

Jones, Lawrence K. *The Encyclopedia of Career Change and Work Issues.* Phoenix: Orax Press, 1992.

Lee, Patricia. *The Complete Guide to Job Sharing.* New York: Walker, 1983.

Mendenhall, Karen. *Making the Most of the Temporary Job Market.* Cincinnati, Ohio: Betterway Books, 1993.

Morin, William J., and James C. Cabrera. *Parting Company: How to Survive the Loss of a Job and Find Another Successfully.* San Diego, CA: HBJ, 1991.

Noble, John. *The Job Search Handbook.* Boston: Bob Adams, Inc., 1988.

Pederson, Laura. *Street Smart Career Guide.* New York: Crown, 1993.

Rushlow, Ed. *Get a Better Job.* Princeton, NJ: Peterson's Guides, 1990.

Wood, Orrin G. *Your Hidden Assets—The Key to Getting Executive Jobs.* Homewood, IL: Dow Jones-Irwin, 1984. Written by the co-founder of a job-changing workshop developed for Harvard Business School alumni; an upscale book.

If you're still in **college** or have recently graduated, the following books will be of particular interest:

Asher, Donald. *From College to Career: Entry Level Resumes for any Major.* Berkeley, CA: Ten Speed Press, 1992.

Briggs, James I. *The Berkeley Guide to Employment for New College Graduates.* Berkeley, CA: Ten Speed Press, 1984.

Gonyea, James C. *Career Selector 2001.* Hauppauge, NY: Barron's, 1993.

Krannich, Ronald L. *Careering & Re-Careering for the 1990's: The Complete Guide to Planning Your Future.* Manassas, VA: Impact Publications, 1989.

La Fevre, John L. *How You Really Get Hired: The Inside Story from a College Recruiter,* 2nd ed. New York: Prentice Hall, 1989.

Osher, Bill, and Sioux Henley Campbell. *The Blue Chip Graduate: A Four Year College Plan for Career Success.* Atlanta: Peachtree Publishers, Ltd., 1987.

Tener, Elizabeth. *Smith College Guide: How to Find and Manage Your First Job.* New York: Pflume, 1991.

For those of you involved in a **mid-life career change,** here are some books that might prove helpful:

Falvey, Jack. *What's Next? Career Strategies After 35.* Charlottesville, VT: Williamson Publishing Co., 1987.

Holloway, Diane, and Nancy Bishop. *Before You Say "I Quit": A Guide to Making Successful Job Transitions.* New York: Collier Books, 1990.

Jeoperson-Anthony, Rebecca, and Gerald Roe. *Over 40 and Looking for Work.* Holbrook. MA: Bob Adams Inc., 1991.

Krannich, Ronald L. *The Educator's Guide to Alternative Jobs and Careers.* Woodbridge, VA: Impact Publications, 1991.

Morgan, John S. *Getting a Job After 50.* Blue Ridge Summit, PA: TAB Books, 1990.

Nyman, Keith D. *Re-Entry: How to Turn Your Military Experience into Civilian Success,* 2nd ed., expanded. Harrisburg, PA: Stockpole Books, 1990.

Otterbourg, Robert. *Its Never Too Late.* New York: Barron's, 1993.

Wolfer, Karen, and Richard G. Wong. *The Outplacement Solution: Getting the Right Job after Mergers, Takeovers, Layoffs, and Other Corporate Chaos.* New York: Wiley, 1988.

For workers who are nearing **retirement age** or have already reached it, here are some books that might be useful:

Danna, Jo. *Starting Over: You in the New Workplace.* Brairwood, NY: Palomino Press, 1990.

Harty, Karen Herkstra. *50 and Starting Over: Career Strategies for Success.* N. Hollywood, CA: Newcastle Pub. Co., 1991.

Strasser, Stephen, and John Sena. *Transitions: Successful Strategies from Mid-Career to Retirement.* Hawthorne, NJ: Career Press, 1990.

And for **handicapped** job seekers, these titles could prove helpful:

Lewis, Adele, and Edith Marks. *Job Hunting for the Disabled.* Woodbury, NY: Barron's, 1983.

Pocket Guide to Federal Help for Individuals with Disabilities. Clearinghouse on the Handicapped. Washington, DC: U.S. Department of Education, 1989.

Witt, Melanie. *Job Strategies for People with Disabilities.* Princeton, NJ: Peterson's Guides, 1992.

For **women** in the work force, these titles will be of interest:

Berryman, Sue E. *Routes Into the Mainstream: Career Choices of Woman & Minorities.* Columbus, OH: Cts. Educational Training Employment, 1988.

Hunter, Janet. *The Smart Woman's Guide to Career Success.* Hawthorne, NJ: Career Press, 1993.

Koltnow, Emily, and Lynne S. Dumas. *Congratulations! You've Been Fired: Sound Advice for Women Who've Been Terminated, Pink-Slipped, Downsized, or Otherwise Unemployed.* New York: Fawcett Columbine, 1990.

How to Get a Job

Morrow, Jodie B., and Myrna Lebov. *Not Just a Secretary: Using the Job to Get Ahead.* New York: Wiley Press, 1984.

Nivens, Beatrice. *The Black Woman's Career Guide.* New York: Anchor Books, 1987.

Shields, Cyndney and Leslie Shields. *Work Sister Work.* New York: Birch Lane Press, 1993.

Thompson, Charlotte E. *Single Solutions—An Essential Guide for the Single Career Woman.* Boston: Branden Pub. Co., 1990.

Wyse, Lois. *The Six-Figure Woman (and How to Be One).* New York: Linden Press, 1984. How to break into top corporate management.

Tips from career counselors for area newcomers

Many of the same job-hunting principles apply no matter if you're looking for a job in Dallas/Fort Worth, Los Angeles, or New York. But to really stand out in the local job market, here are some tips from career counselors. These will be especially helpful as you begin your job marketing campaign, particularly if you're a newcomer:

Dr. Jon Crook, IATREIA/Outpath Institute: "Spend some time assessing your skills so you know what you can do: solve problems, reorganize to cut costs, create new markets. A candidate really impresses an employer when he or she can name their skills clearly and apply them specifically to the company's needs."

Taunee Besson, Career Dimensions: "People who come here and want to find work quickly locate the pivotal individuals in their fields. I've known people who have come to Dallas and in an afternoon get the whole place scoped out. Dallas has some well-established networks, and if you can plug into one of the networks, you can piggyback on it and get around to people you need to talk to.

"People who have similar interests enjoy helping each other out. Look up the local branch of a fraternal organization, sorority, or alumni club, or get involved in church. The fastest way to get plugged in is to get together with people of like minds. Those who are good at networking are going to be more successful."

Eleanor Baldwin of Hour Savers Career Service believes that the "womb to the tomb job is long gone." Contemporary job hunting moves from "project to project," and she encourages action on the individual's part. "When you see the ceiling cracking, you don't stand around waiting for the beams to fall." A consultant to the Texas Employment Commission, Baldwin often lectures to what she terms "stress professionals," suggesting they see "job hunting as theater."

William Helton, an Arlington psychologist:
"Organize in your mind the career areas which
especially appeal to you. Then actively develop
your own network as you participate in a number
of information interviews. Don't hesitate to ask
for names and referrals, and follow up on all
possible leads. The Dallas-Fort Worth Metroplex
has many people who will attempt to be helpful
in your quest for information." ■

Professional Career Analysis

It would be great if there were some vocational assessment that
would confirm without a doubt who you are and precisely what job,
career, or field best suits you. Unfortunately, there isn't. Professionals in vocational planning have literally dozens of tests at their
disposal designed to assess personality and aptitude for particular
careers.

There are basically two approaches to career assessment. The
first measures interests, values, and skills. A variety of assessment
tests evaluate these qualities and provide useful information for the
career changer. This kind of assessment helps answer the questions,
"What do I like to do? What do I believe in? and What have I
developed some measure of expertise in?" These are vitally important questions since many people find that if they are doing what
they enjoy and what is consistent with their beliefs and experiences,
they will do well, excel, and have fun.

The second career assessment method measures aptitudes. Aptitudes are natural abilities in which you excel. These assessments
may measure abilities ranging from manual dexterity to visual
conceptualization (useful for interior design, for example). These
types of assessments help answer the question, "What am I naturally good at?"

Remember that while it's important to engage in work that you
have natural abilities in, many job skills are learned, developed, and
refined in the work setting. It is therefore most important to do work
that you **enjoy**. With the pleasure thus derived, you will find that
your skill development increases.

The test most commonly used is probably the Strong-Campbell
Interest Inventory (SCII). This multiple-choice test takes about an
hour to administer and is scored by machine. The SCII has been
around since 1933. The most recent revision, in 1981, made a serious
and generally successful attempt to eliminate sex bias, and to
introduce a theoretical orientation to career assessment.

The SCII offers information about an individual's interests on
three different levels. First, the test provides a general statement
about the test-taker's interest patterns. These patterns suggest not
only promising occupations but also characteristics of the most
compatible work environments and personality traits affecting work.

Second, the test reports how interested a person is in a specific
work activity compared with other men and women who also completed the SCII. Finally, the occupational scales compare the test-
taker with satisfied workers in some 90 different occupations. If you

17

think you'd enjoy being a librarian, for example, you can compare yourself with other librarians and see how similar your likes and dislikes are. The occupational scales indicate how likely you are to be satisfied with the choice of a particular occupation.

Personality/vocational tests come in a variety of formats. Many are multiple choice; some require you to finish incomplete sentences; others are autobiographical questionnaires. No single test should ever be used as an absolute. Personality tests are important in evaluating your personal style and how well you might enjoy the work environment as well as for generating discussion and for providing data that can be used in making judgments.

In the Dallas/Fort Worth area, vocational guidance and testing are available from a variety of sources. The most comprehensive service is generally provided by private career counselors and career consultants. Their approaches and specialties vary greatly. Some primarily provide testing while others also offer long-term programs that include counseling, resume writing, preparing for the job interview, and developing a job marketing campaign. Fees usually range from $50 to several thousand dollars.

It's best to find a professional who specializes in the type of vocational help you need. You don't want to spend thousands of dollars on long-term consulting when you only need several coaching sessions and tests. On the other hand, if you've had a history of employment problems or are feeling paralyzed in your job search, it is probably well to talk to a career counselor who is also qualified to conduct personal counseling.

The list that follows gives you some idea of what counselors and consultants offer. Telephone these professionals to find out whether their services fit your needs. Although the terms are often used interchangeably, there is a difference between a *career counselor and consultant*. Most professionals can use the title counselor or psychologist only if they have fulfilled educational and professional requirements determined by the State of Texas in order to become a Licensed Psychologist or a Licensed Professional Counselor.

In Texas, you can no longer provide career services without a license. Professionals who aren't licensed often call themselves career consultants and are able to work only under contract to corporations. This field attracts people from a wide variety of backgrounds, education, and levels of competency. That's why it's important to talk to people who have used the service you are considering, and check with the Better Business Bureau to find out if any complaints have been lodged against them.

Because career counseling and consulting firms are private, for-profit businesses with high overhead costs, they usually charge more for testing than local community colleges or social service agencies. A fuller discussion of services offered by career consultants is provided in Chapter 6. Also in Chapter 6 is a list of social service agencies, some of which offer vocational testing.

CAREER COUNSELORS AND CONSULTANTS

Achievement Specialists: IATREIA/Outpath Institute
1152 Country Club Lane
Fort Worth, TX 76112
(817) 654-9600
Contact: Richard Citrin, Ph.D., or Robert Rainey, M.A.
Full service consulting and counseling with knowledgeable experts with
Fortune 100 corporate experience. Help in development of specific career
options for individuals and groups. Program includes in-depth vocational
assessment, marketing plan development, resume preparation, interviewing training utilizing video-taped simulations, job-search skills, and
salary negotiations.

The **Outpath Job Search Club** meets weekly on Thursday evenings.
This is a cost-effective group program conducted by one of our principals.
New groups begin each month. There is a nominal one-time enrollment
fee of $40. Program fees are: 12 weeks - $375, 6 weeks - $215. Initial
exploratory session - $50. Particular expertise in working with mid-life
career changers, displaced middle managers who are seeking new career
options, executives over age 50, and individuals interested in starting
small businesses. Secretarial support provided for resume and job-search
correspondence. Free initial 30-minute consult by appointment with one
of our principals.

AIMS
12160 Abrams Rd., Suite 314, Lock Box 19
Dallas, TX 75243
(214) 234-8378
Non-profit research organization offering battery of tests to determine
what career will be most satisfying according to aptitude. Works with all
adults, college and high school students to help determine long-term
career and educational goals. Fee: $525 for three half-day sessions that
include counseling and evaluation.

Douglas Bellamy, Ed.D., Psychologist
12900 Preston Rd., 717 North Dallas Bank Tower
Dallas, TX 75230
(214) 404-8888
Individualized program that includes psychological testing to determine
which careers are most likely to fit one's values, interests, personality
characteristics, and aptitudes. Career alternatives explored; job-search
strategies developed; and assistance and guidance in implementation,
including resume writing during counseling sessions. Usually one to six
sessions at $80 per hour.

Martin Birnbach & Associates dba/CATS (Career Advisory Team Services)
15150 Preston Rd., Suite 300
Dallas, TX 75248
(214) 490-JOBS
One-on-one career counseling teaches Pro-Active Job Searching. Teaches
how to identify the perfect job and career and then how to pursue the
right company. How to get an interview and how to ask for the job. Fees
vary. Martin is host of KLIF Radio's "Jobs and Careers" show and NBC
Channel 5's news team "Career Choices."

Dr. Tim Branaman
600 W. Campbell Rd., Suite 2

Richardson, TX 75080 or
650 S. Edmonds
Lewisville, TX 76040
(214) 669-1266
Career counseling, testing, and evaluation. Assistance provided for many
different needs, including graduating college students, management and
sales professionals, and women in transition. Fees vary.

Career Action Associates
12655 N. Central Expwy., Suite 512
Dallas, TX 75243
Fort Worth (817) 926-9941
Contact: Rebecca Hayes, Licensed Professional Counselor
Provides full-service career assistance, including assessment, resume
writing, developing job-hunting strategies, interviewing, and networking.
Career/life planning, vocational assessment, and vocational rehabilitation for disabled workers also available. Special help provided for college
students and high school students entering the job market. Also conducts
career/life-planning seminars. Fee: $80 an hour.

Career Design Associates
2818 Country Club Rd.
Garland, TX 75043
(214) 278-4701
Contact: Dr. Helen Harkness
Comprehensive program for career planning and resources for focusing,
restructuring, or changing careers. Two programs are available: Career
Change—one-year retainer required for program designed to include
personal and extensive video taping, testing, career information/re-
sources, and complete job-hunting techniques; Career Reappraisal—
three-to-four-month program focusing on career assessment and information. Prices vary according to need but range from $1,500 to $4,900 with
monthly pay-out available. First discussion is free. Client references
provided.

Career Dimensions
6330 LBJ Frwy., Suite 136
Dallas, TX 75240
(214) 239-1399
Contact: Taunee Besson
Full-service career and life-planning program that includes a self-
directed job search with emphasis on self-assessment, resume writing,
job interviewing, researching job market, networking, salary negotiation.
Offers special help to newcomers, career changers, and international
transfers. Spouse network. Publishes free "Dimensions Associates"
newsletter. Fee: $50 for exploratory session, $100 per hour for counseling, and $600 for 20-hour small-group program.

Career Focus Associates
1700 Coit Rd., Suite 220
Plano, TX 75075
(214) 596-1233
Contact: Jackie Statman
Comprehensive services for teens through seniors that include 4-12-week
programs for career self-assessment with a strong focus on transferable
skills, personality strengths, and personal values/priorities. Writing of
"high-profile" resumes and effective cover letters. Skill training for

information and career position interviews, job-finding strategies, and negotiating salary offers. Fees vary.

Career Management Resources
222 W. Las Colinas Blvd., Suite 2114
Irving, TX 75039
(214) 556-0786
Contact: Mary Holdcroft, Licensed Professional Counselor
Comprehensive career counseling service, including testing, skill assessment, resume preparation, and interviewing techniques. Identification of potential employers, networking, and introductions provided. Specialize in spouse relocation assistance, outplacement, individual career management, career/life planning, and facilitating successful career changes. Secretarial support provided, including resumes and job-search correspondence. Fees vary.

Dr. Carrell Chadwell
3500 Oak Lawn, Suite 400
Dallas, TX 75219
(214) 526-3505
Contact: Carrell Chadwell, Ph.D.
Individualized career evaluation, testing, and counseling. Generally 2 to 6 sessions. Fees vary.

Corporate Dynamics
511 E. Carpenter Freeway, Suite 270
Irving, TX 75062
(214) 869-2470
Contact: Richard Poth
In-depth personal assessment and career counseling for the professional engaged in reevaluation of career and life direction. Individualized programs include assessment, counseling, resume writing, videotaping mock job interviews, researching the job market, and support throughout the job campaign. Fees vary.

Creative Career Counseling
703 Shadywood Lane
Richardson, TX 75080
(214) 235-4689
Contact: Joan Youngblood, M.A.
Customized counseling process designed for career changers, work-reality-shocked graduates, reentry homemakers, people who have lost a job, and others who are recareering. The program enables clients to define occupational direction, create a quantified, accomplishment resume, and connect with career resources: Fee: Sliding scale based on income.

Cross Roads Career Consultants
The Metroplex Affiliate of The Five O'Clock Club
222 W. Las Colinas Blvd., Suite 2114
Irving, TX 75039
(214) 432-1935
Contact: Linda Davidson
Managerial, professional, and executive job-search group with professional counselors. Meet weekly on Monday evenings. With the counselor and group input you learn The Five O'Clock Club method, set definite job targets and make contacts that lead to employment. Fee 10 sessions - $350, 5 sessions $200, and $60 one-time fee. Sample session - $40.

How to Get a Job

Metroplex Affiliate career consultants are available for private coaching on issues such as solving current job problems, preparing your resume, and enabling career change. Fee: $75 per hour.

Darlene Davis & Associates
5909 Luther Lane, Suite 1400
Dallas, TX 75225
(214) 363-5169
Contact: Darlene Davis
Offers complete career counseling, testing and assessment for all disciplines through senior executive, including our proprietary Strategic Career Mapping used to develop a career path based on each client's unique personal profile and characteristics. Programs include a five-week group Career Workshop series and individual private counseling for Strategic and Tactical Job Search Career Guidance. "Making It On My Own Again" is a twelve-week course specifically designed for those who have been displaced by a divorce, widowed, or reentering the work force after a prolonged absence. Fees vary.

Carol Duncan Enterprises
North Dallas Bank Tower
12900 Preston Rd., Suite 500
Dallas, TX 75230
(214) 385-1130
Contact: Carol Duncan, a Licensed Career Counselor
Custom-designed program to fit individual needs. Included with career counseling is lifestyle planning, individual assessment through self-identity, job opportunities, resume writing, interview skills, salary negotiations, and follow-up support. Specialties include assisting people with a major career change, transitional counseling, helping women return to the workforce, and assisting graduating college students to develop strategies for their career and lifestyle. Fee: $60 per hour.

William Helton and Associates
Fielder Professional Park
721 N. Fielder Rd., Suite C
Arlington, TX 76012
(817) 460-5831
Contact: William M. Helton, Ph.D.
Offers career and life planning counseling, which emphasize assisting people in identifying their "essence"—those activities which naturally create a sense of satisfaction. A series of personal interviews is intertwined with an individualized battery of tests on personality, values, interests, and abilities to reveal future career and leisure options that can lead to a balanced life.

Hour Savers Career Services
(214) 349-2992
Contact: Eleanor Baldwin
Package deal includes resume, improving job-hunting skills, and interviewing techniques. Also offers career workshops, outplacements, career and employment consultations, corporate outplacements, and public speaking on employment issues. Fee: $99-$259.

22

How to market yourself

Rob Rainey of the IATREIA/Outpath Institute in Fort Worth advises job seekers to think of themselves as a product about to be reintroduced to the market as the "new and improved version."

"Position yourself as the solution to a potential employer's problem. Most other candidates will be looking for a job and focusing on their own needs. The smart candidate will show the buyer (employer) what's in it for him. Take time to think about your special features and benefits so that when asked, 'why should I hire you?' by an employer, you'll be prepared to list all the things you can do that will make money, save money, or improve the quality of the organization in a way the employer does not have the time or ability to do on his own." ■

Johnson O'Connor Research Foundation
4950 N. O'Connor Blvd., Suite 250
Irving, TX 75062
(214) 541-0650
Metro (214) 791-0330
Contacts: Wendy Finan, Bill Stroud, or Bill Claunch
National non-profit educational organization that tests aptitude during three sessions. Interpretation of results helps clients make vocational and educational decisions. Fee: $450, which includes an additional counseling session within the first year after initial testing.

Professional Counseling Services
1221 Abrams Rd., Suite 227
Dallas, TX 75081
(214) 699-0774
Contact: Peggy Donohue, M.A., C.P.C., N.C.C.
Offers vocational testing plus interest skills and personality inventories to help clients prepare for a career or the job hunt. Help with resume preparation and job interviewing techniques can be utilized. Marketing and job-search strategies; job opportunities are explored. Fees: Negotiable.

Rehabilitation Services Associates
Dallas/Fort Worth Regional Office
3505 Turtle Creek Blvd., Suite 312
Dallas, TX 75219-9800
(214) 520-9800
Contact: Robert Boudreaux, Carol Bennett, or Susan Laszynski
Assists the general public and persons with medical restrictions by providing counseling, vocational assessment, labor market information, job-seeking skills, and job placement. Comprehensive program includes analyzing work history, helping clients in job-seeking skills, resume writing, labor market surveys to identify openings in entry-level positions. Fee: $85 an hour.

Richland College Career Assessment Services
12800 Abrams Rd.
Dallas, TX 75243-2199

How to Get a Job

(214) 238-6020
Contact: Peggy J. Davis, Ph.D.
Offers a Career Center designed for the adult professional in the business community who is dealing with issues surrounding career planning and changes. Serves all adults within the Dallas business community.

Margaret Thompson
3813 Crestwood Ter.
Fort Worth, TX 76107
(817) 626-7023
Contact: Margaret Thompson, Licensed Professional Counselor
Vocational testing and career assessments are primary services. Most appointments are scheduled on Saturday. Fee: Averages $300 for five hours of tests, report, and follow-up conference.

Dr. Jerry Weiss
6750 Hillcrest Plaza Dr., Suite 308
Dallas, TX 75230
(214) 458-8111
Offers a scientifically developed program that uses particular interests, aptitudes, skills, and personality to help people choose the career path that fits them. The two-step program begins with an assessment and then offers information about choosing the right career and pursuing it through job-hunting techniques, resume hints, and interviewing techniques. Fees vary.

**Who's good?
Who's not?**

A listing in this book does not constitute an endorsement of any consulting firm, search firm, or employment agency. Before embarking on a lengthy or expensive series of tests, try to get the opinion of one or more people who have already used the service you're considering.

In Texas, employment agencies and career consultants who charge individuals a fee for finding jobs must be licensed by the Texas Department of Labor. No license is required if the employer pays the cost. If you want to find out if a firm has a license, call the State of Texas, Department of Licensing and Regulation, Licensing Division, (817) 261-3800 or 1-800-252-8026.

Before hiring professional services, check with the Better Business Bureau. It's also a good idea to check with the City of Dallas Action Center or State Attorney General's office to find out if any complaints have been filed there. You can call, write, or drop by those offices for information.

Better Business Bureau of Metropolitan Dallas
2001 Bryan Tower, Suite 850
Dallas, TX 75201
(214) 220-2000

Better Business Bureau of Tarrant County
1612 Summit Ave., Suite 260
Fort Worth, TX 76102
(817) 332-7585

Action Center City of Dallas
1500 Marilla St. C2/1N
Dallas, TX 75201
(214) 744-3600

State Attorney General
714 Jackson, Suite 800
Dallas, TX 75202
Toll free (214) 263-2685 ■

What To Expect from a Career Counselor

What kind of help can you expect from a career counselor that you can't find on your own?

The first thing you'd probably notice is that a counselor really listens to you. They are trained to understand, not to judge. You may find yourself being more candid with a counselor after 30 minutes than you would be with a friend you've know for 30 years. The result of this type of interaction is that you're likely to end up knowing yourself better.

While counselors are trained to understand and support you, they are not there simply to stroke your ego. Your mother or best friend might agree with your plan to change from sales to engineering. A counselor might point out that you've never managed to pass a course in mathematics.

A counselor will understand that career planning is an ongoing lifelong process that manifests itself differently in the various stages of human development that each of us must negotiate. It is a very different thing to hunt for a job at ages 21, 41, and 61. Tests aren't the whole answer, but they can be a part of the answer. Counselors know how to interpret tests.

Career counselors aren't locked in to outmoded job-search strategies. They can give you ideas on how to make more contacts, write a better resume, and interview with impact. They can spot where your approach needs beefing up more readily than a non-professional.

For most people, a job search is a demanding, if not downright stressful time. A counselor can provide both emotional support and expert advice. Career counselors and consultants provide many different types of services. When you're looking for professional help, make sure you find someone who can best meet your needs.

Career counselor Mary Holdcroft, who heads up Career Management Resources, suggests that individuals ask these questions when checking out services:

1. What type of individuals does the counselor work with most often?

2. What services are provided?
3. Does the counselor help focus on career selections, including research sources?
4. Does the counselor provide development and implementation of a job-search plan?
5. For newcomers to the area, how quickly can the plan be implemented?

Job Help for Women

"Conducting a job search requires a stronger, more aggressive approach through learning tools and techniques that help job seekers stand out from their competition, which is vital in today's changing job market," said Paula Pryor, employment services director of **The Women's Center of Tarrant County.**

The Women's Center offers numerous programs to help people identify new employment opportunities. The Center's Jobs Now Program is a good place to begin because it's designed to help people improve job-search skills to find employment in a fairly short time. Programs start every three weeks. Anyone participating in the program can use their job bank, containing an average of over 4,000 current job openings each month.

Extra help is provided through the Center's Mentors Network, offering women an opportunity to receive advice from people in their field. Mentors are available from a variety of professions, ranging from fast-food managers, attorneys, and construction workers to hairdressers.

Other programs are designed to meet a variety of needs. Employment counseling may be sought by some who want special help, and others will want to check on self-sufficiency assistance for low-income mothers, a long-term training and employment program.

"We provide a positive atmosphere and empower women and their families to gain control over their lives and improve the quality of their lives," Pryor said.

The employment services are provided free of charge and are available to men as well as women. About 20 percent of the participants are men. The Center is located at 1723 Hemphill St., Fort Worth, TX 76110, (817) 927-4050.

Here are five additional resource centers mainly oriented toward assisting women in job searches and counseling.

Adult Resource Center
Richland College
Crockett Hall, First Floor
12800 Abrams Rd.
Dallas, TX 75243
(214) 238-6034 or
(214) 238-6331
Special personal and employment counseling provided free of charge to low-income single parents. Referrals are made to special courses and programs at the community college.

Explore
Dallas County Phone: (214) 783-6665

Tarrant County Phone: (817) 861-4454
All-volunteer, non-profit organization that offers eight-week seminars for women who want to boost their self-esteem, grow professionally, and find ways to accomplish their goals.

Woman's Center in Richardson
515 Custer Rd.
Richardson, TX 75080
(214) 238-9516
Variety of free programs, sessions on finding potential, considering lifework planning, and preparing for the job hunt. Three-part program includes doing a vocational self-assessment, teaching job-search skills, and exploring crossroads. When requested in advance, child care is provided for program participants.

Women's Center of Dallas
3505 Turtle Creek Blvd.
Dallas, TX 75219
(214) 821-8388
Mainly an advocacy program that sponsors special programs throughout the year on employment-related topics.

YWCA Women's Resource Center
4621 Ross Ave.
Dallas, TX 75204
(214) 821-9595
Employment services available at the YWCA's headquarters at 4621 Ross Ave. and at six branches in Dallas County. Services include individual career counseling, testing, job banks, support groups, quarterly YWCA breakfasts, and bimonthly lunches with networking opportunities and guest speakers. The YWCA's Explore course is offered in the spring and fall. The self-discovery program includes eight sessions at several Dallas County locations.

Colleges Offering Vocational Testing and Guidance

Students don't often realize how much help is available through college and university career and placement centers. At several area community colleges, non-students can benefit as well. Several of the Dallas County Community College District campuses have extended services to assist everyone, whether or not they are enrolled. The extent of assistance varies from campus to campus.

Many of the colleges and universities offer non-credit and credit courses as well as special lectures and seminars to help individuals prepare for the job hunt and explore options in the work world. In recent years, schools also have offered more practical courses that are designed to help individuals acquire job skills or brush up on ones they already have.

Current or prospective students can also see what's available at career centers to help them plan what to do after graduation. By getting on track early, students can avoid the frustration of taking the wrong courses. After graduation, many colleges and universities continue to work with alumni through the placement office and in career centers.

How to Get a Job

Check with each school to find out what's available and who is eligible for assistance. Here's a list of area colleges offering vocational help and a description of basic services:

COLLEGES WITH VOCATIONAL PROGRAMS

Brookhaven College
3939 Valley View Lane
Farmers Branch, TX 75244
(214) 620-4830
Free counseling and testing for students enrolled in at least one credit course. Computer job bank located in the placement office. Credit and non-credit courses, seminars, and workshops assist individuals in many phases of career exploration. Adult center provides career symposiums, support programs, and resources for individuals, including single parents, displaced homemakers, and women returning to work. Call (214) 620-4849 for subsidized child-care information.

Cedar Valley College
3030 N. Dallas Ave.
Lancaster, TX 75134
(214) 372-8262
Free counseling on academic level. Testing fees apply to non-students. Employment service for students and alumni and prospective students. Computerized job listings. Human development credit courses assist individuals making career decisions.

Eastfield College
3737 Motley Dr.
Mesquite, TX 75150
(214) 324-7039
Career Planning and Placement Center offers free career counseling and testing for students and former students of the Dallas County Community College District. Career counseling and testing available for non-students through the Continuing Education Office. Fees are based upon testing (People Place/Adult Resource Center, (214) 324-7113). District computer job bank and employment listings available to students and former students. Career and job fair scheduled every April, along with employment seminars and other special programs.

EL Centro College
Main and Lamar Sts.
Dallas, TX 75202
(214) 746-2415
Free career testing and counseling for students. Non-students pay fees for tests ranging from $5 to $25. Employment openings listed in computer job bank and on the career center bulletin board. Numerous references and books available in the Career Resource Center. Human development courses offered on career planning and exploration.

Mountain View College
4849 W. Illinois Ave.
Dallas, TX 75211
(214) 333-8606
Free testing for currently enrolled students and prospective students; $40 for non-students. Counseling and the Career Center's job bank are free and available to students and alumni.

28

North Lake College
5001 N. MacArthur Blvd.
Irving, TX 75062
(214) 659-5210
Academic advisement, career counseling, and educational planning are available free of charge for currently enrolled students at Career Planning and Placement Center. Testing available through a human development course. Counseling center has resource library and computer services for students and non-students. Job Placement Center assists alumni and students enrolled in credit and non-credit courses with job placement through a computerized job bank. Call Center for Returning Adults at (214) 659-5373 about brown-bag luncheons that are open to the public.

Richland College
12800 Abrams Rd.
Dallas, TX 75243
(214) 238-6986
Free career counseling and testing for currently enrolled students. The Career Resource Library has hundreds of resources on career planning, occupational research, and employment skill development. It also houses the student job placement computerized system and other computer-aided systems. The Career Resource Library is available free of charge to currently enrolled and former Richland College students. An educational and career-planning course is available through the Continuing Education Office. Career assessment services are offered to Dallas Community residents for a small fee, which includes career counseling and career assessment tests. Special help provided in the Adult Resource Center to low-income single parents.

Southern Methodist University
131 Strong Hall, 3315 Daniel
Dallas, TX 75275
(214) 768-2797
Services offered free to students and to alumni during two years after graduation. Other alumni pay $50 charge for six-month counseling and testing service. Computerized self-assessment program prepares individuals for exploring career options. Career Center offers individual and group counseling and information about job openings.

Tarrant County Junior College—Northeast Campus
828 Harwood Rd.
Hurst, TX 76054
(817) 788-6661
Free career counseling, testing, and placement for currently enrolled students and former students. $10 fee for applying for admission to service. SIGI computer program assists in making vocational choices. Non-students assisted through community college courses and spring job fair.

Tarrant County Junior College—Northwest Campus
4801 Marine Creek Pkwy.
Fort Worth, TX 76179
(817) 232-7788
Counseling and Career Placement Center offers free standard vocational tests and counseling for students and alumni. Also assists in helping locate part-time, seasonal, and full-time work. Special services provided

How to Get a Job

for the handicapped. Students meet with professionals in their field through the Rotary Club Career Counseling Program.

Tarrant County Junior College—South Campus
5301 Campus Dr.
Fort Worth, TX 76119
(817) 531-4551
Comprehensive Career Planning and Placement Center. Some career and job search resources available to public. Career counseling for current, former, and prospective students. Special course in career planning for women in transition.

Texas Christian University
Career Planning and Placement Center
2800 S. University Dr., 220 Student Center
Fort Worth, TX 76129
(817) 921-7860
The Career Planning and Placement Center offers a full range of free testing, counseling, and placement services for students and alumni. Special programs include videotaping mock job interviews, career fairs and summer job fairs, as well as more than 40 workshops on all aspects of employment. Assistance in self-assessment and decision-making provided by a computerized program. Job listings for students and alumni are published weekly in "The Career Connection" bulletin. Subscribers pay a minimal fee for postage.

Texas Wesleyan University
1201 Wesleyan St.
Fort Worth, TX 76105
Metro (817) 429-7104 or (817) 531-4432
Counseling and Testing Center provides free testing for currently enrolled students; alumni pay a fee for testing. Special help offered to those who are undecided about a major, going through a career change, or want to pursue additional graduate studies. Placement office regularly updates job listings on bulletin board, sponsors job fairs, and sets up interviews with employers for graduating seniors.

University of Texas at Arlington
703 W. Nedderman Dr.
Arlington, TX 76019-0156
(817) 273-3671
The Office of Counseling and Career Development assists current UTA students and graduates with all phases of career exploration and development. Seminars cover resume writing, interviewing skills, and the job-search process. On-campus interviewing is conducted twice each year—spring and fall—for full-time professional positions. A weekly newsletter describing current, full-time job openings in the metroplex is available to new graduates and alumni registered for this service. A nominal fee is charged for use of these services. Student Employment Services assists currently enrolled students and their spouses with part-time, temporary, summer, internship, and co-op positions. UTA holds a campus-wide career fair each spring and participates in the Texas MBA Consortium, a "Hire-in" for MBA students from 21 Texas universities.

University of Texas at Dallas
2601 Floyd Rd.
Richardson, TX 75080
(214) 690-2943

Office of Career Planning and Placement offers career counseling, testing, and placement assistance for students and alumni. Nominal fees charged for registration and vocational tests. Computerized guidance information available. Special services include career development library, career information fairs, job-search seminars, and information about employers. Students and alumni are encouraged to bring resumes and attend job fairs during fall and spring semesters, along with the summer career fair. Job fairs are open to the public.

Thinking of Starting Your Own Small Business?

Many basic questions about starting your own small business can be answered by the U.S. Small Business Administration. The Dallas/ Fort Worth Regional office is located in Fort Worth at the address listed below. Professional staff at the facility are ready to help you evaluate your start-up requirements. You can obtain a free copy of the publication *Directory of Business Development,* which details the services of the SBA. Topics include everything from borrowing, recordkeeping, and marketing to managing employees. Specific documents and other material can be ordered from this publication at a nominal cost.

Basic questions can be answered over the phone, but you'll learn more by dropping by the main office to meet with staff members or volunteers from SCORE (Service Corps of Retired Executives). You'll be matched up with a retired professional in your field who can share information that will help you get started. Special help is offered to veterans, minorities, and women.

The SBA offers a free seminar on the third Saturday of every month at the Clarion Hotel located at 1241 Mockingbird Lane in Dallas. The seminar is open to the public but a reservation is advisable. Contact the SBA at the number listed below for more details.

Two excellent resources for help in establishing, setting up, and operating your small business are The Priest Institute in Dallas and the Automation & Robotics Research Institute (ARRI) located in Fort Worth.

The Priest Institute offers a two-hour free orientation seminar every Tuesday morning. During the seminar, each participant will be assessed as to their needs and assigned to a staff consultant or referred to the SBA or other outside consultants who can help. The Priest Institute works with established companies as well as start-up businesses. They also have extensive resources to help companies develop business contracts with local, state, and federal government agencies.

The Automation & Robotics Research Institute in Fort Worth is a joint effort with the Small Business Administration and others to enhance manufacturing competitiveness by transferring advanced technology and philosophy to small and medium-sized manufacturing firms. Actually any small firm interested in developing business with the federal government can take advantage of the help offered by ARRI. Advice and assistance about funding for a prototype product, information on potential government utilization of a product or service, and how to do business with the government are among the services offered by the ARRI staff.

More information can be obtained at the following offices.

Small Business Administration—Dallas/Fort Worth Regional Office
4300 Amon Carter Blvd., Suite 114
Forth Worth, TX 76155
Metro (817) 355-1933

The Bill J. Priest Institute for Economic Development
1402 Corinth St.
Dallas, TX 75215
(214) 556-5700
Contact: Vera Tanner

Automation & Robotics Research Institute
7300 Jack Newell Blvd. S.
Fort Worth, TX 76118
(817) 794-5965
Contact: Michele Y. Reed

Starting a small business takes courage

Ron Childs and Bob Wehr, both in their mid-40s and upper-level managers for a Dallas aerospace firm, were caught in a downsizing due to reduced government spending. With help from career counselor Rob Rainey of the IATREIA/Outpath Institute in Fort Worth, they assessed their background, experience, and contacts and after serious thought prepared a business plan.

They formed CW Aerotech in Arlington to market technically innovative products in the aviation industry. They also planned to broker European manufactured aviation parts in the United States as well as doing some consulting. The first nine months were the toughest, says Childs, "but once we got some momentum going we were in a reasonable profit position by the end of the first year."

Both Ron and Bob will tell you that starting and running your own small business takes tremendous courage, long hours, and a willingness to take risks. They also agree that working for themselves provides far more satisfaction than working for a large corporation. ∎

Writing a Resume That Works

Volumes have been written about how to write a resume. That's because, in our opinion, generations of job seekers have attached great importance to the creation and perfection of their resumes. Keep in mind that no one ever secured a job offer on the basis of a resume alone. The way to land a good position is to succeed in the employment interview. You have to convince a potential employer that you're the best person for the job. No piece of paper will do that for you.

The resume also goes by the name of *curriculum vitae* (the course of one's life), or *vita* (life) for short. These terms are a little misleading, however. A resume cannot possibly tell the story of your life, especially since, as a rule, it shouldn't be more than two pages long. The French word *résumé* means "a summing up." But in the American job market, a resume is a concise, written summary of your work experience, education, accomplishments, and personal background—the essentials an employer needs to evaluate your qualifications.

A resume is nothing more or less than a simple marketing tool, a print ad for yourself. It is sometimes useful in generating interviews. But it is most effective when kept in reserve until after you've met an employer in person. Sending a follow-up letter after the interview, along with your resume, reminds the interviewer of that wonderful person he or she met last Thursday.

The Basics of a Good Resume

The resume is nothing for you to agonize over. But since almost every employer will ask you for one at some point in the hiring process, make sure that yours is a good one.

What do we mean by a good resume? *First, be sure it's up to date and comprehensive.* At a minimum it should include your name, address, and phone number; a complete summary of your work experience; and an education profile. (College grads need not include their high school backgrounds.)

In general, your work experience should include the name, location, and dates of employment of every job you've held since leaving school, plus a summary of your responsibilities and, most important, your accomplishments on each job. If you're a recent graduate, or have held several jobs, you can present your experience chronologically. Begin with your present position and work backward to your first job. If you haven't had that many jobs, organize your resume to emphasize the skills you've acquired through experience. Other resume formats are also acceptable, as you will see later in this chapter.

A second rule of resume-writing is to *keep the resume concise.* Most employers are very busy and would prefer not to read more than two pages, but up to three pages is acceptable for someone with twenty or more years of experience. Remember, you cannot give your entire life history and include everything but the kitchen sink in your resume; yet you must be sure to include the most relevant aspects of your background.

It is okay to have more than one resume. Some of our clients have as many as three versions, each focused a little differently to appeal to different types of employers or industries. In most cases your resume will be scanned, not read in detail. Describe your experience in short, pithy phrases. Use action words to describe your accomplishments. Avoid large blocks of copy. Your resume should read more like a chart than a short story.

There are no hard and fast rules on what to include in your resume besides work experience and education. A statement of your objective and a personal section containing hobbies, marital status, and so on, are optional. An employer wants to know these things about you, but it's up to you whether to include them in your resume or bring them up during the interview. If you have served in the military, you ought to mention that in your resume.

Your salary history and references, however, should not be included in your resume; these should be discussed in person during the interview.

Keep in mind that a resume is a sales tool. Make sure that it illustrates your unique strengths in a style and format you can be comfortable with. Indicate any unusual responsibilities you've been given, or examples of how you've saved the company money or helped it grow. Include any special recognition of your ability. For example, if your salary increased substantially within a year or two, you might dramatize the increase by stating it in terms of a percentage.

Third, keep your resume honest. Never lie, exaggerate, embellish, or deceive. Tell the truth about your education, accomplishments, and work history. You needn't account for every single work day that elapsed between jobs, however. If you left one position on November 15 and began the next on February 1, you can minimize gaps by simply listing years worked instead of months.

Fourth, your resume should have a professional look. If you type it yourself or have it typed professionally, use a word processor or high-quality office typewriter with a plastic ribbon (sometimes called a "carbon" ribbon). Do not use a household or office typewriter with a cloth ribbon.

If your budget permits, consider having your resume typeset professionally on a computer. You then will have a choice of type faces, such as boldface, italics, and small caps. You can also request that the margins be justified (lined up evenly on both sides, although the marketing experts tell us it is best to left justify and allow a ragged right edge). If using a computer or word processor, have the final draft laser printed.

A benefit of storing your resume on disk is that updating is easy, and you can make quick changes to customize your resume for different applications.

Universal Resume Format

The following format will work for virtually all job seekers. But remember, there are no concrete rules in resume preparation. Modify this guide as necessary to make the most favorable impression.

NAME
Address, City, State, Zip
Phone

Job Objective: Vital piece of information. Many employers use as screening device or to signal job match; should grab attention and motivate employer to read further. If at all possible, the Objective should be tailored to the job you are seeking.

Employment: Place strongest of the two sections, Employment or Education, first. This is particularly important to the recent graduate especially if she or he graduated from one of the more prestigious schools such as Harvard. The more impressive your work history, the more prominently you should display it. Remember, what the employer is really buying is your experience.

List jobs in reverse chronological order, putting the most promotable facts—employer or job title—first.

Give functional description of job if work history is strong and supports job objective.

Accomplishments: The real proof of your value to a prospective employer is illustrated in your accomplishments. These are succinct statements of what you actually contributed to your current and former employers. Accomplishments are usually expressed in quantified terms, such as dollars or percentages. They typically follow each specific job and relate to your contributions to that employer. Here's an example of an accomplishment: "Successfully reduced direct manufacturing cost by $300,000.00 per year through the development and implementation of a new automated drying process."

Skills: You may embed these in the employment section. Put skills section first for career changers. Choose skills that are most relevant to job objective.

Give short statements to support skills. Make support statements results oriented. Position most marketable skills first and demonstrate their value to the prospective employer in your accomplishment statements.

Education: List in reverse chronological order, putting the most promotable facts—school or degree—first. Mention any honors or achievements, such as high GPA or Dean's List.

Miscellaneous: Call this section anything applicable—Interests, Activities, Accomplishments, or Achievements. Give only information that promotes your candidacy for the position you're applying for.

You can also include community service activities, which either enhance your work skills or would bring credit to the company.

References: Furnished upon request. Don't waste space on names and addresses. Keep them on a separate sheet. Employers know that this information will be furnished at an appropriate time.

Three Popular Resume Formats

There are a number of different methods for composing a quality resume. Every career counselor and resume compiler has his or her own favorite method and style. As the person being represented by the resume, you must choose the style and format that best suits and sells you. Many resume books will use different terms for the various styles. We will highlight the three most popular types.

1. **The chronological resume** is the traditional style, most often used in the workplace and job search; that does not mean it is the most effective. Positive aspects of the chronological resume include the traditionalist approach that employers may expect. It also can highlight past positions that you may wish your potential employer to notice. This resume is also very adaptable, with only the reverse chronological order of items as the essential ingredient.

2. **The functional resume** is most common among career changers, people reentering the job market after a lengthy absence, and those wishing to highlight aspects of their experience not related directly to employment. This resume ideally focuses on the many skills one has used at his or her employment and the accomplishments one has achieved. It shows a potential employer that you can do and have done a good job. What it doesn't highlight is where you have done it. The implicit danger of this format is that professional resume screeners have come to view this style with suspicion and wonder what the writer is trying to hide.

3. **The combination resume** combines the best features of a functional resume and a chronological resume. This allows job seekers to highlight skills and accomplishments while still maintaining the somewhat traditional format of reverse chronological order of positions held and organizations worked for.

No matter what format you use to prepare your resume, be sure to proofread it before sending it to the printer. A misspelled word or typing error reflects badly on you, even if it's not your fault. Read every word out loud, letter for letter and comma for comma. Get a friend to help you.

Sample resumes and cover letters appear at the end of this chapter.

Printing Your Resume

Do not make copies of your resume on a photocopy machine. Have it quick printed professionally. If it is on a disk, use a laser printer. The resume you leave behind after an interview or send ahead to obtain an interview may be photocopied several times, and copies of copies can be very hard to read.

You should also avoid such gimmicks as using colored paper (unless it's very light cream or light gray) or using a paper size other than 8½ x 11". A recent survey we conducted of our corporate clients indicated a preference for plain bright white paper followed by a light cream or ivory.

What NOT To Do with Your Resume Once You Have It Printed

Do not change your resume except to correct an obvious error. Everyone to whom you show the resume will have some suggestion for improving it: "Why didn't you tell 'em that you had a scholarship?" or "Wouldn't this look better in italics?" The time to consider those kinds of questions is before you go to the typesetter. Obviously, if you have saved your resume on a floppy disk, it will be easier to revise. Even then, it's probably not worth the trouble to make a lot of nitpicking changes. Remember, there is no such thing as a perfect resume. Except typographically. Also, it is okay to have more than one version, each containing slightly different aspects or slants of your background that may be important to potential employers in different industries.

A second point to remember: DO NOT send out a mass mailing. If you send letters to 1,000 company presidents, direct mail consultants tell us that you can expect a response of from 1 to 2 percent—and 95 percent of the responses will be negative. The shotgun approach is expensive; it takes time and costs money for postage and printing. You'll get much better results if you are selective about where you send your resume. We'll discuss this at greater length in Chapter 5. The important thing is to concentrate on known hiring authorities in whom you are interested.

Our purpose here is not to tell you how to prepare the ideal resume (there is no such thing), but rather to provide some general guidelines. The following books contain even more how-to information.

BOOKS ON RESUME WRITING & COVER LETTERS

Beatty, Richard. *The Perfect Cover Letter*. New York: John Wiley and Sons, 1989.

Bostwick, Burdette. *Resume Writing: A Comprehensive How-To-Do-It Guide*. New York: John Wiley and Sons, 1990.

Coxford, Lola M. *Resume Writing Made Easy for High Tech*. Scottsdale, AZ: Gorsuch Scarisbrick, 1987.

Eyler, David. *Resumes that Mean Business*. New York: Random House, 1993.

Fournier, Myra, and Jeffery Spin. *Encyclopedia of Job Winning Resumes*. Ridgefield CT: Round Lake Publishing, 1993.

Foxman, Loretta D. *Resumes That Work*. New York: John Wiley and Sons, 1989.

Jackson, Tom. *The Perfect Resume*. New York: Anchor/Doubleday, 1990.

Krannich, Ronald L., and Cheryl Rae Krannich. *Dynamite Resumes: 101 Great Examples and Tips for Success*. Manassas, VA: Impact Publications, 1992.

Lewis, Adele. *How to Write a Better Resume*. Woodbury, NY: Barron's Educational Series, 1989.

Nadler, Burton Jay. *Liberal Arts Power: How to Sell It on Your Resume*. Princeton, NJ: Peterson's Guides, 1989.

Parker, Yana. *Damn Good Resume Guide: 200 Damn Good Examples*. Berkeley: Ten Speed Press, 1988.

Rosenburg, Arthur, and David Hizer. *The Resume Handbook: How to Write Outstanding Resumes & Cover Letters for Every Situation.* Holbrook, MA: Bob Adams, 1990.

Tepper, Ron. *Power Resumes.* New York: John Wiley and Sons, 1992.

Yates, Martin. *Resumes that Knock 'em Dead.* Holbrook, MA: Bob Adams, 1988.

How to choose a professional

According to Darlene Davis, a Dallas Career Counselor, before engaging a professional to help you write your resume, run through the following checklist of questions.

What will it cost? Some firms charge a set fee. Others charge by the hour. Though many firms will not quote an exact price until they know the details of your situation, you should obtain minimum and maximum costs before you go ahead.

What does the price include? Does the fee cover only writing? Or does it include typesetting? Most firms will charge extra for printing.

What happens if you're not satisfied? Will the writer make changes you request? Will changes or corrections cost extra?

How do this writer's fees and experience stack up against others? It's wise to shop around before you buy writing services, just as you would when purchasing any other service.

Never allow a resume writer to sell you anything other than a standard bright white or pale ivory paper. Making your resume stand out by using unusual colors or textures is the kiss of death. Business people are conservative and expect an equally conservative but professional resume. The only exception to this rule is if you are in a glamor industry where the exception is expected. ■

Should You Hire Someone Else to Write Your Resume?

In general, if you have reasonable writing skills, it's better to prepare your own resume than to ask someone else to do it. If you write your own job history, you'll be better prepared to talk about it in the interview. "Boiler plate" resumes also tend to look and sound alike.

On the other hand, a professional resume writer can be objective about your background and serve as a sounding board on what you should and shouldn't include. You might also consider a professional if you have trouble writing in the condensed style that a good resume calls for.

Here is a list of area firms that will assist you in preparing your resume. Remember that a listing in this book does not constitute an endorsement. Before engaging a professional writer, ask for a recommendation from someone whose judgment you trust—a personnel director, college placement officer, or a knowledgeable friend. Check with the Better Business Bureau and other consumer advocates listed in Chapter 2 to see if there have been any complaints made about the resume service you are considering.

PROFESSIONAL RESUME PREPARERS

Achievement Specialists—IATREIA/Outpath Institute
1152 Country Club Lane
Fort Worth, Texas 76112
(817) 654-9600
Includes a two-hour consultation with a professional consultant with Fortune 100 experience and 50 laser printed copies of the final resume. Extensive experience working with executives, mid-life career changers, and displaced middle managers.
Fee: $200
Contact: Rob Rainey

A Better Answer
Gateway Tower II, Suite 787
Dallas, TX 75251
(214) 234-3833
Fee: 1- page resume $25; $50 for up to 3 pages, and includes 10 copies. Retained on diskette for 6 months.
Contact: Liz Moore

Accurate Type
1506 W. Pioneer Pkwy., Suite 105
Arlington, TX 76103
(817) 861-5695
Fee: $25 and up depending on level of service required. Offers resume typesetting, review and assessment, and consultation. Develops effective cover letters. Provides targeted mailings to employers. Career testing and consulting, and online national database of employers and contact names. Offers lifetime storage of disks.
Contact: Sherri Gay

Action Business Services
533 Hambrick Rd.
Dallas, TX 75218
(214) 348-0681
Fee: $10 and up per page for resumes and cover letters depending on needs. Evening appointments available.
Contact: Rubye Dawson

A Professional Resume Place
13601 Preston Rd., Suite 414 W
Dallas, TX 75240
(214) 960-8363 for office nearest you.
Offers custom writing and career development service. Complimentary consultations to assess individual needs. Ten offices in Dallas-Fort Worth area.
Contact: Toni Stuffel

Executive Resume Service
4912 WestLake
Fort Worth, TX 76103

(817) 292-3307
Also: 700 Northeast Loop 820
Hurst, TX 76053
Fee: Averages $65-$100 for resume composition and printing.

Executive Services
1401 W. Pioneer Pkwy., Suite 112
Arlington, TX 76013
(817) 277-7643
Fee: $25 for one page, $35 for two pages. $5.50 for cover letter. $25 consultation fee. Member of Professional Association of Resume Writers and National Resume Bank. Deluxe embossed papers and folders, typesetting, and laser fax and transcription services available.
Contact: Cindy Holmes

Hour Savers Career Services
(214) 349-2992
Unique package deal includes resume, improving job-hunting skills, and interview techniques. Also offers career workshops, career and employment consultations, corporate outplacements, and public speaking on employment issues.
Contact: Eleanor Baldwin

Resume Specialist of Arlington
1408 E. Mitchell St.
Arlington, TX 76016
Metro (817) 469-6500
Includes resume counseling, marketing, composition, typesetting, printing, and salary histories. Lifetime update available.
Contact: Peter Ots

Resumes Plus
3201 Airport Frwy.
Bedford, TX 76021
(817) 283-2849
Fee: $35 for one-page resume with 15 copies. Also provides cover and thank-you letters. Offers counseling, networking assistance, laser printing, typesetting, writing assistance, and brochure-style resumes.
Contact: Bill Mueller

Resumes That Win
845 E. Arapaho Rd., Suite 107
Richardson, TX 75081
(214) 234-2274
Offers a commitment to positive professional writing. Other area locations.
Fee: Ranges from $50-$250, depending on needs for composition and printing of resumes and cover letters.

Top O' The Stack
1300 E. Arapaho Rd., Suite 112
Richardson, TX 75081
(214) 907-8639
Fee: $12 and up for resume preparation and typing. Offers laser printing.

The Word Factory
2167 W. Seminary Dr.
Fort Worth, TX 76115
(817) 924-6720
Fee: $20 for one page, $10 for each additional page for resume typing and
printing. Lifetime storage on computer disk.
Contact: Mike Hartley

SAMPLE CHRONOLOGICAL RESUME

GEORGE P. BURDELL
200 SILICON DRIVE
DALLAS, TEXAS 75204
(214) 555-4545

OBJECTIVE

Position in technical management.

PROFESSIONAL EXPERIENCE

SAMPO CORPORATION   1988-Present
Dallas, Texas

Manager, Marketing & Planning (Taiwan)   1990-Present
- **Supervised** operations & staff of new products development.
- **Instrumental** in making decisions regarding OEM new products with clients such as: IBM, NCR, TI, Xerox, Quadram, etc.
- **Developed** 4 new products: Low-cost display monitor, oscilloscope, and two DEC-compatible terminals.
- **Increased** IPD sales volume in 1993: $45,000,000; 90% increase from 1989.

Manager, Southwestern Sales (Richardson, TX)   1988-1990
- Generated $3,000,000 in sales of OEM display monitors to IBM(NC), NCR(SC), Quadram, Digital Control, & other local accounts.

EDWARDS ELECTRONICS   1980-1988

Sales Engineer (Garland, TX)   1985-1988
- Successfully collaborated with OEM engineers to **develop monitors** for computer & laser games such as Jungle King & Dragon's Lair.

Production Engineer (Dallas, TX)   1980-1985
- Key member of team credited with **building** Texas's first TV manufacturing plant.
- **Involvement** in this $7,000,000 project ranged from conceptualization to production of 600, 19" color sets daily.

EDUCATION

Southern Methodist University: **MBA in Marketing,** 1988
University of Texas at Arlington: BS in Electrical Engineering, 1980

REFERENCES

Furnished upon request.

43

SAMPLE FUNCTIONAL RESUME

KATHY SANCHEZ
4000 Greenwood Drive, NE
Dallas, TX 75238
(214) 555-5648

OBJECTIVE: Seek position as an administrative supervisor, utilizing administrative, organizational, and computer skills.

SKILLS

Administrative
- Independently evaluated and restructured a major client's account for an advertising agency.
- Managed accounting procedures for a non-profit corporation in excess of $80,000.
- Supervised nine professional and four support personnel.

Organizational
- Established procedure for assigned experiments and procured equipment for a research laboratory.
- Planned course syllabi, assessed weaknesses of individual students to facilitate learning.

Computer
- Developed and wrote application programs for accounting, marketing, and manufacturing departments, utilizing COBOL.
- Completed advanced courses in COBOL, FORTRAN, and BASIC.

EMPLOYMENT

Programmer/Analyst, American Eurocopter Inc.,
Grand Prairie, TX (1992-Present)
Account Administrator, The Bloom Agency/Dallas (1988-90)
Instructor, Eastfield College Math Dept., Mesquite, TX (1982-85)

EDUCATION

M.S. Mathematics, Southern Methodist University (1982)
B.S. Mathematics, University of Texas (1978)

REFERENCES

Furnished upon request.

SAMPLE COMBINATION RESUME

SUSAN SKINNER
122 Pine Street
Fort Worth, TX 76262
(817) 555-0000

OBJECTIVE: Software development position.

EDUCATION: University of North Texas
M.S., Information and Computer Science;
GPA 3.7/4.0 12/88

Texas Christian University
B.A., Mathematics;
GPA 3.5/4.0 5/83

QUALIFICATIONS:
Career-related projects:
▪ Designed and implemented multi-tasking operating system for the IBM-PC.
▪ Implemented compiler for Pascal-like language.
▪ Designed electronic mail system using PSL/PSA specification language.

Languages and operating systems:
▪ Proficient in Ada, Modula-2, Pascal, COBOL.
▪ Working knowledge of IBM-PC hardware and 8088 assembly language.

WORK EXPERIENCE:
Neil Araki Programming Services
Fort Worth, TX—10/88-Present
▪ **UNIX Programmer**—Responsible for supporting MS-DOS database applications to IBM-PC/AT and system administration.

Strathmore Systems
Hurst, TX—10/85-9/88
Computer Programmer
▪ Performed daily disk backup on Burroughs B-1955 machine.
▪ Executed database update programs and checks.

From 8/83 to 9/85, held full-time positions as Box Office Manager and Accountant for arts organizations in Fort Worth.

REFERENCES:

Furnished upon request.

The power of action verbs

Gary J. has been an engineer in Dallas for 20 years. During those years he has changed jobs seven times, enhancing his career with each move. Gary realized early that using powerful, action verbs to describe his accomplishments made his resume stand out. Here are some sample verbs that job seekers in various career areas should use to help build a more effective resume.

Management
Controlled
Directed
Supervised
Headed
Implemented

Methods and Controls
Coordinated
Restructured
Cataloged
Verified
Systematized

Public Relations/ Human Relations
Monitored
Counciled
Sponsored
Integrated

Creative
Devised
Developed
Originated
Conceived

Advertising/ Promotion
Generated
Targeted
Tailored
Sparked

Communications
Facilitated
Edited
Consulted
Disseminated

Resourcefulness
Rectified
Pioneered
Achieved

Negotiations
Engineered
Mediated
Proposed
Negotiated ■

The Cover Letter

Whether you are answering a want ad or following up an inquiry call or interview, you should always include a cover letter with your resume. If at all possible, the letter should be addressed to a specific person—the one who's doing the hiring—and not "To Whom It May Concern." You can generally track the right person down with a few phone calls to the company in question.

A good cover letter, like a good resume, is brief—usually not more than three or four paragraphs. No paragraph should be longer than three or four sentences. If you've already spoken to the contact person by phone, remind him or her of your conversation in the first paragraph. If you and the person to whom you are writing know someone in common, the first paragraph is the place to mention it.

You should also include a hard-hitting sentence about why you're well qualified for the job in question.

In the next paragraph or two, specify what you could contribute to the company in terms that indicate you've done your homework on the firm and the industry.

Finally, either request an interview or tell the reader that you will follow up with a phone call within a week to arrange a mutually convenient meeting.

Remember that the focus of your job search is to sell yourself as a match to fit an employer's needs. You should emphasize that you match the company's needs throughout all your communication—your resume, any phone calls, and cover letters and follow-up letters.

SAMPLE COVER LETTER FOR AN
EXECUTIVE POSITION

2441 Safehaven Blvd.
Carrollton, Texas
(214) 555-7902

Mr. Ogden King   November 8, 1994
President
NASH Enterprises
1655 Carpenter Freeway
Dallas, Texas 79034

Dear Mr. King:

While networking it came to my attention that you may be
looking for a senior-level Human Resources Executive in your
Dallas headquarters. I believe my background may be of interest
to you. I have a unique combination of experience with major
corporations that enables me to resolve many difficult employee
relations problems while simultaneously reducing associated
costs.

I am able to deal with the gamut of sensitive employee problems
occurring on and off the job. I have reduced employee stress levels
and thus increased productivity by twenty percent. I have helped
in the identification and retention of the most valuable employees
through an in-depth assessment review and have helped other
employees gain assignments more suited to their skills and
abilities.

My unique combination of abilities should allow me to make a
significant contribution to the right company.

I look forward to talking with you in the near future concerning
this opportunity and will call your office in the next few days to
set up a personal meeting at your convenience.

Sincerely,

David R. Sellinghard

SAMPLE COVER LETTER FOR A NEW GRADUATE

Valerie S. Jones
3420 Rosedale Ave.
Fort Worth, TX 75421
(817) 555-6886

Ms. Jacqueline Read   June 26, 1994
Wide World Publishing Company
1400 Walnut Hill Lane, Suite 250
Dallas, TX 77237

Dear Ms. Read:

As an honors graduate of The University of North Texas with
two years of copy editing and feature writing experience with a
community newspaper, I am confident that I would make a
successful editorial assistant with Wide World.

Besides my strong editorial background, I offer considerable
business experience. I have held summer jobs in an insurance
company, a law firm, and a data processing company. My famil-
iarity with word processing should prove particularly useful to
Wide World now that you're fully automated.

I would like to interview with you as soon as possible and would
be happy to check in with your office about an appointment. If
you prefer, your office can contact me between the hours of 11:00
a.m. and 3:00 p.m. at (817) 555-6886.

Sincerely,

Valerie S. Jones

SAMPLE COVER LETTER FOR ANSWERING
AN ADVERTISEMENT

May 14, 1994

2239 Forest Park Blvd.
Fort Worth, TX 76345

Box 1826
The Dallas Morning News
Communications Center
Dallas, TX 75265

Dear Employer:

Your advertisement in the May 13 issue of *The Dallas Morning
News* for an experienced accountant seems perfect for someone
with my background. My five years of experience in a small
accounting firm in Fort Worth has prepared me to move on to a
more challenging position in a prestigious firm like yours.

As you can see from my resume, my work experience consists of
both basic accounting services and consulting with a few of our
firm's bigger clients. This experience combined with an appetite
for hard work and enthusiasm makes me a strong candidate for
your consideration.

I would appreciate an opportunity to meet with you to discuss
how my background could meet the needs of your organization. I
will call you within the week to see if we could arrange a convenient time to meet.

Sincerely,

Jim Clark
(817) 555-4414

SAMPLE NETWORKING COVER LETTER

December 2, 1994

228 S. Meadowlark Lane
Dallas, TX 75116
(214) 555-9876

Dear Mike:

Just when everything seemed to be going so well at my job, the company gave us a Christmas present that nobody wanted—management announced that half the department will be laid off before the end of the year. Nobody knows yet just which heads are going to roll. But whether or not my name is on the list, I am definitely back in the job market.

I have already lined up a couple of interviews. But knowing how uncertain job hunting can be, I can use all the contacts I can get. You know my record—both from when we worked together at 3-Q and since then. But in case you've forgotten the details, I've enclosed my resume.

I know that you often hear of job openings as you wend your way about Dallas and Fort Worth and I'd certainly appreciate your passing along any contacts or leads you think might be worthwhile.

My best to you and Fran for the holidays.

Cordially,

Emily Noir

How to Get a Job

Seven ways to ruin a cover letter

1. Spell the name of the firm incorrectly.
2. Don't bother to find out the name of the hiring authority. Just send the letter to the president or chairman of the board.
3. If the firm is headed by a woman, be sure to begin your letter, "Dear Sir." Otherwise, just address it, "To Whom It May Concern."
4. Make sure the letter includes a couple of typos and sloppy erasures. Better yet, spill coffee on it first, then mail it.
5. Be sure to provide a phone number that has been disconnected, or one at which nobody is ever home.
6. Tell the firm you'll call to set up an appointment in a few days; then don't bother.
7. Call the firm at least three times the day after you mail the letter. Get very angry when they say they haven't heard of you. ∎

Researching the Dallas/ Fort Worth Job Market

We've said the key to getting job offers is to convince employers that you match their needs. We'd add that the key to job satisfaction is finding a position whose responsibilities match your interests and abilities. This means you've got to know the job and the company.

Once you've figured out what kind of job you want, you need to find out as much as you can about which specific companies might employ you. Your network of personal contacts can be an invaluable source of information about what jobs are available where. But networking can't do it all; at some point, you'll have to do some reading. This chapter fills you in on the directories, newspapers, and magazines you'll need in your search, and notes the libraries where you can find them.

Libraries

Public libraries are an invaluable source of career information. Everything from books on resume writing to *Standard and Poor's*

53

Register of Corporations, Directors, and Executives can usually be found in the business and economics sections.

DALLAS PUBLIC LIBRARY

The most extensive collection of job-hunting books and reference material can be found in this modern eight-floor downtown library located at 1515 Young St., (214) 670-1700. The 18 branch libraries carry many of the most frequently used guides and directories. Any book that isn't available in one library can be requested through the inter-library loan system.

At the main library, most of the major business directories, magazines, and books can be found in the **business and technology section** on the fifth floor. Few signs are posted, so ask at the main desk for directions on where to find what you're looking for and advice on where else to look for information. Underground parking is available and is convenient and usually safe.

Time invested in finding out as much as possible about a company before a job interview can pay off. For example, if you want to find out about a major business's financial outlook, check its annual report. Hundreds of annual reports, including those for most major Dallas companies, are on microfilm.

The Business Section also keeps an index of newspaper stories written about local companies. The **Infotrack** computer search system will identify stories about companies that have run in trade journals and other sources.

U.S. Securities and Exchange Commission reports on the sixth floor offer additional information about businesses. You may find even more revealing information than what is contained in annual reports, such as the profitability of different divisions within a company.

The sixth floor also includes many government documents, including U.S. Labor Department employment outlooks. You may wonder, for example, about the future for computer programmers during the next decade. Government publications can offer some predictions.

The first and eighth floors have stacks with general career books, such as *What Color Is Your Parachute?* and other popular guides. Information about government jobs and samples of qualifying tests are kept on the eighth floor.

Gail Bialas, the library's public information officer, highlights the library as an asset. "Lots of people tell us how helpful the library was in helping them find a job," Gail adds. "For one thing, it's one of the few resources that's free. And that can be a big help to someone who is out of work."

Dallas Branch Libraries

Audelia Road: 10045 Audelia Rd. (214) 670-1350
Casa View: 10355 Ferguson Rd. (214) 670-8403
Dallas West: 2332 Singleton Blvd. (214) 670-6445

Forest Green: 9015 Forest Lane (214) 670-1335
Fretz Park: 6990 Belt Line Rd. (214) 670-6420
Hampton-Illinois: 2210 Illinois Ave. (214) 670-7646
Highland Hills: 3624 Simpson Stuart Rd. (214) 670-0987
Martin Luther King, Jr., Library-Learning Center: 2922 Martin
   Luther King, Jr., Blvd. (214) 670-0344
Lakewood: 6121 Worth St. (214) 670-1376
Lancaster-Kiest: 3039 S. Lancaster Rd. (214) 670-1952
North Oak Cliff: 302 W. Tenth St. (214) 670-7555
Oak Lawn: 4100 Cedar Springs Rd. (214) 670-1359
Park Forest: 3421 Forest Lane (214) 670-6333
Pleasant Grove: 1125 S. Buckner Blvd. (214) 670-0965
Polk-Wisdom: 7151 Library Lane (214) 670-1947
Preston Royal: 5626 Royal Lane (214) 670-7128
Renner Frankford: 6400 Frankford Rd. (214) 670-6400
Skyline: 6006 Everglade Rd. (214) 670-0938
Walnut Hill: 9495 Marsh Lane (214) 670-6376

How to conduct a rock-bottom computer search

Let's say you have an interview with the sales director of XYZ Corporation, a company that has the perfect job opportunity. You've done your homework by searching through the directories listed in this chapter, you've familiarized yourself with the appropriate trade magazines, and you have an information file with the XYZ Corporation's annual report and product brochures.

You know where the sales director went to college and even what sorority she joined. But you need more up-to-date information on what has happened to the company during the past six months.

One quick way to find out is through the Dallas Public Library's on-line search service available in the Information and Reference Section at (214) 670-1608. All reference questions are funnelled through this department in the central library located at 1515 Young St.

The library has access to more than 200 databases, including DIALOG, Dun & Bradstreet, and Dow Jones. A computer search on XYZ Corporation will go through these databases and print out a bibliography of recent articles that have been written about that company.

The cost for the service is determined by the number of sources and time involved in doing the search. Minimum charge is $25. You first tell the librarian the maximum amount of money you can spend on the search. The public isn't charged for the librarian's time, making this offering one of the best values in town. ∎

Using the Dallas Public Library's On-Line Information Service

You have hundreds of resources at your fingertips through the Dallas Public Library's community information database, called **APL/CAT.**
Say you want to find out the names of major professional organizations in your field of interest. Go to a computer terminal at any one of the Dallas city libraries and use the on-line information service to find more than 300 listings under professional organizations. You also will be given cross-reference listings for more sources.

APL/CAT can be especially useful to job seekers who may want to know about social services, employment agencies, women's programs, day-care centers for child care, and organizations that provide food and clothing for the unemployed. Dozens of major categories are listed in the information service that contains more than 6,000 single entries.

Printouts of some of the categories are available through the **Urban Information Center** on the sixth floor of the main library at 1515 Young St. Charges start at $10 and increase, depending on the number of listings. Call in advance to order.

Ask any librarian to help you learn to use APL/CAT. You can call the main reference desk at (214) 670-1700 to ask a librarian for information you need from the database. New listings are continuously added to APL/CAT. Most of the data is for the City of Dallas, although some entries are listed for Dallas County suburbs.

FORT WORTH PUBLIC LIBRARY

The downtown Fort Worth Public Library and its nine branches are invaluable resource for job hunters. Many library staff members go out of their way to help people who are looking for work.

The largest collection of material can be found in the **Business and Technology Section** in the lower level of the downtown library at 300 Taylor St. Many of the 10-K reports on major corporations, government study guides, and self-help material are available. A list of City of Fort Worth job openings can be found here.

Limited information is provided by calling the Business and Technology section at (817) 871-7727. You'll gather much more from dropping by one of the libraries.

When you do, be sure to ask for a librarian's help. It's common for people to flounder if they aren't familiar with what's available in the library, says Sally McCoy, manager of the Business and Technology Section. That's why she likes to help point people in the right direction, so they can make the best use of the resources.

The main library and several of the branches have **Adult Learning Centers** that can be very useful to people who want to upgrade skills, prepare for taking the GED exam, or get help when English is their second language. The program, coordinated by the Fort Worth Independent School District, assists adults in getting the extra boost they need to find better jobs.

You can also find job-hunting information at the following Fort Worth branch libraries.

Fort Worth Branch Libraries

Diamond Hill/Jarvis: 1300 NE 35th St. (817) 624-7331
East Berry: 4300 E. Berry St. (817) 536-1945
Meadowbrook: 5651 E. Lancaster Ave. (817) 451-0916
North Side: 601 Park St. (817) 626-8241
Ridglea: 3628 Bernie Anderson Ave. (817) 737-6619
Riverside: 2913 Yucca Ave. (817) 838-6931
Seminary South: 501 E. Bolt St. (817) 926-0215
Shamblee: 959 E. Rosedale St. (817) 870-1330
Southwest Regional Library: 4001 Library Lane (817) 782-9853
Wedgwood: 3816 Kimberly Lane (817) 292-3368

MAJOR SUBURBAN LIBRARIES

Arlington: 101 E. Abram St. (817) 459-6900
Balch Springs: 4301 Pioneer Rd. (214) 286-8856
Bedford: 1805 L. Don Dodson Dr. (817) 952-2160
Burleson: 216 SW Johnson Ave. (817) 295-6131
Carrollton: 2001 Jackson Rd. (214) 466-3353
Cedar Hill: 225 Cedar St. (214) 291-7323
DeSoto: 211 E. Pleasant Run Rd. (214) 230-9656
Duncanville: 103 E. Wheatland Rd. (214) 780-5052
Euless: 201 N. Ector Dr. (817) 685-1480
Everman: 118 W. Trammell (817) 551-0726
Farmers Branch: 13613 Webb Chapel Rd. (214) 247-2511
Forest Hill: 6619 Forest Hill Dr. (817) 483-9811
Garland Nicholson Memorial Library: 625 Austin St.
  (214) 205-2500
Grand Prairie: 901 Conover Dr. (214) 264-1571
Grapevine: 1201 S. Main (817) 481-0336
Haltom City: 3201 Friendly Lane (817) 831-6431
Highland Park: 4700 Drexel Dr. (214) 521-4150
Hurst: 901 Precinct Line Rd. (817) 788-7300
Hutchins-Atwell: 300 N. Denton St. (214) 225-4711
Irving: 801 W. Irving Blvd. (214) 721-2606
Lake Worth: 3801 Adam Grub (817) 237-9681
Lancaster: 220 W. Main St. (214) 227-1081

Mansfield: 110 S. Main St. (817) 473-4391

Mesquite: 300 W. Grubb (214) 216-6220

Newark: Ramhorn Hill Rd. (817) 489-2224

North Richland Hills: 6720 NE Loop 820 (817) 581-5700

Richardson: 900 Civic Center Dr. (214) 238-4000

Richland Hills: 6724 Rena Dr. (817) 595-6630

River Oaks: 4900 River Oaks Blvd. (817) 626-5421

Rowlett: Main St. at Skyline Dr. (214) 412-6161

Sachse: 3033 6th St. (214) 530-8966

Saginaw: 355 W. McLeroy (817) 232-2100, ext. 170

Seagoville: 702 N. Hwy. 175 (214) 287-7720

Sunnyvale: 402 Tower Place (214) 226-4491

Watauga: 7109 Whitley Rd. (817) 428-9412

White Settlement: 8215 White Settlement Rd. (817) 367-0166

Wilmer: 205 E. Belt Line Rd. (214) 225-6620

Directories

When you're beginning your homework, whether you're researching an entire industry or a specific company, there are four major sources of information with which you should become familiar.

Standard and Poor's Register of Corporations, Directors, and Executives (Standard and Poor's Publishing Co., 25 Broadway, New York, NY 10004) is billed as the "foremost guide to the business community and the executives who run it." This three-volume directory lists more than 50,000 corporations and 70,000 officers, directors, trustees, and other bigwigs.

Each business is assigned a four-digit number called a Standard Industrial Classification (S.I.C.) number, which tells you what product or service the company provides. Listings are indexed by geographic area and also by S.I.C. number, so it's easy to find all the companies in Texas that produce, say, industrial inorganic chemicals.

You can also look up a particular company to verify its correct address and phone number, its chief officers (that is, the people you might want to contact for an interview), its products, and, in many cases, its annual sales and number of employees.

If you have an appointment with the president of XYZ Corporation, you can consult *Standard and Poor's Register* to find out where he or she was born and went to college—information that's sure to come in handy in an employment interview. Supplements are published in April, July, and October.

The **Thomas Register of American Manufacturers** and the **Thomas Register Catalog File** (Thomas Publishing Co., One Penn Plaza, New York, NY 10001) are published annually. This 23-volume publication is another gold mine of information. You can look up a particular product or service and find every company that provides it. (Since this is a national publication, you'll have to weed out companies that are not in the Dallas/Fort Worth area, but that's easy.) You can also look up a particular company to find out about branch offices, capital ratings, company officials, names, addresses, phone numbers, and more. The *Thomas Register* even contains five volumes of company catalogs. Before your appointment with XYZ Corporation, you can bone up on its product line with the *Thomas Register*.

Moody's Complete Corporate Index (Moody's Investor Service, 99 Church St., New York, NY 10007) gives you the equivalent of an encyclopedia entry on more than 20,000 corporations. This is the resource to use when you want really detailed information on a particular company. *Moody's* can tell you about a company's history—when it was founded, what name changes it has undergone, and so on. It provides a fairly lengthy description of a company's business and properties, what subsidiaries it owns, and lots of detailed financial information. Like the directories above, *Moody's* lists officers and directors of companies. It can also tell you the date of the annual meeting and the number of stockholders and employees.

The Million Dollar Directory (Dun & Bradstreet, Inc., 3 Sylvan Way, Parsippany, NJ 07054) is a five-volume listing of approximately 160,000 U.S. businesses with a net worth of more than half a million dollars. Listings appear alphabetically, geographically, and by product classification and include key personnel. Professional and consulting organizations such as hospitals, engineering services, credit agencies, and financial institutions other than banks and trust companies are not generally included.

So much for the Big Four directories. The following list contains more than five dozen additional directories and guides that may come in handy. Many are available at area libraries.

OTHER USEFUL DIRECTORIES

Accounting Employers of Texas
(Texas Society of CPA's Education Fund, 1421 W. Mockingbird Lane, Suite 100, Dallas, TX 75247.) A directory of company profiles.

Accounting Firms and Practitioners
(American Institute of Certified Public Accountants, 1211 Avenue of the Americas, New York, NY 10036.) Covers about 25,000 certified public accounting firms belonging to the Institute, as well as member accountants with independent practices.

Advertising Research Foundation Yearbook
(Advertising Research Foundation, 3 E. 54th St., New York, NY 10022.) Lists 375 member advertising agencies, research organizations, trade associations, advertisers, academic institutions, and broadcasting and publishing firms.

Adweek Agency Directory
(A/S/M Communications, Inc., 49 E. 21st St., New York, NY 10010.) Lists ad agencies, media and media buying services, key personnel, major accounts.

How to Get a Job

The Almanac of American Employers: A Guide to America's 500 Most Successful Large Corporations
(Contemporary Books, 180 N. Michigan Ave., Chicago, IL 60601.)
Alphabetical profiles of major corporations, including information about benefits, job turnover, and financial stability.

Americas Corporate Families
(Dun & Bradstreet, Inc., 3 Century Drive, Parsippany, NJ 07054.)
Directory of 8,000 parent companies and 48,000 divisions and subsidiaries.

Apparel Trades Book
(Dun & Bradstreet, One Diamond Hill Rd., Murray Hill, NJ 07974.) Lists about 175,000 apparel retailers and wholesalers. Separate editions for each.

Aviation Telephone Directory
(Directional Media Systems, Inc., 535 W. Lambert Rd., Suite D, Brea, CA 92621.) Suppliers of aviation products and services, airports, and fixed-base operators.

Bacon's Publicity Checker
(Bacon's Publishing Company, 332 S. Michigan Ave., Chicago, IL 60604.)
Covers over 7,800 trade and consumer magazines, 1,700 daily newspapers, and 8,000 weekly newspapers in the United States and Canada.

Best's Insurance Reports, Property, Casualty, Life, and Health
(A.M. Best Company, Ambest Rd., Oldwick, NJ 08858.) Addresses in depth analysis, operating statistics, financial data, ratings and listings of 1,300 major companies with names of key officers.

Billion Dollar Directory: America's Corporate Families
(Dun and Bradstreet, Inc., 3 Sylvan Way, Parsippany, NJ 07054-3896.)
Lists 7,800 U.S. parent companies and their 44,000 foreign and domestic subsidiaries. Organized alphabetically by name of parent company.

Book of Lists
(Dallas Business Journal, 4131 N. Central Expwy., Suite 310, Dallas, TX 75204.) Lists of the top 25 companies in all major industries, along with the 100 largest public companies and 50 largest employers for Dallas, Tarrant, and Austin counties.

Book of Lists
(The Business Press, Tarrant County's Business Journal, 501 Jones St., Fort Worth, Texas 76102.) Lists of the top companies in all major industries, along with lists of the largest public companies and largest employers in Tarrant County.

Career Guide: Dun's Employment Opportunity Directory
(Dun's Marketing Services, 3 Sylvan Way, Parsippany, NJ 07054-3896.)
Designed for those beginning a career; describes job prospects at hundreds of companies.

College Placement Annual
(College Placement Council, 62 Highland Ave., Bethlehem, PA 18017.)
Directory of the occupational needs of 1,200 corporations and government employers. Lists names and titles of recruitment representatives.

Consultants and Consulting Organizations Directory
(Gale Research Co., 835 Penobscot Bldg., Detroit, MI 48226; $85.)
Contains descriptions of 16,000 firms and individuals involved in
consulting; indexed geographically.

Corporate Technology Directory
(Corporate Technology Information Services, Inc., 12 Alfred St., Suite
200, Woburn, MA 01801.) Profiles of 23,000 high-technology corporations,
manufacturers, and developers in the U.S., including address, phone,
ownership, history, brief description, sales, number of employees,
executives, and products. Indexed by company names, geography,
technology, and product.

Dallas Chamber of Commerce Publications
(Greater Dallas Chamber Information Department, 1201 Elm St., Suite
200, Dallas, TX 75270.) The following publications are available:
Dallas Area Employment Trends and Economic Indicators.
Dallas At a Glance.
Directory of Foreign-Owned Companies lists Dallas/Fort Worth
  foreign-owned companies by country of origin, including year of
  local establishment and area employment.
Directory of High-Technology Firms lists high-technology firms in the
  Dallas/Fort Worth area.
Greater Dallas Business and Industry Guide.
Greater Dallas Office Real Estate Journal.
Minority Business Development Handbook.

Dallas County Business Guide
(Business Extension Bureau, 4802 Travis St., Houston, TX 77002.) Major
Dallas-area businesses listed alphabetically and according to business
category.

Data Sources: Hardware-Data Communications Directory and Data Sources: Software Directory
(Ziff-Davis Publishing Co., 20 Brace St., Suite 110, Cherry Hill, NJ
08034.) Two-volume guide to most products, companies, services, and
personnel in the computer industry.

Dictionary of Occupational Titles
(U.S. Dept. of Labor, Washington, DC 20210.) Occupational information
on job duties and requirements; describes almost every conceivable job.

Directories in Print
(Gale Research Company, 835 Penobscot Bldg., Detroit, MI 48226.)
Contains detailed descriptions of all published directories: what they list,
who uses them, and who publishes them.

Directory of Corporate Affiliations
(National Register Publishing Co., Inc., 3004 Glenview Rd.,Wilmette, IL.
60091.) Primarily a who owns who directory. Detailed information about
changes in ownership due to mergers and acquisitions. Lists 4,000
corporations and their subsidiaries.

Directory of Executive Recruiters
(Consultants News, Kennedy Publishers Inc., Templeton Rd., Fitzwilliam
NH 03447.) Lists more than 2,000 executive search recruiters by company name, function, location, retainer and contingency categories of
search.

Directory of Chain Restaurant Operators
(Business Guides, Inc., 425 Park Ave., New York, NY 10022.) Listings of chain restaurants, chain hotels, and food services.

Directory of Community Resources for Fort Worth and Tarrant County
(United Way of Metropolitan Tarrant County, 210 E. 9th St., Fort Worth, TX 76102.) Major social service agencies in Tarrant County listed alphabetically.

Directory of Construction Associations
(Metadata, Inc., Box 585, Locust, NJ 07760.) Lists about 2,500 local, regional, and national professional societies, technical associations, trade groups, manufacturer bureaus, government agencies, labor unions, and other construction information sources. Arranged by topic.

Directory of Industry Data Sources: U.S. & Canada
(Ballinger Publishing Co., Harper & Row Publishers, 54 S. Church St. Cambridge, MA 02138.) Three-volume set is a directory to published document and research services for 65 industries. Does not reference material prior to 1979.

Directory of Services
(Community Council of Greater Dallas, 2121 Main St., Suite 500, Dallas, TX 75201.) Lists agencies and services for residents of Dallas and Collin counties and the Lewisville Independent School District.

Directory of Texas Manufacturers
(Bureau of Business Research, The University of Texas, P.O. Box 7459, Austin, TX 78712.) Texas manufacturers listed alphabetically and according to SIC number and major product.

Electronic News Financial Fact Book and Directory
(Fairchild Publications, Inc., 7 E. 12th St., New York, NY 10003.) Background and financial information about leading companies in the electronics industry.

Employment Opportunities Directory
(Dun's Marketing Services, 1 Penn Plaza, New York, NY 10119.) Designed for those beginning a career; describes job prospects at hundreds of companies.

Encyclopedia of Associations: National Organizations in the U.S.
(Gale Research Co., 835 Penobscot Bldg., Detroit, MI 48226.) Lists 14,000 local and national associations, professional clubs, and civic organizations by categories; includes key personnel. Indexed geographically.

Encyclopedia of Business Information Sources
(Gale Research Co., 835 Penobscot Bldg., Detroit, MI 48226.) Lists each industry's encyclopedias, handbooks, indexes, almanacs, yearbooks, trade associations, periodicals, directories, computer databases, research centers, and statistical sources.

Engineering, Science and Computer Jobs
(Peterson's Guides, P.O. Box 2123, Princeton, NJ 08543.) Lists of specific companies within these industries.

Everybody's Business
(Doubleday, 10 E. 53rd St., New York, NY 10022; available at bookstores
for $10.) Candid profiles of 400 American manufacturers of well-known
brand-name products.

Fairchild's Financial Manual of Retail Stores
(Fairchild Books, Fairchild Publications, Inc., 7 E. 12th St., New York,
NY 10003.) Lists 275 publicly held companies in the U.S. and Canada
that deal partly or exclusively in retail sales. Arranged alphabetically.

Fairchild's Textile and Apparel Financial Directory
(Fairchild Books, Fairchild Publications, Inc., 7 E. 12th St., New York,
NY 10003.) Lists 275 publicly owned textile and apparel corporations.
Arranged alphabetically.

Finding A Federal Job Fast
(Impact Publications, 9104-N Manassas Dr., Manassas Park, VA 22111.)
Secrets to finding jobs. Helpful in locating job vacancies, marketing
oneself, and getting hired.

Finding a Job in the Nonprofit Sector
(The Taft Group, 12300 Twinbrook Parkway, Suite 450, Rockville, MD
20852.) Overview of employment trends, job-hunting tips, and contact/
employment information for 5,000 of the largest nonprofits in the U.S.

**Fort Worth Chamber of Commerce Membership Directory &
Buyer's Guide**
(Fort Worth Chamber of Commerce, 777 Taylor St., Suite 900, Fort
Worth, TX 76102.) Membership roster, classified listings, and business
index.

Fortune Double 500 Directory
(Time, Inc., Time & Life Bldg., Rockefeller Center, New York, NY 10020.)
Lists the 500 largest corporations, as well as the 500 largest U.S. non-
industrial corporations and the top 100 service companies in diversified
financial services and banking. Arranged by annual sales.

Franchise Opportunities Handbook
(U.S. Government Printing Office, Superintendent of Documents,
Washington, DC 20402.) Lists over 1,200 franchise companies in the U.S.
Includes information on their operation, size, history, capital needed, and
various forms of assistance available.

Gale Directory of Publications
(Gale Research, Inc., 835 Penobscot Bldg., Detroit MI 48226-4094.) Lists
national, local, and trade magazines alphabetically and by state.

Gale Directory of Publications and Broadcast Media
(Gale Research Inc., 835 Penobscot Bldg., Detroit, MI 48226.) Lists
35,000 publications and broadcast stations as well as the feature editors
of major daily newspapers.

**Greater Dallas Chamber Membership Directory and
Business Guide**
(Greater Dallas Chamber Information Dept., 1201 Elm St., Suite 200,
Dallas, TX 75270.) Chamber of Commerce members listed alphabetically
and according to products and services.

Guide to American Directories
(B. Klein Publications, P.O. Box 8503, Coral Springs, FL 33065.) Includes listing and descriptions of 6,000 directories in more than 300 major classifications.

Guide to Special Issues and Indexes of Periodicals
(Special Libraries Association, 235 Park Ave. S., New York, NY 10003.) Alphabetical listing of consumer, trade, and technical periodicals.

Hispanic Media & Markets Directory
(Standard Rate & Data Service, 3004 Glenview Rd., Wilmette, IL 60091.) Provides company, subsidiary, and branch names, addresses, phone, and key personnel for over 600 Spanish-language publications and broadcast stations.

Hispanic Media USA
(Media Institute, 3017 M St. NW, Washington, DC 20007.) Provides company name, address, phone, and names of key personnel for 250 print, TV, and radio stations whose primary language is Spanish.

Hotel and Motel Management—Buyer's Directory
(Harcourt General Inc., 27 Boylston St. Chestnut Hills, MA 02167.) Lists about 2,100 companies that supply goods and services to the lodging market; includes separate sections for hotel chains, related associations, manufacturers' representatives, franchise and referral organizations, consulting firms, personnel agencies, publishers, and schools.

International Advertising Association—Membership Directory
(IAA, 342 Madison Ave., Suite 2000, New York, NY 10017.) Covers 2,700 member advertisers, advertising agencies, media, and other firms involved in advertising. Arranged geographically and by function or service.

International Association for Personnel Women—Membership Roster
(IAPW, P.O. Box 969, Andover, MA 01810.) Lists 1,500 members-at-large and members of affiliated chapters.

International Television and Video Almanac
(Quigley Publishing Company, Inc., 159 W. 53rd St., New York, NY 10019; $42.) Lists television networks, major program producers, major group station owners, cable television companies, distributors, firms serving the industry, equipment manufacturers, casting agencies, literary agencies, advertising and publicity representatives, and television stations.

National Directory of Magazines
(Oxbridge Communications, Inc., 150 Fifth Ave., New York, NY 10011.) Profiles 29,000 magazines by interest categories; includes key staff names, circulation, and description. Cross-indexed by subject. Indexed alphabetically by title.

National Directory of Women-Owned Business Firms
(Business Research Services, Inc., 2 E. 22nd St., Suite 202, Lombard, IL 60148.) Lists 20,000 women-owned firms, providing name, address, phone, products and services, and name and title of contact.

National Trade and Professional Associations
(Columbia Books, Inc., 1212 New York Ave. NW, Suite 3000, Washington, DC 20005; $30.) Lists all associations and labor unions in the U.S. and Canada; indexed geographically and by key words.

Newsletters in Print
(Gale Research Co., 835 Penobscot Bldg., Detroit, MI 48226.) Reference guide to national and international information and financial services, association bulletins, and training and educational services.

Occupational Outlook Handbook
(Bureau of Labor Statistics, 441 A St. NW, Washington, DC 20212.) Describes in clear language what people do in their jobs, the training and education they need, earnings, working conditions, and employment outlook.

O'Dwyer's Directory of Public Relations Firms
(J.R. O'Dwyer & Co., 271 Madison Ave., New York, NY 10016.) Describes 1,500 public relations firms in the U.S., their key personnel, local offices, and accounts; indexed geographically.

Oil & Gas Directory
(Geophysical Directory, Inc., P.O. Box 130508, Houston, TX 77219.) Directory of 5,200 producers, purchasers, gatherers, transporters, and other oil service companies worldwide.

Peterson's Job Opportunities for Engineering, Science, and Computer Graduates
(Peterson's Guides, Inc., P.O. Box 2123, Princeton, NJ 08540; $13.25.) Describes 1,000 government agencies, technical firms, and manufacturers that hire engineers, computer scientists, and physical scientists.

Polk's Bank Directory
(R.L. Polk Company, 2001 Elm-Hill Pike, Nashville, TN 37202.) Major detailed directory, listing banks and other financial institutions as well as government agencies by address.

Printing Trades Directory
(A.F. Lewis & Co., Inc., 79 Madison Ave., New York, NY 10016.) Printing plants, bookbinders, typesetters, plate makers, paper merchants and manufacturers, printing machinery manufacturers and dealers, and others serving the graphic arts industry.

QED's Guide to School Districts
(Quality Education Data, 1600 Broadway, 12th Floor, Denver, CO 80202.) Public and private elementary and secondary schools, including basic data and dollars per student, percent minority enrollment, educational specializations of key personnel, VCR units, number of microcomputers, other data.

The Red Book of Housing Manufacturers
(McGraw-Hill, 24 Huntwell Ave., Lexington, MA 02173.) Listings of companies involved in the production of everything from dwelling units to small components.

Reference Book of Corporate Management
(Dun & Bradstreet, Inc., 3 Sylvan Way, Parsippany, NJ 07054.) National directory of 2,400 companies with at least $20 million in sales; listed by

name. Also lists biographies of key personnel and directors, including schools attended and past jobs.

Rotan-Mosle/Paine-Webber Guide
(Scholl Communications, Inc., P.O. Box 560, Deerfield, IL 60015; $26.95.) Directory of major publicly held corporations and financial institutions headquartered in Texas and Oklahoma.

Sheldon's Department Stores
(Phelon, Sheldon & Marsar, 15 Industrial Ave., Fairview, NJ 07022.) Directory of the largest department stores, women's specialty stores, chain stores, and resident buying offices. Geographical listings, plus alphabetical index.

The Sibbald Guide to the Texas Top Two-Fifty
(The Sibbald Guide, 5725 E. River Rd., Suite 575, Chicago, IL 60631.) Profile of the state's leading public companies and financial institutions.

Standard Directory of Advertising Agencies
(National Register Publishing Co., 3004 Glenview Rd., Wilmette, IL 60091.) *The Red Book* of 5,000 advertising agencies and their 60,000 accounts.

Texas Almanac and State Industrial Guide
(A.H. Belo Corp., Communications Center, Dallas, TX 75265.) Information on business and industry, transportation, education, and other essential facts.

Texas Association of Realtors Referral Directory
(Texas Association of Realtors, P.O. Box 14488, Austin, TX 78761.) Texas Association of Realtors members listed by city.

Texas Banking Red Book
(Bankers Digest, Inc., 6440 N. Central Expwy., Suite 215, Dallas, TX 75206; $15.75.) Lists banks, federal deposit insurance corporations, holding companies, and other banking institutions.

Texas Fact Book
(Bureau of Business Research, University of Texas at Austin, Austin, TX.) Includes economic profiles, business information, employment, and manufacturing. Begins in 1989 with yearly supplements.

Texas Food Industry Association Directory
(Texas Retail Grocers Association, 7333 Hwy. 290 East, Austin, TX 78723.) List of Texas Retail Grocers Association members, sponsors, exhibitors, and advertisers.

Texas Insurance Directory (North and South)
(Insurance Field Co., 4325 Old Shepherdsville Rd., Louisville, KY 40218.) Annual list of facilities and services of licensed property, liability, and life companies and agencies in Texas.

Texas Savings & Loan Directory
(Texas Savings & Loan League, 408 W. 14th St., Austin, TX 78701.) Includes statistical information, regulatory agencies, industry associations, annual reports, and members.

Texas Trade and Professional Associations
(Bureau of Business Research, The University of Texas at Austin.) Lists trade and professional associations.

Travel Industry Personnel Directory
(Capital Cities Media, 7 W. 34th St. New York, NY 10001.)
Lists air and steamship lines, tour operators, bus lines, hotel representatives, foreign and domestic tourist information offices, and trade associations.

Underwriter's Handbook
(National Underwriter Co., 420 E. 4th St., Cincinnati, OH 45202.)
Lists Insurance agents, agencies, adjusters, field representatives, consultants, appraisers, audit and inspection services, and related insurance groups and associations.

U.S. Industrial Directory
(Cahners Publishing Company, 270 Saint Paul St., Denver, CO 80206.) A four-volume set for identifying suppliers, manufacturers, and distributors etc. Lists brief bios for key company executives.

Ward's Business Directory of U.S. Private and Public Companies
(Gale Research Inc., 835 Penobscot Bldg., Detroit, Mich 48226.) Covers nearly 85,000 privately owned companies representing all industries.

Who's Who in the Motion Picture Industry and Who's Who in Television
(Packard Publication Co., 7623 Sunset Blvd., Hollywood, CA 90046.)
Names and addresses of hundreds of directors, producers, production companies, and network executives.

Women Helping Women: A State by State Directory of Services
(Women's Action Alliance, 370 Lexington Ave., New York, NY 10017.)
Covers 180 career counseling centers, services for battered women and rape victims, displaced homemakers programs, planned parenthood clinics, skilled trades training centers, women's centers, women's commission, and women's health services.

Women's Guide to Career Preparation: Scholarships, Grants and Loans
(Anchor Press, Doubleday Publishing Company, 245 Park Ave., New York, NY 10017.) Lists organizations that provide counseling, scholarships, and other assistance to older women and minority women who are returning to work or seeking a career change.

Yearbook of International Organizations
(Union of International Associations and International Chambers of Commerce, Rue Washington 40, B-1050, Brussels, Belgium.) Lists 27,000 truly international organizations (active in at least 3 countries); indexed by name, address, and description.

Newspapers

Answering want ads is one of several tasks to be done in any job search, and generally among the least productive. According to *Forbes* magazine, only about 10 percent of professional and technical people find their jobs through want ads. The typical response is 300 or more resumes per ad. Like any other long shot, however, answering want ads sometimes pays off. Be sure to check not only the classified listings but also the larger display ads that appear in the Sunday business sections of the major papers. These ads are usually for upper-level jobs.

Help-wanted listings generally come in two varieties: open advertisements and blind ads. An open ad is one in which the company identifies itself and lists an address. Your best bet is not to send a resume to a company that prints an open ad. Instead, you should try to identify the hiring authority (see Chapter 5) and pull every string you can think of to arrange an interview directly.

The personnel department is in business to screen out applicants. Of the several hundred resumes that an open ad in a major newspaper is likely to attract, the personnel department will probably forward only a handful to the people who are actually doing the hiring. It's better for you to go to those people directly than to try to reach them by sending a piece of paper (your resume) to the personnel department.

Blind ads are run by companies that do not identify themselves because they do not want to acknowledge receipt of resumes. Another reason companies run blind ads is to obtain a quick and relatively inexpensive salary survey of what a particular job is being paid in the local market. By running the ad they are able to obtain several hundred resumes of individuals from many competing companies at no risk and little expense. Since you don't know who the companies are, your only option in response to a blind ad is to send a resume.

This is among the longest of long shots and usually pays off only if your qualifications are exactly suited to the position that's being advertised. Just remember that if you depend solely on ad responses, you're essentially conducting a passive search, waiting for the mail to arrive or the phone to ring. Passive searchers usually are unemployed a long time.

Newspaper business sections are useful not only for their want ads but also as sources of local business news and news about personnel changes. Learn to read between the lines. If an article announces that Mega-Bucks, Inc., has just acquired a new vice-president, chances are that he or she will be looking for staffers. If the new veep came to Big Bucks from another local company, obviously that company may have at least one vacancy and possibly several.

MAJOR NEWSPAPER RESOURCES

The Dallas Morning News
Communications Center
Dallas, TX 75265
(214) 977-8222
The *News* purchased the *Dallas Times Herald* in late 1991, making Dallas a one-newspaper city. The *News* carries an extensive Sunday classified section. A bulldog Sunday edition is sold on Saturday. Extensive business coverage is carried in the daily business sections.

Fort Worth Star-Telegram
400 W. 7th St.
Fort Worth, TX 76101
Metro (817) 429-2655
The *Star-Telegram* publishes a "Tarrant Business" section on Monday,
which includes business news and features for Fort Worth and the Mid-
Cities area.

National Business Employment Weekly
Box 300
Princeton, NJ 08543-0300
(609) 520-4305
The weekly is published by *The Wall Street Journal*. It reprints recruitment ads from the *Journal's* four regional editions as well as articles and
editorials about the business community.

The Wall Street Journal
1233 Regal Row
Dallas, TX 75247
(214) 631-7250
The nation's leading weekday business publication has a Southwest
edition, which is published locally. Its classified section usually carries
ads for mid- to upper-level management positions. The *Journal* only
covers news about the business community—everything from the
economy to personnel changes in the country's major corporations. If you
really want to do your homework on the business community, the
Journal is the place to start.

SUBURBAN AND COMMUNITY NEWSPAPERS

Most of the following newspapers carry want ads.

**Addison/North Dallas
Register**
4950 Keller Springs Rd.,
Suite 160
Addison, TX 75248
(214) 553-7401
Published on Thursday.

Arlington Citizen-Journal
1111 W. Abram St.
Arlington, TX 76012
(817) 548-5400
Sunday publication is inserted in
the Arlington edition of the *Fort
Worth Star-Telegram.*

Arlington News
1000 Ave. H East
Arlington, TX 76011
Metro (817) 695-0500
Published Thursday, Friday, and
Sunday by the Dallas/Fort Worth
Suburban Newspapers.

Carrollton Chronicle
1712 Belt Line Rd.
Carrollton, TX 75006
(214) 446-0303
Published on Wednesday.

Cedar Hill Chronicle
708 Cedar St.
Cedar Hill, TX 75104
(214) 291-4223
Published on Thursday.

The Colony Leader
5110 Paige Rd., Suite 102
The Colony, TX 75056
(214) 625-6397
Published on Wednesday.

Coppell Gazette
1712 Belt Line Rd.
Carrollton, TX 75006
(214) 446-0303
Published on Wednesday.

How to Get a Job

Dallas Post Tribune
2726 S. Beckley Ave.
Dallas, TX 75224
(214) 946-7678
Published on Thursday. A good
resource for the minority
community.

Duncanville Suburban
606 Oriole
Duncanville, TX 75116
(214) 298-4211
Published on Thursday.

El Sol de Texas
P.O. Box 803402
Dallas, TX 75380
(214) 386-9120
Spanish-language newspaper
published on Thursday, with
news about Dallas, Fort Worth,
and Latin countries.

Farmers Branch Times
1712 Belt Line Rd.
Carrollton, TX 75006
(214) 446-0303
Published on Thursday.

The Garland News
613 State St.
Garland, TX 75040
(214) 272-6591
Published Thursday, Friday, and
Sunday by the Dallas/Fort Worth
Suburban Newspapers.

Grand Prairie News
1000 Ave. H East
Arlington, TX 76011
Metro (817) 695-0500
Published Thursday, Friday, and
Sunday by the Dallas/Fort Worth
Suburban Newspapers.

Grapevine Sun
332 Main St.
Grapevine, TX 76051
(817) 488-8561
Published Thursday and Sunday.

Irving News
1000 Ave. H East
Arlington, TX 76011
Metro (817) 695-0500
Published Thursday, Friday, and
Sunday by the Dallas/Fort Worth
Suburban Newspapers.

Lancaster News
303 W. Pheasant Run
Lancaster, TX 75146
(214) 227-6033
Published on Thursday.

Lewisville Daily Leader
102 Lakeland Plaza
Lewisville, TX 75067
(214) 436-3566
Published Wednesday and
Saturday.

Lewisville News
131 W. Main St.
Lewisville, TX 75067
(214) 436-5551
Published Wednesday, Friday,
and Sunday.

Mesquite News
303 N. Galloway Ave.
Mesquite, TX 75149
(214) 285-6301
Published Thursday.

Metrocrest News
1720 Josey Lane, Suite 100
Carrollton, TX 75006
(214) 418-9999
Published on Thursday, Friday,
and Sunday by the Dallas/Fort
Worth Suburban Newspapers for
Carrollton, Farmers Branch,
Addison, and Coppell.

Mid-Cities News
1000 Ave. H East
Arlington, TX 76011
Metro (817) 695-0500
Published Thursday, Friday, and
Sunday for Hurst, Euless,
Bedford, Haltom City, North
Richland Hills, and Richland
Hills by the Dallas/Fort Worth
Suburban Newspapers.

Oak Cliff Tribune
2303 W. Ledbetter Professional
Bldg., Suite 200
Dallas, TX 75224
(214) 339-3111
Published on Thursday.

70

Park Cities News
8115 Preston Rd., Suite 120
Dallas, TX 75225
(214) 369-7570
Published on Thursday for
Highland Park and University
Park.

Park Cities People
6116 N. Central Expwy.,
Suite 230
Dallas, TX 75206
(214) 739-2244
Published on Thursday for
Highland Park and University
Park.

Plano Daily Star-Courier
801 E. Plano Pkwy., Suite 100
Plano, TX 75074
(214) 424-6565
Published Wednesday through
Sunday, with a special "Working
Section" on Sundays.

Richardson Daily
409 Belle Grove, Suite 101
Richardson, TX 75083
(214) 234-3198
Published Thursday, Friday, and
Sunday by the Dallas/Fort Worth
Suburban Newspapers.

Seagoville Suburbia News
115-A Hall Rd.
Seagoville, TX 75159
(214) 287-3277
Delivered Thursday for Balch
Springs, Combine, Crandall, and
Seagoville.

Suburban Tribune
3008 F. Balch Springs Rd.
Balch Springs, TX 75180
(214) 286-8850
Published Thursday and mailed
to residents in the Southeast
Dallas area.

The White Rocker News
10809 Garland Rd.
Dallas, TX 75218
(214) 327-9335
Published on Thursday for the
White Rock area.

General Business Magazines

The smart job seeker will want to keep abreast of changing trends in
the economy. These periodicals will help you keep up with the
national and Dallas/Fort Worth business scenes.

Business Week
1221 Avenue of the Americas
New York, NY 10020
(212) 997-1221
Weekly.

Dallas Business Journal
4131 N. Central Expwy.,
Suite 310
Dallas, TX 75204
Metro (214) 988-7106
Weekly business publication
(Fridays).

Forbes
60 5th Ave.
New York, NY 10011
(212) 620-2200
Bi-weekly.

Fort Worth Business Press
303 Main
Third Floor
Fort Worth, TX 76102
(817) 336-8300
Weekly business publication
(Fridays).

Fortune
Time & Life Bldg.,
Rockefeller Center
New York, NY 10020
(800) 621-8000
Published 27 times per year.

Money
Time & Life Bldg.,
Rockefeller Center
New York, NY 10020
(800) 633-9970
Monthly.

Newsweek
444 Madison Ave.
New York, NY 10022
(800) 631-1040
Weekly. Includes business
coverage.

Smart Money
1790 Broadway
New York, NY 10019
(800) 444-4204

Success
230 Park Ave.
New York, NY 10169
(800) 234-7324

Time Magazine
1271 Avenue of the Americas
New York, NY 10022
(212) 586-1212
Weekly. Includes business
coverage.

Working Woman
230 Park Ave.
New York, NY 10169
(212) 551-9500
Monthly.

Job-Hunt-Related Publications

The following newspapers and magazines contain only job listings
and job-related information and advice.

AAR/EEO Affirmative Action Register
8356 Olive Blvd.
St. Louis, MO 63132
(314) 991-1335
"The only national EEO recruitment publication directed to females,
minorities, veterans, and the handicapped." Monthly magazine consists
totally of job listings.

Black Employment & Education
2625 Piedmont Rd.
Atlanta, GA 30324
(404) 469-5891
Contact: Ed Admont, General Manager
Magazine publishes career opportunities nationwide. Stores resumes on
database to be accessed by employers.

Career Pilot
Future Aviation Professionals of America
4959 Massachusetts Blvd.
Atlanta, GA 30337
(800) JET-JOBS
Monthly magazine outlines employment opportunities for career pilots.
Organization provides hiring information, salary surveys, monthly job
reports, and counseling to prepare for interviews.

Community Jobs
50 Beacon St.
Boston, MA 02108
(617) 720-5627
The employment newspaper for the non-profit sector.

Contract Engineer Weekly
CE Publications, Inc.
P.O. Box 97000
Kirkland, WA 98083
(206) 823-2222
Weekly magazine of job opportunities for contract engineers.

Federal Jobs Digest
310 N. Highland Ave.
Ossining, NY 10562
Elaborate listing of job opportunities with the federal government.
Published bi-weekly.

International Employment Hotline
P.O. Box 6170
McLean, VA 22106
Monthly listing of overseas jobs. Provides a resume service for subscribers.

Legal Employment Newsletter
P.O. Box 36601
Grosse Point, MI 48236
Newsletter lists open legal positions as well as career opportunities in
the public-private sector.

National and Federal Legal Employment Report
1010 Vermont Ave., NW
Washington, DC 20005
(202) 393-3311
Monthly in-depth listings of attorney and law-related jobs in federal
government and with other public and private employers throughout the
U.S.

Opportunities in Non-Profit Organizations
ACCESS: Networking in the Public Interest
67 Winthrop St.
Cambridge, MA 02138
Monthly listing of non-profit jobs around the country, organized by type
of non-profit.

**Widening
opportunities for
African-Americans**

S. Barry Hamdani, publisher of *Black Employment & Education* magazine (see above), says jobs are increasing in health care throughout the U.S. Likewise, careers in education are becoming more available.

"I can offer two tips for our readers seeking business management opportunities," says Hamdani. "Before the interview make sure you know more about the employer than they know about you—research the company. Next be sure several key people within the company have your resume before the interview. You'll need all the inside influence you can get." ■

Local Trade and Special Interest Magazines

Every industry or service business has its trade press—that is, editors, reporters, and photographers whose job it is to cover an industry or trade. You should become familiar with the magazines of the industries or professions that interest you, especially if you're in the interviewing stage of your job search. Your prospective employers are reading the industry trade magazines; you should be too.

Trade magazines are published for a specific business or professional audience; they are usually expensive and available by subscription only. Many of the magazines we've listed here are available at major Dallas/Fort Worth area libraries. For those not to be found at the library, call up the magazine's editorial or sales office and ask if you can come over to look at the latest issue.

The following magazines have editorial offices in the Dallas/Fort Worth area, reporting area news about the people and businesses in their industry. Many carry local want ads and personnel changes. For a complete listing of the trade press, consult the *Ayer Directory of Publications* at the library.

Adweek/Southwest
2909 Cole Ave., Suite 220
Dallas, TX 75204
(214) 871-9550
Weekly advertising, public relations, and marketing trade publication.

Bankers Digest
6440 N. Central Expwy.,
Suite 215
Dallas, TX 75206
(214) 373-4544
Weekly Texas banking publication.

Builder Insider
640 North Central Expwy.,
Suite 215
Dallas, TX 75206
(214) 871-2913
Tabloid for builders, architects, and remodelers.

Daily Commercial Record
706 Main St.
Dallas, TX 75202
(214) 741-6366
Newspaper covering business, legal, and real estate interests.

The Cattleman
1301 W. 7th St.
Fort Worth, TX 76102
(817) 332-7155
Monthly cattlemen's magazine.

Cotton Gin and Oil Mill Press
3638 Executive Blvd.
Mesquite, TX 75149
(214) 288-7511
Bi-weekly cotton industry publication.

Farm Journal
811 S. Central Expwy., Suite 525
Richardson, TX 75080
(214) 231-6033
Regional editorial office for monthly farm industry publication.

Greenhouse Manager
120 St. Louis Ave.
Fort Worth, TX 76104
(817) 332-8236
Monthly worldwide publication for greenhouse growers.

Impressions
15400 Knoll Trail Dr., Suite 112
Dallas, TX 75248
(214) 239-3060
Monthly publication for the
imprinted sportswear and textile
screen printing industries.

The Insurance Record
2730 Stemmons Frwy., Suite 507
Dallas, TX 75207
(214) 630-0687
Bi-weekly insurance trade
publication.

**Journal of Petroleum
Technology**
222 Palisades Creek Dr.
Richardson, TX 75080
(214) 952-9393
Monthly publication for drilling,
exploration, production engineers, and managers.

Legal Assistant Today
Legal Assistant Today, Inc.
6060 North Central Frwy.
Dallas, TX 75206
(214) 369-6868
Professional news and information magazine for legal assistants.

Nursery Manager
120 St. Louis Ave.
Fort Worth, TX 76104
Metro (817) 429-1494
Monthly worldwide publication
for nursery industry.

Oil & Gas Journal
4849 Greenville Ave., Suite 660
Dallas, TX 75206
(214) 739-3338
Weekly petroleum industry
publication.

Performance
1203 Lake St., Suite 200
Fort Worth, TX 76102
(817) 338-9444
Weekly international touring
talent magazine.

Pipeline & Gas Journal
5787 S. Hampton, Suite 230
Dallas, TX 75232
(214) 467-3933
Monthly petroleum industry
publication.

**SAF-The Center for Commer-
cial Horticulture**
1601 Duke St.
Alexandria, VA 22314
(800) 366-4743
Monthly florist industry publication.

Texas Contractor
2510 National Dr.
Garland, TX 75041
(214) 271-2693
Weekly publication and daily
newsletter for heavy construction
industry.

Well Servicing
Workover/Well Servicing
Publications, Inc.
6060 North Central Frwy.
Dallas, TX 75206
(214) 692-0771
Oil journal.

General Interest Magazines and Newspapers

In your job search, you'll find it helpful to know as much about the
Dallas/Fort Worth area as possible. The following publications will
help you become better informed:

American Way
P.O. Box 619640
DFW Airport, TX 75261
Metro (817) 967-1804
American Airlines' semi-weekly
inflight magazine.

Aura of Fort Worth
2917 Morton
Fort Worth, TX 76107
(817) 332-3548
Bi-monthly magazine for Tarrant
County.

Baptist Standard
2343 Lone Star Dr.
Dallas, TX 75212
(214) 630-4571
Weekly publication for Southern
Baptists.

Buddy Magazine
11258 Goodnight Lane
Dallas, TX 75229
(214) 484-9010
Monthly music magazine with a
special edition for the Dallas/Fort
Worth area that includes entertainment listings.

Dallas Business Journal
4131 N. Central Expwy.,
Suite 310
Dallas, TX 75204
Metro (214) 520-1010
Weekly business publication.

Dallas Child
3330 Earhart Dr., Suite 102
Carrollton, TX 75006
(214) 960-8474
Monthly magazine for parents.

Dallas Cowboys Weekly
Cowboys Center
1 Cowboys Pkwy.
Irving, TX 75063
(214) 556-9972
Dallas Cowboys publication,
distributed weekly during
football season and monthly
during off-season.

Dallas Observer
3211 Irving Blvd., Suite 110
Dallas, TX 75247
(214) 637-2072
Weekly entertainment, lifestyles,
and current events publication.

Fort Worth Business Press
303 Main St.
Fort Worth, TX 76106
(817) 336-8300
Weekly business publication
(Fridays).

Key Magazine
2915 LBJ Frwy., Suite 136
Dallas, TX 75234
(214) 484-6383
Monthly visitor's magazine.

Private Clubs
3030 LBJ Frwy., Suite 600
Dallas, TX 75234
(214) 243-6191
Bi-monthly magazine for Club
Corporation of America members.

SR Texas
11551 Forest Central Dr.,
Suite 305
Dallas, TX 75243
(214) 341-9429
Monthly publication for people
over the age of 50.

**The Texas Catholic
Newspaper**
3725 Blackburn, P.O. Box 190347
Dallas, TX 75219
(214) 528-8792
Bi-weekly publication with local
and international news for
Catholics.

Texas Jewish Post
11333 N. Central Expwy.,
Suite 213
Dallas, TX 75243
(214) 692-7283
Weekly publication with local
and international news for the
Jewish faith.

The Texas Lawyer
1 Ferris Plaza
400 S. Record St., Suite 1400
Dallas, TX 75202
(214) 744-9300
Weekly publication for the legal profession.

Travelhost Magazine
10701 N. Stemmons Frwy.
Dallas, TX 75220
(214) 691-1163
A guide placed in 22,000 area motel rooms, with advertising for entertainment and restaurants along with some real estate ads.

Vitality Magazine
8080 N. Central L.B. 78
Dallas, TX 75206
(214) 691-1480
Weekly travel magazine, with features on real estate, entertainment, health, wellness, and dining available at area hotels.

Telephone Job Banks

Here's a way to find out about job openings by "letting your fingers do the walking." Just dial any one of the numerous telephone job banks and listen to the taped recordings that describe available positions and how to apply.

There is no charge for most of these job hotlines other than what you might spend for a telephone call. The following is a list of area telephone job banks.

City of Dallas (214) 670-5908

City of Fort Worth (817) 871-7760

Communicators' Job Bank (214) 684-8301

Dallas County Community College District
(214) 746-2438

Federal Job Information Line (214) 767-8035

Network of Hispanic Communicators and DFW ABC Job Line
(214) 977-6635

Southern Methodist University (214) 768-1111

Tarrant County Junior College (817) 335-6721

Texas Christian University (817) 921-7791

Texas Instruments (214) 995-6666

The right job may be only a phone call away

The **Communicators' Job Bank,** (214) 684-8301, is a joint service project of the local International Association of Business Communicators (IABC) and the Public Relations Society of America (PRSA). Each week, job bank coordinator Joan Hammond updates a telephone recording that relays information about openings in public relations, advertising, marketing, design, and related fields. She describes the job, qualifications, and salary range, but no company name is disclosed.

To apply for openings through the Communicators' Job Bank, you request that your resumes be sent to the job listings of your choice. To register with the Communicators' Job Bank a small fee is charged that covers the cost of mailing your resumes to an unlimited number of employers during a three-month period. IABC and PRSA members pay $10, and non-members are charged $20. An average of 30 jobs are usually on file each week.

In addition to the above service, the groups also sponsor the "Communicators Career Connection," which is a monthly speakers meeting concerning specific job-search techniques and is open to members at a nominal fee. Contact R.V. Baugus (214) 252-0404 ■

Developing a Strategy: The ABCs of Networking

The successful job search doesn't happen by accident. It's the result of careful planning. Before you rush out to set up your first interview, it's important to establish a strategy, that is, to develop a plan for researching the job market and contacting potential employers.

This chapter and Chapter 7 will cover specific techniques, such as networking, that you'll find useful in your search. But before we get to them, a few words are in order about your overall approach.

It's Going to Take Some Time

Looking for a new job is no easy task. It's as difficult and time-consuming for a bright young woman with a brand-new MBA as it is for a fifty-year-old executive with years of front-line experience. Every once in a while someone lucks out. One of Rob Rainey's clients established a record at IATREIA/Outpath by finding a new position in ten days. But most people should plan on two to six months of full-time job-hunting before they find a position they'll really be happy with.

According to *Forbes* magazine, the older you are and the more you earn, the longer it will take to find what you're looking for—in fact, up to six months for people over 40 earning more than $40,000. People under 40 in the $20,000-$40,000 bracket average two to four months.

Your line of work as well as local market demand will also affect the length of your search. Usually, the easier it is to demonstrate tangible bottom-line results, the faster you can line up a job. Lawyers, public relations people, and advertising executives are harder to place than accountants and sales people, according to Bill Wheeler an executive search recruiter in Dallas.

Be Good to Yourself

Whether or not you're currently employed, it's important to nurture your ego when you're looking for a new job. Rejection rears its ugly head more often in a job search than at most other times, and self-doubt can be deadly.

Make sure you get regular exercise during your job search to relieve stress. You'll sleep better, feel better, and perhaps even lose a few pounds.

Take care of your diet and watch what you drink. Many people who start to feel sorry for themselves tend to overindulge in food or alcohol. Prescription medications may not be as helpful as sharing your progress with your family or a couple of close friends.

Beef up your wardrobe so that you look and feel good during your employment interviews. There's no need to buy an expensive new suit, especially if you're on an austerity budget, but a new shirt, blouse, tie, pair of shoes, or hairstyle may be in order.

Maintain a positive outlook by developing a support system of friends and family who can be available and supportive when needed. Unemployment may not be the end of the world; however it may feel like it is to you if this is your first experience, just remember that few people complete a career without losing a job at least once. Keep a sense of humor, too. Every job search has its funny moments. It's OK to joke about your situation and share your sense of humor with your friends and family.

Life goes on despite your job search. Your spouse and kids still need your attention. Try not to take out your anxieties, frustrations, and fears on those close to you. At the very time you need support and affirmation, your friends may prefer to stay at arm's length. You can relieve their embarrassment by being straightforward about your situation and by telling them how they can help you.

Put Yourself on a Schedule

Looking for work is a job in itself. Establish a schedule for your job search and stick to it. If you're unemployed, work at getting a new job full-time—from 8:30 a.m. to 5:30 p.m., five days a week; and from 9 a.m. to 12 noon on Saturdays. During a job search, there is a temptation to use "extra" time for recreation or to catch up on household tasks. Arranging two or three exploratory interviews will prove a lot more useful to you than washing the car or cleaning out the garage. You can do such tasks at night or on Sundays, just as you would if you were working.

Don't take a vacation during your search. Do it after you accept an offer and before you begin a new job. You might be tempted to "sort things out on the beach." But taking a vacation when you're unemployed isn't as restful as it sounds. You'll spend most of your time worrying about what will happen when the trip is over.

Even if you're currently employed, it's important to establish regular hours for your job search. If you're scheduling interviews, try to arrange several for one day so that you don't have to take too much time away from your job. You might also arrange interviews for your lunch hour. You can make phone calls during lunch or on your break time. You'd also be surprised at how many people you can reach before and after regular working hours.

Tax-deductible job-hunting expenses

Deidre Wells, a certified public accountant in Arlington, Texas, offers the following tips on deducting job-hunting expenses on your income tax form. To qualify for certain deductions, you must hunt for a job in the same field you just left, or in the field that currently employs you. For example, someone who has worked as a public school teacher could not be compensated for the cost of getting a real estate license and seeking a Realtors job.

If you are unemployed or want to switch jobs, expenses can be itemized on Schedule A of Form 1040. Expenses you probably can deduct include preparing, printing, and mailing resumes; and vocational guidance counseling and testing. You might also be able to take the standard government reimbursement for miles driven to and from job interviews. Telephone, postage, and newspaper expenses may also be deductible.

While seeking work out of town, additional deductions might be allowed for transportation, food, and lodging.

Another good bit of advice: tax laws are subject to change, so always check with your local Internal Revenue Service office. ∎

Watch Your Expenses

Spend what you have to spend for basic needs such as food, transportation, and housing. But watch major expenditures that could be delayed or not made at all. The kids will still need new shoes, but a $200 dinner party at a fancy place could just as well be changed to sandwiches and beer at home.

Keep track of all expenses that you incur in your job search, such as telephone and printing bills, postage, newspapers, parking, transportation, tolls, and meals purchased during the course of interviewing. These may be tax deductible.

Networking Is the Key to a Successful Job Search

The basic tasks of a job search are fairly simple. Once you've figured out what kind of work you want to do, you need to know which companies might have such jobs and then make contact with the hiring authority. These tasks are also known as researching the job market and generating leads and interviews. Networking, or developing your personal contacts, is the best technique for finding out about market and industrial trends and is unsurpassed as a way to generate leads and interviews.

Networking is nothing more than asking the people you already know to help you explore the job market and meet the people who are actually doing the hiring. Each adult you know has access to at least 30 people you do not know. Of course, a lot of them will not be able to do much in the way of helping you find a job. But if you start with, say, 20 or 30 people, and each of them tells you about 3 other people who may be able to help you, you've built a network of 60 to 90 contacts.

Mark S. Granovetter, a Harvard sociologist, reported to *Forbes* magazine that "informal contacts" account for almost 75 percent of all successful job searches. Agencies find about 9 percent of new jobs for professional and technical people, and ads yield another 10 percent or so. Since 75% of all successful job searches are the result of networking, you would be well advised to concentrate about the same percentage of effort in this area as well. Others may be going the passive route by answering ads and waiting for agencies to call them. You can seize the initiative by going after specific jobs only you know about from your networking.

Here's an example of a networking letter

Box 7457
The University of Dallas
Irving, TX 75033
(214) 555-2468

April 11, 1994

Dr. Norman Hartman
President
Combined Opinion Research
300 Progress Ave.
Irving, TX 75008

Dear Dr. Hartman:

Dr. Robert Brown, with whom I have studied these past two years, suggested that you might be able to advise me of opportunities in the field of social and political research in the Dallas/Fort Worth area.

I am about to graduate from the University of Dallas with a B.A. in American History, and am a member of Phi Beta Kappa. For two of the last three summers I have worked in the public sector as an intern with Citizens for a Better Government. Last summer I worked as a desk assistant at *Newsweek's* Dallas office.

I am eager to begin work and would appreciate a few minutes of your time to discuss employment possibilities in the field of social and political research. I will be finished with exams on May 24 and would like to arrange a meeting with you shortly thereafter.

I would appreciate an opportunity to visit with you about your firm and its activities and will call next week. Dr. Brown sends his warmest regards.

Sincerely,

Steven Sharp ■

How to Start

To begin the networking process, draw up a list of all the possible contacts who can help you gain access to someone who can hire you for the job you want. Naturally, the first sources, the ones at the top of your list, will be people you know personally: friends, colleagues, former clients, relatives, acquaintances, customers, and club and church members. Just about everyone you know, whether or not he or she is employed, can generate contacts for you.

Don't forget to talk with your banker, lawyer, insurance agent, dentist, and other people who provide you with services. It is the nature of their business to know a lot of people who might help you in your search. Leave no stone unturned in your search for contacts. Go through your Christmas card list, alumni club list, and any other list you can think of.

On the average, it may take 10 to 15 contacts to generate one formal interview. It may take 5 or 10 of these formal interviews to generate one solid offer. And it may take 5 offers before you uncover the exact job situation you've been seeking. You may have to talk to as many as 250 people before you get the job you want.

Don't balk at talking to friends, acquaintances, and neighbors about your job search. In reality, you're asking for advice, not charity. Most of the people you'll contact will be willing to help you, if only you tell them how.

The Exploratory Interview

If I introduce you to my friend George at a major downtown bank, he will get together with you as a favor to me. When you have your meeting with him, you will make a presentation about what you've done in your work, what you want to do, and (most importantly) you will ask for his advice, ideas, and opinions. That is an exploratory interview. As is true of any employment interview, you must make a successful sales presentation to get what you want. You must convince George that you are a winner and that you deserve his help in your search.

The help the interviewers provide is usually in the form of suggestions to meet new people or contact certain companies. I introduced you to George. Following your successful meeting, he introduces you to Tom, Dick, and Mary. Each of them provides additional leads. In this way, you spend most of your time interviewing, not staying at home waiting for the phone to ring or the mail to arrive.

A job doesn't have to be vacant in order for you to have a successful meeting with a hiring authority. If you convince an employer that you would make a good addition to his or her staff, the employer might create a job for you where none existed before. In this way, networking taps the "hidden job market."

To make the most of the networking technique, continually brush up on your interviewing skills (we've provided a refresher course in Chapter 7). Remember, even when you're talking with an old friend, you are still conducting an exploratory interview. Don't treat it as casual conversation.

Developing Professional Contacts

Friends and acquaintances are the obvious first choice when you're drawing up a list of contacts. But don't forget professional and trade organizations, clubs, and societies—they are valuable sources of contacts, leads, and information. In certain cases, it isn't necessary for you to belong in order to attend a meeting or an annual or monthly lunch, dinner, or cocktail party.

Many such groups also publish newsletters, another valuable source of information on the job market and industry trends. Some professional associations offer placement services to members, in which case it may be worth your while to join officially. At the end of this chapter, we've provided a list of selected organizations that might prove useful for networking purposes.

If you're utterly new to the area and don't as yet know a soul, your job will naturally be tougher. But it's not impossible. It just means you have to hustle that much more. Here are some first steps you should take. Start attending the meetings of any professional society or civic organization of which you've been a member in the past. Find a church, temple, or religious organization that you're comfortable with and start attending. Join a special interest group. It could be anything from The Sierra Club to Parents Without Partners.

If you're just out of college (or even haven't finished yet), work through your alumni association to find out who else in the area attended your alma mater. If you were in a fraternity or sorority, use those connections. If you're not a member of any of the groups mentioned above, now's the time to join—or to investigate some of the networking groups that follow.

Once you've taken the trouble to show up at a meeting, be friendly. Introduce yourself. Tell people you talk to what your situation is, but don't be pushy. You've come because you're interested in this organization and what it stands for. Volunteer to serve on a committee. You'll get to know a smaller number of people much better, and they'll see you as a responsible, generous person, a person they'll want to help. Do a bang-up job on your committee and they'll want to help all the more.

Take charge of your career search!

Martin Birnbach conducts a weekly call-in career and job show on KLIF radio every Sunday afternoon. Martin is particularly knowledgeable about training opportunities, companies looking for employees, and who you need to contact.

He adds, "Answering ads, networking, joining counseling groups—these are all reactive job hunting. Identify companies and industries, target specific hiring authorities in each company, and try to create your own openings and secure interviews. This way you are the only candidate under consideration and you have greatly enhanced your chances of getting hired—*be pro-active.* ∎

Keeping Yourself Organized

The most difficult part of any job search is getting started. You can get a Day Runner or comparable Time Management System at most office supply stores at a reasonable cost. It has been our experience over the years that this can be one of your best investments and insurance against missed appointments and lost information.

In a short time you will generate many letters and be waiting for a number of return calls. Nothing is more embarrassing or destructive to your candidacy than to finally get an important return call or response to one of your letters and then not remember the individual, ad, or circumstance the person is calling about. With the information neatly entered in your Day Runner, a quick glance in the alphabetical section brings you immediately up to date.

If you're on a tight budget, a pocket calendar or engagement diary that divides each work day into hourly segments is an inexpensive method to address this need. You will also want to keep a personal log of calls and contacts. You may want to develop a format that's different from the one shown here. Fine. The point is to keep a written record of every person you contact in your job search and the results of each contact.

Your appointment calendar (it can be a notebook from the convenience store) will help keep you from getting confused and losing track of the details of your search. If you call someone who's

out of town until Tuesday, say, your log can flag this call so it won't
fall between the cracks. It may also come in handy for future job
searches.

Your log's "disposition" column can act as a reminder of additional sources of help you'll want to investigate. You'll also have a
means of timing the correspondence that should follow any interview.

CALLS AND CONTACTS

Date	Name & Title	Company	Phone	Disposition
2/10	Chas. Junior, V.P. Sales	Top Parts	(214) 689-5562	Interview 2/15; 9 a.m.
2/10	E. Franklin Sales Manager	Frameco	(214) 876-0900	Out of town until 2/17
2/10	L. Duffy Dir. Marketing	Vassar Inc.	(817) 744-8700	Out of office. Call in aft.
2/10	P. Lamm Dir. Sales	Golfco Ent.	(817) 834-3000	Busy to 2/28 Call then.
2/10	E. Waixel VP Mktg. & Sales	Half'n'Half Foods	(214) 342-1200	Interview 2/14; 2 p.m.

If you're unemployed and job hunting full time, schedule yourself
for two exploratory interviews a day for the first week and three to
five completed networking phone calls per day. Each meeting should
result in at least three subsequent leads. Leave the second week
open for the appointments you generated during the first. Maintain
this pattern as you go along in your search.

We can't emphasize too strongly how important it is that you put
yourself on a job-searching schedule, whether or not you're currently
employed. A schedule shouldn't function as a straitjacket, but it
ought to serve as a way of organizing your efforts for greatest
efficiency. Much of your job-hunting time will be devoted to developing your network of contacts. But you should also set aside a certain
portion of each week for doing your homework on companies that
interest you (see Chapter 4) and for pursuing other means of
contacting employers (we'll get to these in a minute).

As you go through your contacts and begin to research the job
market, you'll begin to identify certain employers in which you're
interested. Keep a list of them. For each one that looks particularly
promising, begin a file that contains articles about the company, its
annual report, product brochures, personnel policy, and the like.
Every so often, check your "potential employer" list against your log
to make sure that you're contacting the companies that interest you
most.

Go for the Hiring Authority

The object of your job search is to convince the person who has the power to hire you that you ought to be working for him or her. The person you want to talk to is not necessarily the president of the company. It's the person who heads the department that could use your expertise. If you're a salesperson, you probably want to talk with the vice president of sales or marketing. If you're in data processing, the manager of operations is the person you need to see.

How do you find the hiring authority? If you're lucky, someone you know personally will tell you whom to see and introduce you. Otherwise, you'll have to do some homework. Some of the directories listed in Chapter 4 will name department heads for major companies in the Dallas/Fort Worth area. If you cannot otherwise find out who heads the exact department that interests you, call the company and ask the operator. (It's a good idea to do this anyway since directories go out of date as soon as a department head leaves a job.)

Use an introduction wherever possible when first approaching a company—that's what networking is all about, anyway. For those companies that you must approach "cold," use the phone to arrange a meeting with the hiring authority beforehand. Don't assume you can drop in and see a busy executive without an appointment. And don't assume you can get to the hiring authority through the personnel department. If at all possible, you don't want to fill out any personnel forms until you have had a serious interview. The same goes for sending resumes (see Chapter 3). In general, resumes are better left behind, after an interview, than sent ahead to generate a meeting.

Telephone Tactics

Cold calls are difficult for most job seekers. Frequently, a reception-ist or secretary, sometimes both, stands between you and the hiring authority you want to reach. One way around this is to call early in the morning before the support staff arrive or about a half-hour after closing. There's a good chance that the secretary will be gone, and the boss will still be finishing up the XYZ project report. Only now there will be no one to run interference for him or her.

Generally, you're going to have to go through a support staffer, so the first rule is to act courteously and accord him or her the same professional respect you'd like to be accorded yourself. This person is not just a secretary. Often, part of his or her job is to keep unsolicited job hunters out of the boss's hair. You want this interme-diary to be your ally, not your adversary. If possible, sell what a wonderfully qualified person you are and how it will be to the company's advantage to have you aboard.

If you're not put through to the hiring authority, don't leave your name and expect a return call. If you leave a message and the executive doesn't know you, he may or may not return the call, and if he does there is a good chance you won't be there when he does. A busy executive rarely calls a stranger back twice. To maintain control of your search, ask when there's a convenient time you might call back, or allow yourself to be put on hold. You can read job-search literature or compose cover letters while you wait. Be sure and keep your target's name and title and the purpose of your call on a card before you, however. You don't want to be at a loss for words when you're finally put through.

Before actually starting your networking calls, take a little time to adjust your attitude and prepare a brief script about who you are and why you are calling. There are two important things to keep in mind before you start:

1. *Never* ask a contact, for a job! Always decompress the person in your initial contact, which is usually by phone, and make it clear that your objective is advice, ideas, and information. Few, if any, will be able to offer you a job or even a legitimate lead, so don't create embarrassment by making them the heavy when they have to reject you. Your first objective is to make a friend and put your contact at ease.

2. You may feel very uncomfortable about asking for help. However, most people are more than happy to help if you ask—and it makes them feel good in the process. A lot of them will identify with your situation and may be thinking, "It wasn't long ago that I was in the same boat."

During the turbulent 90s with lots of people trying to network into new jobs, avoid the pitfall of trying to network with highly visible public figures and well-known executives. These people tend to be "over-networked" and will set up some very challenging barriers to maintain their privacy. Your best bet with this type of person is to arrange through a mutual friend to call them at a pre-set time and with a very specific and well-organized agenda. Most do not suffer unfocused fishing expeditions well and will appreciate your efforts at being brief and organized.

Once you make the call, you must be prepared to get right to the point. If possible, set up an appointment and get off the phone before you find yourself in a telephone interview. The objective of such a phone interview, obviously, will be to establish reasons why your target should not grant you a meeting. Avoid this trap if you can. If you do find yourself involved in a phone interview, do your best to demonstrate how you can contribute to your interviewer's company.

When calling one of your primary contacts, that is, some one you know on a first-name basis, you might say:

"John, I've decided to leave Universal Electronics. I've been giving a lot of thought to career options and what I would like to do next. I've put together a preliminary marketing strategy and I'd like to drop by for a few minutes and get your impressions and ideas. You're pretty knowledgeable about the electronics industry and you've known me for quite a while. Would it be convenient to meet for 20-30 minutes later this week?" (Total elapsed time 30 seconds)

When calling a secondary contact, that is, someone who you have been referred to but have never met, you might say:

"Ms. Hartley, my name is David Sellinghard, and our mutual friend, John Overstreet, referred me to you. I'm planning to leave

Universal Electronics in the next few months, and I've put together a career plan focused toward the medical robotics field. John said you had a lot of insight into this emerging field, and he thought you might be willing to give me your impressions of my marketing plan. I've done quite a bit of research in the field and I'm really excited about what's been accomplished in such a short time. I also believe there is a lot for me to learn. Could we get together for 20-30 minutes at a convenient time next week?" (Total elapsed time 30 seconds)

Your worst case scenario may be the necessity to "cold call" a target executive. While technically this is not networking, it may be the only way to reach some key individual in your field of interest. In this instance you must create interest by using your "five minute commercial":

"Mr. Bighammer, my name is David Sellinghard, and I'm an electronics engineer with Universal Electronics. I'm planning a career move, and I've developed a strategy for applying robotics technology to the medical field. Your name has come up several times during networking conversations as an expert in government grants for innovative technology. I was wondering if you would be willing to spend a few minutes with me, sharing your experience and ideas. I'd particularly appreciate hearing about companies who seem to be on the leading edge in this field. Could we meet for 20-25 minutes sometime early next week?" (Total elapsed time 40 seconds)

You will need to write out your initial approaches and practice them until you feel comfortable and they sound smooth and articulate.

Other Tactics for Contacting Employers

Direct contact with the hiring authority—either through a third-party introduction (networking) or by calling for an appointment directly—is far and away the most effective job-hunting method. Your strategy and schedule should reflect that fact, and most of your energy should be devoted to direct contact. It's human nature, however, not to put all your eggs in one basket. You may want to explore other methods of contacting potential employers, but they should take up no more than a quarter of your job-hunting time.

Calling or writing to personnel offices may occasionally be productive, especially when you know that a company is looking for someone with your particular skills. But personnel people, by the nature of their responsibility, tend to screen out rather than welcome newcomers to the company fold. You're always better off going directly to the hiring authority.

Consider the case of a company that runs an ad in *The Wall Street Journal*. The ad may bring as many as 600 responses. The head of personnel asks one of the secretaries to separate the resumes into three piles according to educational level. The personnel chief automatically eliminates two of the three stacks. He or she then flips through the third and eliminates all but, say, eight resumes. The personnel specialist will call the eight applicants, screen them over the phone, and invite three for a preliminary interview. Of those three, two will be sent to the hiring authority for interviews. That means 598 applicants never even got a chance to make their case.

Statistically, fewer than one out of four job hunters succeed by going to personnel departments, responding to ads (either open or blind), or using various employment services. Some do find meaningful work this way, however. We repeat, if you decide to use a method other than networking or direct contact, don't spend more than 25 percent of your job-hunting time on it.

Fort Worth Post Office sheds light on blind ads

Often, ads ask a candidate to send a resume to a P.O. Box. If you decide to reply, you face several challenges. What company is involved? To whom should I address my cover letter? What is the company's position in the market?

The office of the Postmaster in Fort Worth states that if the holder of a post office box does business with the public, the post office must release the information it possesses on the holder. This information enables you to personalize your response and do some research to tailor your resume to a specific firm. It avoids a blind response.

Call the Post Office with the zip code and box number indicated in the ad to get the facts—and get a competitive edge on other applicants. ■

As you might expect, many books have been written on job-hunting strategy and techniques. Here is a list of selected resources.

SELECTED BOOKS ON JOB-HUNTING STRATEGY

Baldwin, Eleanor. *300 Ways to Get a Better Job*. Holbrook, MA: Bob Adams, Inc., 1991.
Ball, Ben. *Manage Your Career: A Self Help Guide to Career Choice/Change*. Oakland, CA: Beckman Publishers, 1989.
Bastress, Frances. *Relocating Spouse's Guide to Employment*, 3rd ed. Chevy Chase, MD: Woodley Publications, 1989.
Baxter, Rogene, and Marcelle Brashear. *Do It Yourself Career Kit: A Career Planning Tool*. Maraga, CA: Bridgewater Press, 1990.
Beatty, Richard H. *The Complete Job Search Book*. New York: John Wiley & Sons, 1988.
Boldt, Lawrence. *Zen and the Art of Making a Living*. New York: Penguin Books, 1993.
Bolles, Richard N. *The Three Boxes of Life and How to Get Out of Them*. Berkeley, CA: Ten Speed Press, 1983.
Bolles, Richard N. *What Color Is Your Parachute?* Berkeley, CA.: Ten Speed Press, 1994. The bible for job hunters and career changers, this book is revised every year and is widely regarded as the most useful and creative manual available.
Camden, Thomas M. *The Job Hunter's Final Exam*. Chicago: Surrey Books, 1990.
Ciabattari, Jane. *Winning Moves: How to Come Out Ahead in a Corporate Shakeout*. New York: Rawson Associates, 1988.

Dubin, Judith A., and Melonie R. Keveles. *Fired for Success.* New York: Warner Books, 1990.

Harkavy, Michael. *One Hunderd One Careers: A Guide to the Fastest Growing Opportunities.* New York: John Wiley & Sons, 1990.

Hiam, A., and S. Angle. *Adventure Careers,* New York: Career Press, 1992.

Hirsch, Arlene S. *Careers Checklists.* Lincolnwood, IL: National Textbook, 1990.

Jackson, Tom. *Guerrilla Tactics in the Job Market.* New York: Bantam Books, 1991. Filled with unconventional but effective suggestions.

Johnson, William Courtney. *The Career Match Method.* New York: John Wiley and Sons, 1992.

Jones, Lawrence K. *The Encyclopedia of Career Change and Work Issues.* Phoenix, AZ: Orax Press, 1992.

Kennedy, Joyce Lane, and Darryl Laramore. *Joyce Lane Kennedy's Career Book.* Lincolnwood: VGM Career Horizons, 1993.

Kleiman, Carol. *The 100 Best Jobs for the 1990s & Beyond.* Chicago: Dearborn Financial Publishing, 1992.

Lee, Patricia. *The Complete Guide to Job Sharing.* New York: Walker, 1983.

Morin, William J., and James C. Cabrera. *Parting Company: How to Survive the Loss of a Job and Find Another Successfully.* San Diego, CA: HBJ, 1991.

Noble, John. *The Job Search Handbook.* Boston: Bob Adams, Inc., 1988.

Pederson, Laura. *Street Smart Career Guide.* New York: Crown Trade Publishing, 1993.

Riehle, Kathleen. *What Smart People do When Losing Their Jobs.* New York: John Wiley and Sons, 1991.

Rogers, Henry C. *Roger's Rules for Businesswomen.* New York: St. Martin's Press, 1988.

Rushlow, Ed. *Get a Better Job.* Princeton, NJ: Peterson's Guides, 1990.

Wood, Orrin G. *Your Hidden Assets—The Key to Getting Executive Jobs.* Homewood, IL: Dow Jones-Irwin, 1984. Written by the co-founder of a job-changing workshop developed for Harvard Business School alumni; an upscale book.

There follows a selected list of organized groups ready-made for networking. Pick those that fit best into your career game plan, and work through them to land the job you want. At the end of the chapter is a special listing of network groups for women and minorities.

SELECTED DALLAS/FORT WORTH PROFESSIONAL ORGANIZATIONS, TRADE GROUPS, NETWORKS, CLUBS, AND SOCIETIES

Administrative Management Society
Dallas Chapter
1400 Corporate
Irving, TX 75038
(214) 580-0400
President: Donna Geel
Professional society for office managers, personnel professionals, and field operations managers. Publishes a newsletter and conducts monthly meetings.

Administrative Management Society
Fort Worth Chapter
1320 S. University Dr., Suite 400
Fort Worth, TX 76107
(817) 336-2565
President: Ronald B. Woods
Parallels Dallas chapter.

Advertising Club of Fort Worth
P.O. Box 820376
Fort Worth, TX 76182
(817) 283-3615
Contact: Grace Collins, Executive Director
Organization for professionals in the advertising business. Meets weekly and publishes a monthly newsletter with job openings.

American Association of Medical Assistants
Garland Chapter
726 Twilight Dr.
Garland, TX 75040
(214) 272-2052
Contact: Linda Coena
Offers aid to people who want to be certified and provides continuing education programs.

Dallas Chapter
2510 Moreland
Mesquite, TX 75150
(214) 270-5226

Fort Worth Chapter
4100 Frawley Dr.
Fort Worth, TX 76180
(817) 284-2204

American Association of Petroleum Landmen
4100 Fossil Creek Blvd.
Fort Worth, TX 76137
(817) 847-7700
Contact: Jack Deeter, Executive Vice President and chief operating officer.

American Association for Respiratory Care
11030 Ables Lane

Dallas, TX 75229
(214) 243-2272
Executive Director: Sam Giordano
National headquarters for respiratory care practitioners. Publishes two magazines with job listings and provides a job hotline for members only.

American Guild of Organists
Dallas Chapter
7159 Wildgrove Ave.
Dallas, TX 75214
(214) 327-2742
Contact: Richard DeLong
National and local placement for members; publishes a newsletter.

American Institute of Architects
Dallas Chapter
2811 McKinney Ave., LB104, #20
Dallas, TX 75204
(214) 871-2788
Contact: Gloria Wise
Professional organization of licensed architects, affiliates, and associates in related fields. Conducts monthly meetings and publishes a newsletter. Keeps resumes on file, has job referral service, offers state and national networking opportunities.

American Institute of Architects
Fort Worth Chapter
1319 Ballinger
Fort Worth, TX 76102
(817) 338-4668
Executive Director: Suzie Adams
Same membership requirements as Dallas Chapter. Conducts monthly meetings and publishes a newsletter. Local distributor for AIA documents.

American Marketing Association
Dallas/Fort Worth Chapter
P.O. Box 515144
Dallas, TX 75251
Schedules monthly educational programs; publishes a newsletter, provides a job bank, and conducts seminars. Contact by mail.

American Medical Women's Association
5445 La Sierra Dr., #W7
Dallas, TX 75231
(214) 691-3100
Contact: Dr. Gretchen Megowan
Informal networking opportunities available at episodic social functions, and continuing medical education.

American Planning Association
North Central Texas Section
P.O. Box 8030309
Richardson, TX 75083
(214) 238-4240
President: Monica Willard
Organization of city planners. Publishes a bimonthly newsletter with job openings; national journal lists job opportunities.

American Society of Civil Engineers
Dallas Branch
2209 Wisconsin St., Suite 100
Dallas, TX 75229
(214) 620-8911
Contact: John Hillhouse
Publishes monthly newsletter with job listings. Informal networking
opportunities at monthly meetings.

American Society of Interior Designers
Texas Chapter
1909-C Hi Line Dr.
Dallas, TX 75207
(214) 748-1541
State Administrator: Sherri Hendrix
Meets monthly and publishes a newsletter. Offers job bank for members,
resumes kept on file for members only.

American Society of Landscape Architects
D/FW Section, Texas Chapter
5910 N. Central Expwy., Suite 1000
Dallas, TX 75206
(214) 891-2204
State Treasurer: Rosanna Brown
Conducts monthly meetings and publishes a newsletter. National
association's newsletter advertises job openings. Texas chapter also has a
newsletter.

American Society of Mechanical Engineers
Southern Regional Office
1950 Stemmons Frwy., Suite 5037C
Dallas, TX 75207
(214) 746-4900
Regional Director: David Cook
Professional organization with more than 1,500 members in North Texas
(Dallas County) and West Texas (Tarrant County) sections. Each section
has monthly meetings and publishes a newsletter. Provides national job
bulletin free of charge to its members upon request, published two times
a month. Provides informal job referrals.

American Society for Training and Development
P.O. Box 541193
Dallas, TX 75354
(214) 242-3991
Contact: Ronnie Norvell
National association for trainers, developers, and human resource
managers. Networking opportunities at monthly meetings. Publishes a
monthly newsletter and offers job referrals to members.

American Subcontractors Association
North Texas Chapter
2615 Avenue E. East, Suite 110
Arlington, TX 76011
(817) 640-8275
Executive Director: Linda White
Professional association of building subcontractors.
Meets monthly and publishes a newsletter.

American Women in Radio & Television
Dallas Chapter
7700 John Carpenter Frwy.
Dallas, TX 75247
President: Sherry Gardner
Meets monthly and publishes a newsletter with some job listings.
Provides networking opportunities. Contact by mail.

American Women in Radio & Television
Fort Worth Chapter
P.O. Box 2495
Fort Worth, TX 76113
(817) 261-3344
President: Teddi Wiggins
Same as Dallas chapter. Has a nationwide job bank.
Contact: Gary Hill

Apartment Association of Greater Dallas
4230 LBJ, Suite 140
Dallas, TX 75244
(214) 385-9091
Contact: Donna Derden
Organization for apartment managers. Conducts monthly educational
meetings, keeps resumes on file for six months, publishes a newsletter,
and has a job bank.

Appraisal Institute
P.O. Box 801807
Dallas, TX 75380-1807
(214) 233-2244
Executive Director: Ruth Kelton
Job-wanted notices published in local newsletter. Conducts monthly
professional development meetings. Provides educational programs for
real estate appraisal industry.

Associated General Contractors
Dallas Chapter
11111 Stemmons Frwy.
Dallas, TX 75229
(214) 247-9962
Education Director: Raleigh Roussell
Schedules regular meetings, maintains a resume file, and publishes a
newsletter.

Association of Human Resource Systems Professionals
P.O. Box 801646
Dallas, TX 75380
(214) 661-3727
Contact: James Stroop
Leading professional organization dedicated to serving the specialized
needs of individuals who manage or use human resource information and
technology.

Association for Women Journalists
P.O. Box 2199
Fort Worth, TX 76113
(817) 390-7539 (Hollace Weiner) Fort Worth
(214) 977-8493 (Sherri Jacobson) Dallas

How to Get a Job

Twice a year mini-conference, annual awards and scholarships, quarterly newsletter, monthly networking breakfast.

Beau Monde League
2670 Belknap Ave.
Dallas, TX 75216
(214) 948-7066
Contact: Louise Richardson
Association of cosmetologists. Awards scholarships and keeps a resume file.

Book Publishers of Texas Association
3404 S. Ravinia Dr.
Dallas, TX 75233
(214) 330-9795
Contact: Pam Lang
Trade organization of booksellers, writers, librarians, publishers, and agents. Publishes newsletter with job advertisements.

Builders Association of Fort Worth-Tarrant County
6464 Brentwood Stair
Fort Worth, TX 76112
(817) 457-2864
Contact: Ross Calhoun
Trade organization for builders and associated personnel. Meets monthly, sponsors seminars and workshops, and publishes a newsletter.

Building Owners and Managers Association of Dallas
1717 Main, #LB19
Dallas, TX 75201
(214) 744-9020
Executive Director: Joe Morchart
Trade association for commercial property managers. Job referrals for members only.

Business and Professional Women of Dallas
P.O. Box 125
Dallas, TX 75221
(214) 361-8841
President: Stephanie Cole
Regular meetings and networking opportunities scheduled by Dallas and other area organizations.

Certified Public Accountants
Dallas Chapter
12222 Merit Dr., Suite 300
Dallas, TX 75251
(214) 960-8311
Executive Director: Margaret Cartwright
Promotes professional education and publishes a newsletter with job advertisements. Keeps resumes on file.

Certified Public Accountants
Fort Worth Chapter
1701 River Run, Suite 607
Fort Worth, TX 76107
(817) 335-5055

Executive Director: Christi Stinson
Parallels Dallas Chapter.

Christian Medical and Dental Society
National Administrative Office
P.O. Box 830689
Richardson, TX 75083
(214) 783-8384
Contact: Don Kencke
A fellowship organization of Christian medical students, physicians, and dentists. Promotes spiritual growth and evangelism.

Dallas Advertising League
5485 Beltline Rd., Suite 370
Dallas, TX 75240
(214) 934-3251
Trade association for professionals in the advertising business. Holds monthly meetings. Publishes a newsletter with a want-ad section.

Dallas Association of Black Women Attorneys
P.O. Box 50633
Dallas, TX 75250
(214) 767-3465
President: Joyce Shalten
Has job bank and makes informal employment referrals. Participates in community projects.

Dallas Association for the Education of Young Children
P.O. Box 12854
Dallas, TX 75225
(214) 638-1703
Contact: Donna Cooper
Organizes training sessions for directors of children's centers.

Dallas Association of Educational and Office Personnel
P.O. Box 123
Dallas, TX 75204
(214) 557-6213
President: Barbara Riley
Organization of secretaries, clerks, and data processors who work for the Dallas Independent School District.

Dallas Association of Law Librarians
P.O. Box 50183
Dallas, TX 75250
(214) 604-2867
President: Elena Carvojal
Offers a placement service and a consulting service free of charge. Holds spring and fall institutes on various aspects of law librarianship.
Contact: Dianne George.

Dallas Association of Legal Secretaries
3425 Lindhurst
Garland, TX 75044
(214) 969-1152
Contact: Sharon Lee
Professional organization of paralegals. Has a job bank and newsletter with employment notices.

Dallas Association of Life Underwriters
12655 N. Central Expwy., Suite 313
Dallas, TX 75243
(214) 991-2364
Executive Director: Karen True
Offers monthly membership meetings, where industry speakers from across the nation are present. Monitors and tracks the industry legislatively.

Dallas Association of Young Lawyers
2101 Ross Ave.
Dallas, TX 75201
(214) 969-7675
President: Beverly Godbey
Organization for lawyers under the age of 36.

Dallas Bar Association
2101 Ross Ave.
Dallas, TX 75201
(214) 969-7066
Executive Director: Georgia Franklin
Organization for attorneys. Provides continuing education and publishes a newsletter.

Dallas Beauticians Association
2617 Martin Luther King Blvd.
Dallas, TX 75215
(214) 946-8947
Executive Director: J.L. Boykin
Organization of beauticians who meet monthly.

Dallas Business League
5980 Arapaho Rd., Suite 32E
Dallas, TX 75248
(214) 980-4294
Contact: Virginia Altman
Association of business people, primarily in banking, law, and sales. Conducts monthly meeting with speakers.

Dallas Communications Council
6304 N. O'Connor Rd., Suite 103
Dallas, TX 75039-3597
(214) 869-0222
Executive Director: Lee Duncan
Association of professionals in film, tape, talent, recording, and other communications industries. Promotes the local communications industry, schedules monthly meetings, raises funds, and publishes a monthly newsletter.

Dallas County Chiropractic Society
818 N. Main, Suite B
Duncanville, TX 75116
(214) 283-9355
Contact: Dr. John Freeman
Sponsors educational programs and keeps a resume file.

Dallas County Dental Society
4100 McEwen Rd., #141

Dallas, TX 75244
(214) 386-5741
Contact: Linda Hill
Professional organization to educate dentists and to educate and serve
the public.

Dallas County Funeral Directors Association
6000 S. R.L. Thornton
Dallas, TX 75232
(214) 371-1336
President: Charles Rawell
Provides informal job referrals.

**Turning volunteer
work into a job**

When Hollace Weiner, now a reporter for the *Fort Worth Star-Telegram*, graduated from the University of Maryland and got married, she figured her journalism career was ending as she embarked on a career as wife and mother. But 13 years later when she was serving as a volunteer on the Board of the Women's Center of Tarrant County, Hollace was asked to take over editorial responsibilities for the Women's Center newsletter. She found herself breaking news stories on sexual abuse and on actions the state legislature took on women's issues.

While in Austin, she found support and comradery among women in the journalism pool. Hollace's confidence began to soar as she realized her writing could go beyond the newsletter. She decided to venture out. Soon she was writing freelance articles for local magazines and the newspaper. Within a year after her articles began appearing she was hired as a staff reporter for the *Fort Worth Star-Telegram*. ■

Dallas County Rental Association
4401 N. Belt Line Rd.
Mesquite, TX 75150
(214) 266-7017
President: Cliff Kellogg
Organization of general rental store managers. Schedules monthly
meetings and has local newsletters.
Contact: C.W. Duncan.

Dallas County Veterinary Medical Association
P.O. Box 797406
Dallas, TX 75379-7406
(214) 669-9237
Professional association of veterinarians. Promotes continuing education
and publishes a monthly newsletter with employment notices.

Dallas Dietetic Association
1414 James Dr.
Cedar Hill, TX 75104
(214) 291-9484

President: Ann John
Professional organization for registered/licensed dieticians and those in
related fields. Career guidance committee assists job hunters.

**Dallas/Fort Worth Association of Metroplex Personnel
Consultants**
6211 W. Northwest Hwy., Suite C261
Dallas, TX 75225
(214) 691-3485
President: Henry Wright
Trade association of account executives of personnel service companies.
Assists people who are looking for help with the job search. Individuals
should call for referrals to job fairs, employment seminars, and agencies
that specialize in their field.

Dallas Geological Society
1 Energy Square, Suite 170
Dallas, TX 75206
(214) 373-8614
President: Dorothy Newsom
Conducts continuing education programs and has an employment
committee that keeps a resume file.

Dallas Group Psychotherapy Society
2505 Wycliff Ave.
Dallas, TX 75219
(214) 528-9240
Dean of Training: Juanita Kirby
Professional organization that provides two-year training program every
two years for members and non-members.

Dallas Human Resource Management Association
P.O. Box 118335
Carrollton, TX 75011
(214) 420-8775
President: Preston Weaver
Meets regularly, has an annual conference, and maintains a resume file.

Dallas Metropolitan Black Nurses Association
P.O. Box 4104
Dallas, TX 75208
(214) 374-7438
President: Doris Foreman
International organization of black nurses who support racial equality.
Newsletter lists job-wanted ads.

Dallas Producers Association
P.O. Box 190769
Dallas, TX 75219
(214) 696-9040
President: Chip Richie
Organization of corporate and commercial film/video producers. Holds
monthly meetings and publishes a newsletter.

Dallas Professional Photographers Association
(214) 289-1851
President: Christian Waits

Professional organization for photographers. Publishes a newsletter with employment information.

Dallas Psychological Association
12900 Preston Rd.
Dallas, TX 75230
(214) 386-4362
Employment Chairperson: Sandy Cook
Organization of psychologists, psychological associates, and students. Provides state-wide employment information.

Dallas Restaurant Association
12770 Coit Rd., Suite 1160
Dallas, TX 75251
(214) 233-2733
Executive Director: Dawn Jantsch
Organization for the food and beverage industry. Provides information about the restaurant industry during monthly meetings, publishes a newsletter and magazine, and awards scholarships.

Dallas School Administrators Association
3031 Allen St., Suite 204
Dallas, TX 75204
(214) 871-7056
President: Robert Watkins
Supports professional development programs and sponsors seminars.

Dallas Society of Illustrators
4409 Maple Ave.
Dallas, TX 75219
(214) 521-2121
President: David Spurlock
Networking organization for graphic and commercial artists who meet monthly.

Dallas Society of Visual Communications
3530 High Mesa
Dallas, TX 75243
(214) 241-2017
Executive Director: Sue Reynolds
Conducts monthly meetings and provides employment referral service.

Dallas Women Lawyers Association
2101 Ross Ave.
Dallas, TX 75201
(214) 969-7066
Contact: Tresi Moore Freemyer
Holds monthly meetings and publishes a newsletter.

Desk and Derrick Club of Dallas
717 N. Harwood, #3430
Dallas, TX 75201
(214) 369-9266
President: Madonna Nuckolls
Organization of individuals employed in petroleum and allied industries. Has an employment committee that assists members only.
Contact: Madonna Nuckolls.

How to Get a Job

Desk and Derrick Club of Fort Worth
815 W. 10th St.
Fort Worth, TX 76102
(817) 332-1377
President: Nina Bright
Parallels Dallas chapter.

Direct Marketing Association of North Texas
4020 McEwen Rd., Suite 105
Dallas, TX 75244-5019
(817) 640-7018
Contact: Ellen Reagan
Organization for list brokers, printers, catalogers, and others in direct marketing industry. Provides a monthly newsletter which includes job listings. Conducts monthly meetings.

Meetings are for meeting people

Laid off during a real estate slump, one enterprising 32-year-old escrow officer decided he would build up his finances by doing something he enjoyed—carpentry. After a few phone calls to friends and former business associates, his newly formed Home Carpentry Service was launched.

At the same time, he attended every possible escrow association meeting, dinner, and other professional events.

"I set a goal," he recalls, "to contact at least three escrow company owners at each meeting, to let them know I was looking and available. Afterward, I'd write a letter to give them my phone number in case they wanted to get in touch right away."

About four months after his first dinner meeting, an officer from one of the larger title companies called him for an interview. "He couldn't get me working on that desk fast enough," he remembers. "The $15 I'd spent on that dinner ticket was the best investment I ever made." ∎

Electrical Women's Round Table
North Texas Chapter
P.O. Box 89 Lewisville, TX 75067
(214) 317-5110
Contact: Gloria Roberts
Professional organization that provides networking in electrical and allied fields.

Fort Worth District Dental Society
3123 McCart Ave.
Fort Worth, TX 76110
(817) 923-9337
Contact: Charles McCluer III, D.D.S.
Professional organization to educate dentists and to educate and serve the public.

Fort Worth Florist's Association
c/o Myles Florist
9423 Hwy. 377 S.
Fort Worth, TX 76126
(817) 249-6346
Contact: Theresa Maddox
Organization for florists in the retail, wholesale, and wire-service floral industry. Promotes industry, organizes civic projects, and design seminars. Conducts monthly meetings and publishes a newsletter.

Fort Worth Human Resources Association
P.O. Box 17508
Fort Worth, TX 76102
(817) 496-8005
President: Michael Brodie
Schedules monthly meetings.

Fort Worth Legal Secretaries Association
550 Bailey Ave., Suite 570
Fort Worth, TX 76107
(817) 338-1707
Contact: Connie Shrouder
Professional association for legal secretaries and legal support staff. Provides continuing education, conducts monthly meetings, and publishes a newsletter.

Fort Worth Professional Women's Organization
316 Main St.
Fort Worth, TX 76102
(817) 870-1737
President: Kathryn T. Bryan
Network for business women in managerial positions.

Fort Worth/Tarrant County Young Lawyers Association
2015 Texas Building
306 W. 7th St., Suite 850
Fort Worth, TX 76102-4906
(817) 338-4092
President: Patricia Riley
Professional organization for young lawyers under the age of 36. Publishes a newsletter with job openings and has resume file and job bank.

Fort Worth, Texas Association of Occupational Health Nurses
2304 Ridgeview St.
Fort Worth, TX 76119
(817) 777-8180
President: Linda Lawrence
Maintains standards of occupational nursing practices to preserve the health and safety of employed workers.

Grand Prairie Educational Paraprofessionals Association
401 E. Grand Prairie Rd.
Grand Prairie, TX 75051
(214) 262-6785
President: Kaye Gilbert
Organization of paraprofessionals in Grand Prairie School District. Conducts monthly meetings.

Home & Apartment Builders Association of Metropolitan Dallas
8730 King George Dr.
Dallas, TX 75235
(214) 631-4840
Executive Vice President: Simon McHugh
Trade association for residential builders and developers. Publishes newsletter with employment ads and keeps resumes on file.

Home Economists in Business
North Texas Chapter
2139 N. Stemmons, #896
Lewisville, TX 75067
(214) 317-5110
President: Gloria Roberts
Monthly meetings scheduled from September through May. Publishes a newsletter.

Independent Insurance Agents of Dallas
8140 Walnut Hill Lane, Suite 707
Dallas, TX 75231
(214) 360-0666
Executive Director: Debi Ryan-Johnson
Schedules seminars and educational meetings.

Institute of Business Designers
North Texas Chapter
1400 Turtle Creek Blvd., Suite LB30
Dallas, TX 75207
(214) 742-4250
Association for designers, architects, and facilities management personnel. Conducts monthly meetings, has job bank, and publishes newsletter and annual membership roster.

Insurance Women of Dallas
P.O. Box 12204
Dallas, TX 75225
(214) 258-6820
Contact: B.J. Ellis
Has monthly meetings and publishes a newsletter.

Insurance Women of Fort Worth
P.O. Box 13672
Arlington, TX 76094
(817) 860-3566
President: Jerry Sheeran
Keeps resumes on file.

International Association of Business Communicators
Dallas Chapter
P.O. Box 2681
Dallas, TX 75221
(214) 701-2732
President: Gale Porter
Meets regularly for continuing education programs. Co-sponsors telephone job bank. Call (214) 978-8070 to hear recording of job openings.

International Association of Business Communicators
Fort Worth Chapter

c/o Fort Worth Clean City
P.O. Box 17033
Fort Worth, TX 76102
(817) 870-1692
President: Susan Campbell
Continuing professional development; call (214) 301-8301.
Parallels Dallas chapter.

International Customer Service Association
Dallas Chapter
P.O. Box 214238
Dallas, TX 75221
(214) 855-7676
Contact: Dawn Kale
Organization for managers and professionals engaged in customer
service. Conducts monthly meetings and publishes a newsletter.

International Furnishings and Design Association
Southwest Chapter
P.O. Box 58045
Dallas, TX 75258
(214) 747-2406
Contact: Pamela Donohow
Organization for those seeking executive level opportunities. Conducts
monthly meetings with networking opportunities.

Irving Association of Educational Office Personnel
513 Huntington
Irving, TX 75061
(214) 253-5144
President: Sue Burk
Organization for all Irving Independent School District office personnel.
Conducts meetings from September through May.

Jung, C.G., Society of North Texas
12810 Hillcrest Rd., Suite 222
Dallas, TX 75230
(214) 701-8971
Secretary: Shirley McElya
Monthly meetings and lectures open to the public. Publishes a newslet-
ter. Educational meetings and seminars scheduled twice a year.
Contact: Diane Tasian.

Mesquite Educational Paraprofessional Association
405 E. Davis St.
Mesquite, TX 75149
(214) 288-6411
Contact: Kaye Jones
Professional organization for secretaries in education field.

National Association of Accountants
P.O. Box 214417
Dallas, TX 75221
(214) 444-2100
President: Joe Zimmerman
Provides employment service, conducts bi-weekly meetings, and pub-
lishes a newsletter.

National Association of Bank Women
Greater Fort Worth Chapter
1001 E. Berry St.
Fort Worth, TX 76110
(817) 926-5411
Professional organization for women executives in the banking industry.
Provides informal job referrals, schedules educational programs, and
awards scholarships.

National Association of Black Social Workers
Dallas Chapter
P.O. Box 150243
Dallas, TX 75315
(214) 375-6484
Contact: Willie Hucks
Addresses needs of black community, including unemployment. Sched-
ules monthly meetings and sponsors educational projects.

National Association of Social Workers
Dallas Unit
10645 Longmeadow Dr.
Dallas, TX 75238
(214) 739-1558
Contact: Sherin Kline
Conducts monthly meetings and publishes a bi-monthly newsletter with
job openings. Keeps jobs listings on file.

National Association of Women in Construction
Dallas Chapter
17610 Midway, #134
Dallas, TX 75287
(214) 407-0227
President: Shirley Brown
Organization conducts educational meetings, awards scholarships, and
maintains a job bank through a referral committee.

National Association of Women in Construction
Fort Worth Chapter
327 S. Adams St.
Fort Worth, TX 76104
(817) 877-5551
Executive Director: Paula Clements
Parallels Dallas Chapter.

Network for Executive Women
P.O. Box 2612
Fort Worth, TX 76113
(817) 491-5356
President: Vickie Wallace
Career-oriented women meet twice weekly in Fort Worth, Arlington, and
Mid-Cities area. Job openings are announced and employment-related
topics are discussed at meetings.

Network of Hispanic Communicators
P.O. Box 222313
Dallas, TX 75222
(214) 977-8456
President: Mercedes Olivera

Organization for journalists, advertising, and public relations professionals. Schedules monthly meetings, publishes newsletter with ads, and
awards scholarships.

New Car Dealers Association of Metropolitan Dallas
2777 N. Stemmons Frwy., Suite 841
Dallas, TX 75207
(214) 637-0531
President: Drew Campbell
Trade association, promoting new car dealers by sponsoring car shows.
Job referrals made.

Newspaper Advertising Sales Association
400 W. Saint Paul, Suite 1300
Dallas, TX 75201
(214) 969-0000
President: Rick Jones
National organization of newspaper advertising salespeople. Offers
informal employment network and schedules monthly meetings.

North Texas Optometric Society
1334 E. Pioneer Pkwy.
Arlington, TX 76010
(817) 461-4453
President: Dr. Wiley Curtis
Organization of optometrists. Publishes a newsletter. State journal lists
job openings.

**Don't overlook the
watering holes**

You can't beat weekday happy hours at local
bars as an informal way of making contacts.

In Dallas, **journalists** divide their time
between Louie's (1839 N. Henderson St.) and
Joe Miller's (3531 McKinney Ave.). Both are
great places to congregate and pick up leads for
stories from lawyers, politicians, and public
relations execs.

Many downtown **professionals** opt for Dick's
Last Resort (1701 N. Market St.) or The Mucky
Duck (3102 Welborn St.) in Oak Lawn, which is a
great place to relax.

La Suprema, owned by Lucy Taylor Ford,
6311 N. O'Conner Rd., serves as an oasis in the
middle of Las Colinas in Irving for **film, video,
and audio types.**

In Fort Worth, **attorneys, legal secretaries,
and bankers** tip oversize drinks during happy
hour at Billy Miner's Saloon (150 W. 3rd St.).
Others mix and mingle downtown at Juanita's,
(115 W. 2nd St.)

Creative types—artists, writers, and musicians—have adopted J&J Blues Bar (937
Woodward), with the unforgettable telephone
number: 870-BEER.

Although the White Elephant (101 E. Exchange Ave.) is popular with **tourists,** locals have adopted it as a favorite hang-out. ■

Pan-African Business Federation
P.O. Box 2815
Dallas, TX 75221
(214) 376-8392
Contact: E. Hosea-Minor
Educational and business training organization.

PBX Telecommunicators of Dallas
10106 Kirkhaven
Dallas, TX 75238
(214) 341-5106
Sponsors workshops and fund-raising projects.

PBX Telecommunicators of Fort Worth
2201 Primrose Ave.
Fort Worth, TX 76111
(817) 572-6760
President: Jana Johnson
Parallels Dallas chapter.

Press Club of Dallas
2927 Maple Ave., Suite 1107
Dallas, TX 75201
(214) 740-9988
Executive Director: Carol Wortham
Sponsors the annual Dallas Gridiron Show, which raises scholarship money, hosts annual Katie Awards, schedules annual roasts, social functions, and professional development meetings. Publishes a newsletter and provides informal job referrals.

Printing Industries Association of Texas
910 W. Mockingbird Lane, Suite 200
Dallas, TX 75247
(214) 630-8871
Executive Director: Nolan Moore
Promotes continuing education at meetings. Job placement service for members and non-members.

Professional Secretaries International
Big D Chapter
P.O. Box 681
Dallas, TX 75221
(214) 480-5308
President: Virginia K. Palazzo
Provides job referrals for members. Meets monthly, conducts seminars, and publishes a bulletin.

Professional Secretaries International
Fort Worth Chapter
201 Main St., Suite 2500
Fort Worth, TX 76102
(817) 332-2500, ext. 457

President: Linda Gerch
Parallels above chapter.

Professional Secretaries International
Garland Chapter
1820 Meadowview Dr.
Garland, TX 75043
(214) 565-5801
President: Shirley Woefle
Parallels above chapter.

Pro-Musica
4237 E. Purdue
Dallas, TX 75225
(214) 368-8669
President: Shirley Kochman
Organization of professional women musicians. Schedules regular meetings and awards scholarships.

Public Library Administrators of North Texas
2001 Jackson Rd.
Carollton, TX 75104
(214) 291-7323
Contact: Beth Little
Informal group of library directors who meet ten times a year.

Internships can lead to permanent relationships

Working as an intern for a Dallas TV station proved to be the most valuable experience for a senior at Southern Methodist University.

Eric said, "I was in the office five days a week working for a top-rated station. I learned how to focus my goals, manage my time, and work under pressure. When a full-time position opened up, I was first in line. When the producer realized that I had been doing a lot of the work anyway, knew the ropes, and knew the people, my internship ended with an offer for a permanent job."

Although Eric was not paid for his work as an intern, some interns do receive a small stipend. Keep in mind also that internship programs are not limited to students. For more information, check the *Directory of Internships,* available at the public library. ■

Sales and Marketing Executives of Dallas
4100 McEwen St., Suite 101
Dallas, TX 75244
(214) 991-0516
Conducts monthly meetings, publishes a newsletter, keeps resumes on file, and awards scholarships.

Sales and Marketing Executives of Fort Worth
5600 Colleyville Blvd.
Colleyville, TX 76034

(817) 656-9111
Executive Director: Charnan Logan
Professional organization for sales and marketing professionals and
students.

Society of Children's Book Writers and Illustrators
North Central Texas Chapter
6840 Fortune Rd.
Fort Worth, TX 76116
(817) 738-5390
Contact: Betty Stone
Organization for children's book writers. Offers monthly meetings and bi-
monthly newsletter.

Society of Petroleum Engineers
P.O. Box 833836
Richardson, TX 75083
(214) 952-9393
Executive Director: Dan Adamson
Publishes a publication with an employment section.

Society for Theatrical Artists Guidance and Enhancement
(S.T.A.G.E.)
4633 Insurance Lane
Dallas, TX 75225
(214) 559-3917
Executive Director: Merri Brewer; and Kelly Smith, Editor and Publicity
Coordinator
A non-profit service and support organization serving the theatrical and
film community of North Texas. S.T.A.G.E. offers classes, auditions, job
call boards, showcases, and a script library. Also area theater ticket
discounts and *Center Stage,* the monthly trade paper for the North Texas
area.

Southwest Home Furnishings Association
P.O. Box 581207
Dallas, TX 75258
(214) 741-7632
Contact: Al Stillman
Trade association for the retail home furnishings industry.

Southwestern Association of Advertising Agencies
c/o Alexander Scot
13740 Midway Rd., Suite 506
Dallas, TX 75244
(214) 385-7222
Executive Director: Valerie Grimes
Association of advertising agency owners and managers. Publishes
membership directory and quarterly newsletter. Sponsors professional
workshops and educational seminars.

TRW Information Services
P.O. Box 64728
Dallas, TX 75243
(214) 699-6169
Contact: Scott Chilton or Keith Blue, (214) 699-6168
Non-profit organization for credit bureau members. Hosts quarterly
meetings.

Tarrant County Bar Association
306 W. 7th., Suite 850
Fort Worth, TX 76102
(817) 335-2246
President: Edwin Bell
Professional association of lawyers.

Tarrant County Home Economics Association
3820 London Lane
Fort Worth, TX 76118
(817) 921-7494
President: Kim Kamin
Meets three times a year and sponsors training programs.

Tarrant County Women's Bar Association
1120 Broad St.
Fort Worth, TX 76107
(817) 335-4417
President: Linda Todd
Professional organization for women lawyers. Maintains job bank.

Texas Association of Film & Tape Professionals
3101 N. Fitzhugh Ave., #420
Dallas, TX 75204
(214) 520-2600
Office Manager: Jane Sibley
Association of film and video freelancers who work in the motion picture, video, and commercial production industry. Publishes the annual *Texas Film/Tape Directory* and sponsors meetings and seminars.

Texas Association of Teachers of Dancing
402 Park Forest
Dallas, TX 75234
(214) 827-1934
Examination Chairman: Jackie Troup Miller
Organization of members from five-state area who pass an examination to qualify for membership. Supplies informal job referrals, sponsors meetings, and publishes a newsletter.

Texas Environmental Health Association
North Texas Association
2561 Matlock
Arlington, TX 76015
(817) 792-7274
Executive Secretary: Debra Laster
Organization of sanitary engineers and inspectors. Six regional chapters meet regularly. Employment opportunities listed in local and state newsletters.

Texas Nurses Association
District 4
515 Texas American Bank Building
Dallas, TX 75235
(214) 357-6227
President: Lucy Norris
Professional organization for registered nurses. Holds monthly meetings and publishes newsletter with occasional job listings.

How to Get a Job

Texas Recreation & Park Society
P.O. Box 905
Arlington, TX 76004
Metro (817) 261-0876
Executive Director: Dianne Darrell
Professional organization for municipal park and recreation personnel.

Texas Society of Professional Engineers
Dallas Chapter
8333 Douglas Ave., Suite 820
Dallas, TX 75225
(214) 361-7900
Executive Secretary: John Burkhoff
Conducts monthly meetings. Involved in local, state, and national legislative issues.

Texas Society of Professional Engineers
Fort Worth Chapter
6808 Kirk Dr.
Fort Worth, TX 76116
(817) 731-9802
President: Scott Adams
Professional organization for engineers in all fields.

Texas Society of Professional Surveyors
North Central Texas Chapter
P.O. Box 2114
Fort Worth, TX 76101-2214
(817) 335-3000
President: Mickey Nowell
Conducts monthly meetings.

Urban Management Assistants of North Texas
c/o North Central Texas Council of Governments
P.O. Box 5888
Arlington, TX 76005
(817) 640-3300
Contact: Mary Hartsell
Organization of individuals in entry-level and mid-management positions in local governments. Conducts regular meetings and publishes newsletter with job openings.

Women in Communications
Dallas Professional Chapter
6839 Gaston Ave.
Dallas, TX 75214
(214) 490-2246
President: Shannon Rust
Professional organization for men and women in all fields of communication. Has a career advisory committee that keeps resume file and solicits jobs for members. Schedules monthly meetings and publishes a newsletter.

Women in Communications
Fort Worth Professional Chapter
P.O. Box 9858
Fort Worth, TX 76147
(817) 332-4628

President: Lucile Davis
Parallels Dallas chapter. Also provides a job bank for members and non-members.

Women in Computing
P.O. Box 741174
Dallas, TX 75374
(214) 373-2277
Contact: Lisa Pratt, President
Professional organization for women in computing and data processing. Awards scholarships, publishes a newsletter, holds monthly dinner meetings to promote professional development and career networking.

Women's Association of Allied Beverage Industries
1325 Cornell St.
Lancaster, TX 75134
(214) 944-9024
President: Sue Prather
Service-oriented organization of employees in the alcoholic beverage industry. Schedules monthly meetings, makes informal job referrals, and publishes a newsletter.

What professional organizations can do for you

"To begin networking with professional organizations, all it takes is a few phone calls to the president and a couple of other members," says a past president of a Dallas professional society. "These people often have their fingers on the pulse of the job market."

"Because of the fluctuations in the job market, professional organizations are sensitive to employment issues. Regularly scheduled meetings focus on career change, job-hunting skills, and other topics that help people who are out of work. During meetings, members often discuss who's looking for work and what's available.

"In one instance an engineer sent me a very impressive resume, but when I tried to convince the manager of an industrial engineering company that he should talk to the engineer, I hit a roadblock. The manager said he didn't have any openings. I urged him to at least meet with the engineer.

"Sure enough, once the manager talked to the engineer, he created a job for him." ∎

25 NETWORK GROUPS FOR WOMEN AND MINORITIES

American Women in Radio & Television
Tarrant County Chapter
1148 W. Pioneer Pkwy., Suite C
Arlington, TX 76103
(817) 261-3344

Business & Professional Women of Dallas
P.O. Box 125
Dallas, TX 75221
(214) 361-8841

Dallas Association of Black Women Attorneys
P.O. Box 50633
Dallas, TX 75250
(214) 767-3465

Dallas Metropolitan Black Nurses Association
P.O. Box 4104
Dallas, TX
(214) 374-7438

Dallas Women Lawyers Association
2500 Tierra Dr.
Irving, TX 75038
(214) 255-7454

Downtown Network of Career Women
8637 Turtle Creek Blvd.
Dallas, TX 75225
(214) 393-1080

Electrical Women's Round Table
North Texas Chapter
P.O. Box 896
Lewisville, TX 75067
(214) 317-5110

Executive Women of Dallas
P.O. Box 515546
Dallas, TX 75251

Explore
Dallas County (214) 343-0165
Tarrant County (817) 861-4454

Fort Worth Professional Women's Organization
316 Main St.
Fort Worth, TX 76102
(817) 870-1737

Insurance Women of Dallas
P.O. Box 12204
Dallas, TX 75225
(214) 258-6820

Irving Women's Network
1033 McCoy Dr.
Irving, TX 75062
(214) 254-7047

National Association of Black Social Workers
P.O. Box 150243
Dallas, TX 75315
(214) 670-6359

National Association of Black Women
1001 E. Berry St.
Fort Worth, TX 76111
(817) 926-5411

National Association of Female Executives
P.O. Box 516291
Dallas, TX 75251
(214) 601-1404

National Association of Women in Construction
17610 Midway Rd., Suite 134
Dallas, TX 75287
(214) 407-0227

National Association of Women in Construction
327 S. Adams Street
Fort Worth, TX 76104
(817) 877-5551

Network of Executive Women
P.O. Box 2612
Fort Worth, TX 76113
(817) 336-9333

**Network of Hispanic
Communicators**
P.O. Box 222313
Dallas, TX 75222
(214) 921-7425

**Pan African Business
Federation**
P.O. Box 2815
Dallas, TX 75221
(214) 376-8392

Women's Center of Dallas
3505 Turtle Creek Blvd.
Dallas, TX 75219
(214) 521-9606

**Womens Center in
Richardson**
515 Custer Rd.
Richardson, TX 75080
(214) 238-9516

Women in Communications
6839 Gaston Ave.
Dallas, TX 75214
(214) 327-0068

Women in Communications
P.O. Box 9858
Fort Worth, TX 76147
(817) 594-8031

**YWCA Women's Resource
Center**
4621 Ross Ave.
Dallas, TX 75204
(214) 821-9595

115

Using Professional
Employment Services

Finding a good job is hard work. So your first impulse may be to turn that job over to professional employment services. After all, don't the pros have all the job listings? Unfortunately, they don't.

Yes, it's smart to use every available resource to generate leads and interviews. But professional employment services vary, from agencies that specialize in temporary clerical help to executive recruiters who deal primarily with top-management types. Employment agencies, career consultants, and executive recruitment firms differ greatly in the kinds of services they offer and in how—and by whom—they get paid. You can save yourself a lot of time, effort, and possibly money if you're familiar with the different kinds of professional employment services. One handbook that might prove useful is the *Directory of Approved Counseling Services* (American Association of Counseling Development, 5201 Leesburg Pike 400, Falls Church, VA 22041).

**Who's good?
Who's not?**

"It pays to check out an employment service," says Ron Berry, president of the **Better Business Bureau of Metropolitan Dallas.**

You can call the BBB at (214) 220-2000 in Dallas or (817) 332-7585 in Fort Worth to ask if any complaints have been filed against the company. If they have, summaries of reports are read over the telephone. Or, you can write and ask them to mail the information to you.

Berry advises talking to several people who have recently used the employment service to find out if they were satisfied. "If you don't know someone, ask the company for several references and call them," he suggests.

Also, carefully read the employment contract and find out if the employment service charges a fee or if the employee pays the fee, says BBB operations director Betsy McKinney. There are a lot of misunderstandings by people who don't find out in advance who has to pay a fee.

Ask if an employment agency is registered by the Texas Department of Labor and Standards. "Don't use one that isn't registered or one that claims to guarantee employment," McKinney adds.

"Be especially wary of the work-at-home schemes that request money in advance to set up the business. Most of these operations collect the money and provide nothing in return, or they advise people to recruit other people for work-at-home operations so the system perpetuates itself," McKinney says.

Once you think you have a good job prospect, call the Better Business Bureau to check on the company. The time to find out about customer complaints or law enforcement action is before you go to work there, not after you have accepted the position. ∎

Employment Agencies

Employment agencies act as intermediaries in the job market between buyers (companies with jobs open) and sellers (people who want jobs). Agencies are paid for placing people. The fee may be paid by the company, but in many cases it is paid by the worker. Agencies that specialize in restaurant and domestic help, for example, often charge the worker a fee. Usually the placement fee amounts to a certain percentage of the worker's annual salary. In many cases, it should not be necessary for you to pay a fee for placement. Keep searching for a firm that won't charge a fee.

Employment agencies seldom place a candidate in a job that pays more than $30,000 a year. Most employment agencies concentrate on support jobs. Supervisory openings may be listed, too, but employment agencies usually don't handle middle- or upper-management positions. In the computer field, for example, computer operators, programmers, and perhaps systems analysts could find work through an agency. But directors of data processing or MIS (management information systems) would go to an executive search firm, or they would job hunt on their own.

A company that's looking for a secretary gains certain advantages by going to a reputable agency. It doesn't have to advertise or screen the hundreds of resumes that would probably pour in from even a small want ad in the Sunday *Dallas Morning News*. A good employment agency will send over only qualified applicants for interviews. Referrals are made quickly, and there is no cost to the company until it hires the secretary. For many companies, it's worth it to pay an agency fee to avoid the hassle of prescreening dozens, if not hundreds, of applicants.

The advantage to the agency of a successful placement (besides the fee) is repeat business. After two or three referrals work out well, an employment agency can generally count on receiving future listings of company vacancies.

The value to the job seeker of using an employment agency depends on a number of factors, including the quality of the agency, the kind of work you're looking for, how much experience you have, and how broad your network of personal and business contacts is. In addition, employment agencies, especially those providing office personnel, will provide training to prospective employees. This training, which could be worth hundreds of dollars, can prepare the job hunter for a number of different positions.

In general, an agency's loyalty will be to its source of income. Agencies are more interested in finding you a job than in finding you job satisfaction. Agencies are likely to pressure you to accept a job you don't really want, just so they can collect their fee. With few exceptions, an agency probably can't do much more for you than you could do for yourself in an imaginative and energetic job search. (Of course, there's the rub—conducting an imaginative and energetic job search.) If a company has to pay a fee to hire you, you're at a disadvantage compared with applicants who are "free." Giving an employment agency your resume could also be a serious mistake if you're trying to conduct a confidential job search.

On the other hand, a good agency can help its candidates develop a strategy and prepare for employment interviews. This training can be most valuable to people who are inexperienced in job-hunting techniques. Of course, you can probably learn job-search strategy and skills more inexpensively by reading this book, plus some of those in our bibliographies. Agency pros should know the market, screen well, and provide sound advice. A secretary who tries to investigate the Dallas/Fort Worth market on his or her own will very likely take longer to get the "right" job than someone who uses a quality agency.

Historically, certain employment agencies engage in practices that can only be called questionable at best, and the field as a whole is trying to polish up a somewhat tarnished image. A few unscrupulous firms have charged outrageous up-front fees in exchange for an uninspired resume, a pep talk on job-search strategies, and a list of job openings that were public domain. There are, of course, a number of reputable, highly professional employment agencies. But, as in any profession, there are also crooks. It's still a practice in some agencies to advertise non-existent openings to attract applicants for other, less desirable positions.

So much for the pros and cons of employment agencies. If you decide to try one, be sure it's a reputable firm. Ask people in your field to recommend a quality agency, and consult the Better Business Bureau and other resources listed in Chapter 2 to see if there have been any complaints about the agency you're considering.

Most important, be sure to read the contract thoroughly, including all the fine print, before you sign it. If you have any questions, or if there's something you don't understand, don't be afraid to ask. It's your right. Make sure you know who is responsible for paying the fee and what the fee is. Remember that *in some cases, an agency's application form is also the contract.*

When you go to an employment agency, treat it the same way you'd treat a job interview. Don't misrepresent yourself, but you want them to think of you as highly marketable. If the agency sees you as very difficult to place, they won't consider you a cost-effective client. If you've paid up-front money, too bad. Even if you haven't, you may have just wasted time that could be better spent conducting your own effective job search.

Here, then, is a selective listing of Dallas/Fort Worth employment agencies, including their areas of specialty.

EMPLOYMENT AGENCIES

Accountants on Call and Accountants Executive Search
5520 LBJ Frwy., Suite 310
Dallas, TX 75240
(214) 980-4184
Accounting and financial.

Accounting Action Personnel
3010 LBJ Frwy., Suite 710
Dallas, TX 75234
(214) 241-1543
Accounting.

ADIA Personnel Services
4100 Spring Valley Rd., Suite 103
Dallas, TX 75244
(214) 661-1356
Administrative, accounting, legal, light industrial, and word processing.

Aware Affiliates
3004 W. Lancaster Ave.
Fort Worth, TX 76107
(817) 870-2590
Office, clerical, professional, and semi-professional sales and management training.

5|24

Babich & Associates
6060 N. Central Expwy., Suite 544
Dallas, TX 75206
(214) 361-5735
Sales, administrative, and technical.

Brown and Keene Personnel Consultants
5910 N. Central Expwy., Suite 1350
Dallas, TX 75206
(214) 987-5050
Administrative support.

Carrollton Employment Services
1925 Belt Line Rd., Suite 409
Carrollton, TX 75006
(214) 416-8708
Secretaries, word processing, and light industrial sales.

Datapro Personnel Consultants
13355 Noel Rd., Suite 2001
Dallas, TX 75240
(214) 661-8600
Data processing.

Robert Half and Accountemps
1300 Summit Ave., Suite 408
Fort Worth, TX 76102
Metro (817) 870-1200
Accounting, financial, bookkeeping, and data processing.

Management Recruiters of Fort Worth-Arlington
1009 W. Randol Mill Rd., Suite 209
Arlington, TX 76012
Metro (817) 469-6161
Technical sales, data processing, medical, insurance, electronics, engineering, technical, and manufacturing.

Marshall Career Service
6500 W. Frwy., Suite 200
Fort Worth, TX 76116
(817) 737-2645
Executive and mid-management placements, specializing in accounting, financial, and operations positions.

Peggy Miller Personnel Consultants
3516 Royal Lane
Dallas, TX 75229
(214) 357-0541
Administrative support.

5|24

Opportunity Unlimited Professional Placement
2720 W. Mockingbird Lane
Dallas, TX 75235
(214) 357-9196
Engineering and computer science, mainly working with aerospace, electronics, and telecommunications.

The Personnel Connection
16479 Dallas Pkwy., Suite 110

Dallas, TX 75248
(214) 713-9900
Temporary clerical service.

Snelling & Snelling
8350 N. Central Expwy.
Dallas, TX 75206
(214) 363-8800
Clerical, administrative, and legal secretaries.

Technology Recruitment
1701 N. Greenville Ave.
Dallas, TX 75206
(214) 669-8170
Engineering, electronics, and software.

Be firm with an agency

A friend of ours had this to say about her experience with employment agencies during her recent job search.

"I've been working as a secretary for 25 years," says Marietta. "When I decided to change jobs, I knew my qualifications supported my desire to work for someone at the level of president or chief executive officer. Unfortunately, I went on a lot of job interviews that I knew were not right for me. The salaries, job descriptions, and locations were all wrong. But I went because the agency suggested I do so.

"Now that I've found a job as administrative assistant to the president of an internationally based manufacturing firm, I'd like to offer this advice to fellow job searchers. Don't hesitate to be assertive with an agency. Demand that they arrange interviews that suit your qualifications and needs. If they can't, take your business elsewhere. Your time is valuable and should not be wasted on mismatched job interviews." ■

Career Consultants

If you open the employment section of the Sunday *Dallas Morning News, Fort Worth Star-Telegram,* or the Southwest edition of *The Wall Street Journal,* you'll see several ads for career consultants (also known as career counselors or private outplacement consultants). The ads are generally directed to "executives" earning yearly salaries of anywhere between $30,000 and $400,000. Some ads suggest that the consultants have access to jobs that are not listed elsewhere. Others claim, "We do all the work." Most have branch offices throughout the country.

Career consultants vary greatly in the kind and quality of the services they provide. Some may offer a single service, such as vocational testing or preparing resumes. Others coach every aspect of the job search and stay with you until you accept an offer. The fees vary just as broadly and range from $100 to several thousand dollars. You, not your potential employer, pay the fee.

There are many reputable consulting firms in the Dallas/Fort Worth area. But as is true of employment agencies, some career consultants have been unethical.

A qualified career consultant can be a real asset to your job search. But no consultant can get you a job. Only you can do that. You are the one who will participate in the interview, and you are the one who must convince an employer to hire you. A consultant can help you focus on an objective, develop a resume, research the job market, decide on a strategy, and/or train you in interviewing techniques. But you can't send a consultant to interview in your place. It just doesn't work that way.

Don't retain a career consultant if you think that the fee will buy you a job. The only reason you should consider a consultant is that you've exhausted all the other resources we've suggested here and still feel you need expert and personalized help with one or more aspects of the job search. The key to choosing a career consultant is knowing what you need and verifying that the consultant can provide it.

Check references. A reputable firm will gladly provide them. Check the Better Business Bureau and other resources listed in this book. Has anyone lodged a complaint against the firm you're considering? Before you sign anything, ask to meet the consultant who will actually provide the services you want. What are his or her credentials? How long has the consultant been practicing? Who are the firm's corporate clients?

Read the contract carefully before you sign it. Does the contract put the consultant's promises in writing? Has the consultant told you about providing services that are not specified in the contract? What does the firm promise? What do you have to promise? Are all fees and costs spelled out? What provisions are made for refunds? For how long a time can you use the firm's or consultant's services? A professional firm will be willing to work on an hourly basis as well as a fixed fee basis and will grant you a free 30-minute initial consultation for evaluation purposes.

Be sure to do some comparison shopping before you select a consultant, find someone you're comfortable with, one who is experienced and knowledgeable in the business world as well as having good credentials. If you feel you're being pressured with fear tactics and predictions of failure without the consultant's help, it's time to find a new consultant. A listing of area career counselors and consultants appears in Chapter 2.

Executive Search Firms

An executive search firm is retained and paid by a company to locate an executive with specific qualifications that meet a precisely defined employment need. The typical search is usually for a position at the senior management level, paying in excess of $65,000/year. The usual fee for a search assignment is 30 percent of the first year's salary of the person to be hired, plus out-of-pocket expenses. During difficult economic times such as these, many search firms have become more flexible in designing their fee structure. Some are even offering flat fees and hourly rates. The advantages of using a search firm are many: confidentiality and the intense effort to deliver qualified candidates in a short time frame are just a few.

Search firms work only for their client companies and really do not have much interest in meeting with individuals who are in transition. It is very difficult to get an appointment with a search consultant unless the consultant feels it would be beneficial to his or her firm to do so. A brief meeting can be very helpful in providing advice and strategy. It is a good idea to attempt to develop a relationship with a number of executive recruiters while still employed, as it is very difficult to get their attention when your unemployed.

If you don't know the search firms in your area or in the geographic area of your interest, the **Directory of Executive Search Consultants,** known as the **Red Book,** is available in the research section of most public libraries.

Sending your resume to every search firm in the Dallas/Fort Worth area is usually not worth the effort and expense. Most firms receive dozens of unsolicited resumes each day. Although most are reviewed, unless you happen to have the exact qualifications for an active search, yours will most likely be discarded. Occasionally, a resume or two will be kept for anticipated projects or business development. It's a long shot, similar to answering blind want ads.

Executive search firms take "broker" role

Bill Wheeler, Director of Wheeler Resources, an executive search consultant located in Lake Whitney, Texas, offers this advice when working with a search consultant. "Be straightforward and candid in all your dealings with the search community. Many excellent job opportunities have been lost by individuals who played games with the search consultant. Remember, there are more qualified candidates than positions. A good recruiter will know more about the company than the candidate knows, and more about the candidate than the company knows. That's why he can act as broker to bring the two together." ■

EXECUTIVE SEARCH FIRMS

R.J. Dishaw and Associates
5440 Harvest Hill Rd., Suite 125
Dallas, TX 75230
(214) 788-1740

Heidrick and Struggles
1999 Bryan St., Suite 1919
Dallas, TX 75201
(214) 220-2130

Hayman & Co.
400 N. Olive St., Suite 2101
Dallas, TX 75201
(214) 953-1900

Henard Associates
15303 Dallas Pkwy., Suite 970
Dallas, TX 75248
(214) 991-7151

Ward Howell International
1601 Elm St., Suite 900
Dallas, TX 75201
(214) 749-0099

Hyde Danforth & Co.
5950 Berkshire Lane, Suite 1600
Dallas, TX 75225
(214) 691-5966

Michael James & Associates
4340 Spring Valley Rd.
Dallas, TX 75244
(214) 386-0547

Korn/Ferry International
3950 Lincoln Plaza
500 N. Akard St., Suite 3950
Dallas, TX 75201
(214) 954-1834

Lamalie Associates
1601 Elm St., Thanksgiving
Tower, Suite 4246
Dallas, TX 75201
(214) 754-0019

Meador Wright Associates
6211 W. Northwest Hwy.,
Suite C261
Dallas, TX 75225
(214) 691-3485

Odell & Associates
12700 Park Central Place,
Suite 1800
Dallas, TX 75251
(214) 458-7900

Page-Wheatcroft & Co.
The White House
 on Turtle Creek
2401 Turtle Creek Blvd.
Dallas, TX 75219
(214) 522-2700

Peat Marwick
200 Crescent Ct., Suite 300
Dallas, TX 75201
(214) 754-2000

Paul R. Ray & Company
301 Commerce St., Suite 2300
Fort Worth, TX 76102
(817) 334-0500

Russell Reynolds Assoc.
2001 Ross Ave.
1900 Trammel Crow Center
Dallas, TX 75201
(214) 220-2033

Spencer Stuart
1717 Main St., Suite 5300
Dallas, TX 75201
(214) 658-1777

Wheeler Resources
R.R. #3, Box 592 H
Lake Whitney, TX 76692
(817) 694-7937

Social Service Agencies

Unlike professional employment agencies, career consultants, and executive search firms, social service agencies are not-for-profit. Many concentrate on aiding the indigent, handicapped people, and those with minimal financial resources. Social service agencies offer a wide range of services, from counseling and vocational training to job placement and follow-up—and their services, in general, are free.

SOCIAL SERVICE AGENCIES

The Bethlehem Foundation
P.O. Box 764026
Dallas, TX 75376-4026
(214) 371-3407
Job referral and counseling for the economically disadvantaged.

Better Influence Association
4616 E. Lancaster Ave.
Fort Worth, TX 76103
Metro (817) 429-9462
Fees: Sliding scale
Career development and employment services for residents of the
Southside, Poly, Stop Six, Eastwood, Forest Hill, and Highland Hill
neighborhoods.

Citizen's Development Center
8800 Ambassador Row
Dallas, TX 75247
(214) 637-2911
Vocational evaluations, work adjustment training, job placement,
supportive employment and follow-up for disabled persons who are at
least 16 years old.

Dallas Inter-Tribal Center
209 E. Jefferson Blvd.
Dallas, TX 75203
(214) 941-1050
Job training, counseling, and placement through job bank for American
Indians and others in Dallas and Tarrant County.
Offers nutrition, food, medical, and dental services. Also has Job Training Partnership Administration programs and drug and alcohol abuse
counseling.

Dallas Urban League
624 N. Hall St., Suite 700
Dallas, TX 75219
(214) 376-0396
Assists minority groups and economically disadvantaged in vocational
counseling and employment. Sponsors Seniors in Community Service
Employment Program for older workers.

EXPANCO
3005 Wichita Ct.
Fort Worth, TX 76140
(817) 293-9486
Provides a controlled work environment for people who are at least 16
years old and not employable in other industries.

Family Service of Tarrant County
Central Office
1424 Hemphill St.
Fort Worth, TX 76104
(817) 927-8884
One of seven area offices offering counseling and an employee assistance
program.

Girls Incorporated of Metropolitan Dallas
3107 Cole Ave.
Dallas, TX 75204
(214) 979-9430
Provides education and counseling for girls 6-18. Pre-employment
programs and job placement for girls up to 18 years old.

How to Get a Job

Goodwill Industries of Dallas
2800 N. Hampton Rd.
Dallas, TX 75112
(214) 638-2800
Vocational counseling, training, and job placement for multi-handicapped adults through the Job Training Partnership Administration.

Jewish Family Service
13140 Coit Rd., Suite 400
Lock Box 137
Dallas, TX 75240
(214) 696-6400
Assistance provided to Jewish people in job assessment, guidance, work readiness, and job search. Help provided for vocationally handicapped adults, elderly, new residents, displaced homemakers, or workers displaced by industrial or technological changes. Also runs a food bank.

Loaves and Fishes
1709 E. Hattie St.
Fort Worth, TX 76104
(817) 334-0903
Day labor service. Provides daily lunch and serves as distributor of food bank collections.

Metrocrest Service Center
1002 S. Broadway St.
Carrollton, TX 75006
(214) 446-2100
Job search and assistance program for residents of Addison, Carrollton, Coppell, and Farmers Branch. 24 hour hotline for family violence counseling. Emergency assistance provided.

M.O.V.E. Employment Resources
4350 Sigma
Dallas, TX 75244
(214) 991-2245
Employment assistance for people "labeled" mentally retarded. Includes job development, placement, on-the-job training, and post-training support in full- and part-time jobs.

Multicultural Community Center
4301 Bryan, Suite 206
Dallas, TX 75204
(214) 828-9891
Administers the Texan Training and Employment Center programs for refugee women and youths and the U.S. Catholic Conference Refugee Job Placement program. Provides youth training and social services.

Project Link/Mainstream
717 N. Harwood, Suite 890
Dallas, TX 75201
(214) 969-0118
Job placement services for disabled persons who are at least 16 years old and have marketable job skills.

Tarrant County Employment and Training Administration
2601 Scott Ave.
Fort Worth, TX 76103

126

(817) 531-5680
Provides employment assistance, a strong focus on training, and placement for those meeting low-income requirements.

Washington Street Presbyterian Mission
2009 Carver
Dallas, TX 75204
(214) 824-6801
Employment and job training for homeless and needy. Provides a summer youth employment center, day care, home study center from September to May for youth in public school, and computer classes. Child development center Monday-Friday, 7-5:30, for 3-5-year-old children, $50.00 a month.

Woman's Center
515 Custer Rd.
Richardson, TX 75080
(214) 238-9516
Variety of programs, including Pathways to Achievement sessions on finding potential, considering lifework planning, and preparing for the job hunt. Three-part program includes doing a vocational self-assessment, learning job-search skills, and exploring crossroads. Women-in-Transition program helps individuals reenter the job market after losing spouse through death, divorce, or separation. Befrienders program offers immediate job-search assistance. Resource center and informal network help women locate employment.

Women's Center of Tarrant County
1723 Hemphill St.
Fort Worth, TX 76110
(817) 927-4050
Employment assistance through Job Search Club that starts every two weeks. Participants can use a job bank that contains an average of 1,700 job openings. Extra help provided through Mentors Network. Many other programs are offered, including one for assisting low-income single parents with young children.

Women's Resource Center
Young Women's Christian Association
4621 Ross Ave., 3rd Floor
Dallas, TX 75204
(214) 821-9595
Employment service available at YWCA's headquarters at 4621 Ross Ave. and at nine Dallas County branches. Offers individual career counseling, testing, support groups, quarterly YWCA breakfasts, and bimonthly lunches with networking opportunities. Explore course is offered in the spring and fall. The self-discovery program includes eight sessions at several Dallas County locations.

The Working Connection
4200 S. Frwy., Suite 2300
Fort Worth, TX 76115
(817) 871-5300
Provides assessment, training, and placement assistance for applicants who meet economically disadvantaged criteria.

Help for vets

The work of the **Vietnam Veterans of America** in establishing memorials to Vietnam veterans is well-known. But many people do not realize that the group also has established more than 100 outreach centers nationwide. The main objective of these centers is to help men and women veterans of the Vietnam War readjust to civilian life.

The centers offer a variety of services. They solicit job listings from both the public and private sectors. Veterans who need additional help are referred to appropriate counseling groups, health agencies, and other organizations.

For more information, contact the Vet Center in Dallas at (214) 361-5896 or the Vietnam Veterans of America Center of Fort Worth at (817) 249-1414. ■

Government Agencies

Many job seekers do not take advantage of the employment listings available through local, state, and federal government agencies because they assume most of the positions will be for lower-paying, unskilled jobs. Actually, that's not always the case. Most of these services are free, so you may as well stop by one or more of the following offices and see what is available.

American G.I. Forum/Veteran's Outreach Program
1025 S. Jennings, Suite 100
Fort Worth, TX 76104
(817) 870-9068
Assistance service, including job placement for Vietnam-era veterans.

Dallas County Community Action Committee
2121 Main St., Suite 100
Dallas, TX 75201
(214) 939-0588
Provides programs that include the Senior Worker Program for low-income individuals who are at least 55 years old. Also provides some financial assistance for utilities. Also has rental assistance and computer classes.

Dallas County Department of Human Services/ Private Industry Council Of Dallas
Employment and Training Division
3625 N. Hall St., Suite 900
Dallas, TX 75219
(214) 522-7291
Employment and training program through the Job Training Partnership Act for low-income or dislocated workers of Dallas or residents who live in Dallas County. Programs include in-school youth employment, classroom vocational training, job placement, and on-the-job training with private sector employers. Four area offices in Garland, Grand Prairie, Lancaster, and Mesquite.

Dallas SER
Jobs for Progress
1575 W. Mockingbird Lane, Suite 650
Dallas, TX 75235
(214) 630-7811
Offers English classes, summer youth programs, clerical skills, job-search assistance, on-the-job training, and counseling for Spanish-speaking Dallas/Fort Worth-area residents. One of four branch offices.

Deaf Action Center
3115 Crestview Dr.
Dallas, TX 75235
(214) 521-0407
Career Center, with assistance in job placement for deaf and multi-disabled adults. Sponsors summer youth program and sign-language classes. Provides literacy program to assist deaf adults in reading and computer training. Advocacy counseling; senior citizen's program.

Garland Neighborhood Service Center
210 Corver St.
Garland, TX 75040
(214) 205-3310
Employment referral and placement. G.E.D. and E.S.L. classes. Provides a senior citizen's yard care program.

Private Industry Council of Dallas/ Dallas County Department of Human Services Employment and Training Division
3625 N. Hall St., Suite 900
Dallas, TX 75219
(214) 522-7191
Provides job training for disadvantaged Dallas youths and adults through the Job Training Partnership Act. Offers vocational classroom instruction, on-the-job training, English instruction, and recruitment.

Rehabilitation Hospital of North Texas
3200 Matlock Rd.
Fort Worth, TX 76015
(817) 468-4000
Work adjustment training for physically and mentally disabled adults through on-the-job training, vocational evaluation, and follow-up.

Senior Community Service Employment Program
2727 Inwood Rd., Suite 100
Dallas, TX 75235
(214) 520-6380
On-the-job training in community service and non-profit agency leads to permanent jobs in the public or private sector. Promotes meaningful, part-time work for persons 55 years and older whose income doesn't exceed U.S. Department of Labor guidelines.

Tarrant County Employment and Training (JTPA)
2601 Scott Ave., Suite 218
Fort Worth, TX 76103
(817) 531-5680
Provides training, placement, and employment for economically disad-vantaged Tarrant County residents who live outside of Fort Worth, Arlington, Euless, Haltom City, and White Settlement. Helps economi-cally disadvantaged youths who are at least 18 years old and dislocated

workers. Also provides summer youth training for 14 to 21-year-olds and an in-school youth program providing after-school jobs.

Texas Commission for the Blind
4200 S. Frwy., Suite 307
Fort Worth, TX 76115-1404
(817) 926-4646 (TDD & VOICE)
A vocational rehabilitation agency offering job guidance, training, and placement services for blind and visually impaired individuals in an 11-county area.

Texas Employment Commission
Dallas / Fort Worth Regional Office
P.O. Box 569460
Dallas, TX 75356-9460
(214) 631-6050
Provides counseling, job bank, unemployment insurance, and special assistance at nine area centers. Special help provided for veterans, disabled workers, and ex-offenders.

Texas Employment Commission
Dallas / Fort Worth Regional Office
P.O. Box 569460
Dallas, TX 75356-9460
(817) 335-5111
Parallels Dallas office. Has two other area centers.

Texas Rehabilitation Commission
3636 Lemmon Ave., Suite 100
Dallas, TX 75219
(214) 528-1919
One of four offices in Dallas that provides job training, evaluation, placement, and follow-up to help disabled individuals return to the workplace.

U.S. Department of Labor
Employment and Training Administration
525 Griffin St., Suite 502
Dallas, TX 75202
(214) 767-4993
Offers job referrals through apprenticeship program.

U.S. Department of Labor
Women's Bureau
525 Griffin St., Suite 731
Dallas, TX 75202
(214) 767-6985
Referrals made to other Labor Department services.

U.S. Office of Personnel Management
Federal Job Information Center
Dallas Area Office
1100 Commerce St.
Dallas, TX 75242
(214) 767-8035
Conducts recruiting and examining for federal employment. Provides information on how to apply for federal jobs and advertises job openings in the Dallas/Fort Worth area.

Veterans Administration
1100 Commerce St., Room 1B29
Dallas, TX 75242
(214) 824-5440
Job assistance program to link veterans with employment and training opportunities. Provides special help for educationally disadvantaged and service-disabled veterans.

Working Connection
4200 S. Frwy., Suite 2300
Fort Worth, TX 76115
(817) 871-5300
Provides assessment, on-the-job training, job club, and job placement. Skill training for auto mechanics, account clerks, machinists, clerk/typists, and stenographers.

How To Succeed In an Interview

If you've read straight through this book, you already know that networking (see Chapter 5) is one of the most important and useful job-hunting techniques around. Networking is nothing more or less than using personal contacts to research the job market and to generate both exploratory and formal job interviews.

Networking and interviewing go hand in hand; all the contacts in the world won't do you any good if you don't handle yourself well in an interview. No two interviews are ever identical, except that you always have the same goal in mind: to convince the person to whom you're talking that he or she should help you find a job or hire you personally. An interview is also an exchange of information. But you should never treat it as you would a casual conversation, even if the "interviewer" is an old friend.

Preparing for the Interview: The 5-Minute Resume

Whether you're talking to the housewife next door about her brother-in-law who knows someone you want to meet or going through a final, formal interview with a multinational corporation, you are essentially making a sales presentation—in this case, selling yourself. Your goal is to convince the interviewer that you have the interest, ability, experience, personality, maturity, and other characteristics required to do a good job and to enlist the interviewer's help in getting you that job.

In an informal interview you'll be talking first to friends and acquaintances. Most of the people you'll be talking to will want to help you. But they need to know who you are, what you've done, what you want to do, and most important, *how* they can help you.

To prepare for any interview, first perfect what we like to call the five-minute resume. Start by giving a rough description, not too detailed, of what you're doing now (or did on your last job) so that when you're telling your story, the listener isn't distracted by wondering how it's going to end.

Then go all the way back to the beginning—not of your career, but of your life. Very briefly talk about where you were born, where you grew up, what your folks did, whether or not they're still living, what your brothers and sisters do, and so on. Then trace your educational background, again briefly, and, next, outline your work history from your first job to your latest.

Finally, tell the interviewer why you happen to be there today. In other words, if you left your last job because of a reduction in force, now is the time to address this, before the interviewer does. In this way you turn a potential negative into a positive. If there were some problems, you can tell your story in the best light. Don't let the interviewer ask first.

Your purpose is to draw the listener into your story, to make him or her interested enough in you to work for you in your search. You want the interviewer to know not only who you are and what you have achieved but also what you are capable of. You also want to establish things in common with the listener. The more you have in common, the harder your listener will work for you.

Co-author Tom Camden, we are not ashamed to admit, is a master of the five-minute resume. Here's how he would begin a presentation to someone whom he thought could help him.

"Would it be all right with you if I gave you a broad-brush review of my background? Let you know what I've done, what I'd like to do? That'll give us some time to talk about how I should go about this job search. Maybe I could pick your brain a little about how you can help me. OK?

"Currently, I'm president of Camden Associates, an outplacement personnel agency.

"Originally, I'm from the Southwest Side of Chicago, near Midway Airport. I'm 54 years old, married with five grown children.

"My father was a security guard at IIT Research Institute; my mother is retired. She used to work for Walgreens—made aspirins,

133

vitamins, and other pills. I'm the oldest of four children. My brother John does the traffic 'copter reports for a Chicago radio station. My sister Connie is a consultant for an industrial relations firm.

"I went to parochial schools. When I was 14, I left home and went into a monastery. I stayed there until I was 19. Then I went to Loyola University, studied psychology, got my degree in '59. I was also commissioned in the infantry.

"I started my graduate work in Gestalt psychology. In 1960 Kennedy called up troops for the Berlin crisis. That included me, so I spent a year on active duty. Following that, I came back and continued my graduate work in industrial relations…"

Tom took exactly a minute and a half to make this part of his presentation, and he's already given his neighbor several areas in which they may have something in common. He's volunteered enough information not only to get the neighbor interested in his story but to let the neighbor form judgments about him. People don't like to play God, says Tom. Yet it's a fact of life that we constantly form judgments about each other. In an interview—even an exploratory, informal one—you may as well provide enough information to be judged on who you are rather than on what someone has to guess about your background. What does it mean to be the oldest of four kids? What can you deduce from Tom's middle-class background?

The typical personnel professional will tell you that the number of brothers and sisters you have has nothing to do with getting a job. Technically, that's true. The law says that an employer can't ask you how old you are, your marital status, and similar questions. Yet anyone who's considering hiring you will want to know those things about you.

The typical applicant begins a presentation with something like, "I graduated from school in June, nineteen-whatever, and went to work for so-and-so." Our task in this book is to teach you how not to be typical. Our experience has convinced us that the way to get a job offer is to be different from the rest of the applicants. You shouldn't eliminate the first 20 years of your life when someone asks you about your background! That's the period that shaped your basic values and personality.

Neither should you spend too much time on your personal history. A minute or two is just about right. That gives you from three to eight minutes to narrate your work history. Most exploratory interviews, and many initial employment interviews, are limited to half an hour. If you can give an oral resume in 5 to 10 minutes, you have roughly 20 minutes left to find out what you want to know (more on that shortly).

Zeroing in on special strengths

Co-author Richard Citrin advises that "you have to accomplish two main points in your contact with a potential employer. First you must convince this hiring person that you are a 'positive can-do person' and second you must convince him that you can make his life easier if he hires you.

"I remember that when I first moved to the Metroplex I went around telling potential employers that I was a new Ph.D. and really didn't know much about how things worked in these parts. But after not getting to first base, I quickly changed my focus to identify my strengths in the areas of career development.

"Within several months, I had job offers in both the corporate and the academic worlds. Now potential employers saw me as someone with a lot of energy who could help them organize their programs and was willing to work long hours." ■

A word about your work history. If you've done the exercises in Chapter 2, or written your own resume, you ought to be able to rattle off every job you've had, from the first to the latest, pretty easily. In the oral resume you want especially to emphasize your successes and accomplishments in each job. This will take some practice. We are not accustomed to talking about ourselves positively. From childhood we're conditioned that it's not nice to brag. Well, we are here to tell you that if you don't do it in the interview, you won't get the offer.

We repeat: the interview is a sales presentation. It's the heart of your job search, your effort to market yourself. In an exploratory interview, the listener will be asking, "Should I help this person?" In a formal interview, the employer will be asking, "Should I hire this person?" In either case, the answer will be "yes" only if you make a successful presentation, only if you convince the interviewer that you're worth the effort.

So, the first step in preparing for any interview, formal or informal, is to practice your five-minute resume. Go through it out loud enough times so that you're comfortable delivering it. Then work with a tape recorder and critique yourself. Try it out on a couple of friends.

When you're preparing for a formal employment interview, do your homework on the company. This advice is merely common sense. But it's surprising how many candidates will ask an interviewer, "What does this company do?" Don't be one of them. Before you go in for an employment interview, find out everything you can about the company—its history, organization, products and services, and growth expectations. Get hold of the company's annual report, catalogs, and brochures. If you do any investing, your stock broker is an excellent source of information about the financial status of any publicly traded company. Consult your networking contacts, and use the resources in Chapter 4.

Steps to a Successful Interview

Before the Interview
- Self-assessment: identify strengths, goals, skills, etc.
- Research the company.
- Rehearse what you plan to say. Practice answers to common questions.
- Prepare questions to ask employer.

During the Interview
- Make sure you arrive a few minutes early.
- Greet the interviewer by his/her last name; offer a firm handshake and a warm smile.
- Be aware of non-verbal communication. Wait to sit until you are offered a chair. Sit straight, look alert, speak clearly and forcefully but stay relaxed. Make good eye contact, avoid nervous mannerisms, and try to be a good listener as well as a good talker. Smile.
- If the interviewer offers you a cup of coffee or a soft drink, accept it. *Never* smoke under any circumstances.
- Follow the interviewer's lead, but try to get the interviewer to describe the position and duties to you fairly early in the interview so you can then relate your background and skills in context.
- Be specific, concrete, and detailed in your answers. The more information you volunteer, the better the employer gets to know you.
- Offer examples of your work that document your best qualities and may relate to the needs of the organization.
- Answer questions as truthfully and as frankly as you can. Do not appear to be "glossing over" anything. On the other hand, stick to the point and do not over-answer questions. The interviewer may steer the interview into ticklish political or social questions. Answer honestly, trying not to say more than is necessary.

Closing the Interview
- Don't be discouraged if no definite offer is made or specific salary discussed.
- If you get the impression that the interview is not going well and that you have already been rejected, do not let your discouragement show. Once in a while, an interviewer who is genuinely interested in you may seem to discourage you to test your reaction.
- A typical interviewer comment toward the close of an interview is to ask if you have any questions. Prepare several questions in advance, and ask those that weren't covered during the interview.
- At the conclusion of your interview, ask when a hiring decision will be made. Also thank your interviewer for his or her time and express your interest in the position.

After the interview

▮ Take notes on what you feel you could improve upon for your next interview.

▮ Even if you are not interested in the position, type a brief thank-you letter to the interviewer, indicating your appreciation for his or her time. Of course, if you are interested, express enthusiasm (see "Following the Interview" near the end of this chapter).

▮ If offered the position, one to two weeks is a reasonable amount of time to make a decision. All employment offers deserve a written reply whether or not you accept them.

How to dress

A young friend of ours who wanted to break into real estate finally landed her first big interview—with Coldwell Banker. It was fairly easy for her to do her homework on a company of that size. Two days before the interview, however, it suddenly dawned on her that she had no idea how to dress. How did she solve her problem?

"It was pretty easy, actually, and fun, too," says Susan. "All I did was go and hang around outside the office for 15 minutes at lunchtime to see what everyone else was wearing."

However, we recommend that even if the office attire is casual, one should still dress professionally. One career counselor recommends that one should "always dress one step above the attire of those in the office where you are interviewing." ▮

What Interviewers Look For

▮ **General Personality:** Ambition, poise, sincerity, trustworthiness, articulateness, analytical ability, initiative, interest in the firm. (General intelligence is assumed.) Different firms look for different kinds of people—personalities, style, appearance, abilities, and technical skills. Always check the job specifications. Don't waste time talking about a job you can't do or for which you do not have the minimum qualifications.

▮ **Personal Appearance:** A neat, attractive appearance makes a good impression and demonstrates professionalism. Invest in a copy of *Dress for Success* by John Malloy if you are not sure what is acceptable business and interview attire.

▮ **Work Experience:** Again, this varies from job to job, so check job specifications. If you've had work experience, be able to articulate the importance of what you did in terms of the job for which you are interviewing and in terms of your own growth or learning. Even if the work experience is unrelated to your field, employers look upon knowledge of the work environment as an asset. The more you can relate accomplishments and contributions to your last employer's bottom line the better.

■ **Verbal Communication Skills:** The ability to express yourself articulately is very important to most interviewers. This includes the ability to listen effectively, verbalize thoughts clearly, and express yourself confidently.

■ **Skills:** The interviewer will evaluate your skills for the job, such as organization, analysis, and research. It is important to emphasize the skills that you feel the employer is seeking and to give specific examples of how you developed them. This is the main reason why it is important to engage in self-assessment prior to the interview.

■ **Goals/Motivation:** Employers will assess your ability to articulate your short-term and long-term goals. You should seem ambitious, yet realistic about the training and qualifications needed to advance. You should demonstrate interest in the functional area or industry and a desire to succeed and work hard.

■ **Knowledge of the Interviewer's Company and Industry:** At a minimum, you really are expected to have done some homework on the company. Don't waste interview time asking questions you could have found answers to in printed material. Know the firm's position and character relative to others in the same industry. General awareness of media coverage of a firm and its industry is usually expected.

Handling the Interview

In an exploratory, or informal, interview most of the people you'll talk with will want to help you. But they need to know how. After you've outlined your personal and work history, ask your contact how he or she thinks your experience fits into today's market. What companies should you visit? Specifically, what people should you contact?

When someone gives you advice or a recommendation to call someone else, do it! Few things can be more irritating than to provide free counsel to someone who then ignores it. If your contact suggests that you call Helen Smith, call her!

In a formal employment interview, there are several typical questions you can expect to encounter, though not necessarily in this order:

Tell me about yourself. (This is your cue for the five-minute resume.)

Why do you want to change jobs?

What kind of job are you looking for now?

What are your long-range objectives?

What are your salary requirements?

When could you be available to start here?

Tell me about your present company.

What kind of manager are you?
How would you describe yourself?
What are your strengths and weaknesses?
Why should I hire you?

In the course of his career, Rob Rainey of IATREIA/Outpath has posed this last question to untold numbers of applicants. "As strange as it may sound, many candidates just sit there and look puzzled as if it were patently obvious." This question is the interviewer's way of seeing if you can contrast and compare your background and experience to the company's needs. It's your opportunity to cut to the heart of the matter, show your "smarts," and ask for the job.

Describe your present boss.
To whom can I talk about your performance?
Are you open to relocation?
How long have you been looking for a new job?
Why are you interested in this company? (This is your golden opportunity to show the interviewer that you've done your homework on the company.)

Practice your answers to these questions *before* you go in for the interview. Anticipate other questions you might be asked, and develop answers for them. In general, keep your responses positive. Never volunteer a negative about yourself, another company, or a former employer. Even if you hate your present boss, describe your areas of disagreement, if you must, in a calm, professional manner. You are selling yourself, not downgrading others. Even if you're not particularly interested in the company, always conduct the interview as if you were dead set on getting the job.

The interviewer will apply your responses to the questions he or she *really* wants answered:

Does the applicant have the ability to do the job?
Can he or she manage people?
How does he or she relate to people?
What kind of person is this? A leader? A follower?
What strengths does he or she have that we need?
Why the number of job changes so far?
Where is he or she weak?
How did the applicant contribute to present and past companies?
What are his or her ambitions? Are they realistic?
Is he or she too soft or too tough on subordinates?
What is this person's standard of values?
Does he or she have growth potential?
Is there a health problem anywhere?
What is the nature of the "chemistry" between us?

What will the department manager think of this applicant as opposed to the others?

Should this person get an offer?

The interview should not be a one-sided affair. Don't treat it like a trip to the dentist and force the interviewer to pull the answers out of you. Questions that you should ask the interviewer are equally important in this exchange of information. For example, you have to know about the job, the company, and the people in your future employment situation. It's necessary to use your judgment to determine how and when to ask questions in an interview. But without the answers, it will be next to impossible for you to make a sound decision if you receive an offer. Some of the questions you want answered are:

What are the job's responsibilities?

What is the company's recent history? Its current objectives? Its market position?

Where are its plants located? What distribution systems does it use?

To whom will I report? What's his or her background?

How much autonomy will I have to get the job done?

Why is the job available?

Where does the job lead?

What about travel requirements?

Where is the job located?

Are there any housing, school, or community problems that will develop as a result of this job?

What is the salary range? (Do not raise the question of explicit salary at this point.)

What is the detailed benefit picture?

What is the company's relocation policy?

When will an offer decision be made?

What references will be required?

When would I have to start?

What is the personality of the company?

What's the next step?

If I come to work here, what areas of the job would you want me to address first?

Following the Interview

Many job seekers experience a kind of euphoria after a good interview. Under the impression that a job offer is imminent, a candidate may discontinue the search. This is a serious mistake. The decision may take weeks, or may not be made at all. On the average, about six weeks elapse between the time a person makes initial contact with a company and when he receives a final answer. If you let up on the search, you will prolong it. Maintain a constant sense of urgency. Get on with the next interview. Your search isn't over until an offer is accepted and you actually begin the new job.

Always follow up an interview with correspondence. The purpose of the letter is to supplement the sales presentation you made. Thank the interviewer for his or her time and hospitality. Express interest in the position (ask for the order). Then mention three additional points to sell yourself further. Highlight how your specific experience or knowledge is directly applicable to the company's immediate needs. Try to establish a date by which a decision will be made.

If you think you could benefit from professional counseling in interviewing skills, consider the resources suggested in Chapter 2 and in Chapter 6. You may also find it helpful to refer to some of the following books.

BOOKS ON INTERVIEWING

Allen, Jeffery. *How to Turn an Interview Into a Job.* New York: Simon & Schuster, 1988.

Biegeleisen, J.I. *Make Your Job Interview a Success: A Guide for the Career-Minded Job Seeker.* New York: Arco, 1991.

Chapmen, Jack. *How to Make $1000 a Minute.* Berkeley, CA.: Ten Speed Press. 1987.

Fear, Richard A. *The Evaluation Interview.* 4th ed. New York: McGraw-Hill, 1990.

King, Norman. *The First Five Minutes: The Successful Opening Moves in Business, Sales and Interviews.* New York: Prentice Hall, 1987.

Kohlmann, James D. *Make Them Choose You: The Executive Selection Process.* Englewood Cliffs, NJ: Prentice Hall, 1987.

Krannich, Caryl R. *Dynamite Answers to Interview Questions.* San Luis Obispo, CA: Impact, 1991.

Leeds, Dorothy. *Smart Questions: Interview Your Way to Success.* New York: Harper, 1993.

Marcus, John J. *The Complete Job Interview Handbook.* 2nd ed. New York: Harper & Row, 1988.

Medley, H. Anthony. *Sweaty Palms: The Neglected Art of Being Interviewed.* Berkeley: Ten Speed Press, 1991.

Smart, Bradford D. *The Smart Interviewer.* New York: John Wiley & Sons, 1989.

Yates, Martin. *Knock 'em Dead with Great Answers to Tough Questions.* Holbrook, MA: Bob Adams, 1991.

Yeager, Neil, and L. Power Hough. *Interviews.* New York: John Wiley & Sons, 1991.

**How to get the
most from your
references**

According to Linda Turner, a Fort Worth career counselor, references should be kept confidential and never revealed until a company is close to making you an offer, and you want to receive one.

Always brief your references *before* you supply an interviewer with their names and numbers. Tell the references what company you're interviewing with and what the job is. Give them some background on the company and the responsibilities you'll be asked to handle.

Your references will then be in a position to help sell your abilities. It is a good idea to help them a little by providing a brief synopsis of your accomplishments, strengths, and a minor weakness that makes you seem human but won't sink your boat.

Finally, don't abuse your references. If you give their names too often, they will lose enthusiasm for your cause. It's just as easy to lose a job offer by being damned by faint praise as it is to be condemned outright. ■

What To Do If Money Gets Tight

Any job search takes time. One particularly pessimistic career counselor we know suggests you plan to spend about two weeks of search time for every thousand dollars you want to earn per year. (Pity the poor soul who wants to make $60,000!) A more optimistic estimate for a job search is around three months, provided the search is conducted full time.

If you already have a full-time job, it will take you longer to find a new one. But at least you will be receiving a paycheck while you're looking. This chapter is intended for those who are unemployed and facing the prospect of little or no income during the search.

When the financial squeeze is on, the first thing to do is make a thorough review of your liquid assets and short-term liabilities. Ask yourself how much cash you can expect to receive during the next three months from the following sources, plus any others you might come up with:

Savings

Securities

Silver and gold

Insurance loan possibilities

Second mortgage possibilities

Unemployment compensation

Severance pay

Accrued vacation pay

Personal loan sources (relatives, friends)

Sale of personal property (car, boat, stamp collections, etc.)

Then you should consider exactly what bills absolutely must be paid. Don't worry about your total outstanding debt. Many creditors might be willing to make arrangements to forgo principal as long as interest payments are made. It is vitally important to talk to your creditors as soon as possible to avoid being hounded and to assure them that you are working with them.

The final step is easy—if sometimes painful. You compare the amount of money you have on hand or expect to receive with the amount you know you'll have to spend. The difference tells you exactly what kind of financial shape you're in.

Part-Time Employment

The old adage has it that it's better to be unemployed than underemployed. If you can afford it, it's wise not to take a part-time or temporary job. The more time you spend looking for a good full-time position, the sooner you're likely to succeed. But if the cupboard looks pretty bare, it may be necessary to supplement your income any way legally possible in order to eat during the search.

Financial advice for job seekers

Bob Vacker, of Financial Network Investment Corporation, a certified financial consultant in Fort Worth, offers the following advice for the cash-strapped job changer.

"Review your current living expenses and reduce them to the lowest possible level by eliminating unnecessary expenditures. Next, review your credit card debt and reduce or eliminate it entirely because of the high cost of borrowing via a credit card. Assess your total assets and note which assets could be used to cover living expenses until a new job is located.

"Rollover your retirement plan funds directly from your previous employer into an IRA to defer current taxes and also allow the funds to grow tax-deferred until you need them in the future. If you need funds for living expenses until you locate a job, use your non-retirement plan assets first. Use your IRA funds sparingly because there will be early withdrawal penalties (as well as income tax) if withdrawn before age 59 1/2.

"Once you get the new job, reassess your financial position, and contribute the maximum you can to your new employer's 401K retirement plan and still have sufficient funds for your monthly living expenses. Remember, all that you will have for retirement is what you send ahead.

"You should be able to continue your medical benefits from your last employer for up to 18 months at a reasonable fee. Keep your credit card debt to a minimum, and attempt to pay off the balance each month. Remain thrifty because job security isn't what it used to be for any of us." ■

Try to find part-time or temporary work that leaves you as free as possible to interview during the day. For this reason, many people choose to drive a cab at night or work in a bar or restaurant during the evenings. This kind of job gives you the advantage of flexible hours, but the pay is not always desirable. Commissioned sales positions abound in almost every industry. But if your personality isn't suited to sales work, don't pursue it. You'll find it very frustrating.

It's best if you can locate part-time work in your chosen field. The pay is usually more attractive, and you can continue to develop your network of contacts. Many professionals can freelance. An administrative assistant, for example, might be able to find part-time work at a law firm. An accountant might be able to do taxes on a part-time basis and still gain access to new referrals.

Another option for those of you with an entrepreneurial flair is to hire out on a contractual basis to employers when you interview with them. Say you're a computer programmer. A company might not have enough computer work to justify hiring someone to fill a full-time position. So you suggest they hire you on a temporary basis until the project is complete. Or suggest one day a week, because that's all the time it will take, or on an as needed basis. The advantage to a company is that they don't have to pay you any benefits (except those you're able to negotiate). The advantage to you is income in your chosen field.

People with technical skills can work themselves into becoming full-time freelancers in just this way. They might even talk an employer OUT of hiring them full time and negotiate contract work in order to maintain the freedom of their self-employed status.

Here are some additional sources to consider when money is really tight and you need part-time or temporary work.

SELECTED SOURCES FOR PART-TIME AND TEMPORARY WORK

Accountants on Call
2828 Routh, Suite 690
Dallas, TX 75201
(214) 979-9001
Temporary and permanent
placement for all levels of
accounting and financial individuals.

Accountemps
Three North Park East, Suite 200
Dallas, TX 75231
(214) 363-3300
Accountants, bookkeepers, and
data processors.

Adia
600 N. Pearl St., Suite 203
Dallas, TX 75200
(214) 953-1430
Clerical, secretarial, communications, legal, marketing, and
accounting. Has six local offices.

ASA Services
2310 Ridge Rd., Suite C
Dallas, TX 75087
(214) 771-5656
Legal secretaries, word processors, receptionists, paralegals,
court runners, and file clerks.

**Availability Temporary
Services**
400 N. St. Paul St.
Dallas, TX 75201
(214) 979-0097
Office, light industrial, and
bookkeeping.

**Burns International Security
Services**
8150 Brookriver Dr., Suite 103A
Dallas, TX 75247
Metro (214) 638-1666
Security guard service.

CDI Temporary Services
3030 LBJ Frwy., Suite 240
Dallas, TX 75234
(214) 241-6111
Data processing, word processing,
and clerical.

**Continental Personnel
Service**
6060 N. Central Expwy.,
Suite 630
Dallas, TX 75200
(214) 363-5296
Sales, management, accounting,
insurance, and medicine.

Firstword Temporaries
10000 N. Central Expwy.,
Suite 122
Dallas, TX 75231
(214) 788-4900
General office, legal secretaries,
and data processors.

Global Technical Services
P.O. Box 161127
Fort Worth, TX 76161
(817) 831-7765
FAX: (817) 831-6915
Contract labor services, specializ-
ing in engineers, designers,
drafters, and aircraft personnel.

Kelly Services
6200 LBJ Frwy., Suite 180
Dallas, TX 75240
(214) 233-9093
Office, word processing, records
management, and light
industrial.

Kelly Services
6000 Western Place, Suite 115
Fort Worth, TX 76107
(817) 731-0785
Light industrial, technical and
professional, office, clerical, and
general labor.

Key Temporaries
3501 Airport Frwy.
Fort Worth, TX 76111
(817) 838-7788
Clerical.

Labor Force
4248 Harry Hines Blvd.
Dallas, TX 75219
(214) 528-0186
General labor.

Manpower Temporary Services
12001 N. Central Expwy.
Dallas, TX 75243
(214) 490-0222
Office, light industrial, sales promotion, and data processing.

Manpower Temporary Services
2000 E. Lamar St., Suite 400
Arlington, TX 76006
(817) 277-7522
Same as Dallas office.

Norrell Temporary Services
16475 Dallas Pkwy., Suite 150
Dallas, TX 75248
(214) 631-0397
Light industrial.

Norrell Temporary Services
301 Commerce St., Suite 1310
Fort Worth, TX 76102
(817) 870-1999
Word processing and clerical.

Olsten Word Processing Temps
9400 N. Central Expwy.,
Suite 112
Dallas, TX 75231
(214) 373-7400
Secretarial, word processing, technical, legal, marketing, light industrial, and accounting.

Peakload Temporary Services
118 Hemphill St.
Fort Worth, TX 76102
Metro (817) 654-4409
Industrial help, contract payrolling services.

The Personnel Connection
8701 Bedford Euless Rd.,
Suite 530
Hurst, TX 76053
Metro (817) 589-1741
Clerical, secretarial, and technical labor.

Pinkertons
1150 Empire Central Place,
Suite 112
Dallas, TX 75247
(214) 631-5934
Security guard service.

Prime Timers
312 Main St.
Fort Worth, TX 76102
(817) 338-1050
(214) 386-8040
Temporary placement of people over 40 in accounting, word processing, and general office work.

Southwest Temporaries
2710 Ave. E East
Arlington, TX 76011
(817) 649-7000
Secretarial, legal, data processing, and accounting.

Temporaries Inc.
5949 Sherry Lane., Suite 785
Dallas, TX 75225
(214) 922-9229
Clerical, customer service, light industrial.

Temporary Employment Associates
University Tower
6440 N. Central Expwy., Suite 603
Dallas, TX 75206
(214) 987-0047
Secretarial, data processing, and payroll.

Today's Temporary
2001 Bryan Tower
Dallas, TX 75201
(214) 969-7333
Two specialty branches: legal secretarial and financial.

Today's Temporary
3840 Hulen, Suite 125
Fort Worth, TX 76107
(817) 735-1091
Word processing, secretarial, accounting, general office work.

Yellow Cab of Dallas
1610 S. Ervay St.
Dallas, TX 75215
(214) 565-9132
Taxicab leasing.

Yellow Checker Cab
2200 S. Riverside Dr.
Fort Worth, TX 76104
(817) 534-7777
Taxicab leasing.

SELECTED BOOKS ON PART-TIME AND FLEXIBLE EMPLOYMENT

Arden, Lynie. *The Work at Home Sourcebook*. Boulder, CO: Live Oak
  Publications, 1987.
Bird, Caroline. *Second Careers: New Ways to Work After 50*. New York:
  Little, Brown and Company, 1992.
Davidson, Christine. *Staying Home Instead: Home Business Alternatives
  to the Two Paycheck Family*. New York: Little, Brown and Company,
  1992.
Lowman, Kaye. *Of Cradles and Careers*. Franklin Park, IL: La Leche
  League, 1984.
Magid, Renee Y. *When Mothers and Fathers Work: Creative Strategies for
  Balancing Career and Family*. New York: AMACOM, 1987.
New Ways to Work. *Flexibility: Compelling Strategies for a Competitive
  Workplace*. San Francisco: New Ways to Work, 1993.
New Ways to Work. *Change At The Top: Working Flexibly at Senior and
  Management Levels*. London: New Ways to Work, 1991.
O'Hare, Bruce. *Put Work in Its Place*. Victoria, BC, Canada: Work Well,
  1988.
Olmstead, Barney, and Suzanne Smith. *The Job Sharing Handbook*.
  Walnut Creek, CA: Ten Speed Press, 1983.
Olmstead, Barney, and Suzanne Smith. *Creating A Flexible Workplace*.
  New York: AMACOM, 1989.
Rothberg and Cook. *Part-Time Professional*. Washington, DC: Acropolis
  Books, 1985.

Government Assistance Programs

If you've exhausted all your resources and can't find part-time or
temporary work, you might consider government or private assistance. Many people bridle at the mere mention of "charity" or
"welfare." But the help you receive may be needed—and temporary.
It's a way of bridging the gap until you land a job. More people take
advantage of these sources of assistance than you might imagine. In
the case of state and federal aid, your tax dollars have helped to
provide the benefits. Your taxes have also paid for the salaries of the
people distributing the benefits.

Don't pass judgment on the merits of the following sources until
you talk with the professionals who administer their respective
programs. Pros can advise you on eligibility and benefits and can also
provide you with other ideas and resources.

The **Texas Department of Human Services** has offices in
Dallas and Tarrant counties. It administers Medicaid, Food Stamps,
and Aid to Families with Dependent Children (welfare) programs.
Some funds are available for limited emergency assistance. Check
with the local office to see if you are eligible.

Dallas and Tarrant **County Health Departments** operate
programs for child health, pre-natal and postpartum care, and
family planning, as well as immunization, dental health, adult
health, chronic disease, sexually transmitted diseases (STD), stroke
and heart attack prevention, community care (elderly), and environmental health programs.

The following organizations represent some major sources of aid
available in the Dallas/Fort Worth area:

GOVERNMENT AID SOURCES

City of Dallas Action Center
Dallas City Hall, 2/A
1500 Marilla St.
Dallas, TX 75201
(214) 744-3600
Central clearinghouse for residents seeking information about city services. Provides assistance in contacting county, state, and federal agencies.

City of Dallas Health and Human Services
City Hall, 7/A/North
1500 Marilla St.
Dallas, TX 75201
(214) 670-5216
Provides referrals to divisions or special programs provided by the city of Dallas.

Dallas County Community Action Committee
2121 Main St., Suite 100
Dallas, TX 75201
(214) 939-0588
Neighborhood centers offer limited emergency assistance, food, and clothing. Promotes self-sufficiency among low-income individuals and families in Dallas County through the senior work program and youth job search assistance programs. Has two other branches.

Dallas County Health Department
1936 Amelia Court
Dallas, TX 75235
(214) 920-7900
Public health services for Dallas County residents who live outside Dallas city limits.

Dallas County Public Welfare
4917 Harry Hines Blvd.
Dallas, TX 75235
(214) 920-7850
Financial assistance for individuals and families who have health problems or meet other eligibility requirements. One-time-only assistance provided to unemployed heads of households in paying utilities. Also offers employment and training programs.

Martin Luther King Jr. Community Center
2922 Martin Luther King Jr. Blvd.
Dallas, TX 75215
(214) 670-8367
Multi-purpose center, offering counseling, health, employment, child care, senior citizen, and other community services. A Dallas County nutrition program offers noon meals. Employable individuals who meet requirements receive some emergency assistance for paying utilities. Also houses branch of the Texas Employment Commission.

Neighborhood Resources Development Program
City of Fort Worth
1000 Throckmorton St.

Fort Worth, TX 76102
(817) 871-7543
Information and referral service to local agencies. Energy crisis program funds available to help individuals retain utility services.
Tarrant County Centers:
Como Office, 4900 Horne St., (817) 731-0521
Martin Luther King, Jr., 5565 Truman Dr., (817) 457-2076
Mansfield Office, 341 Debbie Lane, (817) 473-0253
North Tri-ethnic, 2950 Roosevelt St., (817) 625-8257
Riverside Office, 201 S. Sylvania Ave., (817) 831-0355
Sansom Park NRD Center, 5428 Cowden St., (817) 624-3139
Southside NRD Center, 959 E. Rosedale St., (817) 332-7786
Worth Heights Office, 3551 New York Ave., (817) 921-5321

Parkland Memorial Hospital
5201 Harry Hines Blvd.
Dallas, TX 75235
(214) 590-8000
Low-cost medical services for Dallas County residents, including emergency, surgical, psychiatric, and outpatient care.

John Peter Smith Hospital
1500 S. Main St.
Fort Worth, TX 76104
(817) 429-5156
Health care to Tarrant County residents on a sliding fee scale for patients who meet federal guidelines.

Social Security Administration
Dallas Area Office
10910 N. Central Expwy.
Dallas, TX 75231
(800) 234-5772
Cash and health benefits through social security retirement and survivor's insurance, disability insurance, supplemental security income, and Medicare.

Social Security Administration
Fort Worth Area Office
Federal Building
819 Taylor St., Room 1A07
Fort Worth, TX 76102
(800) 234-5772
Parallel services to Dallas office.

Tarrant County Department of Human Services
3206 Miller Ave.
Fort Worth, TX 76119
(817) 640-5090
Financial assistance through vouchers for food, rent, and utility payments. Referrals, counseling, and shelter for eligible homeless families with children.
Branch offices:
Arlington, 501 W. Main St., (817) 459-6869
Bedford, 813 Brown Ter., (817) 285-0044
Fort Worth, 3206 Miller Ave., (817) 531-5620

Texas Department of Health
Public Health Region 5
2561 Matlock Rd.
Arlington, TX 76015
Metro (817) 261-2911
Provides information and referrals to inexpensive health service pro-
grams, including chronically ill and disabled children's services program,
early childhood intervention program, and social work services.

Texas Department of Human Services
Region Five
631 106th St.
Arlington, TX 76011
(817) 640-5090
Food stamps, medical, and social services for adults and children who
meet income guidelines.
Food Stamp program offered at the following Fort Worth sites:
308 E. 4th St., (817) 335-5171
3128 S. Riverside Dr., (817) 921-5511
2526 Jacksboro Hwy., (817) 625-2161
1010 Lamar, Suite101, (817) 460-6491

Texas Employment Commission
Dallas District Office
8300 John Carpenter Frwy.
Dallas, TX 75247
(214) 631-6050
Provides unemployment insurance for those who are eligible and cannot
find employment through the commission's job bank.
Special help provided for elderly, youths, handicapped, ex-offenders, and
women with dependent children.

Texas Employment Commission
Fort Worth District Office
310 W. 13th St.
Fort Worth, TX 76102
(817) 335-5111
Parallel services to Dallas District Office.

Check the T.E.C. for Jobs and Unemployment Benefits

Here are three good reasons to check with the Texas Employment
Commission (addresses above): 1) there's no charge for any of the
services; 2) you'll probably find leads for better jobs than you
expected; and 3) you may qualify for one of the programs assisting
special groups.

An average of 2,000 available positions are listed in the TEC's
computerized job bank. On weekdays, you can contact any one of the
13 area offices to check on what's available. At least 50 percent are
professional, clerical, and sales jobs. And a majority are permanent,
full-time positions.

The government-funded public employment agency also provides free proficiency testing and counseling and makes referrals to
social agencies. Special assistance is provided to veterans.

Job Search Seminars are offered in the downtown Fort Worth, downtown Dallas, and Richardson-Plano offices. Anyone is eligible to attend the five-day workshop. Participants prepare for the job search by watching a video job-hunting course. In addition, they learn to communicate more effectively with employers by having mock job interviews videotaped so they can see where they need to improve.

The TEC also helps people find seasonal employment. Several weeks before the State Fair of Texas opens in October, a TEC booth is set up on the Dallas fairgrounds to sign up as many as 1,000 people for temporary jobs. The TEC also assists store owners in large shopping malls to find workers for the Christmas rush.

Anyone who is unemployed can register at the TEC for unemployment insurance. The amount of money individuals are eligible to receive depends on their former income and reasons for their last job separation. The TEC requires people to search actively for a job while they receive unemployment compensation. Checks are mailed twice a month for up to 26 weeks.

To sign up for benefits, bring personal identification, such as a driver's license or military identification, and evidence of work eligibility, such as a social security card. Also, bring the name and mailing address of your last employer to one of the 12 TEC offices in the Dallas/Fort Worth area. If you were employed outside of Texas during the past 24 months, you will need the names and addresses of all the companies you worked for during that time.

For more information, call the Fort Worth office at (817) 335-5111 or the Dallas office at (214) 631-6050.

TEC OFFICES IN THE DALLAS AREA:

Dallas East Office, 4625 Eastover Dr., Mesquite, (214) 388-5840
Garland, 217 N. 10th St., (214) 276-8361
Grand Prairie, 202 W. Hwy. 303, (214) 264-5881
Irving, 2925 N. Skyway, (214) 258-0114
Kessler Hills, 1050 N. Westmoreland Rd., Suite 316, (214) 330-5183
Martin Luther King Jr. Community Center, 2922 Martin Luther King Jr. Blvd., (214) 421-2460
Lancaster-Kiest Office, Oak Cliff, 4243 S. Pope (214) 372-1471
Northwest-Carrollton, 1718 Trinity Valley Dr., (214) 620-1351
Richardson-Plano, 1222 E. Arapaho Rd., (214) 234-5391

TEC OFFICES IN TARRANT COUNTY:

Arlington, 979 N. Cooper St., (817) 265-8431
Bedford, 1809 Forest Ridge Dr., (817) 545-1809
Downtown Fort Worth, 301 W. 13th St., (817) 335-5111

Private Charitable Organizations

If you have exhausted all your resources, the following are major sources of aid in the Dallas/Fort Worth area:

American Red Cross
2300 McKinney Ave.
Dallas, TX 75201
(214) 871-2175
Limited financial aid and shelter for families, service personnel, and others experiencing short-term crisis.

Arlington Charities
811 Secretary St.
Arlington, TX 76015
(817) 275-1511
Clothing, household items, and food provided on a short-term basis for Arlington residents.

Catholic Charities
Dallas Office
3725 Blackburn, P.O. Box 190507
Dallas, TX 75219
(214) 520-6590
Limited emergency financial aid to low-income families in East Dallas provided by Brady Social Service Center, 4009 Elm St., (214) 826-8330.

Catholic Charities
Fort Worth Office
1404 Hemphill St.
Fort Worth, TX 76104
(817) 921-5381
Food and emergency financial assistance for travelers and Tarrant County residents.
Other sites:
813 Brown Ridge Trail., Bedford, (817) 282-6646
2024 N. Houston St., Fort Worth, (817) 626-3402
2801 Miller, Fort Worth, (817) 543-5610
401 W. Sandford, Fort Worth, (817) 274-2560
349 N.W. Renfro St., Burleson, (817) 295-6252

Community Council of Greater Dallas
Information and Referral Services
2121 Main St., Suite 500
Dallas, TX 75201
(214) 747-3711
24-hour emergency referral service to health, welfare, and social service agencies.

Consumer Credit Counseling Service of Greater Dallas
8737 King George Dr., Suite 200
Dallas, TX 75235
(214) 638-2227
Credit counseling for financially distressed individuals. No fee for counseling; small fee for debt liquidation.
Branch Offices:
201 E. Abram, Suite 730, Arlington, (817) 461-2227
1525 N. Interstate 35, Suite 206, Carrollton, (214) 242-6548

7125 Marvin D. Love Frwy., Suite 102, Duncanville, (214) 709-3000
100 N. Central Expwy., Suite 400, Richardson, (214) 437-6252

Jewish Family Service
13140 Coit Rd., Suite 400
Dallas, TX 75240
(214) 696-6400
Provides guidance counseling.

Salvation Army
6500 Harry Hines Blvd.
Dallas, TX 75235
(214) 353-2731
Meals, lodging, and casework service for transient men, women, and children. Temporary emergency assistance for families who do not meet public agencies' requirements.

SEARCH (Southeast Area Churches Association)
3301 E. Rosedale
Fort Worth, TX 76105
(817) 531-2211
Emergency food, clothing, transportation, medical, and utility assistance.

YWCA of Fort Worth and Tarrant County
512 W. 4th St.
Fort Worth, TX 76102
(817) 332-6191
Permanent housing up to six months $30-$55. Low-cost meals served. Child care provided for a fee.

Where To Turn If Your Confidence Wilts

Recently a bank fired a loan officer who had worked there for more than 10 years. The employee was 50 years old, about five feet, six inches tall, weighed almost 300 pounds, and did not have a college degree. His written communication skills were negligible. His poor attitude and appearance, lack of enthusiasm, and dismal self-esteem suggested he would be unemployed a long time.

The bank decided to use IATREIA/Outpath's outplacement service to help the person get another job. "There wasn't much we could do about changing his age, education, size, or communication skills," Rob Rainey recalls. "But we certainly could—and did—work with him on improving his self-esteem and changing his attitude toward interviewing for new jobs."

After a four-month search, the loan officer succeeded in landing a position that exactly suited his needs. His new job even was located in the neighborhood where he lived. It seemed like a typical success story—until the bank informed Tom Camden about how dissatisfied that person was with the counsel he had received. The man told the bank that they would have been better off paying him the consulting fee instead of retaining outside help.

"He was really angry," Rob recalls. "And also full of stress, guilt, fear, anxiety, desire for vengeance, and a host of other emotions."

Such feelings, unfortunately, are not at all unusual. In fact, they're a normal part of any job search, particularly for those who have been laid off or fired. That's because rejection, unfortunately, is inevitable in any job search.

If you've read Chapter 5, you know that you may speak with up to 300 people on a formal or informal basis while you're looking for suitable work—and a healthy percentage of those people will be unable or unwilling to help you. Every job seeker must anticipate rejection—it comes with the territory. Being turned down in an interview is a painful experience, and it's normal to feel hurt. The trick is to keep those hurt and angry feelings from clouding your judgment or affecting your behavior.

What To Do If You Get Fired

Being fired ranks just after the death of someone you love or divorce when it comes to personal traumas. If it should happen to you, take time to evaluate the bad news before accepting a settlement offer. If you quickly accept what your employer has to offer, it will be much more difficult to change your situation later. Tell the boss you want some time to think about a settlement. Then go back in a day or two and negotiate.

Stay on the payroll as long as you can, even if your pride hurts. Find out if you are eligible for part-time work or consulting jobs to tide you over until you find your new job. You may be able to hang on to insurance and other benefits until you've found new employment.

Try to negotiate a generous severance payment. In the last five years, severance agreements have risen dramatically in some industries. What the company offers at first may not be their maximum. Negotiation doesn't always work, but you certainly ought to try to get the most for your years of service.

Check with your personnel office to make sure you're getting all the benefits to which you are entitled, such as vacation pay and profit sharing. Check your eligibility for unemployment compensation before you accept an offer to resign instead of being terminated.

Don't attack management during your termination interview. It may cost you good references and hurt your chances of finding a new job.

Take advantage of any outplacement assistance that is offered. Don't reject the company's offer to help even if your pride has been stung.

Dealing with Emotional Stress

If you're beginning to feel your confidence wilt, reread the tips in Chapter 5 for treating yourself well. Put yourself on a regular schedule. Make sure you're eating healthy foods and getting enough rest and exercise. Don't punish yourself for being unemployed or losing a job offer. These things happen to everyone during the job search process.

One of the worst things that can happen in any job search is to let rejection undermine your self-confidence. Like the little boy at the door who asks, "You don't want to buy a magazine, do you?" a person who doesn't feel good about himself will not easily convince an employer that he should be hired. Each new rejection further erodes self-esteem, and the job search stalls or takes a nose dive: "Maybe I am a loser. Perhaps I was lucky to have my old job as long as I did. Maybe my sights are set too high. I suppose I should look for something less responsible at a lower salary."

Thoughts such as these cross most people's minds at some time or other in the job search. As we've said, it's normal to feel hurt, angry, and depressed after a series of rejections. It's important, however, to recognize these feelings and learn to work them out in some non-destructive way. It is not normal to let such feelings sabotage your job search. Just because you're unemployed or looking for a new job doesn't mean you're a bad or worthless person. The only thing "wrong" with you is that you haven't found the offer that you want.

When your confidence starts to wilt, turn to a trusted friend or relative. Talk about your feelings frankly. Get mad or sad or vengeful. Then get back to work on your job search. Don't let fear of rejection keep you from making that next call. It may be just the lead you're looking for.

There are no hard and fast rules on when to seek professional counseling and support, but we can offer certain guidelines. If you seriously think you need professional help, you ought to investigate two or three sources. Besides the ones we've listed below, check with your minister, priest, or rabbi.

If you feel you have nowhere else to turn, or if you don't want to share your feelings with anyone you know, you should consider professional counseling. If you're not making calls, not preparing for interviews, or not doing what you know you have to do to get the job you want, you could probably use some counseling.

Everybody feels bad about being rejected. But if you allow those feelings to overwhelm you, or if they're interfering with finding a job, it's probably time to talk with a professional. Another sure sign is if you're waking up most mornings too sick or lethargic from overeating, over drinking, or abusing some other substance to do what you have to do.

Where To Find Help for Emotional Problems

A listing in this book does not constitute an endorsement of any institution, therapist, or school of therapy. Therapy depends a great deal on the "chemistry" between therapist and patient—something only you can evaluate. It is quite acceptable to call a therapist and ask for a few minutes to visit before setting an appointment. You may have a few general questions to ask such as "what is your therapeutic orientation" and "what do you know about job hunting and career development." There are many therapists who have career development skills, and this should certainly be a part of any counseling at this time in your life.

Therapy is offered by quite a variety of people, from psychiatrists and psychologists with years of postgraduate training to master's-level professionals such as social workers, licensed professional counselors, and marriage and family therapists. Before engaging a therapist, check his or her credentials. Is the therapist licensed? Where was the therapist trained? What degrees does the therapist hold? How long has the therapist been practicing? Does he or she belong to any professional associations? Do they have any experience in working on career development issues?

Dr. Sheila Collins, Clinical Director of the IATREIA Institute, recommends that you interview several therapists before you enter therapy—even if you have to buy 15 minutes of their time. Ask about cost, credentials, whether your health insurance covers their fees, the type of therapy they practice, the length of time they anticipate would be required to deal with your concerns. The answers to all of these questions are important. But equally important is the sense of rapport you feel. It is vital that you feel comfortable confiding in this person.

There are a number of professions that practice counseling and therapy. The following rundown is arranged more or less in order of years of training, which in turn usually determines the fee charged. A psychiatrist is an M.D. and is able to prescribe medication. In fact most psychiatrists will generally see you for just medication evaluation and management. Don't be afraid to consider medication, especially if you're experiencing depression. Short-term uses of antidepressant medication can be extremely helpful in focusing and energizing your career search.

A psychologist usually has a Ph.D. and has completed a five-year graduate training program. Psychologists often have specialized career development skills and can offer comprehensive assessment and counseling.

A clinical social worker has a master's degree in social work and has conducted therapy under supervision while in training. There are also licensed professional counselors, psychiatric nurses, and pastoral counselors.

In these days of changing health care policies, many people will find that counseling services are often covered under their family health insurance policy. Although career counseling is not a covered service, emotional counseling is covered, especially if provided within a short-term treatment model. Your insurance company usually maintains a list of providers who are in their managed care network, and you can consider calling them for possible referrals.

One of the best ways to find out who might be helpful for you is to ask your friends for recommendations. If someone you know well has been helped and swears by a therapist, that's a strong testimonial. There are, unfortunately, a bewildering variety of schools of therapy. Each one has its detractors and its supporters. What worked for your friend might not work for you. Ask your friend how the therapist worked, and try to envision yourself going through a similar process. Today many therapeutic interventions offer relatively rapid relief. Plan on about six to eight sessions to help you get back on your feet. For references to counseling services, you can all these two resources:

Mental Health Association of Dallas County
2929 Carlisle St.
Dallas, TX 75204
(214) 871-2420
Referrals and information for counseling and self-help groups that deal with a variety of concerns. Provides several different types of support services as well as telephone assistance.

Mental Health Association of Tarrant County
3136 W. 4th St.
Fort Worth, TX 76107
(817) 335-5405
Referrals and information for counseling and self-help groups that deal with a variety of concerns. Provides educational programming, monthly mental health forums, and telephone assistance.

Church groups offer support

Churches are taking a more active role in helping the unemployed. One of the largest organizations is the **Inter-Faith Job Search Council** that meets in different churches every Saturday morning in both Dallas and Fort Worth except on holidays. This is a non-denominational organization of volunteers. Churches provide the space.

Most meetings include a motivational speaker to help boost morale. Other sessions are provided on a variety of topics that rotate each week. Among the most frequently discussed subjects are resume writing, marketing yourself, interviewing, networking, managing your finances, and how to cope emotionally if you lose your job.

An important part of the session is networking, which gives people an opportunity to pass out resumes and to exchange job leads. The atmosphere is friendly and casual, with free donuts and coffee served at the half-day sessions.

Many of the larger churches provide reference books and job-hunting material in their libraries that also can be helpful. Notices of the meetings are run in church calendars.

For more information, call Craig Foster, Chairman, at (214) 754-0550, ext. 214, Bob Mahoney, Vice Chairman at (214) 754-0550, or Valton Holley, Director of Public Relations, at (214) 348-8943. ∎

RELIGIOUS ORGANIZATIONS OFFERING COUNSELING

Azle Pastoral Counseling Center
229 S. Stewart St.
Azle, TX 76020
(817) 444-2929
Individual and group counseling for marriage, family, and personal life adjustment. Initial fee of $20, plus testing expenses, and then a sliding scale fee for other visits.

Catholic Charities
3725 Blackburn
Dallas, TX 75219
(214) 528-4870
A variety of programs provided, including emergency help for refugees and migrants. Counseling billed on sliding scale.

First United Methodist Church Counseling Service
800 W. 5th St.
Fort Worth, TX 76102
(817) 924-8521
Counseling for couples, individuals, codependency, adult children of alcoholics, and smoking. Alcohol and drug use assessments available. Workshops in assertiveness, marriage enrichment, divorce adjustment, stress management, retirement, communications, and listening skills. Fees vary from $45 for individual counseling to sliding scale. Also provides workshops on Alzheimer's and self-esteem, grief recovery, and discovering your inner child. Fees vary from $0-35.

Interfaith Job Search Council of Dallas County
(214) 754-0550 ext. 214
Conducts weekly job-search seminars free of charge.

Jewish Family Service
13140 Coit Rd., Suite 400
Dallas, TX 75240
(214) 696-6400
Individual and family counseling. Assessment, guidance, and vocational counseling services. Sliding scale fees.

Richland Hills Church of Christ Counseling Center
6250 NE Loop 820
Richland Hills, TX 76180
Metro (817) 498-1722
Provides job bank, food bank, and clothing room. Individual, couples, depression, stress management, divorce recovery, and grief recovery counseling. Various self-help groups. Fee $50.00. Offers free support groups.

SELECTED CRISIS CENTERS AND INSTITUTIONS

AIDS Outreach Center
1125 W. Petersmith St.
Fort Worth, Tx. 76102
(817) 335-1994
Offers a variety of services for persons with AIDS and their loved ones. Information & referral by phone and in person.

Alcoholics Anonymous
Fort Worth Central Office
316 Bailey Ave.
Fort Worth, TX 76107
(817) 332-3533
Offers referrals to numerous AA groups in Tarrant County. Free.

Alcoholics Anonymous
Metropolitan Dallas
13500 Midway Rd., Suite 100
Dallas, TX 75244
(214) 239-4599
Provides information and referrals for alcoholics and their families.
Offers support groups. Free.

American Indian Center
818 E. Davis St.
Grand Prairie, TX 75050
(214) 262-1349
Crisis counseling for American Indians and a halfway house for alcohol
rehabilitation. Free.

CONTACT—Dallas
Telephone Counseling
P.O. Box 800742
Dallas, TX 75380-0742
Administration: (214) 233-0866
Counseling Line: (214) 233-2233
Teen Line: (214) 233-TEEN
Trained volunteers provide 24-hour telephone counseling and referrals
for distressed individuals. Provides referrals to emergency aid, including
food, shelter, and prescription medicine.

CONTACT—Tarrant County
P.O. Box 1431
Arlington, TX 76004
Administration: (817) 277-0071
Counseling Line: (817) 277-2233
Parallels Dallas office.

Crisis Intervention
1424 Hemphill
Fort Worth, TX 76104
Counseling Hotline: (817) 927-5544
Trained volunteers provide 24-hour telephone counseling and referrals.

Dallas Council on Alcoholism and Drug Abuse
4525 Lemmon Ave., Suite 300
Dallas, TX 75219
24-hour assistance line: (214) 522-8600
Provides public education, information and referrals, employee assistance program. Sliding scale fees.

Family Guidance Center
2200 Main St.
Dallas, TX 75201
(214) 747-8331
Counseling for individuals, couples, and families. Psychiatric consulta-

tion and psychological testing. Outreach to minority and low-income neighborhoods. Sliding scale fees.

Fort Worth Veterans' Counseling Center —The Vet Center
1305 W. Magnolia St.
Fort Worth, TX 76104
(817) 921-3733
Outpatient psychological counseling, specializing in treatment of delayed combat stress. Psychological counseling available in alcohol/drug abuse, marital stress, and for psychiatric treatment. Offers information and referrals for employment, veterans' benefits, homeless veterans, and other readjustment needs. Free.

Nexus
8733 La Prada Dr.
Dallas, TX 75228
(214) 321-0156
Residential and day programs for adolescents and women who are dealing with alcohol and drug-abuse problems. In and outpatient services available. Individual and employment counseling available. Sliding scale fees.

Oak Lawn Community Services
3434 Fairmount
Dallas, TX 75219
HOTLINE: in English and Spanish (214) 263-AIDS
Therapeutic individual, couple, group, and family counseling for gay men and lesbians. Offers education programs, professional consultation, outpatient drug/alcohol recovery program, and provides adult day care for people with AIDS. Sliding scale fees.

The Salvation Army
5302 Harry Hines Blvd.
Dallas, TX 75235
(214) 688-4494
Administrative center for services that include counseling and work therapy for unattached, disabled, and transient men. Some services available for women and families. Free.

The Suicide and Crisis Center
2808 Swiss Ave.
Dallas, TX 75204
(214) 828-1000 (Crisis Line)
24-hour telephone crisis counseling for individuals contemplating suicide or facing a crisis. Community education and preventative services are offered. Survivors of suicide support group is also provided. Accepts contributions.

Turtle Creek Manor
2707 Routh St.
Dallas, TX 75201
(214) 871-2454
Vocational and group counseling for people 18-60 with mental/emotional problems and/or chemical dependency. Job readiness training. Sponsored by the Texas Rehabilitation Commission, Adult Probation, and VA Hospital.

Career transition issues

According to Sharon Rush a professional counselor at the IATREIA Institute, for most people, conducting a job search constitutes a crisis of sorts. Strong feelings will be aroused, and action must be taken if the crisis is to be resolved. While it's normal to have all of the following emotional responses during the course of your job search, you must manage your emotions or they'll manage you.

Anger—You must not let the fact you were fired or treated indifferently by some interviewer make you hostile on your next interview. Be aware of the object of your anger. Don't displace it onto someone else.

Depression—Of course, you're going to get disappointed and frustrated at times, but don't give in to self-pity. Your next employer wants a go-getter, not a poor-me-er.

Social withdrawal—When you're down and out it's very tempting to avoid others. Don't become a hermit. You need all the friends and contacts you can maintain. Don't apologize for being out of work. It has happened to most people.

The best antidote against getting bogged down in your own emotional turmoil is to take action:

1. Stay physically active. Research has shown that regular, vigorous aerobic activity combats depression and anxiety.

2. Come up with a good plan for finding a job and stick to it. Give your self lots to do every day. Impose deadlines on yourself. As you start making progress, you'll start feeling better.

3. Join a support group for other job seekers. Not only will you get encouragement, you'll also get leads and advice.

4. Make finding a good job a full-time job. You'll feel better and find the right position quicker. ■

Selecting the Right Job
for You

Welcome to the most pleasant chapter of this book. You've figured out what you want to do, developed an acceptable resume, and used your network of contacts and other resources to research the job market and generate all sorts of interviews. If you haven't received a reasonable offer yet, you're close to it.

You have a nice kind of problem if a company makes you an offer and insists on an immediate response while you're still investigating other promising leads. The employer making this offer is essentially telling you, "We think you have everything we're looking for, and we want you to start as soon as possible." Remember, at this point you have more power with this company than at any other time in the job search, and you should not be afraid to flex it in a responsible manner.

It can be difficult to stall or delay your acceptance just because other promising leads still haven't yielded firm offers. You have to use your best judgment in such a case, but you owe it to both yourself and the people who interviewed you to bring in all outstanding possibilities and *then* make your decision. Unless you're absolutely desperate, there's no reason to jump at the first offer you receive. In fact, many career specialists feel you should not take the first offer unless it is a great fit for you.

Ask the employer for a period of time, three to seven days, to review the offer and consider your options. Contact the other companies with which you were talking, and inform them that you have a pending offer. Ask them to get back to you within a set period of time (you set the time!) with a response.

If a company wants you badly enough, they'll wait a reasonable length of time for you to decide. In the meantime, use your offer to "encourage" other companies to reach a decision about your candidacy. We're not suggesting that you play hardball. That probably won't work and might even work against you. But it makes perfect sense to inform other companies who are interested in you that you have an offer. If you're sure you'd rather work for them, say so. But also say that you'll have to accept the first offer if you don't hear from them within the allotted time. Don't lie about your intentions. If you don't intend to accept the first offer, don't say that you do. Otherwise, the second (and better) company might write you off, assuming that you won't be available by the time they're ready to decide.

A job involves much more than a title and base salary. For any firm offer, be sure you understand what your responsibilities will be, what benefits you'll receive besides salary (insurance, vacation, profit sharing, training, tuition reimbursement, and the like), how much overtime is required (and whether you'll be paid for it), how much travel is involved in the job, who your superior will be, how many people you'll be supervising, and where the position might lead. (Is it a dead-end job, or are people in this slot often promoted?) In short, find out anything and everything you need to know to evaluate the offer.

For many positions, especially those requiring several years' experience, it's appropriate to ask for an offer in writing. Such a document would specify the position's title, responsibilities, reporting relationship, compensation, and include a statement of company benefits.

At the very least, before you make a firm decision, be sure to obtain a copy of the company's personnel policy. It will fill you in on such details as the number of paid sick days, overtime and vacation policy, insurance benefits, profit sharing, and the like. These so-called fringe benefits can really add up. Be certain to assign a dollar value to them to help you evaluate the financial pros and cons of each offer.

It seems obvious to us that it's unwise to choose a job exclusively on the basis of salary and benefits. You spend more of your waking hours at work than at any other activity. Don't condemn yourself to working for an impossible boss, with colleagues and subordinates you can't stand, doing work that you find boring, to accomplish goals you don't believe in.

Finding the Right Culture

Carolyn Grant, a coordinator of job-search training for the Texas Employment Commission, warns that you ignore a company's culture at your own peril. You can find a position that suits you to a T but still be unhappy if you don't fit the culture of the company that hires you. It takes some doing to assess an organization's culture, but it's worth your while.

Some signs are fairly obvious: What do people wear? What is the furniture like? Are office doors kept open or closed? Are there any minorities or women in positions of power? How friendly are people to you? To each other? Does anybody laugh? A very important question to ask—Do I feel comfortable here?

There are five aspects of an organization's culture to consider. Try to find out as much as you can about each.

1. What is the relationship between a company and its environment? Does it control its own destiny, or must it depend on the mood of an adversarial home office? You probably wouldn't be wise to work for a municipal bus company if they were phasing out bus service.

2. How does a company view human nature? Good or evil? Changeable or immutable? Answers to these questions determine how employees are treated, how much supervision and control is exerted. How openly will employees communicate? Will there be opportunities for training and development?

3. What are the philosophy and mission of a company? Printed brochures are often good indicators. A good company is clear on what business it's in.

4. How do people relate to each other in a company? Is there a formal flow chart? Are there many vertical levels (defense industry)? Or is power more evenly and horizontally spread out (some new hi-tech firms)? The more horizontal, the more informal, and things generally get done through relationships.

5. How are decisions made, who makes them, and upon what basis? Facts and reason? Politics? Ideology? Good old boy or old girl network? The whims of an autocrat at the top?

The answers to these questions will determine the working atmosphere for most companies.

Compare the Offers on Paper

You've talked with each employer and taken notes about the responsibilities and compensation being offered. Where possible, you've obtained a job offer in writing. You have also read through the company's personnel policy. Now, make yourself a checklist for comparing the relative merits of each offer. We've provided a sample here, but if another format suits your purposes better, use it. The idea is to list the factors that you consider important in any job, and then assign a rating for how well each offer fills the bill in each particular area.

We've listed some of the factors that we think ought to be considered before you accept any offer. Some may not be relevant to your situation. Others that we've left out may be of great importance to you. So feel free to make any changes you want.

Once you've listed your factors, make a column for each job offer you're considering. Assign a rating (say, 1 to 5, with 1 the lowest and 5 the highest) for each factor and each offer. Then, total the score.

The offer with the most points is not necessarily the one to accept. The chart doesn't take into account the fact that "responsibilities" may be more important to you than "career path." Nevertheless, looking at the pros and cons of each offer in black and white should help you make a much more methodical and logical decision.

Factor	Offer A	Offer B	Offer C
Responsibilities	_____	_____	_____
Company reputation	_____	_____	_____
Salary	_____	_____	_____
Health Insurance	_____	_____	_____
Paid vacation	_____	_____	_____
Pension	_____	_____	_____
Profit sharing	_____	_____	_____
Tuition reimbursement	_____	_____	_____
On-the-job training	_____	_____	_____
Career path (where can you go from this job?)	_____	_____	_____
Company future	_____	_____	_____
Quality of product or service	_____	_____	_____
Location (housing market, schools, transportation)	_____	_____	_____
Boss(es)	_____	_____	_____
Other workers	_____	_____	_____
Travel	_____	_____	_____
Overtime	_____	_____	_____
Other	_____	_____	_____
TOTAL POINTS	_____	_____	_____

Salary Strategy

Before you accept an offer—or dicker over salary—you need to know what other people who fill similar positions are making. If you are a professional, check with the local professional association. Most associations conduct an annual salary survey in the local market to determine how their members are doing. This can be an excellent source of compensation data.

Another source of information is *The American Almanac of Jobs and Salaries* by John Wright, published by Avon.

For college graduates, your college career center will have an up-to-date *Salary Survey* published by the College Placement Council, which contains salary information by occupations, industries, and college majors.

What you really need to know is what other people with your qualifications and experience are making in Dallas/Fort Worth for working the job you're considering. Once you have this information, you are in an excellent position to evaluate any offers you receive. Probably the best source of all for salary information is—you guessed it—your network of contacts.

BOOKS ON SALARY NEGOTIATION

Chapmen, Jack. *How to Make $1,000 a Minute.* Berkeley: Ten Speed Press, 1987.
Cohen, Herb. *You Can Negotiate Anything.* New York: Bantam Publishing Co., 1983.
Derek, Robert, *The Cost of Talent.* New York: Free Press, 1993.
Fisher, Roger, and William Ury. *Getting to Yes.* New York: Penguin Books, 1983.
Graham, Lawrence, *The Best Companies for Minorities.* Pflume, 1993.
Kennedy, Marilyn Moats. *Getting the Job You Want and the Money You're Worth.* Piscataway, NJ: American College of Physician Executives, 1987.
Levering, Robert, and M. Moskowitz. *The 100 Best Companies to Work for in America.* New York: John Wiley & Sons, 1993.
Washington, Thomas. *The Hunt.* Belview, WA: Mt. Vernon Press, 1992.
Wendleton, Kate. *Through the Brick Wall.* New York: Villard Books, 1992.

A Final Word

Once you have accepted a job, it's important that you notify each of the people in your network of your new position, company, address, and phone number. Be sure to thank these people; let them know you appreciated their assistance. After all, you never know when you may need to ask them to help you again. You've spent weeks building up a network of professional contacts. *Keep your network alive.*

On each anniversary date of your new job, take the time to run through the self-appraisal process to evaluate your situation and the progress you are making (as measured by job satisfaction, increased salary, responsibilities, and abilities). Consider how they compare with the objectives you set at the start of your search. Although you may be completely satisfied in your new assignment, remember that circumstances can change overnight, and you must always be prepared for the unexpected. So make an employment "New Year's Resolution" to weigh every aspect of your job annually and compare the result with what you want and expect from your life's work.

We hope that you have made good use of the job-search techniques outlined in this book. Indeed, we hope that the resulting experiences not only have won you the job you want but—equally important—also have made you a wiser person. Perhaps the next time you talk to an unemployed person or someone who is employed but seeking a new job, you will look at that person with new insight gained from your own search experiences. We hope you'll gladly share what you've learned about how to get a job in Dallas/Fort Worth.

Zeroing in on a great place to work

How do you know when you've found a great place to work?

We asked business writer Robert Levering, co-author of *A Great Place to Work: What Makes Some Employers So Good and Some So Bad* and *The 100 Best Companies to Work for in America,* what he considered the key to evaluating a job proposal.

"Before you accept a job," Levering insists, "you ought to ask yourself, 'what kind of relationship am I going to have with the people I work for, with the people I'm going to work with, and with my work itself?'"

When he was tracking down "the 100 best employers in America," the rankings were based on five tangibles: pay, benefits, job security, opportunities for promotion, and ambiance. Now, however, he believes the values that rest behind the perks may be more significant than the perks themselves. Levering states, "You must trust the people you work for, have pride in what you do, and enjoy the people you work with. Simply put, the criteria for a great place to work are trust, pride, and fun."

That doesn't mean that salary range, stock options, or a gourmet corporate cafeteria are irrelevant. Levering explains, "If you feel that you're being cheated or that the company is not paying you as much as it could, it's not just an issue of money. How your employer compensates you for your time tells you about how your employer values you, and that concerns trust.

"Similarly, pride translates into systems that let people develop their skills. Pride ensures that employees have the tools they need to do their jobs. Pride means workers get credit for their accomplishments. And if your co-workers

are relaxed, pleasant to be with, and basically
compatible, work is fun. Often that comes down
to how much corporate politics permeates the
office."

Are companies—other than the 100 best—
willing to create a corporate culture based on
trust, pride, and fun?

"There are positive signs," Levering says.
"Businesses know that the work force has
changed. Employees are now more highly
educated and looking for the best job possible.
Employers want to attract and retain the best
people, so they want to treat their employees
well. A hell of a lot of companies would like to
be on the list of the 100 best places to work." ■

Where Dallas/Fort Worth Works

This chapter contains the names, addresses, and phone numbers of the area's top 1,500 employers of white-collar workers. The companies are arranged in categories according to the major products and services they manufacture or provide. Where appropriate, entries contain a brief description of the company's business and the name of the personnel director or other contact.

This listing is intended to help you survey the major potential employers in fields that interest you. It is *selective,* not exhaustive. We have not, for example, listed *all* the advertising agencies in the area, as you can find that information in the *Yellow Pages.* We have simply listed the top twenty-five or so, that is, the ones potentially with the most jobs.

The purpose of this chapter is to get you started, both looking and thinking. This is the kickoff, not the final buzzer. Browse through the whole chapter, and take some time to check out areas that are unfamiliar to you. Many white-collar skills are transferable. People with marketing, management, data processing, accounting, administrative, human resources, secretarial, and other talents are needed in a huge variety of businesses and industries.

Ask yourself in what area your skills could be marketed. Use your imagination, especially if you're in a so-called specialized field. A dietician, for instance, might look first under Health Care, or maybe Hotels. But what about Insurance companies, Museums, Banks, or the scores of other places that run their own dining rooms for employees or the public? What about food and consumer magazines? Who makes up all those recipes and tests those products?

The hints and insider interviews that are scattered throughout this chapter are designed to nudge your creativity and suggest additional ideas for your job search. Much more detailed information on the area's top employers, and other, smaller companies, can be found in the directories and other resources suggested in Chapter 4. We can't stress strongly enough that you have to do your homework when you're looking for a job, both to unearth places that might need a person with your particular talents, and to succeed in the interview once you've lined up a meeting with the hiring authority.

A word about hiring authorities: if you've read Chapter 5, you know that the name of the game is to meet the person with the power to hire you, or get as close to that person as you can. You don't want to go to the chairman or the personnel director if the person who actually makes the decision is the marketing manager or customer service director.

Obviously, we can't list every possible hiring authority in the area's "Top 1,500." If we tried, you'd need a wagon to haul this book around.

Besides, printed directories go out of date—even those that are regularly and conscientiously revised. So always double-check a contact whose name you get from a book or magazine, including this one. If necessary, call the company's switchboard to confirm who heads a particular department or division. Here, then, are Dallas/Fort Worth's greatest opportunities. Happy hunting!

The Dallas/Fort Worth area's top 1,500 employers are arranged in the following categories:

Accounting/Auditing Firms
Advertising/Public Relations
Aircraft and Aerospace
Apparel and Textiles
Architectural Firms
Auto/Truck/Transportation Equipment
Banks/Savings and Loans/Credit Unions
Book Publishers and Distributors
Broadcasting and Television
Chemicals
Computers: Data Processing
Computers: Hardware/Software

Contractors/Construction
Drugs/Biological Products
Educational Institutions
Electronics
Energy, Oil, and Gas Companies
Engineering Firms
Entertainment
Environmental Services
Film, Video, Recording, and Talent Services
Food/Beverage Producers and Distributors
Furniture and Fixtures Manufacturers
Government
Health Care
Hotels/Motels/Conventions
Human Services
Insurance
Law Firms
Management Consultants
Manufacturers
Media: Print
Metal Products
Museums and Art Galleries
Paper/Packaging/Allied Products
Printers
Real Estate
Recreation/Sports/Fitness
Restaurant Chains
Retailers/Wholesalers
Stock Brokers/Investment Bankers
Telecommunications
Travel/Transportation/Shipping
Utilities

Accounting/Auditing Firms

You may also want to check the sections on **Banks** and **Stock Brokers**

For networking in accounting and related fields, check out the following professional organizations listed in Chapter 5:

PROFESSIONAL ORGANIZATIONS:

Certified Public Accountants
National Association of Accountants

For additional information, you can contact:

American Institute of CPAs
Harbor Cite Financial Center
201 Plaza Three
Jersey City, NJ 07311
(201) 938-3000

American Society of Women Accountants
1755 Lynn Field, #222
Memphis, Tn. 38119
(901) 680-0470

Institute of Management Accountants
10 Paragon Dr.
Montvale, NJ 07645
(201) 573-9000

National Association of Black Accountants
7249-A Hanover Pkwy.
Greenbelt, MA 20770
(301) 474-6222

National Society of Public Accountants
1010 N. Fairfax St.
Alexandria, VA 22314
(703) 549-6400

PROFESSIONAL PUBLICATIONS:

Accounting News
CPA Journal
CPA Letter
Journal of Accountancy
National Public Accountant

DIRECTORIES:

Accounting Firms and Practitioners (American Institute of
  Certified Public Accountants, New York, NY)
Emerson's Directory of Leading U.S. Accounting Firms
  (Emerson's, Seattle, WA)
National Directory of Accounting Firms & Accountants (Gale
  Research, Inc., Detroit, MI)
National Directory of Certified Public Accountants (Peter Norbach
  Publishing Co., Princeton, NJ)
Texas Society of Certified Public Accountants Directory (Texas
  Society of Certified Public Accountants, Dallas, TX)
Who Audits America (Data Financial Press, Menlo Park, CA)

EMPLOYERS:

Andersen, Arthur, & Co.
Dallas Office
901 Main St., Suite 5600
Dallas, TX 75202
(214) 741-8300
Division Head of Management and Services: Scot Wilson

Andersen, Arthur, & Co.
Fort Worth Office
777 Main St., Suite 1100
Fort Worth, TX 76102
(817) 870-3000
Contact: Same as Dallas office

BDO Seidman
2400 Plaza of the Americas
600 N. Pearl St.
Dallas, TX 75201
(214) 220-3131
Contact: Department Head

Bailey Vaught Robertson & Co.
1999 Bryan St., Suite 2500
Dallas, TX 75201
(214) 979-0390
Contact: Prefer mail inquiries only

Belew, Averitt & Co.
700 N. Pearl St.
Plaza of the Americas
Dallas, TX 75201
(214) 969-7007
Contact: Personnel

Bland Garvey & Taylor
1202 Richardson Dr., Suite 203

Richardson, TX 75080
(214) 231-2503
Contact: Mail resume to John Garvey

Candy & Schonwald
3116 Live Oak St.
Dallas, TX 75204
(214) 826-6660
Personnel: Pam Green

Cheshier & Fuller
14175 Proton Rd.
Dallas, TX 75244
(214) 387-4300
Contact: Personnel

Cohen, Martin W., & Co.
1600 W. Pacific Ave., Suite 1900
Dallas, TX 75201
(214) 953-3000
Contact: Personnel

Coopers & Lybrand
Dallas Office
1999 Bryan St., Suite 3000
Dallas, TX 75201
(214) 754-5000
Personnel Director: Don Barr

Coopers & Lybrand
Fort Worth Office
301 Commerce St., Suite 1900
Fort Worth, TX 76102
Metro (817) 429-2410
Administrator: Carolyn Drews

Deloitte and Touche
Texas Commerce Tower
2200 Ross, Suite 1600
Dallas, TX 75201
(214) 777-7000
Recruitment Director: Lindsey Green

Ernst & Young
Dallas Office
2001 Ross Ave., Suite 2800
Dallas, TX 75201
(214) 979-1700
Consulting Positions: Dottie Gricius
Audit and Tax Positions: Molly Cook

Ernst & Young
Fort Worth Office
500 Throckmorton St., Suite 2200
Fort Worth, TX 76102
Metro (817) 335-1900
Partner: Turner Almond

Hoffman, McBryde & Co.
7950 Elmbrook Dr., Suite 200
Dallas, TX 75247
(214) 631-4758
Contact: Miriam McBryde

Lane, Gorman Trubitt & Co.
1909 Woodall Rogers Frwy., Suite 400
Dallas, TX 75201
(214) 871-7500
Administrator: Nancy Caudill

Leventhal, Kenneth, & Co.
2200 Ross Ave., Suite 1100
Dallas, TX 75201
(214) 969-0900
Human Resources Director: Tim Durie

KPMG Peat, Marwick
Dallas Office
200 Crescent Ct., Suite 300
Dallas, TX 75201
(214) 754-2000
Recruiter: Michelle Robertson

KPMG Peat, Marwick
Fort Worth Office
301 Commerce St.
2500 City Center Tower II
Fort Worth, TX 76102
(817) 335-2655
Partner: John Anderson

Price Waterhouse
Dallas Office
1700 Pacific Ave., Suite 1400
Dallas, TX 75201
(214) 922-8040
Human Resources Director: Terry Kepler

Price Waterhouse
Fort Worth Office
1700 City Center Tower II
301 Commerce St.
Fort Worth, TX 76102

(817) 870-5500
Sr. Manager: John B. Esch

Tannenbaum Bindler & Co.
2323 Bryan St., Suite 700
Lock Box 107
Dallas, TX 75201
(214) 969-6990
Personnel Manager: Margaret Bentley

Thornton, Grant
1445 Ross Ave., Suite 800
Dallas, TX 75202
(214) 855-7300
Office Manager: B.L. Zavatsky

Travis, Wolf, and Co.
5580 LBJ Frwy., Suite 400
Dallas, TX 75240
(214) 661-1843
Office Manager: Walter de Vlught

Vogel, Philip, & Co.
12221 Merit Dr., Suite 1200
Dallas, TX 75251
(214) 386-4200
Managing Partner: Buddy Raden

Weaver & Tidwell
1500 Commerce Building
307 W. 7th St.
Fort Worth, TX 76102
(817) 332-7905
Partner: W.M. Mack Lawhon

Advertising/Public Relations

For networking in **advertising/public relations** and related fields, check out the following professional organizations listed in Chapter 5:

PROFESSIONAL ORGANIZATIONS:

Advertising Club of Fort Worth
American Marketing Association
Dallas Advertising League
Dallas Professional Photographers Association
Dallas Society of Illustrators
Dallas Society of Visual Communications
Direct Marketing Association of North Texas
International Association of Business Communicators
Press Club of Dallas
Southwestern Association of Advertising Agencies
Texas Association of Film & Tape Professionals
Women in Communications

For additional information, you can contact:

The Advertising Council
261 Madison Ave.
New York, NY 10016
(212) 922-1500

American Advertising Federation
1101 Vermont Ave., NW, Suite 500
Washington, DC 20005
(202) 898-0089

American Association of Advertising Agencies
666 Third Ave.
New York, NY 10017
(212) 682-2500

Direct Marketing Association
11 W. 42nd St.
New York, NY 10036
(212) 768-7277

Public Relations Society of America
33 Irving Place, 3rd Floor
New York, NY 10003
(212) 995-2230

PROFESSIONAL PUBLICATIONS:

Advertising Age
Adweek/Southwest
Direct Marketing Magazine
Industrial Marketing
Journal of Advertising Research
Journal of Marketing Research
Journal of Public Relations
Madison Avenue
Marketing and Media Decisions
Marketing Week
PR Quarterly
Public Relations News
Public Relations Review

DIRECTORIES:

Bradford's Directory of Marketing Research Agencies (Bradford Directory of Marketing Research Agencies, Centerville, VA)
International Directory of Market Companies and Services Green Book (American Marketing Association, New York, NY)
Marketing Consultants Directory (American Business Directories, Omaha, NE)
O'Dwyer's Directory of Corporate Communications and O'Dwyer's Directory of Public Relations Firms (J.R. O'Dwyer Company, New York, NY)
Public Relations Career Directory (Career Press, Hawthorne, NJ)
Public Relations Journal—Register Issue (Public Relations Society of America, New York, NY)
Standard Directory of Advertising Agencies (National Register Publishing Co., Wilmette, IL)
Who's Who in PR (P.R. Publishing Co., Exeter, NH)

EMPLOYERS:

Anderson Fischel Thompson
Prestonwood Tower
5151 Belt Line Rd., Suite 700
Dallas, TX 75240
(214) 233-8461
Chairman of the Board: Joe Anderson
Advertising and public relations.

Berry-Brown Advertising
3100 McKinnon, Suite 1100
Dallas, TX 75201-1046
(214) 871-1001
Personnel Manager: Virdie Horton
Advertising and public relations.

Bloom FCA
P.O. Box 190950
Dallas, TX 75219
(214) 443-9900
Director of Human Resources: Debi Lockhart
Advertising and public relations.

Champney and Associates
1440 W. Mockingbird Lane, Suite 300
Dallas, TX 75247
(214) 631-2535
Personnel: Zafar Khan
Advertising and public relations.

Dally Advertising
1320 S. University Dr., Suite 501
Fort Worth, TX 76107
(817) 332-5299
President: Scott Dally
Advertising and public relations.

Evans/Dallas
4131 N. Central Expwy., Suite 510
Dallas, TX 75204
(214) 521-6400
President: George Arnold
Advertising and public relations.

Goodman & Associates
3633 W. 7th St.
Fort Worth, TX 76107
(817) 735-9333
President: Gerry Goodman
Advertising and public relations.

Hill & Knowlton
2929 Carlisle, Suite 115
350 N. St. Paul
Dallas, TX 75204
(214) 979-0090
Sr. Vice President: Russ Pate
Public relations.

Keller-Crescent/Southwest
102 Decker Ct., Suite 100
Irving, TX 75062
(214) 541-0700
Administrative Assistant: Sue Harper
Advertising and public relations.

Knape & Knape
2501 Cedar Springs, Suite 500

Dallas, TX 75201
(214) 979-5050
Vice President and Director of PR: Steven Silvers
Advertising and public relations.

KNE
501 Elm St., Suite 300
Lock Box 6
Dallas, TX 75202
(214) 741-7500
President: Jim Krause
Advertising.

Larkin, Meeder & Schweidel
2501 Cedar Springs Rd., 4th Floor
Dallas, TX 75201
(214) 688-7070
Office Manager: Mary Graves
Advertising.

Laurey Peat & Associates
2001 Ross Ave., Suite 3020
Dallas, TX 75201-2978
(214) 871-8787
Office Manager: Debbie Meyer
Public relations.

Levinson and Hill
600 N. Pearl, Suite 910
Dallas, TX 75201
(214) 880-0200
Vice President of Client Services: Dixie Pineda
Advertising and public relations.

Main Station Unlimited
901 S. Main St.
Fort Worth, TX 76104
(817) 332-1040
President: Bob Walter
Advertising and public relations.

McCann-Erickson/Dallas
10830 N. Central Expwy., Suite 246
Dallas, TX 75231
(214) 361-1135
General Manager: Santiago Hinojosa
Advertising and public relations.

McKone & Co.
1900 Westridge Dr.
Irving, TX 75038
(214) 550-7433

President: Pete McKone
Advertising and public relations.

Moroch & Associates
3625 N. Hall St., Suite 1200
Dallas, TX 75219
(214) 520-9700
Office Manager: Cathy Beath
Advertising and public relations.

Point Communications
14001 Dallas Pkwy., Suite 450
Dallas, TX 75240
(214) 851-1100
President: Sam Johnson
Advertising and public relations.

PR/Texas
P.O. Box 17210
Fort Worth, TX 76102
Metro (817) 429-4682
President: Jane Schlansker
Advertising and public relations.

Puskar Gibbon Chapin
3500 Maple Ave., Suite 900
Dallas, TX 75219
(214) 528-5400
Principal: Jim Gibbon
Advertising and public relations.

Regian Associates
219 S. Main St.
Fort Worth, TX 76104
(817) 870-1128
Public Relations: Julie Wilson
Advertising and public relations.

Richards Group
10000 N. Central Expwy., Suite 1200
Dallas, TX 75231
(214) 891-5700
Office Manager: Teri Jones
Advertising.

Saunders, Lubinski & White
7610 Stemmons Frwy., Suite 100
Dallas, TX 75247
(214) 630-6160
Office Manager: Tracy Griffin
Advertising and public relations.

Team & Associates Advertising
209 S. Jennings Ave.
Fort Worth, TX 76104
(817) 332-1560
Contact: Personnel Department
Advertising and public relations.

Temerlin McClain
P.O. Box 619200
DFW Airport, TX 75261-9200
(214) 556-1100
Contact: Personnel Department
Advertising and public relations.

Tracy-Locke/Dallas
200 Crescent Court
Dallas, TX 75201
(214) 969-9000
Contact: Personnel Department
Advertising and public relations.

Western International Media
2929 Carlisle St., Suite 260
Dallas, TX 75204
(214) 871-1050
Media Supervisor: Lisa Wettig
Media-buying service.

Witherspoon & Associates
1000 W. Weatherford St.
Fort Worth, TX 76102
(817) 335-1373 (Toll free)
Sr. Vice President: Mike Wilie
Advertising and public relations.

Breaking into public relations

During his senior year in college, Greg, an enterprising friend of ours, began querying companies about job openings in public relations. All responded with a polite form letter, stating he must have prior experience.

Not one to be easily discouraged, he moved to Dallas after graduation, even though he didn't know anyone except his college roommate. He began writing to public relations executives and asking for five minutes of advice on how to get started in the business. He telephoned them to set up appointments and followed up the visits with thank-you notes.

One of the men he contacted was on the Cystic Fibrosis Foundation Board of Directors. When he told him the charity might consider setting up a PR department, he contacted the

184

director and ended up running the new department.

"I'm glad I went to work for a non-profit organization because it was the best experience I could have gotten," he says. "No one was there to spoon feed me. I built the department from scratch."

In addition to regular PR functions, he assisted with fund-raising and made arrangements for the annual dinner. He did such a superb job of setting up the event that one of the guests, a PR agency owner, offered him a job as an account executive. By that time, Greg had two years of experience and was ready to make a move. ■

Tips for landing your first job out of college

Landing that first job out of school is a frightening prospect for many. But there are ways to prepare for entry into the work world.

We asked directors of college and university career centers for the best advice they could give someone who is starting to look for their first job after graduation. Here are their replies:

Dr. Van Parker, Tarrant County Junior College Northeast's Director of Counseling and Testing Services: "Try to get work experience while you're in college. If you wait until you get out, you're already behind. Don't worry about low pay because the experience will more than make up for the difference. Later on you will get back what you didn't receive in pay in terms of the extra boost to your career. Also be sure to get as much experience in writing and English as you can. I have applications from Ph.D.s who can't write or communicate effectively."

Dr. Don Hankins, Tarrant County Junior College South Campus Director of Counseling and Testing: "One of the most important things is to work on communications skills. People who present themselves well do better in getting a job, and once they get out, they get ahead faster than others."

Linda Foley, Eastfield Community College Coordinator of Career Placement: "To be prepared, learn how to get a job. Preparation and research as well as resume writing and interviewing techniques are what can really help you get a job these days. Many people are unaware of how college career centers can help current and former students free or for a nominal fee." ■

Aircraft and Aerospace

You may also want to check out the sections on **Computers** and **Electronics.**

PROFESSIONAL ORGANIZATIONS:

For information, you can contact:

Aerospace Education Foundation
1501 Lee Highway
Arlington, VA 22209
(703) 247-5800

Aerospace Electrical Society
P.O. Box 24883 Village Station
Los Angeles, CA 90024

Aerospace Industries Association of America
1725 De Sales St., NW
Washington, DC 20036
(202) 371-8400

American Institute of Aeronautics and Astronautics
5001 Airport Plaza Dr.
Long Beach, CA 90815

Int'l. Association of Machinists & Aerospace Workers
8411 S. Pioneer
Whittier, CA 90601
(818) 961-9426

National Space Institute
600 Maryland Ave., SW
Washington, DC 20034

PROFESSIONAL PUBLICATIONS:

Aviation Week & Space Technology
Business & Commercial Aviation
Journal of Air Law and Commerce

DIRECTORIES:

Aerospace Industries Association of America-Directory of VTOL Aircraft (Aerospace Industries Association of American, Washington, DC)
Aviation Buyers Guide (Debora, Shelbyville, TN)

Aviation Week & Space Technology, Buyers Guide Issue (McGraw-Hill Publishing Co., New York, NY)
Corporate Technology Directory (Corporate Technology Information Services, Woburn, MA)
World Aviation Directory & Buyers Guide (McGraw-Hill Publishing Co., New York, NY)

EMPLOYERS:

Aerospace Optics
3201 Sandy Lane
Fort Worth, TX 76112
(817) 451-1141
Contact: Personnel Department
Manufactures aircraft switches.

Aerospace Technologies
7445 E. Lancaster Ave.
Fort Worth, TX 76112
(817) 429-7412
Contact: Personnel Department
Manufactures aircraft components.

American Eurocopter
2701 Forum Dr.
Grand Prairie, TX 75051
Metro (214) 641-0000
Contact: Isla Mae Allison, Manager Personnel
Reassembles and modifies helicopters for commercial and government use.

Associated Air Center
8321 Lemmon Ave.
Dallas, TX 75209
(214) 350-4111
Human Resources Coordinator: Stan Zinn
Refurbishing and maintenance of executive and commercial-sized aircraft.

BEI Defense Systems Co.
P.O. Box 1367
Euless, TX 76039
(817) 267-8191
Personnel Manager: Pat McDaniel
Manufactures rocket systems, rocket fuses, warheads, and rocket motors.

Bell Helicopter/Textron
P.O. Box 482
Fort Worth, TX 76101
(817) 280-2011
Contact: P.D. Shabay, Vice President Personnel

Government contractor involved in research and manufacturing of helicopters.

Dyncorp
6801 Calmont Ave.
Fort Worth, TX 76116
(Contact company by mail only)
Employment Manager: Daphne Geary
Government service contractor for aircraft maintenance and modification.

Edward's Aerospace
5100 Airport Frwy.
Irving, TX 75062
(214) 790-1122
Contact: Personnel Administration Manager
Manufactures aircraft parts and equipment, flexible pipe fittings for marine and oil industries, and bonded metal parts.

EDM of Texas
14042 Distribution Way
Farmers Branch, TX 75234
(214) 241-2501
Controller: Bill Wade
Repairs aircraft parts.

GEC Avionics
6410 Southwest Blvd., Suite 128
Fort Worth, TX 76109
(817) 763-0281
Contact: Atlanta office at (404) 448-1947
Develops and produces electronic devices used in aircraft.

General Aviation Industries
P.O. Box 8617
Fort Worth, TX 76124
(817) 284-4848
Personnel Director: Bonnie Nix
Government defense contractor for ground support and spare parts for airplanes.

Glover Machine Co.
P.O. Box 210187
Dallas, TX 75211
(214) 331-8373
Personnel Director: Ygnacio Lopez
Manufactures aircraft parts.

HAC Corp.
537 Camden Dr.
Grand Prairie, TX 75051
(214) 263-4387

Personnel: Dianna Snow
Manufactures aircraft parts and does composite bonding.

K-C Aviation
7350 Cedar Springs Rd.
Dallas, TX 75235
(214) 902-7535
Human Resources Recruiter: Jacque Leopard
Aircraft maintenance and modification.

Lockheed Fort Worth Division
Lockheed Blvd.
Fort Worth, TX 76108
or
P.O. Box 748
Fort Worth, TX 76101
(817) 777-2000
Contact: Employment Office
Major employer and government contractor that manufactures
aircraft, radar systems, and related equipment in the Fort Worth
division.

LTV Aerospace and Defense Company
P.O. Box 655907 Ms49L-06
Dallas, TX 75265
(214) 266-2011
Contact: Employment Office
Government contractor producing aircraft missiles, launch
vehicles, and space vehicle components.

Menasco Aerosystems Division
4000 Hwy. 157
Euless, TX 76040
(817) 283-4471
Manager of Human Resources: Kathy Johnson
Multi-industry firm, producing marine weapons, handling systems, aircraft landing gear, helicopter rotor assemblies, and heat-
treated metals.

Progressive
1030 N. Commercial Blvd.
Arlington, TX 76017
Metro (817) 467-0031
Aircraft machine shop.

Putoma Corp.
5101 E. California Pkwy.
Fort Worth, TX 76119
Metro (817) 429-5416
Office Manager: Wanda Nicholson
Manufactures aircraft parts.

Ryder Aviall
P.O. Box 7199
Dallas, TX 75209
(214) 956-5000
Contact: Personnel Department
Services and repairs turbine engines, installs avionic systems, refurbishes general aviation airframes, and operates terminal hangar and refueling complex at Dallas Love Field. Also distributes engine and aircraft-related parts and supplies.

Stratoflex
220 Roberts Cutoff Rd.
Fort Worth, TX 76114
(817) 738-6543
Employee Relations: Terry Benton
Manufactures hose fittings for aircraft and automobiles.

Texstar
802 Ave. J East
Grand Prairie, TX 75050
(214) 647-1366
Contact: Personnel Department
Manufactures canopies for aircraft.

Apparel and Textiles

You may also want to check the **Retailers/Wholesalers** section.

For networking in the apparel and textile industries and related fields, check out the following professional organization listed in Chapter 5:

PROFESSIONAL ORGANIZATIONS:

American Society of Interior Designers

For additional information, you can contact:

American Apparel Manufacturers Association
2500 Wilson Blvd., Suite 301
Arlington,VA 22201
(703) 524-1864

Association of Bridal Consultant
200 Chestnutland Rd.
New Milford, CT 06776
(203) 355-0464

Counsel of Fashion Designers of America
1412 Broadway
New York, NY 10018
(212) 302-1821

Educational Foundation for the Fashion Industries
227 W. 27th St.
New York, NY 10001

International Association of Clothing Designers
475 Park Ave. S.
New York, NY 10016
(212) 685-6602

Sportswear Apparel Association
450 7th Ave.
New York, NY 10123
(212) 564-6161

Textile Distributors Association
45 W. 36th St.
New York, NY 10018
(212) 563-0400

Textile Research Institute
Box 625

Princeton, NJ 08540
(609) 924-3150

PROFESSIONAL PUBLICATIONS:

Apparel Industry Magazine
Fashion Newsletter
Textile Products
Textile Research Journal
Textile World
Women's Wear Daily

DIRECTORIES:

Apparel Industry Sourcebook (Denyse & Co., Inc., North Holly-
   wood, CA)
Apparel Trades Book (Dunn & Bradstreet, Inc., New York, NY)
Fairchild's Textile & Apparel Financial Directory (Fairchild
   Publications, New York, NY)
Membership Directory (American Apparel Manufacturers Associa-
   tion, Arlington, VA)
Models Mart Directory (Peter Glenn Publications, New York, NY)
Textile Blue Book (Division Publishing Co., Glen Rock, NJ)
Wholesale / Manufacturers Apparel Directory (American Business
   Lists, Omaha, NE)

EMPLOYERS:

Byn-Mar
2952 Ladybird Lane
Dallas, TX 75220
(214) 350-7011
Head Designer: Vicki Inabett
Operations Manager: Sandra Robinson
Manufactures women's clothing.

Cheerleader Supply Co.
2010 Merritt Dr.
Garland, TX 75041
(214) 231-6364
Personnel Director: Sherri McInnis
Manufactures cheerleader's apparel.

Costa, Victor
7600 Ambassador Row
Dallas, TX 75247
(214) 634-1133
Contact: Personnel
Manufactures women's clothing.

Designers Collection
901 Regal Row
Dallas, TX 75247
(214) 634-8040
Contact: Personnel
Manufactures table linens.

Haggar Co., The
6113 Lemmon Ave.
Dallas, TX 75209
(214) 352-8481
Contact: Human Resources
Manufactures men's clothing.

Jerell
1431 Regal Row
Dallas, TX 75247
(214) 637-5300
Contact: Personnel Office
Manufactures women's and juniors' clothing.

Jones of Dallas Manufacturing
8505 Chancellor Row
Dallas, TX 75247
(214) 638-0321
Contact: Personnel
Manufactures women's clothing.

Justin Boot Co.
300 S. Jennings Ave.
Fort Worth, TX 76104
(817) 332-4385
Personnel Manager: Bill Ledbetter
Manufactures cowboy boots.

Niver Western Wear
1221 Hemphill St.
Fort Worth, TX 76104
(817) 336-2389
Office Manager: Dorris Scanlan
Manufactures Western clothing.

Prophecy Corp.
1302 Champion Circle
Carrollton, TX 75006
(214) 247-1900
Contact: Human Resources
Manufactures women's sportswear.

RLM Fashion Industries
1140 Empire Central Place, Suite 104
Dallas, TX 75247

(214) 747-4812
Contact: Personnel
Manufactures women's apparel.

Resistol Hats
601 Marion Dr.
Garland, TX 75042
(214) 494-0511
Contact: Personnel Department
Manufactures cowboy hats and other headwear.

Sidran Sportswear
2875 Merrell Rd.
Dallas, TX 75229
(214) 352-7979
Contact: Personnel Manager
Manufactures men's Western clothing.

Sunny South Fashions
7777 Hines Place
Dallas, TX 75235
(214) 637-4333
Personnel Director: Paula Hultsman
Manufactures women's sportswear.

Williamson-Dickie Manufacturing Co.
509 W. Vickery St.
Fort Worth, TX 76104
(817) 336-7201
Personnel Director: Estelle Lewis
Manufactures women's and men's work clothing.

Wolf, Howard B.
3809 Parry Ave.
Dallas, TX 75226
(214) 823-9941
Sr. Vice President: Eugene Friesen
Manufactures women's clothing.

Architectural Firms

You may also want to check the sections on **Contractors/ Construction, Engineering, and Real Estate.**

For networking in architecture and related fields, check out the following professional organizations listed in Chapter 5:

PROFESSIONAL ORGANIZATIONS:

American Institute of Architects
American Society of Landscape Architects
Institute of Business Designers

For additional information, you can contact:

American Institute of Architects
1735 New York Ave., NW
Washington, DC 20006
(202) 626-7300

AIA Fort Worth
675 N. Henderson St., Suite 800
Fort Worth, TX 76107
(817) 338-4668
Exec. Director: Suzie Adams

AIA Dallas
2811 McKinney St., Suite 20
Dallas, TX 75204
(214) 871-2788
Exec. Director: Gloria Wise

National Association of Minority Architects
101 Broad St.
Richmond, VA 23220
(804) 788-0338

National Council of Architectural Registration Boards (NCARB)
1735 New York Ave., NW
Washington, DC 20006
(202) 783-6500

Society of American Registered Architects
1245 S. Highland Ave.
Lombard, IL 60148
(708) 932-4622

Texas Society of Architects
114 W. Seventh, Suite 1400
Austin, TX 78701
(512) 478-7386

PROFESSIONAL PUBLICATIONS:

AIA Journal
Architecture
Architectural Record
Practicing Architect
Progressive Architecture
Texas Architect

DIRECTORIES:

AIA Membership Directory (American Institute of Architects, New
   York, NY)
Directory of Contract Service Firms (C.E. Publications, Kirkland,
   WA)
National Membership Directory (Society of American Registered
   Architects, Lombard, IL)
Profile: Firm & Membership Directory (American Institute of
   Architects, Washington, DC)

EMPLOYERS:

Benson, Hlavaty & Associates
1717 Main St., Suite 3550
Dallas, TX 75201
(214) 698-2700
President: Martti Benson

Beran & Shelmire
Two Turtle Creek Village, Suite 1313
Dallas, TX 75219
(214) 522-7980
President: Overton Shelmire

Boothe Architects
1111 Foche St. #201
Fort Worth, Tx. 76107
(817) 332-8998
Principal: Ray Boothe

Corgan Associates Architects
501 Elm St., Suite 500
Dallas, TX 75202
(214) 748-2000
Contact: Department Head

Dahl Architects
1825 Market Center Blvd., Suite 520
Dallas, TX 75207-3332
(214) 748-7337
Associate: Jerry Sutton

F&S Partners
3535 Travis St., Suite 201
Dallas, TX 75204
(214) 559-4851
Vice President: Jim Bullock

Good Fulton Farrell
3102 Oak Lawn Ave., Suite 250
Dallas, TX 75219
(214) 528-5599
Principal: Duncan Fulton

Hahnfeld Associates
675 N. Henderson, #100
Fort Worth, TX 76017
(817) 335-1303
Principal: Lee Roy Hahnfeld

Haldeman, Powell, Johns
15303 Dallas Pkwy., Suite 300
Dallas, TX 75248
(214) 701-9000
Contact: Department Head

Hardy McCullah/MLM Architects
12221 Merit Dr., Suite 280
Dallas, TX 75251
(214) 385-1900
Office Manager: Earlene Romano

Harper Kemp Clutts and Parker
4131 N. Central Expwy., Suite 400
Dallas, TX 75204
(214) 528-8644
Contact: Howard Parker

Hatfield Halcomb Architects
14951 Dallas Pkwy., Suite 200
Dallas, TX 75240
(214) 404-1034
Director of Operations: Jim Stuart

Hellmuth/Obata & Kassabaum
6688 N. Central Expwy., Suite 700
Dallas, TX 75206

(214) 739-6688
Sr. Vice President: Dan Jeakins

Henningson, Durham & Richardson
12700 Hillcrest Rd., Suite 125
Dallas, TX 75230
(214) 960-4000
Contact: Executive Vice President

Hodges & Associates
13642 Omega Rd.
Dallas, TX 75244
(214) 387-1000
Contact: Department Head

JPJ Architects
5910 N. Central Expwy., Suite 1200
Dallas, TX 75206
(214) 987-8000
Office Manager: Buddy Mullen

Komatsu/Rangel
550 Bailey Ave. Ste 102
Fort Worth, TX 76107
(817) 332-1914
President: Karl Komatsu

Meier, Frank, Architects
4514 Travis St., Suite 350
Dallas, TX 75205
(214) 528-0020
President: Jim Phillips

OmniPlan
400 S. Record St., # 900
Dallas, TX 75202
(214) 742-1261
Principal: Lionel Morrison

Page Southerland Page
3500 Maple Ave., Suite 700
Dallas, TX 75219
(214) 522-3900
Partner: Cliff Lloyd

Parker/Croston Partnership
3311 Hamilton Ave.
Fort Worth, TX 76107
(817) 332-8464
Contact: Charles Kelley

Rees Associates
511 E. John Carpenter Frwy., Suite 222
Irving, TX 75062
(214) 630-7337
Vice President: Ralph Blackman

RTKL Associates
2828 Routh St., Suite 200
Dallas, TX 75201
(214) 871-8877
AIA Principal: Joe Scalabrin

Shepherd, Phillip, Architects
8235 Douglas Ave., Suite 900
Dallas TX 75225
(214) 691-2900
Contact: Chase Corher

SHWC, Inc.
P.O. Box 619087
Dallas, TX 75261
(214) 550-0700
Partner: Bill Wadley
Inquire by mail.

Smith, Harwood K., & Partners
1111 Plaza of the Americas North
Dallas, TX 75201
(214) 969-5599
Executive Vice President: Wade Driver

Taylor Gahl & Stensland Architects
5001 Spring Valley Rd., Suite 800E
Dallas, TX 75224
(214) 620-9262
Partner: Dallas Taylor

Vestal, Loftis, Kalista Architects
1161 Corporate Dr. W. #300
Arlington, TX 76006
(817) 633-1600
Principal: Jeff Kalista

Womack Architects
3000 McKinney Ave.
Dallas, TX 75204
(214) 754-8700
Personnel Director: Mike Hampton

WRA Architects
7557 Rambler Rd., Suite 400
Dallas, TX 75231

How to Get a Job

(214) 750-0077
President: Raymond Arhelger

Yandell and Hiller
512 Main St., Suite 1500
Fort Worth, TX 76102
(817) 335-3000
President: Roger Yandell
Architecture and engineering design services.

Auto/Truck/Transportation Equipment

You may also want to look at the section on **Travel and Transportation.**

PROFESSIONAL ORGANIZATIONS:

For more information, you can write to:

Automotive Service Industry Association
25 NW Point Blvd.
Elk Grove Village, IL 60007
(708) 228-1310

Society of Automotive Engineers
400 Commonwealth Dr.
Warrendale, PA 15096
(412) 776-4841

PROFESSIONAL PUBLICATIONS:

Auto Age
Autocar & Motor
Automotive Industries
Automotive News
Chilton's Motor Age
Drag Racing News
Four-Wheeler Magazine
Jobber Topics
Motor Trend
Truck & Off-Highway Industries
Trux

DIRECTORIES:

ASIA Membership Directory (Automotive Service Industries
  Association, Elk Grove Village, IL)

Automotive Age, Buyers Guide Issue (Freed-Crown Publishing Co., Van Nuys, CA)

Automotive News, Market Data Book Issue (Crain Communications, Detroit, MI)

Jobber Topics, Annual Marketing Directory Issue (Irving-Cloud Publishing Co., Chicago,IL)

Wards Automotive Yearbook (Ward's Communications, Detroit, MI)

EMPLOYERS:

Big 4 Automotive
400 South Frwy.
Fort Worth, TX 76104
(817) 332-3171
General Manager: Wayne Mitchell
Warehouse distributor for automotive parts.

Cummins Southern Plains
600 N. Watson Rd.
Arlington, TX 76011
Metro (817) 640-6801
Personnel Director: Cindy Baeumler
Distributes and services diesel engines.

Darr Equipment Co.
549 Jim Wright Frwy.
Fort Worth, TX 76108
Metro (817) 429-9226
Contact: Dallas Personnel Office at (214) 445-0060
Caterpillar dealership and parts distributor.

FM Industries
8600 Will Rogers Blvd.
Fort Worth, TX 76140
(817) 293-4220
Personnel Manager: Jack Adams
Manufactures hydraulic cushioning devices for railroad freight cars.

Fruehauf Corp.
4132 Irving Blvd.
Dallas, TX 75247
(214) 263-2266
Contact: Personnel Department
Manufactures semi-trailers.

General Motors Corp.
2525 E. Abram St.
Arlington, TX 76010
(817) 625-2085

How to Get a Job

Contact: Personnel Department
Major manufacturer of Oldsmobiles and Chevrolets.

Interstate Battery System of America
12770 Merit Dr.
Dallas, TX 75251
(214) 991-1444
Recruiter: Janie Britton
Battery distributor.

Long Mile Rubber Co.
6820 Forrest Park Rd.
Dallas, TX 75235
(214) 350-7851
Contact: Personnel Department
Manufactures crude rubber.

Mass Merchandisers
909 W. North Carrier Pkwy.
Grand Prairie, TX 75050
(214) 647-7891
Contact: Department Head
Wholesaler of automotive supplies, housewares, and other non-food items.

SCS Frigette Corp.
1200 W. Risinger Rd.
Fort Worth, TX 76134
(817) 293-5313
Personnel Manager: Jane Turner
Manufactures automotive air conditioners and parts.

TIC United Corp.
4645 N. Central Expwy.
Dallas, TX 75205
(214) 559-0580
Vice President of Personnel: Harrold Hatley
Manufactures farm machinery; steel forgings.

Texas Kenworth Co.
4040 Irving Blvd.
Dallas, TX 75247
(214) 920-7300
Contact: Executive Offices
Heavy-duty truck sales and service.

202

Banks/Savings and Loans/Credit Unions

You may also want to check out the sections on **Accounting** and **Stock Brokers.**

For networking in the banking industry and related fields, check out the following professional organizations listed in Chapter 5:

PROFESSIONAL ORGANIZATIONS:

Dallas Business League
National Association of Bank Women

For additional information, you can contact:

American Bankers Association
1120 Connecticut Ave., NW
Washington, DC 20036
(202) 663-5000

Bank Marketing Association
1120 Connecticut Ave., NW, Third Floor
Washington, DC 20036
(202) 663-5268

Financial Women International
7910 Woodmont Ave., Suite 1430
Bethesda, MD 20814
(301) 657-8288

Mortgage Bankers Association of America
1125 15th St., NW
Washington, DC 20005
(202) 861-6500

National Bankers Association (minority bankers)
1802 T St., NW
Washington, DC 20009
(202) 588-5432

Savings & Community Bankers of America
900 19th St., NW, Suite 400
Washington, DC 20006
(202) 857-3100

PROFESSIONAL PUBLICATIONS:

ABA Banking Journal
American Banker

Bank Administration
Bank Marketing Magazine
Banker & Tradesman
Bankers Magazine
Bankers Monthly
Mortgage Banking
Savings Institutions

DIRECTORIES:

American Bank Directory (McFadden Business Publications,
     Norcross, GA)
American Banker's Guide to the First 5,000 U.S. Banks (American
     Banker, New York, NY)
Money Market Directory (Money Market Directories,
     Charlottsville, VA)
Moody's Bank & Finance Manual (Moody's Investor Service, New
     York, NY)
Polk's Bank Directory (R.L. Polk, Nashville, TN)
Rand McNally Bankers Directory (Thompson Financial Informa-
     tion, Rand McNally, Skokie, IL)
Texas Savings & Loan Directory (Texas State Directory Press,
     Austin, TX)
The U.S. Savings Institutions (Thompson Financial Information,
     Rand McNally, Skokie, IL)

EMPLOYERS:

American Airlines Employees Federal Credit Union
4200 Amon Carter Blvd., Mail Drop 2100
Fort Worth, TX 76155
Metro (817) 963-6000
Contact: Personnel Department

American Federal Bank
14001 Dallas Pkwy.
Dallas, TX 75240
(214) 450-1800
Contact: Human Resources Department

Bank of America
300 E. Carpenter Frwy.
Irving TX 75062
(214) 717-1900
Contact: Personnel Department

Bank of Commerce
P.O. Box 17089
Fort Worth, TX 76089
(817) 332-3261
Contact: Human Resources Department

Bank of North Texas
8701 Bedford Euless Rd.
Hurst, TX 76053
(817) 280-9500
Contact: Annette Stamm

Bank One Texas
1717 Main St.
Dallas, TX 75265
(214) 290-2000
Contact: Human Resources Department

Bluebonnet Savings Bank
3100 Monticello
Dallas,TX 75205
(214) 443-9000
Contact: Personnel Department

Colonial Savings
2626 W. Frwy.
Fort Worth, TX 76102
(817) 390-2000
Personnel Director: Martha Erngy

Comerica Bank—Texas
P.O. Box 650282
Dallas TX 75265
(214) 841-1400
Contact: Personnel Department

Community Credit Union
5400 Independence Pkwy.
Plano, TX 75023
(214) 596-3300
Human Resources Director: Liz German

Cullen/Frost Bank of Dallas
2001 Bryan St.
Dallas, TX 75201
(214) 979-2000
Senior Vice President and Cashier: William R. Mathis, Jr.

Dallas Teachers Credit Union
4600 Ross Ave.
Dallas, TX 75204
(214) 824-6371
Personnel Director: Les McKee

Educational Employees Credit Union
1617 W. Seventh St.
Fort Worth, TX 76102

How to Get a Job

(817) 336-5508
Contact: Human Resources

Federal Reserve Bank of Dallas
2200 N. Pearl
Dallas, TX 75201
(214) 922-5000
Contact: Human Resources Department

Fidelity Bank
100 Main St.
Fort Worth, TX 76102
(817) 332-9797
Contact: Human Resources Department

Guaranty Federal Savings and Loan Assoc.
8333 Douglas Ave., Human Resources, 3rd Floor
Dallas, TX 75225
(214) 360-3360
Employment Coordinator: Janie Chrisenberry

Hibernia National Bank of Texas
P.O. Box 2249
Dallas, TX 75221
(214) 969-6429
Contact: Human Resources Department

Nations Bank
901 Main St.
Dallas, TX 75202
(214) 508-6262

North Dallas Bank & Trust Co.
12900 Preston Rd.
Dallas, TX 75230
(214) 387-1300
Contact: Human Resources Department

NorthPark National Bank
1300 NorthPark Center
Dallas, TX 75225
(214) 890-5100
Vice President of Human Resources: Cathy Reed

Overton Bank & Trust
P.O. Box 16509
Fort Worth, TX 76162
(817) 731-0101
Contact: Personnel Department

Team Bank
P.O. Box 2050

Fort Worth, TX 76113
(817) 884-4000
Contact: Personnel Department

Texas Commerce Bank, NA
500 E. Border St.
Arlington, TX 76004
Metro (817) 469-3100
Personnel: Suzzanne Kittrell

Texas Commerce Bank, NA
2200 Ross Ave., 7th Floor
Dallas, TX 75201
(214) 922-2300
Personnel: Tina Orlando

Texas Independent Bank
5221 N. O'Connor Rd., Suite 1300
Irving, TX 75356
(214) 869-4600
Personnel: Tiffani Burke

Vought Heritage Credit Union
425 W. Jefferson Blvd.
Grand Prairie, TX 75051
(214) 263-5171
Vice President of Personnel: Mike Hedlund

Book Publishers and Distributors

You might also want to check out the section on **Media.**

For networking in book publishing and related fields, check out the following professional organizations listed in Chapter 5:

PROFESSIONAL ORGANIZATIONS:

Society of Children's Book Writers and Illustrators
Women in Communications

For additional information, you can contact:

American Booksellers Association
560 White Plains Rd.
Tarrytown, NY 10591
(914) 631-7800

Association of American Publishers
1718 Connecticut Ave., NW
Washington, DC 20009
(202) 232-3335

PROFESSIONAL PUBLICATIONS:

American Bookseller
Editor & Publisher
Library Journal
Publishers Weekly
Small Press

DIRECTORIES:

American Book Trade Directory (R.R. Bowker, New York, NY)
Editor & Publisher International Yearbook (Editor & Publisher, New York, NY)
Literary Market Place (R.R. Bowker, New York, NY)
Publishers Directory (Gale Research, Detroit, MI)

EMPLOYERS:

Harcourt Brace and Company
8551 Esters Blvd.
Irving, TX 75063
(214) 929-4666
Director of Personnel: Nechelle Harris
Regional sales office of educational publishing company.

Houghton Mifflin Co.
13400 Midway Rd.
Dallas, TX 75244
(214) 980-1100
Contact: Personnel
Regional sales and warehouse division of educational publishing company.

MAPSCO
5308 Maple Ave.
Dallas, TX 75235
(214) 521-2131
Contact: Department Head
Publishes street maps and reference guides.

Prentice Hall School Division
641 W. Mockingbird Lane
Dallas, TX 75247
(214) 631-0955
Regional Sales Manager: Reece Washington
Textbook sales and marketing division.

Summit Group
1227 W. Magnolia Ave.
Fort Worth TX 76104
(817) 654-9511
President: Mark Hulme
Publishes general and self - help books.

Sweet Publishing
3950 Fossil Creek Blvd., Suite 201
Fort Worth, TX 76137
(817) 232-5661
Personnel Director: Kippi Bridger
Publishes Bible school curriculum.

Taylor Publishing Co.
1550 W. Mockingbird Lane
Dallas, TX 75235
(214) 637-2800
Contact: Personnel Department
Publishes yearbooks and general interest books.

Broadcasting and Television

You may also want to look at the section on **Film and Video.**

For networking in TV, radio, cable TV, and related fields, check out the following professional organizations listed in Chapter 5:

PROFESSIONAL ORGANIZATIONS:

Dallas Communications Council
Network of Hispanic Communicators
Press Club of Dallas
Texas Association of Film and Tape Professionals
Women in Communications

For additional information, you can contact:

American Federation of Television & Radio Artists
260 Madison Ave.
New York, NY 10016
(212) 532-0800

Association of Independent TV Stations
1320 19th St., NW, Suite 300
Washington, DC 20036
(202) 887-1970

International Radio & Television Society
420 Lexington Ave.
New York, NY 10170
(212) 867-6650

National Academy of Television Arts and Sciences
111 W. 57th St.
New York, NY 10019
(212) 586-8424

National Association of Broadcasters
1771 N St., NW
Washington, DC 20036
(202) 429-5300

National Cable Television Association
1724 Massachusetts Ave., NW
Washington, DC 20036
(202) 775-3550

Radio-Television News Directors Association
1000 Connecticut Ave., NW, Suite 615

Washington, DC 20036
(202) 659-6510

PROFESSIONAL PUBLICATIONS:

Billboard
Broadcasting Press Digest
Cable Age
Cable Marketing
Cable World
Cablevision Magazine
Communications News
Radio Only
Radio World
Television Broadcast
Variety

DIRECTORIES:

Broadcasting Cable Sourcebook (Broadcasting Publishing Co., Washington, DC)
Broadcasting Yearbook (Broadcasting Publishing Company, Washington, DC)
Television and Cable Fact Book (Warren Publications, Washington, DC)
TV/Radio Age Ten-City Directory (TV Editorial Corporation, New York, NY)

EMPLOYERS:

KAAM-AM
15851 Dallas Pkwy., Suite 1200
Dallas, TX 75248
(214) 263-0008
Personnel Director: Mary Young
Big Band and great singer music.

KCBI-FM
411 Ryan Plaza Dr.
Arlington, TX 76011
Metro (817) 792-3800
Director of Operations: Ron Harris
24-hour religious radio music.

KDAF-TV
8001 John Carpenter Frwy.
Dallas, TX 75247
(214) 634-8833
Contact: Personnel Department
Channel 33 independent TV station.

KDFI-TV
433 Regal Row
Dallas, TX 75247
(214) 637-2727
Contact: Department Head
Channel 27 independent TV station.

KDFW-TV
400 N. Griffin St.
Dallas, TX 76202
(214) 720-4444
Contact: Personnel Department
Channel 4 CBS-TV affiliate.

KEGL-FM
222 W. Las Colinas Blvd., Suite 1400
Irving, TX 75039
(214) 869-9700
Contact: Department Head
Contemporary hits.

KERA-FM
3000 Harry Hines Blvd.
Dallas, TX 75201
Metro (214) 871-1390
PBS-affiliated public affairs programs and jazz/classical radio music.

KERA-TV
3000 Harry Hines Blvd.
Dallas, TX 75201
Metro (214) 871-1390
Channel 13 PBS-TV station.

Public broadcasting job hotline

You can phone **KERA** for a recorded listing of job openings. Just dial (214) 871-1390, ext. 598. Or send your resume to the attention of the Personnel Dept. at the KERA address. You can also come by to fill out an application from 8:00 am to 5:00 pm, Monday to Friday.

Karen Denard, host of KERA's "Karen Denard's Evening Talk Show'" advises broadcasting hopefuls: "I recommend that you volunteer and join professional groups. When you do a little bit for others and include yourself in organizational work, serendipitous things do happen. You hear of opportunities and receive information you might not have gotten otherwise." ∎

KESS-FM
7700 John Carpenter Frwy.

Dallas, TX 75247
Metro (214) 263-0700
Office Manager: Carmen Aguilera
24-hour Spanish radio music.

KFJZ-AM
2214 E. Fourth St.
Fort Worth, TX 76102
Metro (817) 429-1630
General Manager: Joe Vasquez
Spanish music from sunrise to sunset.

KHSX-TV
1957 E. Irving Blvd.
Irving, TX 75060
(214) 721-0104
General Manager: Bradley Foltyn
Channel 49 Christian independent TV station.

KHYI-FM
545 E. John Carpenter Frwy., Suite 1560
Irving, TX 75062
Metro (214) 263-3695
Business Manager: Kelli Fox
Contemporary-hit radio music.

KJMZ-AM/FM
9900 McCree Rd.
Dallas, TX 75238
Metro (214) 263-0400
Contact: Department Head
Urban contemporary radio music.

KKDA-FM
621 N.W. Sixth St.
Grand Prairie, TX 75053
Metro (214) 263-9911
Office Manager: Evelyn Broughton
24-hour urban contemporary radio music.

KLIF-AM
3500 Maple Ave., Suite 1600
Dallas, TX 75219
(214) 526-2400
Personnel Director: Floyd Andrews
24-hour all-talk radio.

KLUV-FM
4131 N. Central Expwy.
Dallas, TX 75204
Metro (214) 263-3187

Contact: Personnel Department
24-hour solid gold radio music.

KMEZ-FM
1229 Corporate Dr. West
Arlington, TX 76006
Metro (817) 691-1075
Contact: Department Head
Easy-listening music.

KMGC-FM
1353 Regal Row
Dallas, TX 75247
Metro (214) 263-2960
Office Manager: Glen Wagner
Light rock/light jazz radio music.

KOAI-FM
5956 Sherry Lane, Suite 2000
Dallas, TX 75225
(214) 691-1075
New age, light jazz radio music.

KPBC-AM
3201 Royalty Row
Irving, TX 75062
Metro (214) 445-1700
Station Manager: Paul Niven
Program Director: Don Evans
24-hour adult Christian contemporary radio music.

KPLX-FM
3500 Maple Ave., Suite 1600
Dallas, TX 75219
Metro (214) 526-2400
Program Director: Brad Chambers
Contemporary country radio music.

KRLD-AM
1080 Metromedia Place
Dallas, TX 75247
Metro (214) 647-5753
News Director: Rick Erickson
Sales Manager: Dan Gorski
All-news radio station, CBS affiliate.

KSCS-FM
1 Broadcast Hill
Fort Worth, TX 76103
Metro (817) 429-2330
General Manager: Victor Sansone
Contemporary country radio music.

KSKY-AM
4144 N. Central Expwy.
Dallas, TX 75204
(214) 827-5759
General Manager: Bill Simmons
24-hour religious radio music.

KSSA-AM
3500 Maple Ave.
Dallas, TX 75219
Metro (214) 528-1600
General Manager: Jorge Sr. Infante
Spanish contemporary radio music.

KTVT-TV
5233 Bridge St.
Fort Worth, TX 76103
Metro (817) 654-1100
Contact: Department Head
Channel 11 independent TV station.

KTXA-TV
1712 E. Randol Mill Rd.
Arlington, TX 76011
Metro (817) 265-2100
Contact: Personnel Department
Channel 21 independent TV station.

KTXQ-FM
4131 N. Central Expwy., Suite 700
Dallas, TX 75204
Metro (214) 263-0804
Contact: Department Head
Album rock radio music.

KVIL-FM
5307 E. Mockingbird Lane, Suite 500
Dallas, TX 75206
Metro (214) 263-6539
Contact: Department Head
Adult contemporary radio music.

KVTT-FM
11061 Shady Trail
Dallas, TX 75229
Metro (214) 263-8713
Station Manager: Raye Nell Thomas
Operations Manager: Devin Wickham
Religious non-commercial radio music.

KXAS-TV
3900 Barnett St.

Fort Worth, TX 76103
Metro (817) 536-5555
Contact: Personnel Department
Channel 5 NBC-TV affiliate.

KXTX-TV
3900 Harry Hines Blvd.
Dallas, TX 75219
(214) 521-3900
Contact: Department Head
Channel 39 independent TV station.

KZPS-FM
15851 Dallas Pkwy., Suite 1200
Dallas, TX 75248
(214) 263-0008
Personnel Director: Mary Young
Classic hit radio music.

Sammons Communication
Dallas Office
3010 LBJ Freeway
Dallas, TX 75234
(214) 484-8888
Contact: Department Head
North Texas cable company.

Southern Baptist Radio-Television Commission
6350 West Frwy.
Fort Worth, TX 76150
(817) 737-4011
Contact: Department Head
Baptist broadcast network producing radio and TV shows.

TCI Cablevision of Texas
1565 Chenault St.
Dallas, TX 75228
(214) 328-2882
Contact: Administrative Office
Cable company with franchise to serve Dallas, Farmers Branch, and Mesquite.

Texas State Network
7901 John W. Carpenter
Dallas, TX 75247
(214) 688-1133
Contact: Department Head
Statewide radio news network.

WBAP-AM
1 Broadcast Hill
Fort Worth, TX 76103

Metro (817) 429-2330
General Manager: John Hare
Country radio music.

WFAA-TV
Communications Center
606 Young St.
Dallas, TX 75202
(214) 748-9631
Personnel Department: Jennifer Barnum
Channel 8 ABC-TV affiliate.

WRR-FM
P.O. Box 159001
Dallas, TX 75315
(214) 670-8888
Assistant Manager: Mary Lou Rodriguez
24-hour classical radio music. Inquire by mail.

**Broadcasting—
tough and
competitive**

If you're fresh out of school and want to break into the Dallas-Fort Worth broadcast market, talk show host and TV commentator Alex Burton has one word of advice, "Wait."

"There's no reason any broadcaster in this market should accept someone without experience. Those with degrees should go to a smaller market so they can unlearn everything they learned in school," Burton says.

While working in smaller towns, get a broad-based education on what makes a radio/TV station run. Volunteer to do EVERYTHING, Burton recommends. That means sales, sports, news, copywriting, deejaying, and even engineering.

"Engineering experience helps you know what is possible, so you're not at the mercy of an engineer, and what to do in case your equipment breaks down," he says.

When you have at least six months of experience, begin building your tape of your best pieces and critique them as if it's someone else's. Then you can take your best work to apply in D/FW's tough broadcast market, which is the ninth largest in the nation.

After working at 20 stations, Burton says, "I would never suggest that anyone go into the broadcasting business. It's such a tenuous life. So few people have contracts. You work long hours, strange hours. It's hard on the wife and kids," he says.

The image of the hard-living, hard-drinking broadcaster is deceptive. "The only people who stay in the business are the ones who do their work straight—all the time," Burton confides. ∎

Chemicals

You may also want to look at the section on **Drugs.**

For information about the chemical industry and related fields, contact the following professional organizations:

PROFESSIONAL ORGANIZATIONS:

American Chemical Society
1155 16th St., NW
Washington, DC 20036
(202) 872-4600

Chemical Manufacturers Association
2501 N St., NW
Washington, DC 20037
(202) 887-1100

Chemical Specialties Manufacturers Association
1913 I St., NW
Washington, DC 20006
(202) 872-8110

PROFESSIONAL PUBLICATIONS:

Chemical Engineering News
Chemical Week

DIRECTORIES:

Analytical Chemistry Lab Guide (American Chemical Society, Washington, DC)
Chemical and Engineering News, Career Opportunities Issue (American Chemical Society, Washington, DC)
Chemical Week: Buyer's Guide Issue (McGraw-Hill, New York, NY)
Chemical Week: Financial Survey of the 300 Largest Companies (McGraw-Hill, New York, NY)
OPD Buyers Directory: The Green Book (Schnell Publishing, New York, NY)

EMPLOYERS:

American Cyanamid Co.
7611 John Carpenter Frwy.
Dallas, TX 75247
(214) 631-2130
Manager: Jerry Elizondo

A diversified corporation with several area divisions: Agriculture, Formica Corp., Household Products, Consumer Health Products, Lederle Laboratories, and Cyro Acrylics.

Ashland Chemical
8201 S. Central Expwy.
Dallas, TX 75241
(214) 371-0794
Personnel Manager: Annie Johnson
Supplies solvents and chemicals and handles hazardous waste disposal.

Atlas Powder Co.
15301 Dallas Pkwy., Suite 1200
Dallas, TX 75248
(214) 387-2400
Contact: Human Resources Manager
Manufactures commercial explosives.

Buckley Oil Co.
1809 Rock Island St.
Dallas, TX 75207
(214) 421-4147
President: Bess Buckley
Buys and sells solvents, motor oils, and lubricants.

Chemical Lime Co.
3700 Hulen St.
Fort Worth, TX 76107
(817) 429-3077
Human Resources: Tom Stokes
Manufactures and distributes powdered lime.

Delta Distributors
11344 Plano Rd.
Dallas, TX 75243
(214) 341-0510
Sales Manager for sales positions: Tom Mrazek
Plant Supervisor for plant positions: Clay Wade
Distributes acetates, acids, ethers, ektones, and pine oil.

Diversey Corp.
8770 S. Central Expwy.
Dallas, TX 75241
(214) 376-6491
Branch Manager: Ron Robbins
Produces industrial and institutional chemicals.

Dow Chemical USA
1 Galleria Tower
13355 Noel Rd., Suite 1025
Dallas, TX 75240

(214) 702-2300
Contact: Company headquarters in Midland, MI, (517) 636-1000,
for sales and lab positions.
Produces agricultural and industrial chemicals, including herbi-
cides, insecticides, plastics, and latex.

Harcros Chemicals
2627 Weir St.
Dallas, TX 75212
(214) 638-8034
Branch Manager: Gary Hutchings
Distributes industrial and oil field chemicals, and laundry products.

Jones-Blair Co.
2728 Empire Central Dr.
Dallas, TX 75235
(214) 353-1600
Human Resources: Jean Lair
Produces and distributes paints and coatings.

NCH Corp.
2727 Chemsearch Blvd.
Irving, TX 75062
(214) 438-0211
Contact: Personnel
Maintenance of industrial and chemical products.

Plastics Manufacturing Co.
2700 S. Westmoreland Rd.
Dallas, TX 75233
(214) 330-8671
Contact: Billy Crow for office positions and C. R. Whited for plant
positions
Produces resin adhesives and plastic dinnerware.

Poly-America
2000 W. Marshall Dr.
Grand Prairie, TX 75051
(214) 647-4374
Contact: Personnel Department
Manufactures polyethylene film for agriculture and commercial
uses.

Southwestern Petroleum Corp.
534 N. Main St.
Fort Worth, TX 76106
(817) 332-2336
Personnel Director: Margaret Castillo
Manufactures protective coatings and specialty lubricants.

Texas Refinery Corp.
840 N. Main St.
Fort Worth, TX 76106
(817) 332-1161
Personnel Manager: Janet May
Produces industrial coatings, lubricants, and industrial cleaners.

Valley Solvents
2573 N.E. 33rd St.
Fort Worth, TX 76111
(817) 831-0001
Branch Manager: Lavon Thompson
Distributes industrial solvents and chemicals.

Virginia KMP Corp.
4100 Platinum Way
Dallas, TX 75237
(214) 330-7731
Personnel: Pat Chaney
Produces water-treating chemicals and manufactures air-conditioning and refrigeration components.

Zoecon Corp.
12005 Ford Rd., Suite 800
Dallas, TX 75234
(214) 243-2321
Contact: Mavonee Jefferies
Two area locations produce a variety of insecticide products, including baited traps and dog and cat flea collars.

Computers: Data Processing

You may also want to look at the sections on **Electronics, Computers: Hardware/Software, Telecommunications.**

For networking in the data processing industry and related fields, you can contact this professional organization listed in Chapter 5:

PROFESSIONAL ORGANIZATIONS:

Women in Computing

For more information about the data processing industry, you can contact:

Data Processing Management Association
505 Busse Highway
Park Ridge, IL 60068
(708) 825-8124

Women in Information Processing
Lock Box 39173
Washington, DC 20016
(202) 328-6161

PROFESSIONAL PUBLICATIONS:

Data Communications
Datamation

DIRECTORIES:

Data Processing Equipment Directory (American Business Directories, Omaha, NE)
Data Processing Services Directory (American Business Directories, Omaha, NE)
Data Sources (Ziff-Davis, New York, NY)
Datamation: The Top 100 Companies in the DP Industry (Cahners Publishing, Newton, MA)
Peterson's Job Opportunies for Engineering, Science, and Computer Graduates (Peterson's Guides, Princeton, NJ)
Thomas Register Office Automation Buyers' Guide (Thomas Publishing, New York, NY)

EMPLOYERS:

AIC Analysts Corp.
9901 E. Valley Ranch Pkwy., Suite 3010, L.B. 27
Irving, TX 75063

(214) 869-1881
Staff Recruiter: Shirley Hollywood
Consulting firm for systems analysts.

Commercial Computer Service
1503 S. University Dr.
Fort Worth, TX 76107
(817) 335-6411
Operations Manager: George Radford
Provides packaged programs, systems programming, and data preparation.

Coopers and Lybrand
2711 LBJ Frwy., Suite 312
Farmer's Branch, TX 75234
(214) 243-1256
Contact: Recruiter
Provides consulting, designing, and programming services.

CompuTrac
222 Municipal Dr.
Richardson, TX 75080
(214) 234-4241
Contact: Department Head
Computerized law firm management systems.

Ceridian Corp.
6700 LBJ Freeway, Suite 3100
Dallas, TX 75240
(214) 385-5750
Contact: Margaret Borszich for customer service positions and Robert Digby for sales positions.
Service bureau company that provides batch services for payroll and other financial needs.

Cutler-Williams
4000 McEwen Rd.
Dallas, TX 75244
(214) 960-7053
Contact: Recruiting
Information management services company.

Electronic Data Systems Corp.
Recruitment Department
5400 Legacy
Plano, TX 75024
(214) 604-6000
Contact: Recruiting
Designs programs, consults, and operates computer services for major commercial and governmental customers worldwide.

Input
813 Greenview
Grand Prairie, TX 75050
(214) 988-3282
President: Charley Havens
Data processing service bureau.

Leardata Info-Services
5910 N. Central Expwy.
Dallas, TX 75206
(214) 360-9008
President: Chris Smith
Provides contract data processing.

Lomas Information Systems
1750 Viceroy Dr.
Dallas, TX 75235
(214) 879-5711
Contact: Human Resources Department
Provides data processing for Lomas Financial Corporation and
contract services for mortgage and savings and loan companies.

Computers: Hardware/Software

You may also want to look at the sections on **Computers: Data Processing, Electronics** and **Telecommunications.**

For networking in the computer and electronics industries, check out these organizations listed in Chapter 5:

PROFESSIONAL ORGANIZATIONS:

**Association of Information Systems Professionals
Women in Computing**

For additional information, you can contact:

Association for Computer Operations Management
742 E. Chapman Ave.
Orange, CA 92666
(714) 997-7966

Association for Computing Machinery
1515 Broadway, 17th Floor
New York, NY 10036
(212) 869-7440

Computer & Communications Industry Association
666 11th St. , NW
Washington, DC 20001
(202) 783-0070

Information Technology Association of America (ITAA)
1616 N. Ft. Myers Dr.
Arlington, VA 22209
(703) 522-5055

Institute of Electrical & Electronic Engineers (IEEE)
345 E. 47th St.
New York, NY 10017
(212) 705-7900

National Association of Desktop Publishers
Boston, MA 02110
(617) 426-2800

PROFESSIONAL PUBLICATIONS:

Byte
Computer World
Electronic Business

Electronic News
MIS News
PC Magazine
PC Week
PC World
Personal Computing

DIRECTORIES:

Directory of Computer Installations (Computer Management
    Research, New York, NY)
Directory of Computer Software and Service Companies
    (ADAPSO, Arlington, VA)
EIA Trade Directory (Electronics Industry Association, Washing-
    ton, DC)
Guide to High Technology Companies (Corporate Technology
    Information Services, Inc., Woburn, MA)
*Peterson's Job Opportunies for Engineering, Science, and Com-
    puter Graduates* (Peterson's Guides, Princeton, NJ)
Who's Who in Electronics (Harris Publications, Twinsburg, OH)

EMPLOYERS:

Amdahl Corp.
900 One Galleria Tower
13355 Noell Rd., L.B. 78
Dallas, TX 75240
(214) 239-8611
Contact: Department Head
Manufactures and sells computers.

Amstrad
1915 Westridge Dr.
Irving, TX 75038
(214) 518-0668
Contact: Department Head
Computer manufacturer.

Apple Computers
1950 Stemmons Frwy., Suite 4038
Dallas, TX 75207
(214) 573-2700
Human Resources Department
Sales office for Apple personal computers.

CE Services
2895 113th St.
Grand Prairie, TX 75050
(214) 641-0070
Contact: Personnel Department
Computer hardware service company.

Computer Language Research
2395 Midway Rd.
Carrollton, TX 75006
(214) 250-7000
Contact: Human Resources Department
Provides time-sharing services for tax applications.

ComTrac Corporation
17950 Preston Rd., Suite 750
Dallas, TX 75252
(214) 733-3911
President: Robert Markovich
Sells computer systems for financial institutions and retailers.

CSC Logic
9330 LBJ Frwy., Suite 500
Dallas, TX 75243
(214) 238-1898
V.P. of Human Resources: Lori Tucker
Provides software for insurance firms.

Digital Equipment
4851 LBJ Frwy., Suite 1100
Dallas, TX 75244
(214) 702-4000
Contact: Personnel Department
Manufacturer of computers and computer devices.

GenRad
1601 N. Collins Blvd.
Richardson, TX 75080
(214) 234-3357
Contact: Human Resources in Concord, MA, (508) 369-4400
Designs and manufactures computer-controlled test, measurement, and development systems in three high-technology markets.

Harris Adacom
1100 Venture Ct.
Carrollton, TX 75006-5412
(214) 386-2000
Contact: Human Resource Department
Manufactures, designs, sells, and services high-technology communications and information processing equipment, including computer terminals, network integration and line printers.

Hogan Systems
5080 Spectrum Dr., Suite 400 E
Dallas, TX 75248
(214) 386-0020
Facilities Administrator: Bill Stapp

Develops, markets, maintains, and supports integrated line of standard banking applications software packages.

International Business Machines Corp.
1507 LBJ Frwy.
Dallas, TX 75234
(214) 280-4000
Contact: Central Employment Office
Manufactures, sells, and services computers and office equipment.

International Business Machines Corp.
Fort Worth Office
201 Main St.
Fort Worth, TX 76102
(817) 870-4000
Contact: Central Employment Office
Computer and electronic components manufacturer and service.

Microny
1901 N. Central Expwy., Suite 400
Richardson, TX 75080
(214) 690-0595
Human Resources Director: Joanna Symmonds
Contact: Jim Shock

NCR Corp.
450 E. John Carpenter Frwy.
Irving, TX 75062
(214) 650-2100
Contact: Personnel Department
Sells and services computer systems and financial and retail terminals.

National Data Corp.
NDC Plaza
Atlanta, GA 30329
(404) 728-2250
Contact: Michael Toth
Sells computer systems and software to banking and health care organizations.

Reynolds & Reynolds Co.
1010 Ave. J. East
Grand Prairie, TX 75050
(214) 647-1722
Regional Human Resources Manager: Scott Brown
Sells and services computers.

Rubicon Corp.
1217 Digital Dr., Suite 125
Richardson, TX 75081

(214) 231-6591
Contact: Personnel Manager
Provides computer software for the medical industry.

Tandem Computers
12770 Merit Dr., Building 8, Suite 200
Dallas, TX 75251
Metro (214) 960-5000
Human Resources Representative
Manufactures, sells, and services computers.

Texas Instruments
13500 N. Central Expwy.
Richardson, TX 75265
(214) 995-3125
Contact: Employment Center

Total Assets Protection
2301 E. Lamar Blvd., Suite 500
Arlington, TX 76006
(817) 640-8800
Contact: Personnel Office
Computer consulting.

Xerox Corp.
222 W. Las Colinas Blvd.
Irving, TX 75039
(214) 830-4000
Contact: Employment Office
One of world's largest manufacturers of copy machines and other
electronic products.

Contractors/Construction

You may also want to look at the sections on **Architecture, Engineering,** and **Real Estate.**

For networking in the construction industry and related fields, check out the following trade and professional organizations listed in Chapter 5:

PROFESSIONAL ORGANIZATIONS:

American Society of Landscape Architects
American Subcontractors Association
Associated General Contractors
Builders Association of Fort Worth/Tarrant County
Home & Apartment Builders Association of Metropolitan Dallas
Mechanical Contractors Association of Dallas
National Association of Women in Construction
Sheet Metal and Air Conditioning Contractors

For additional information, you can contact:

Associated Builders & Contractors
1300 N. 17th St., 8th Floor
Rosslyn, VA 22209
(703) 637-8800

Associated General Contractors of America
1957 E St., NW
Washington, DC 20006
(202) 393-2040

Construction Management Association of America
1893 Preston White Dr., Suite 130
Reston, VA 22091
(703) 391-1200

Construction Specifications Institute
601 Madison St.
Alexandria, VA 22314
(703) 391-1200

National Association of Home Builders of the U.S.
1201 15th St., NW
Washington, DC 20005
(202) 822-0200

National Association of Minority Contractors
1333 F St., NW, #500

Washington, DC 20004
(202) 347-8259

National Association of Women in Construction
327 S. Adams St.
Fort Worth, TX 76104
(817) 877-5551

PROFESSIONAL PUBLICATIONS:

Associated Construction Publications
Builder
Building & Contractor
Building Design & Construction
Construction Review
Constructor
Dixie Contractor
ENR: Engineering News Record

DIRECTORIES:

Associated Builders & Contractors Membership Directory (Associated Builders & Contractors, Washington, DC)
Blue Book of Major Homebuilders (CMR Systems, Crofton, MD)
Construction Equipment, Construction Giants (Cahners Publishing, Des Plaines, IL)
Constructor Directory Issue (Associated General Contractors of America, Washington, DC)
ENR Directory of Contractors (McGraw-Hill, New York, NY)
Who's Who in Engineering (Engineers Joint Council, New York, NY)

EMPLOYERS:

APAC-Texas
1901 Cold Springs Rd.
Fort Worth, TX 76102
(817) 336-0521
Personnel Director: Mike Manning
Contractor for highway, street, and parking facilities.

Austin Industries
3535 Travis St.
Dallas, TX 75204
(214) 443-5500
Personnel Manager: Evelyn Hulshouser
General contractor, including commercial, residential, and road construction.

Brandt, J.W.P., Engineering
11245 Indian Trail

Dallas, TX 75229
(214) 241-9411
Contact: Personnel Department
Commercial and residential contractor.

Byrne, Thomas S.
900 Summit Ave.
Fort Worth, TX 76102
(817) 335-3394
V.P. of Construction: Richard M. Patterson
Commercial construction.

Centex Bateson Construction Co.
10150 Monroe Dr.
Dallas, TX 75229
(214) 357-1891
Contact: Don Sumrell
General contractor.

Centex Corp.
3333 Lee Pkwy.
Dallas, TX 75219
(214) 559-6500
Employee Communications Coordinator: Dianne Clifton
Residential and commercial construction.

Freeman Companies
8801 Ambassador Row
Dallas, TX 75247
(214) 638-6450
Contact: Department Head
Full-service contractor.

Frymire Engineering Co.
2818 Satsuma Dr.
Dallas, TX 75229
Metro (214) 263-0201
Commercial and residential contractor, heating, air conditioning, plumbing, and electrical.

HCB Contractors
1401 Elm St., Suite 4600
Dallas, TX 75202
(214) 747-8541
V.P. of Human Resources: Jerry Cooper
Commercial construction.

Haws & Tingle General Contractors
909 W. Magnolia Ave., Suite 2
Fort Worth, TX 76104
Metro (817) 429-8310
Superintendent of Field Office: Robert Reed

President: Jerry Herman
General contracting.

JRL Birtram Construction and Engineering
107 Harrison Ave.
Arlington, TX 76011
Metro (817) 261-2991
Contact: Personnel Department
Concrete, asphalt, and construction.

LH Lacy Co.
10888 Shady Trail
Dallas, TX 75220
(214) 357-0146
Personnel Director: Mary Wright
Highway and road construction.

Medco
2625 Elm St., Suite 216
Dallas, TX 75226
(214) 820-2492
Contact: Personnel Department
General contractor.

Redman Industries
2550 Walnut Hill Lane, Suite 200
Dallas, TX 75229
(214) 353-3600
Contact: Personnel Department
Mobile home construction.

Speed Fab-Crete Corp.
1150 E. Mansfield Hwy.
Kennedale, TX 76060
(817) 572-0351
Contact: Department Head
General contractor and pre-cast concrete manufacturer.

Walker Building Corp.
3733 Flory St.
Fort Worth, TX 76180
(817) 284-9208
President: Joe Walker
Commercial building construction.

Drugs/Biological Products

You may also want to look at the section on **Chemicals.**

For more information, you can contact:

PROFESSIONAL ORGANIZATIONS:

American Pharmaceutical Association
2215 Constitution Ave., NW
Washington, DC 20037
(202) 628-4410

Association of Biotechnology Companies
1666 Connecticut Ave, Suite 330
Washington, DC 20009

National Association of Medical Suppliers
625 Slaters Lane, # 200
Alexandria, VA 22314
(703) 836-6263

National Association of Pharmaceutical Manufacturers
747 Third Ave.
New York, NY 10017
(212) 838-3720

Pharmaceutical Manufacturers Association
1100 15th St., NW
Washington, DC 20005
(202) 835-3400

PROFESSIONAL PUBLICATIONS:

American Druggist
Biotechnology
Cosmetics and Toiletries
Cosmetic World
Drug Topics
Journal of Pharmaceutical Sciences
PMA Newsletter
Soap / Cosmetics / Chemical Specialties

DIRECTORIES:

Biotechnology Directory (Stockton Press, New York, NY)
Drug Topics Red Book (Medical Economics Data Co., Montvale, NJ)

Genetic Engineering & Biotechnology Related Firms Worldwide Directory (Mega-Type Publishing, Princeton Junction, NJ)
NACDS Membership Directory (National Association of Chain Drugstores, Alexandria, VA)
NAMS Membership Directory (National Association of Medical Suppliers, Alexandria, VA)
NWDA Membership Directory (National Wholesale Druggists Association, Alexandria, VA)
Pharmaceutical Manufacturers of the U.S. (Noyes Data Corp., Park Ridge, NJ)

EMPLOYERS:

AKM Distributing Co.
10681 N. Stemmons Frwy.
Dallas, TX 75220
(214) 869-0595
Vice President: Carolyn McLellan
Manufactures vitamins, health, and beauty aids.

Abbott Laboratories
1921 Hurd Dr.
Irving, TX 75038
(214) 257-6000
Contact: Personnel Department
Mail applications/resumes to:
Placement and Development T1-3
Designs, develops, and manufactures automated diagnostic medical instruments.

Alcon Laboratories
6201 South Frwy.
Fort Worth, TX 76134
(817) 293-0450
Jobline: (817) 551-4575
Contact: Placement Office
Produces opthalmic products, including contact lens solutions and eye care products.

Carrington Lab
2001 Walnut Hill Lane
Irving, TX 75038
(214) 518-1300
Contact: Personnel Department
Produces women's skincare products.

Colgate-Hoyt: GEL-KAM
14335 Gillis Rd.
Dallas, TX 75244
(214) 233-2800
Manufactures dental products.

Dexide
7509 Flagstone Dr.
Fort Worth, TX 76118
(817) 589-1454
Personnel: Roger Cooper
Manufactures surgical scrub devices.

Fox Meyer Drug Co.
1220 Senlac Dr.
Carrollton, TX 75006
(214) 446-9090
Contact: Department Head
Distributes pharmaceuticals.

Johnson & Johnson Medical
2500 Arbrook Blvd.
Arlington, TX 76014
(817) 467-0211
Jobline: (817) 784-4800
Contact: Personnel Department
Johnson & Johnson subsidiary that produces disposable medical products.

Nortex Drug Distributors
1021 N. Central Expwy.
Plano, TX 75075
(214) 424-2127
Contact: Individual store manager
Parent company for Drug Emporium chain.

Quest Medical
4103 Billy Mitchell St.
Dallas, TX 75244
(214) 387-2740
Human Resources Manager: Corinne Olszowka
Develops, manufactures, and markets proprietary disposable products for the health care industry.

Educational Institutions

For networking in education and related fields, check out the
following professional organizations listed in Chapter 5:

PROFESSIONAL ORGANIZATIONS:

Dallas Association for the Education of Young Children
Dallas Association of Educational and Office Personnel
Dallas Music Teachers Association
Dallas School Administrators Association
Irving Association of Educational Office Personnel
Mesquite Educational Paraprofessional Association
Public Library Administrators of North Texas

For additional information, you can contact:

American Association of School Administrators
1801 N. Moore St.
Arlington, VA 22209
(703) 528-0700

American Association of University Women
2401 Virginia Ave., NW
Washington, DC 20037

Association of Independent Colleges and Universities
1 Dupont Circle
Washington, DC 20036

Association of School Business Officials
11401 N. Shore Dr.
Reston, VA 22090
(703) 478-0405

Council for Educational Development and Research
200 L St., NW
Washington, DC 20036
(202) 223-1593

National Education Association
1201 16th St., NW
Washington, DC 20036
(202) 833-4000

PROFESSIONAL PUBLICATIONS:

Chronicle of Higher Education
Education Week
Instructor

School Administrator
Teaching Exceptional Children
Teaching Pre-K-8
Technology and Learning
Today's Catholic Teacher

DIRECTORIES:

College Board Guide to High Schools (College Board, New York,
    NY)
Peterson's Guide to Four Year Colleges (Peterson's Guides,
    Princeton, NJ)
Private Schools of the United States (Market Data Retrieval,
    Shelton, CT)
Public Schools USA (Williamson Publications, Charlotte, NC)
QED's School Guide (Quality Education Data, Denver, CO)

EMPLOYERS, PUBLIC SCHOOL DISTRICTS:

Arlington Independent School District
1203 W. Pioneer Pkwy.
Arlington, TX 76013
Metro (817) 261-2581
Executive Director of Personnel: Denny Dowd
Enrollment: 50,000

Birdville Independent School District
6125 E. Belknap St.
Haltom City, TX 76117
(817) 831-5700
Personnel: Gary Clark and Sue Martin
Enrollment: 20,000

Carrollton-Farmers Branch Independent School District
1445 N. Perry Rd.
Carrollton, TX 75006
(214) 323-5700
Personnel Director: Doug Shouse
Enrollment: 18,000

Castleberry Independent School District
315 Churchill Rd.
Fort Worth, TX 76114
(817) 737-7235
Superintendent: Jerry W. Cook
Enrollment: 3,000

Cedar Hill Independent School District
270 S. Hwy. 67
Cedar Hill, TX 75104
(214) 291-1581

Personnel Director: Kathline Bailey
Enrollment: 4,836

Dallas Independent School District
3700 Ross Ave.
Dallas, TX 75204
(214) 824-1620
Contact: Personnel Department
Enrollment: 130,000

DeSoto Independent School District
200 E. Belt Line Rd.
DeSoto, TX 75115
(214) 223-6666
Personnel Director: Ron Cagle
Enrollment: 6,000

Duncanville Independent School District
802 S. Main St.
Duncanville, TX 75137
(214) 296-4761
Personnel Director: Carl Smith
Enrollment: 10,000

Eagle Mountain-Saginaw Independent School District
1200 Old Decatur Rd.
Saginaw, TX 76179
(817) 232-0880
Deputy Superintendent: Truett Absher
Enrollment: 4,700

Everman Independent School District
608 Townley Dr.
Everman, TX 76140
(817) 568-3500
Personnel Officer: Nelda Winnett
Enrollment: 3,300

Fort Worth Independent School District
100 N. University
Fort Worth, TX 76107
(817) 336-8311
Assistant Superintendent: J.D. Shipp
Enrollment: 75,500

Garland Independent School District
720 Stadium Dr.
Garland, TX 75040
(214) 494-8201
Personnel Director: Roger Harrington (elementary); Gary Reeves
(secondary)
Enrollment: 35,100

Grand Prairie Independent School District
202 W. College St.
Grand Prairie, TX 75053
(214) 264-6141
Assistant Superintendent for Personnel: Michael Hinojosa
Enrollment: 17,000

Grapevine-Colleyville Independent School District
3051 Ira E. Woods Ave.
Grapevine, TX 76051
(817) 488-9588
Personnel: Margaret Montgomery
Enrollment: 10,000

Highland Park Independent School District
7015 Westchester Dr.
Dallas, TX 75205
(214) 521-4103
Contact: Personnel Department
Enrollment: 4,000

Hurst-Euless-Bedford Independent School District
1849 Central Dr.
Bedford, TX 76022
(817) 283-4461
Personnel Department
Enrollment: 18,600

Irving Independent School District
901 N. O'Connor Rd.
Irving, TX 75061
(214) 259-4575
Assistant Superintendent: Jerry Christian
Enrollment: 21,850

Kennedale Independent School District
100 W. Mansfield Hwy.
Kennedale, TX 76060
(817) 478-1166
Contact: Personnel
Enrollment: 1,600

Lake Worth Independent School District
6800 Telephone Rd.
Lake Worth, TX 76135
(817) 237-1491
Administrative Assistant: Mattie Millican
Enrollment: 1,500

Lancaster Independent School District
1105 Westridge Ave.
Lancaster, TX 75146

(214) 227-4141
Contact: Personnel Department
Enrollment: 4,000

Mansfield Independent School District
605 E. Broad St.
Mansfield, TX 76063
(817) 473-5600
Personnel: Martha Reed
Enrollment: 8,000

Mesquite Independent School District
405 E. Davis St.
Mesquite, TX 75149
(214) 288-6411
Personnel: Michael Eddy
Enrollment: 28,000

Plano Independent School District
2700 W. 15th St.
Plano, TX 75075
(214) 519-8100
Personnel: Danny Modisette
Enrollment: 34,000

Richardson Independent School District
400 S. Greenville Ave.
Richardson, TX 75081
(214) 301-3333
Contact: Peg Griffith
Enrollment: 33,150

White Settlement Independent School District
401 S. Cherry Lane
White Settlement, TX 76108
(817) 367-1350
Superintendent: Clabe Welch
Enrollment: 3,965

Wilmer-Hutchins Independent School District
3820 E. Illinois Ave.
Dallas, TX 75216
(214) 376-7311
Personnel: Joyce Aldrige
Enrollment: 4,000

EMPLOYERS, PRIVATE AND PAROCHIAL SCHOOLS:

All Saints Episcopal School
8200 Tumbleweed Dr.
Fort Worth, TX 76108

Head Master: Louis H. Hayden
(817) 246-2413

Bending Oaks High School
13777 N. Central Expwy.
Dallas, TX 75243
(214) 669-0000

Bethesda Christian School
4700 N. Beech St.
Fort Worth, TX 76137
(817) 281-6446

Burton Adventist Academy
4611 Kelly - Elliott Rd.
Arlington, TX 76017
(817) 572-0081

Calvary Academy
1600 W. Fifth St.
Fort Worth, TX 76102
(817) 332-3351

Casserta Learning Center
1400 Hemphill
Fort Worth, TX 76104
(817) 926-1745

Cistercian Preparatory School
One Cistercian Rd.
Irving TX 75039
(214) 438-4956

Dallas Academy
950 Tiffany Way
Dallas, TX 75218
(214) 324-1481

Dallas International School
6039 Churchill Way
Dallas, TX 75230
(214) 991-6379

Episcopal School of Dallas
4100 Merrell Rd.
Dallas, TX 75229
(214) 358-4368

Fair Hill School
16150 Preston Rd.
Dallas, TX 75248
(214) 233-1026

Fort Worth Christian School
7517 Bogart Dr.
Fort Worth, TX 76180
(817) 281-6504

Fort Worth Country Day School
4200 Country Day Lane
Fort Worth, TX 76109
(817) 732-7718

Glenview Christian School
4805 North East Loop 820
Fort Worth, TX 76137
(817) 281-5155

Greenhill School
14255 Midway Rd.
Dallas, TX 75244
(214) 661-1211

Hockaday School
11600 Welch Rd.
Dallas, TX 75229
(214) 363-6311

Jesuit College Preparatory School
12345 Inwood Rd.
Dallas, TX 75244
(214) 387-8700

Lake Country Christian School
7050 Lake Country Dr.
Fort Worth, TX 76179
(817) 236-8703

Lamplighter School
11611 Inwood Rd.
Dallas, TX 75299
(214) 369-9201

Lutheran High School
8494 Stults Rd.
Dallas, TX 75243
(214) 349-8912

Meadowbrook Christian School
6801 Meadowbrook Dr.
Fort Worth, TX 76112
(817) 457-2345

Nolan Catholic High School
4501 Bridge St.

Fort Worth TX 76103
(817) 457-2920

Oak Hill Academy
6464 E. Lovers Lane
Dallas, TX 75214
(214) 368-0664

Oakridge School
5900 Pioneer Pkwy.
Arlington, TX 76013
(817) 451-4994

Owens Highland Academy
1013 N. Gibbons
Fort Worth, TX 76011
(817) 274-8087

Pantego Christian Academy
2210 W. Park Row
Arlington, TX 76013
(817) 460-3315

St. Albins Episcopal School
911 S. Davis St.
Arlington, TX 76013
(817) 460-6071

St. Alcuin Montessori School
6144 Churchill Way
Dallas, TX 75218
(214) 239-1745

St. Andrews Inter-Parochial Catholic School
3304 Dryden Rd.
Fort Worth, TX 76109
(817) 924-8917

St. John the Apostle School
7421 Glenview Dr.
Fort Worth, TX 76180
(817) 284-2228

St. Marie Goretti
1200 S.Davis St.
Arlington, TX 76013
(817) 275-5081

St. Marks School of Texas
10600 Preston Rd.
Dallas, TX 75230
(214) 363-6491

St. Michael School
8011 Douglas Ave.
Dallas, TX 75225
(214) 691-8681

St. Paul Lutheran
1800 W. Frwy.
Fort Worth, TX 76102
(817) 332-4563

St. Rita School
712 Weller Blvd.
Fort Worth, TX 76112
(817) 451-9383

St. Vincent 's Episcopal School
1300 Forest Ridge
Bedford TX 76022
(817) 354-7979

Shelton School
5200 W. Lovers Lane
Dallas, TX 75209
(214) 352-1772

Southwest Christian School
4600-B Alta Masa Blvd.
Fort Worth, TX 76133
(817) 294-0350

Texas Christian Academy
915 Web St.
Arlington, TX 76011
(817) 274-5201

Trinity Christian Academy
17001 Addison Rd.
Dallas, TX 75248
(214) 931-8325

Trinity Valley School
6101 McCart Ave.
Fort Worth, TX 76133
(817) 292-6060

Ursuline Academy
4900 Walnut Hill Lane
Dallas, TX 75229
(214) 363-6551

EMPLOYERS, UNIVERSITIES AND COLLEGES:

Amber University
1700 Eastgate Dr.
Garland, TX 75041
(214) 279-6511
Personnel: Algia Allen
Business and technology undergraduate and graduate university.
Enrollment: 1,500

Baylor College of Dentistry
3302 Gaston Ave.
Dallas, TX 75246
(214) 828-8100
Personnel: John Gilbert
Private college for dentists, dental hygienists, and graduate students.
Enrollment: 400

Baylor University School of Nursing
3700 Worth St.
Dallas, TX 75246
(214) 820-3361
Office Manager: Barbara Worth
Personnel Dean: Phyllis Karns
Four-year R.N. program.
Enrollment: 200

Collin County Community College District
2200 W. University
McKinney, TX 75070
For job listings (214) 881-JOBS
Contact: Personnel Department
Community college.
Enrollment: 10,000

Criswell College
4010 Gaston Ave.
Dallas, TX 75246
(214) 821-5433
Personnel: Leo Bradley
Graduate and undergraduate Bible studies program.
Enrollment: 300

Dallas Baptist University
7777 W. Kiest Blvd.
Dallas, TX 75211
(214) 331-8311
Personnel Department
Private liberal arts school offering undergraduate and graduate programs.
Enrollment: 2,700

Dallas County Community College District
701 Elm St.
Dallas, TX 75202
(214) 746-2149
Jobline: (214) 746-2438
Contact: Individual campus
Offers associate degrees at seven campuses, including
Brookhaven College, Cedar Valley College, Eastfield College, El
Centro College, Mountain View College, North Lake College, and
Richland College.
Approximate enrollment: 144,000

Dallas Theological Seminary
3909 Swiss Ave.
Dallas, TX 75204
(214) 824-3094
Personnel Director: Jim Anderson
Non-denominational graduate seminary.
Enrollment: 1,000

Devry Institute of Technology
4250 N. Belt Line Rd.
Irving, TX 75038
(214) 258-6330
Human Resources Manager: Glyn Williams
Private institution offering training and placement in electronics,
technology, and computer science with associate and bachelor's
degrees.
Approximate enrollment: 2,400

Harris College of Nursing
P.O. Box 32899
Fort Worth, TX 76129
(817) 921-7652
Personnel Dean: Patricia Scearse
Four-year undergraduate nursing program associated with Texas
Christian University.
Enrollment: 400

Southern Methodist University
P.O. Box 232
Dallas, TX 75275
(214) 768-2131
Contact: Personnel Department
Private university offering undergraduate and graduate pro-
grams.
Enrollment: 9,150

Southwestern Baptist Theological Seminary
P.O. Box 22000
Fort Worth, TX 76122
(817) 923-1921

Contact: Personnel Department
World's largest Baptist graduate theological seminary.
Approximate enrollment: 5,000

Tarrant County Junior College District
1500 Houston St.
Fort Worth, TX 76102
(817) 336-7851
Administrative Office Assistant: Martha Martinez
Community college offering associate degrees at TCJC Northeast
Campus, TCJC Northwest Campus, TCJC South Campus, and
Community Campus in downtown Fort Worth.
Approximate enrollment: 28,500

Texas Christian University
2800 S. University Dr.
Fort Worth, TX 76129
Jobline: (817) 921-7791
Contact: Personnel Department
Private university affiliated with the Christian Church, offering
undergraduate and graduate programs.
Enrollment: 7,000

Texas College of Osteopathic Medicine
3500 Camp Bowie Blvd.
Fort Worth, TX 76107
Metro (817) 429-9120
(817) 735-2000
Personnel Director: Rand Horseman
State medical school for osteopathic doctors.
Enrollment: 450

Texas Wesleyan University
1201 Wesleyan St.
Fort Worth, TX 76105
(817) 531-4403
Personnel Department
Private Methodist college, offering undergraduate and graduate
programs.
Enrollment: 1,500

University of Dallas
1845 E. Northgate Dr.
Irving, TX 75062
(214) 445-0110
Personnel Director: Mary Laughlin
Private Catholic university offering undergraduate and graduate
programs.
Enrollment: 2,600

University of Texas at Arlington
701 S. Nedderman Dr.

Arlington, TX 76019
Metro (817) 273-2011
Contact: Personnel Department
Largest area state university, offering undergraduate and graduate programs.
Enrollment: 24,000.

University of Texas at Dallas
2601 N. Floyd Rd.
Richardson, TX 75080
(214) 690-2111
Personnel Director: Jerry Robinson
State university, offering undergraduate and graduate programs.
Enrollment: 8,900

University of Texas Southwestern Medical Center at Dallas
5323 Harry Hines Blvd.
Dallas, TX 75235-9060
(214) 648-3404
Contact: Employment Office
State health science center, which includes the Southwestern Medical School, Southwestern Graduate School of Biomedical Sciences, and the School of Allied Health Sciences.
Enrollment: 2,200

Electronics

Be sure also to look at the sections on **Aircraft and Aerospace, Computers: Hardware/Software,** and **Telecommunications.**

For networking in the electronics industry and related fields, check out this organization listed in Chapter 5:

PROFESSIONAL ORGANIZATIONS:

Electrical Women's Round Table

For additional information, you can contact:

Electronics Industry Association
2001 Pennsylvania Ave., NW
Washington, DC 20006
(202) 457-4900

Institute of Electrical & Electronics Engineers (IEEE)
345 W. 47th St.
New York, NY 10017
(212) 705-7900

North American Telecommunications Association
2000 M St., NW
Washington, DC 20036
(202) 296-9800

PROFESSIONAL PUBLICATIONS:

Communications Week International
Electronic Business
Electronic News
Telecommunications Reports
Telephony

DIRECTORIES:

American Electronics Association Directory (American Electronics
    Association, Santa Clara, CA)
Corporate Technology Directory (Corporate Technology Informa-
    tion Services, Woburn, MA)
Directory of High Technology Firms (Greater Dallas Chamber of
    Commerce, Dallas, TX)
EIA Trade Directory (Electronics Industry Association, Washing-
    ton, DC)

Guide to High Technology Companies (Corporate Technology
   Information Services, Woburn, MA)
Who's Who in Electronics (Harris Publications, Twinsburg, OH)

EMPLOYERS:

AT&T Information Systems
5501 LBJ Frwy., Suite 1009
Dallas, TX 75240
(214) 308-5542
Job hotline: 1-800-562-7288
Employment Supervisor: Bill Henderson
Sales, service, and maintenance for AT&T products.

Airborn Connectors
4321 Airborn Dr.
Addison, TX 75001
(214) 931-3200
Personnel Manager: Evelyn Key
Manufactures electronic connectors.

American Medical Electronics
250 E. Arapaho Rd.
Dallas, TX 75081
(214) 918-8300
Human Resources Director: Lovonne Chimbel
Manufactures proprietary medical equipment.

Business Records Co.
1111 W. Mockingbird Lane
Dallas, TX 75247
(214) 688-1800
Human Resources: Linda Hansen
Micrographically records and electronically indexes special
records. Also has elections services and county data entry service.

Continental Electronics
4212 S. Buckner Blvd.
Dallas, TX 75227
(214) 381-7161
Employment Manager: Marie McGill
Manufactures high-power radio transmitters for radio stations.

E-Systems
1200 S. Jupiter Rd.
Garland, TX 75042
(214) 272-0515
Contact: Staffing Office
Corporate headquarters for major worldwide developer and
producer of high-technology electronic systems and products for
government uses.

Hamilton - Hallmark
11333 Pagemill Dr.
Dallas, TX 75243
(214) 343-5000
Employment Recruiter: Jan Bordman
Distributes electronic components.

Honeywell
830 E. Arapaho
Richardson, TX 75081
(214) 470-4271
Contact: Department Head
Researches, develops, manufactures, and sells advanced technology products for information processing, electronics, automation, and controls industries.

Howell Instruments
3479 W. Vickery Blvd.
Fort Worth, TX 76107
(817) 336-7411
Personnel Manager: Corene Cloud
Manufactures ground test equipment for jet engines.

International Power Machine Corp.
2975 Miller Park North
Garland, TX 75242
(214) 272-8000
Personnel Manager: Judy Hemphill
Manufactures Uninterrupted Power Supply Systems (UPS).

Motorola Mobile Products Division
5555 N. Beach St.
Fort Worth, TX 76137
(817) 232-6000
Staffing Manager: Gary Gillespie
Research and development of cellular phones.

Recognition Equipment
2701 E. Grauwyler Rd.
Irving, TX 75061
(214) 579-6000
Human Resources Manager: Willemia Shaw
Designs and manufactures image processing, OCR, and networking technologies.

Siecor Corp.
9275 Hwy. 377 North
Keller, TX 76248
(817) 431-1521
Personnel Manager: Penny Church
Manufactures telephone apparatus, electronic components, and fiber optics.

Spectradyne
1501 N. Plano Rd.
Richardson, TX 75081
(214) 234-2721
Contact: Human Resources Department
Manufactures, sells, and services television entertainment
systems.

Tandy Corp.
1800 One Tandy Center
Fort Worth, TX 76102
(817) 390-3700
Contact: Personnel Department
Manufactures and sells consumer electronic parts and equipment,
including microcomputers, cellular mobile telephones, and satel-
lite dishes.

Teccor Electronics
1801 Hurd Dr.
Irving, TX 75038
(214) 580-1515
Personnel Manager: Myran Dill
Manufactures semiconductors.

Texas Instruments
13500 N. Central Expwy.
Richardson, TX 75265
(214) 995-3125
Contact: Employment Center
Largest Texas-based high-tech firm. Designs, develops, and
manufactures semiconductor memories, microprocessors, large-
scale integrated circuits, electronic calculators, home and professional computers, electronic data terminals, electro-optics equipment, and various defense systems.

Thermalloy
2021 W. Valley View Lane
Dallas, TX 75234
(214) 243-4321
Contact: Personnel Department
Manufactures electronic components and systems, including
semiconductor equipment and semiconductor insulating covers.

Varo
2800 W. Kingsley Rd.
Garland, TX 75046
(214) 840-5446
Contact: Staffing Office
Manufactures defense systems.

Wiltel Communications Systems
5151 Beltline Rd., Suite 100

Carrollton, TX 75240
(214) 991-3388
Sells and services phone systems.

Energy, Oil, and Gas Companies

For networking in the energy industry and related fields, check
out the following organizations listed in Chapter 5:

PROFESSIONAL ORGANIZATIONS:

Dallas Geological Society
Desk & Derrick Club of Fort Worth
Society of Petroleum Engineers

For more information, you can contact:

American Gas Association
1515 Wilson Blvd.
Arlington, VA 22209
(703) 841-8400

American Petroleum Institute
1201 Main St.
Dallas, TX 75202
(214) 748-3841

Clean Energy Research Institute
219 McArthur Bldg.
Coral Gables, FL 33124
(305) 284-4666

PROFESSIONAL PUBLICATIONS:

Drilling
Engineering & Mining Journal
Gas Digest
Mining Newsletter
National Petroleum News
Oil and Gas Journal
Petroleum Engineer International
Petroleum Marketer
Pipeline
Public Power
Solar Beat
Texas Oil Marketer
World Oil

DIRECTORIES:

Brown's Directory of North American & International Gas Companies (Energy Publications, Dallas, TX)
Energy Job Finder (Mainstream Access, New York, NY)
Mining Companies Directory (American Business Directories, Omaha, NE)
National Petroleum News Factbook (Hunter Publishing, Des Plaines, IL)
Oil and Gas Directory (Geophysical Directory, Houston, TX)
Oil and Gas Exploration and Development Directory (American Business Directories, Omaha, NE)
Solar Industry Journal (Solar Energy Industries Association, Washington, DC)
US Oil Industry Directory (Penwell Publishing, Tulsa, OK)
Whole World Oil Directory (National Register Publishing Company, Wilmette, IL)

EMPLOYERS:

Arch Petroleum Co.
777 Taylor St., Suite II-A
Fort Worth, TX 76102
Metro (817) 429-0691
Contact: Personnel Department
Oil and gas exploration and production.

Atlantic Richfield Company
1601 Bryan St.
Dallas, TX 75201
(214) 880-2500
Vice President Human Resources: Neal Thompson
Domestic oil and gas exploration and production.

Aztec Manufacturing Co.
400 N. Tarrant Rd.
Crowley, TX 76036
(817) 297-4361
Director of Industrial Relations: Bill Arnold
Manufactures oil tubing and processing drilling pipe.

CALTEX Petroleum Corp.
125 E. John W. Carpenter Frwy.
Irving, TX 75039
(214) 830-1000
Contact: Personnel Department
Oil refining and marketing.

Delphi Gas Pipeline Corp.
1700 Pacific Ave., L.B. 10
Dallas, TX 75201
(214) 954-2000

Employment Supervisor: Keith Huffman
Headquarters for drilling company that produces natural gas
from properties.

Dresser Industries
1600 Pacific Ave.
Dallas, TX 75201
(214) 740-6000
Personnel Manager: Danny Sanchez
Supplies technology, products, and services used by energy-
related industries in the development of petroleum, natural gas,
and coal.

Endevco
8080 N. Central Expwy., 12th Floor
Dallas, TX 75206
(214) 691-5536
Payroll Administrator: Becky Erickson
Natural gas transportation company.

ENSERCH Corp.
1817 Wood St.
Dallas, TX 75201
(214) 651-8700
Contact: Employment Office
Petroleum exploration and production, natural gas transmission
and distribution, engineering and construction, oil field services,
and major utilities.

EXXON Capital Corporation
4545 Fuller Dr., Suite 250
Dallas, TX 75038
(214) 650-7000
Contact: Personnel Department
Oil and gas exploration and marketing.

Fina, Inc.
8350 N. Central Expwy., Suite 1300
Dallas, TX 75206
(214) 750-2400
Corporate Recruiter: Paula Green
Exploration and production of petroleum and petrochemical
products.

GNC Energy Corp.
2811 McKinney Ave., Suite 340 West Lobby
Dallas, TX 75204
(214) 979-0353
President: W.H. Hudson
Exploration surveys.

Halliburton Co.
3600 Lincoln Plaza
500 N. Akard St.
Dallas, TX 75201
(214) 978-2600
Vice President Administration: Karen Stewart
Headquarters for one of the world's largest and most diversified
oil field services and engineering and construction organizations.
Also has casualty and life insurance companies.

Harbison-Fischer Manufacturing Co.
901 N. Crowley Rd.
Crowley, TX 76036
(817) 297-2211
Personnel Director: Leon Gregory
Manufactures oil field equipment, subsurface oil well pumps, and
pumping equipment.

Holly Corp.
100 Crescent Ct., Suite 1600
Dallas, TX 75201-1880
(214) 871-3555
Contact: Personnel Director Don Prout in Artesia, NM, (505) 748-
3311
Refining and marketing of petroleum products.

Hunt Oil Co.
1445 Ross at Field
Dallas, TX 75202-2785
(214) 978-8020
Recruiter: Paula Smith
Oil and gas production, real estate, and agribusiness.

ICO
6500 West Frwy., Suite 220
Fort Worth, TX 76116
Metro (817) 429-9005
Benefits Coordinator: Bonnie Wallace
Services oil field equipment.

Knox Oil of Texas
4835 LBJ Frwy., Suite 800
Dallas, TX 75244
(214) 960-9663
Contact: Department Head
Wholesale and retail petroleum production.

LTV Energy Products Co.
2441 Forest Lane
Garland, TX 75042
(214) 487-3000

Supervisor of Compensation and EEO: Joyce Powell
Manufacturer and distributor of oil field supplies.

Maxus Energy Corp.
717 N. Harwood St.
Dallas, TX 75201
(214) 953-2000
Vice President Human Resources Services: Mark Gentry
Oil and gas exploration and production.

Maynard Oil Co.
8080 N. Central Expwy., Suite 660
Dallas, TX 75206
(214) 891-8880
Contact: Katherine Shaffer
Exploration, development, and production of oil and natural gas.

Meridian Oil Co.
801 Cherry St.
Fort Worth, TX 76102
(817) 429-3080
Human Resources Representative: Linda Harris
Oil and gas exploration and production.

Mobil Oil Corp.
1201 Main St.
Dallas, TX 75202
(214) 658-2111
Contact: Employee Relations
Petroleum refining and distribution.

NRM and Edisto Resources
2121 San Jacinto Tower, Suite 2600
Dallas, TX 75201
(214) 880-0243
Contact: Personnel Department
Oil and gas exploration and production.

ORYX Energy Co.
P.O. Box 2880
Dallas, TX 75221-2880
(214) 715-4000
Personnel: Steve Church
Oil and gas exploration and production.

Pacific Enterprises
LTV Center, Suite 1200
1700 Pacific Ave.
Dallas, TX 75201
(214) 953-0088
Contact: Personnel Department

Exploration, development, production, and acquisition of crude oil, natural gas, and other natural resources.

Peerless Manufacturing Co.
2819 Walnut Hill Lane
Dallas, TX 75229
(214) 357-6181
Contact: Personnel Director
Manufactures products for oil and gas industry.

Petro Hunt Corp.
3900 Thanksgiving Tower
Dallas, TX 75201
(214) 922-0135
Personnel: Bill Heidelberg
Oil and gas production.

Schlumberger Well Services
4100 Spring Valley Rd., Suite 600
Dallas, TX 75244
(214) 385-6470
Relocation Coordinator: Valerie Horne
Oil field services.

Statex Petroleum
1801 Royal Lane, Suite 110
Dallas, TX 75229
(214) 869-2800
Executive Vice President: Dhar Carman
Oil and gas exploration and production.

Sunshine Mining Co.
300 Crescent Court, 15th Floor
Dallas, TX 75201
(214) 855-8700
Silver mining and exploration for natural gas.

Teledyne Geotech
3401 Shiloh Rd.
Garland, TX 75041
(214) 271-2561
Human Resources Manager: Ernest Stephens
Manufactures scientific equipment for oil and gas, seismology, and meteorology industries.

Triton Energy Corp.
6688 N. Central Expwy., Suite 1400
Dallas, TX 75206
(214) 691-5200
Contact: Vice President of Human Resources
Oil, gas, and coal exploration and production.

Union Pacific Resources Co.
801 Cherry St.
Fort Worth, TX 76102
(817) 877-6000
Vice President of Human Development: William H. Locke
Petroleum exploration and production.

Whitehall Corp.
2659 Nova Dr.
Dallas, TX 75229
(214) 247-8747
Contact: Department Head
Seismic marine equipment, aircraft maintenance, and electronics.

Woodbine Petroleum
1445 Ross Ave., Suite 3660
Dallas, TX 75202
(214) 855-6263
Vice President: Cricket Livengood
Oil and gas exploration and production.

Engineering Firms

You may also want to look at the sections on **Architecture** and **Contractors/Construction.**

For networking in engineering and related fields, check out the following professional organizations listed in Chapter 5:

PROFESSIONAL ORGANIZATIONS:

American Society of Civil Engineers
American Society of Mechanical Engineers
Texas Environmental Health Association
Texas Society of Professional Engineers

For additional information you can contact:

American Society of Civil Engineers
345 E. 47th St.
New York, NY 10017
(212) 705-7496

American Society of Mechanical Engineers
345 E. 47th St.
New York, NY 10017
(212) 705-7722

Institute of Electrical & Electronics Engineers (IEEE)
345 E. 47th St.
New York, NY 10017
(212) 705-7900

National Society of Professional Engineers
1420 King St.
Alexandria, VA 22314
(703) 684-2800

Society of Women Engineers
120 Wall Street, 11th Floor
New York, NY 10005-3902
(212) 509-9577

PROFESSIONAL PUBLICATIONS:

Building Design & Construction
Chemical Engineering News
Civil Engineering
Construction Weekly
ENR: Engineering News Record
Proceedings

DIRECTORIES:

Directory of Contract Service Firms (C.E. Publications, Kirkland, WA)

Engineering, Science, and Computer Jobs (Peterson's Guides, Princeton, NJ)

IEEE Directory (Institute of Electrical and Electronics Engineers, New York, NY)

Official Register (American Society of Civil Engineers, New York, NY)

Professional Engineering Directory (National Society of Professional Engineers, Alexandria, VA)

Who's Who in Engineering (American Assoc. of Engineering Societies, Washington, DC)

Who's Who in Technology (Gale Research, Detroit, MI)

EMPLOYERS:

ABB Impel Corp
6800 W. Frwy.
Fort Worth TX 76116
(817) 738-0300
Senior Local Executive: Jerry W. Allen
Specialties: Transportation, highways, aviation, rail, and environmental water resources.

Arjo Engineers
4311 Oak Lawn Ave.
Dallas, TX 75219
(214) 520-7799
Chairman of the Board: Ken Argenbright
Specialties: Office buildings, shopping centers, educational facilities, and hospitals.

Black & Veatch Engineering and Architects
5728 LBJ Frwy., Suite 300
Dallas, TX 75240
(214) 770-1500
Recruitment Director: Bill Davis
Specialties: Municipal water and wastewater.

Bridgefarmer & Associates
1300 S. Sherman St., Suite 290
Richardson, TX 75081
(214) 231-8800
Sr. Vice President: John Blackledge
Specialties: Highways, railroads, and bridges.

Brockette Davis Drake
3535 Travis St., Suite 100
Dallas, TX 75204
(214) 522-9540

Contact: Prefer mail inquiries only
Specialties: Surveying, civil, and structural engineering.

Campbell & Associates Consulting Engineers
3625 N. Hall St., Suite 500
Dallas, TX 75219
(214) 559-2600
President: Stephen J. Campbell
Specialties: Mid- and high-rise office buildings and hotels.

Carter & Burgess
1100 Macon St.
Fort Worth, TX 76102
(817) 735-6000
Personnel Supervisor: Ken Pusey
Specialties: Engineering, planning, landscape architecture, and
surveying.

CH2M Hill
5339 Alpha Rd., Suite 300
Dallas, TX 75240
(214) 980-2170
Personnel Director: Jill Lyons
Specialties: Wastewater and hazardous wastes.

Datum Engineering
6516 Forest Park Rd.
Dallas, TX 75235
(214) 358-0174
Engineering Department: Tom Herrin
Specialties: Corporate facilities, universities, and airports.

DeShazo, Tang & Associates
330 Union Station
Dallas, TX 75202
(214) 748-6740
President: John DeShazo
Specialties: Transportation planning and traffic engineering.

Dunn Consulting Engineers
3141 Hood St., Suite 300
Dallas, TX 75219
(214) 521-0038
Vice President of Finance: Wayne Keys
Specialties: Office buildings and health care facilities.

EMCOM Baker-Shifett
5701 E. Loop 820 S.
Fort Worth, TX 76119
(817) 478-8254
Senior Local Executive: Michael M. Shifett

Specialities: Municipal solid waste, integrated waste management systems.

Everage Consultants
2630 W. Frwy., Suite 100
Fort Worth, TX 76102
(817) 429-7562
Senior Local Executive: J.M. Ted Everage
Specialities: Civil , municipal, railroad, and environmental engineering.

Freese and Nichols
6500 W. Frwy.
Fort Worth, TX 76116
(817) 735-7300
President: Robert Herchert
Specialties: Industrial and manufacturing facilities architecture, structural, mechanical, electrical, plumbing, utility infrastructure, and site development.

Gillespie, Cawley & Associates
307 W. Seventh St., Suite 302
Fort Worth, TX 76102
(817) 336-2461
Senior Local Executive: Richard F. Strickland
Specialties: Petroleum engineering.

Graham Associates
616 Six Flags Dr., Suite 400
Arlington, TX 76011
(817) 640-8535
Senior Local Executive: Jim M. Wagon
Specialities: Commercial, residential, land development.

Greiner Engineering Sciences
909 E. Las Colinas Blvd., Suite 1900
Lock Box 44
Irving, TX 75039
(214) 869-1001
Director of Human Resources: Thomas R. Smith
Specialties: Highways and airports.

Gutierrez, Smouse, Wilmut & Associates
11117 Shady Trail
Dallas, TX 75229
(214) 620-1255
Senior Local Executive: Alberto F. Gutierrez
Specialities: Civil, transportation, environmental, water, waste water, and solid waste treatment.

Halff, Albert H., Associates
8616 Northwest Plaza Dr.

Dallas, TX 75225
(214) 739-0094
Contact: Personnel Department
Specialties: Flood plain management, office/industrial parks, and environmental engineering.

Howard Needles Tammen & Bergendoff
14114 Dallas Pkwy., Suite 630
Dallas, TX 75240
(214) 661-5626
Office Coordinator: Claire Caldwell
Specialties: Highway design and municipal engineering.

Huitt-Zollars
3131 McKinney Ave., Suite 600
Dallas, TX 75204
(214) 871-3311
Contact: Bobbie O' Brien
Specialties: Hydrology/hydraulics and land development.

Johnson, Bernard
7800 Stemmons Frwy., Suite 730
Dallas, TX 75247
(214) 631-7200
Sr. Vice President: Bill Glasgow
Specialties: Engineering for city governments and other public groups.

Kimley-Horn and Associates
12660 Coit Rd., Suite 300
Dallas, TX 75251
(214) 386-7007
Personnel Director: Brad Dennard
Specialties: Transportation engineering.

Kirk Voich Gist
1500 Ballinger
Fort Worth, TX 76102
(817) 335-4991
Senior Local Executive: Don W. Kirk
Specialities: Building design architecture, landscape architecture, and engineering.

Knowlton—English—Flowers
1901 Central Dr., Suite 550
Bedford, TX 76021
(817) 283-6211
Senior Local Executive: Kenneth E. English
Specialities: General civil engineering.

Lockwood Andrews & Newnam
2710 N. Stemmons Frwy., Suite 1200

Dallas, TX 75207
(214) 630-1414
Operations Manager: Jack Moseley
Specialties: Public works engineering.

Lockwood Greene Engineers
4201 Spring Valley Rd., Suite 1500
Dallas, TX 75244
(214) 991-5505
Human Resources Manager: Judy Schosield
Specialties: Advanced technology and manufacturing facilities.

Plumber, Allen & Associates
210 W. Sixth St., Suite 400
Fort Worth, TX 76102
(817) 332-4085
Senior Local Executive: John H. Cook
Specialties: Water quality assessment, storm water management.

Rady and Associates
910 Coller
Fort Worth, TX 76102
(817) 335-6511
Senior Local Executive: Darrell Johnson
Specialities: Municipal civil consulting.

Romine, Romine & Burgess
300 Greenleaf St.
Fort Worth, TX 76107
(817) 336-4633
Office Manager: Patti McKittrick
Specialties: Mechanical and electrical engineers.

Schrickel Rollins & Associates
1161 Corporate Dr. W., Suite 200
Arlington, TX 76006
(817)640-8212
Senior Local Executive: Albert W. Rollins
Specialities: Municipal and general civil engineering.

Southwestern Laboratories
2575 Lone Star Dr.
Dallas, TX 75212
(214) 263-1133
President: Bill Harper
Specialties: Industrial, institutional, commercial buildings, and
construction materials testing.

Sverdrup Corp.
4311 Oak Lawn Ave., Suite 300
Dallas TX 75219
(214) 520-2116

Senior Local Executive: Phillip G. Weston
Specialities: Civil, structural, mechanical, electrical, and
architecture.

Teague, Nall & Perkins
915 Florence St.
Fort Worth, TX 76102
(817) 336-5773
Principal: Gary Teague
Specialties: Consulting engineering.

Turner, Collie & Braden
5710 LBJ Frwy., Suite 370
Dallas, TX 75240
(214) 960-9651
Principal: Thomas Burke
Specialties: Highways and airports.

Yandell & Hiller
512 Main St
Fort Worth, TX 76102
(817) 335-3000
Senior Local Executive: Roger L. Yandell
Specialities: Structural, mechanical, electrical, civil engineering,
and architecture.

Wier & Associates
4300 Beltway Plaza, Suite 130
Arlington, TX 76018
(817) 467-7700
Senior Local Executive: John P. Wier
Specialities: Comprehensive civil and municipal engineering, land
planning and surveying.

Entertainment

For networking in the entertainment industry, check out the following professional organizations listed in Chapter 5:

PROFESSIONAL ORGANIZATIONS:

American Guild of Organists
Pro-Musica
Society for Theatrical Artists Guidance and Enhancement (S.T.A.G.E.)

For more information, you can contact:

Academy of Motion Picture Arts & Sciences
8949 Wilshire Blvd.
Beverly Hills, CA 90211
(310) 247-3000

American Federation of Arts
41 E. 65th St.
New York, NY 10021
(212) 988-7700

American Guild of Authors and Composers
6430 Sunset Blvd.
Hollywood, CA 90028

Amusement and Music Operators Association
111 E. Wacker Dr.
Chicago, IL 60601
(312) 245-1021

Arts and Business Council
25 W. 45th St.
New York, NY 10036
(212) 819-9287

PROFESSIONAL PUBLICATIONS:

American Film
ArtCom
Backstage
BAM
Billboard
Mix
Music Journal
Performance
Show Business

Theater Times
TV Radio Age
Variety

DIRECTORIES:

Back Stage Film / Tape / Syndication Directory (Back Stage
Publications, New York, NY)
Blue Book (Hollywood Reporter, Hollywood, CA)
Contemporary Music Almanac (Macmillian Publishers, New York,
NY)
Film Producers, Studios, and Agents Guide (Lone Eagle, Beverly
Hills, CA)
Mass Entertainment Buyers Guide (Billboard Publications,
Nashville, TN)
Music Business Handbook & Career Guide (Sherwood Co., Los
Angeles, CA)
Music Business (Music Industry Resources, San Anselmo, CA)
Theatre Directory (Theatre Communications Group, New York,
NY)
Who's Who in the Motion Picture Industry (Packard House,
Beverly Hills, CA)
Who's Who in Television (Packard House, Beverly Hills, CA)

EMPLOYERS:

Billy Bob's Texas
2520 Rodeo Plaza
Fort Worth, TX 76106
(817) 624-7117
Personnel: Ruth Churkey
World's largest honky-tonk with indoor bull-riding arena, concerts by national entertainers, gift shops, and restaurants.

Caravan of Dreams
312 Houston St.
Fort Worth, TX 76102
Metro (817) 429-4000
General Manager: Alex Petrou
President: Jerry Thompson
Jazz/blues nightclub, featuring local and national entertainers,
theater, and restaurant.

Casa Manana Theatre
3101 W. Lancaster Ave.
Fort Worth, TX 76107
(817) 332-9319
Company Manager: Debbie Brown
Theater with summer musicals, children's plays, and theatrical
productions.

Dallas Alley
2019 N. Lamar St., Suite 200
Dallas, TX 75202
(214) 988-0581
Contact: Fill out applications from 9 a.m.-6 p.m., Monday-Friday
Nightclub complex.

Dallas Opera
3102 Oak Lawn Ave., Suite 450, LB 130
Dallas, TX 75219
(214) 443-1043
Opera association.

Dallas Repertory Theatre
150 NorthPark Center
Dallas, TX 75225
(214) 885-5082
Executive Producer: Douglas Parker
Legitimate theater.

Dallas Symphony Orchestra
2301 Flora St., Suite 300
Dallas, TX 75201-2413
(214) 871-4000
Contact: Personnel

Dallas Theater Center
3636 Turtle Creek Blvd.
Dallas, TX 75219
(214) 526-8210
General Manager: Sean Skeehan
Legitimate theater.

Dallas Zoo
621 E. Clarendon Dr.
Dallas, TX 75203
(214) 946-5154
Contact: Personnel Office
City zoo.

Fort Worth Ballet
6845 Green Oaks Rd.
Fort Worth, TX 76116
(817) 763-0207
Executive Director: David Mallette
Ballet company.

Fort Worth Opera Association
3505 W. Lancaster Ave.
Fort Worth, TX 76107
(817) 731-0833

Director of Development: Pat Crowley
Opera company.

Fort Worth Symphony Orchestra
4401 Trail Lake Dr.
Fort Worth, TX 76109
(817) 921-2676
General Manager: John Toohey

Fort Worth Zoological Park
19819 Colonial Pkwy
Fort Worth, TX 76110
(817) 871-7050
Assistant Director: Elaine McGowan
More than 4,000 animals and exhibits.

Funny Bone Comedy Club
2525 E. Arkansas Lane, Suite 253
Arlington, TX 76010
Metro (817) 265-2277
Manager: Debra Esparza
Comedy club with local and national entertainers.

Hip Pocket Theatre
1627 Fairmount Ave.
Fort Worth, TX 76104
(817) 927-2833
General Manager: Holly Leach
Outdoor theater.

Shakespeare Festival of Dallas
3630 Harry Hines Blvd., Suite 306
Dallas, TX 75219
(214) 559-2778
Contact: Executive Director
Produces annual Shakespeare play series.

Showco
201 Regal Row
Dallas, TX 75247
(214) 263-5944
Contact: Mail resume
Sound and lighting company.

Six Flags Over Texas
2201 Road To Six Flags
Arlington, TX 76010
Metro (817) 640-8900
Contact: Personnel Office
Family theme park.

How to Get a Job

Stage West
3055 S. University Dr.
Fort Worth, TX 76109
(817) 924-5938
Artistic Director: Jerry Russell
Legitimate theater.

State Fair of Texas
P.O. Box 150009
Dallas, TX 75315
(214) 565-9931
Contact: Personnel for staff positions and Texas Employment
Commission for seasonal jobs during annual fair in October.

Texas Stadium
2401 E. Airport Frwy.
Irving, TX 75062
(214) 438-7676
Director of Operations: Ron Underwood
Major stadium for Dallas Cowboys football games and other
events.

Theatre Three
2800 Routh St.
Dallas, TX 75201
(214) 871-2933
Director of Administration: Chris Hansdorff
Chief of Operations: Thurman Moss
Non-profit legitimate theater.

Wet 'N Wild
1800 E. Lamar St.
Arlington, TX 76006
Metro (817) 265-3356
Contact: Personnel department at Arlington and Garland water
parks

Theatrical career often noble but low paying

Theatre Three Executive Producer and Director
Jac Alder appreciates the struggle involved when
people pursue a career in the theater. He was
an architect for seven years before his avocation
became his vocation.

His interests motivated him to get more
involved in the theater, although he says, "I have
not given up architecture. In the service of the
theater, I design sets. I use every bit of training I
got as an architect on virtually a daily basis.
Right now I'm standing over a computer doing a
spread sheet on construction costs."

Alder describes how terrified parents have
approached him and said, "My God, my son or
daughter is in theater. What's going to happen?"

272

"They can't see it as a paying profession and they are right," he says.

He tells parents that the theater teaches young people to work in a team situation, meet deadlines, and deal with great ideas of the Western World.

"My feeling is that any task can be followed with a sense of ethics and a sense of industry," Alder says. "If any job offers you an opportunity to do that, you've got a wonderful life. Theater involves creativity, responsibility, and all the things that we think are important." ■

Environmental Services

Also Check the section on **Engineering.**

For information about careers in environmental services and related fields, you can contact:

PROFESSIONAL ORGANIZATIONS:

Alliance for Environmental Education
10751 Ambassador Dr., Suite 201
Manassas, VA 22110
(703) 335-1025

American Wilderness Alliance
7600 E. Arapahoe Rd., Suite 114
Englewood, CO 80112
(303) 771-0380

The Conservation Foundation
1250 24th St., NW
Washington, DC 20037
(202) 293-4800

Environmental Careers Organization
286 Congress St.
Boston, MA 02210
(617) 426-4783

National Association of Environmental Professionals
5165 MacArthur Blvd., NW
Washington, DC 20016
(202) 966-1500

National Solid Waste Management Association
1730 Rhode Island Ave., NW

Washington, DC 20036
(202) 659-4613

Sierra Club
730 Polk St.
San Francisco, CA 94109
(415) 776-2211

Water Environmental Federation
601 Wythe St.
Alexandria, VA 22314
(703) 684-2400

PROFESSIONAL PUBLICATIONS:

Buzzworm
E, The Environmental Magazine
Earth Watch
Environmental Watch
Pollution Engineering
Water Engineering & Management
Water and Wastes Digest

DIRECTORIES:

The Complete Guide to Environmental Careers (The CEIP Fund,
Island Press, Washington, DC)
Conservation Directory (National Wildlife Federation, Washing-
ton, DC)
Directory of National Environmental Organizations (U.S. Envi-
ronmental Directories, St. Paul, MN)
EI Environmental Services (Environmental Information Ltd.,
Bloomington, MN) Lists over 400 waste handling facilities,
1700 consultants, 470 labs, 700 transportation firms, 375 spill
response firms.
Guide to State Environmental Programs (Deborah Hitchcock
Jessup, ed. The Bureau of National Affairs, Inc.)
Listing of Awardee Names: Active Awards (Dept. of Energy,
Washington, DC) Lists 2400 companies, organizations, agen-
cies receiving funding from the Department of Energy.
Management of World Wastes—Buyers Guide Issue (Communica-
tion Channels, Inc. Atlanta, GA)
Manufacturers List (Synergy, New York) Lists 3000 manufactur-
ers of renewable energy equipment.

EMPLOYERS:

Black & Veatch
5728 LBJ Frwy., Suite 300
Dallas, TX 75240
(214) 770-1500

Contact: Charles Duncan, Director
Water and wastewater treatment.

Carter & Burgess
1100 Macon St.
Fort Worth, TX 76102
(817) 335-2611
Contact: Employment Office
Water/waste water resources, hazardous waste assessments, and permits.

Gutierrez, Smouse, Wilmut & Associates
1117 Shady Trail
Dallas, TX 75229
(214) 620-1255
Contact: Alberto Gutierrez, Founder
Water & solid waste.

Plummer, Allen, & Associates
801 W. Mitchell
Arlington, TX 76013
(817) 461-1491
Contact: Alan Plummer
Water quality assessment, toxicity reduction evaluations, environmental site assessment.

Rone Engineers
11234 Goodnight Lane
Dallas, TX 75229
(214) 241-4517
Contact: Charles Jackson
Environmental and geotechnical, environmental exploration.

USA Waste Services
5000 Quorum Dr., Suite 445
Dallas, TX 75240
(214) 233-4212
Contact: Personnel Director
Engaged in non-hazardous solid waste management.

Waste Recovery
2606 Gaston Ave.
Dallas, TX 75226
(214) 741-3865
Contact: Thomas Earnshaw
Engaged in the processing of scrap tires into a refined fuel supplement.

Film, Video, Recording, and Talent Services

You may also want to look at the section on **Broadcasting and Television.**

For networking in film, video, and related fields, check out these professional organizations listed in Chapter 5:

PROFESSIONAL ORGANIZATIONS:

Dallas Communications Council
Dallas Producers Association
Texas Association of Film & Tape Professionals
Texas Association of Teachers of Dancing

For additional information, you can contact:

Academy of Motion Picture Arts & Sciences
8949 Wilshire Blvd.
Beverly Hills, CA 90211
(310) 247-3000

American Film Institute
2021 N. Western Ave.
Hollywood, CA 90028
(213) 856-7600

PROFESSIONAL PUBLICATIONS:

American Film
Back Stage
Billboard
Box Office
Film Comment
Film Journal
Variety

DIRECTORIES:

Audio-Visual Buyer's Guide (PTN Publishing Company, Melville, NY)
Audio-Visual Communications: Who's Who (Media Horizons, New York, NY)
Back Stage Shoot/Commercial Production (Knowledge Industry Publications, White Plains, NY)
Billboard International Buyers Guide (Billboard Publishers, New York, NY)

Film Producers, Studios, and Agents Guide (Lone Eagle, Beverly
  Hills, CA)
Who's Who in the Motion Picture Industry (Packard House,
  Beverly Hills, CA)

EMPLOYERS:

AVW Audio Visual
2241 Irving Blvd.
Dallas, TX 75207
(214) 634-9060
Contact: Department Head
Sells and leases equipment; produces tapes for customers.

Dallas Communications Complex
The Studios at Las Colinas
6301 N. O'Connor Rd.
Irving, TX 75039
(214) 869-0700
Vice President: Mike Childress
Film and sound studios, manages offices for support services for
the commercial and entertainment film business.

Dallas Sound Lab
Four Dallas Communications Complex, Suite 119
6305 N. O'Connor Rd.
Irving, TX 75039
(214) 869-1122
Accepts resumes by mail only.
Contact: Johnny Marshall
Specializes in post-production audio services for film and video,
including film/video interlock and scoring; mixing, demos, and
albums.

Dawson, Kim, Agency
P.O. Box 585060
Dallas, TX 75258
(214) 638-2414
Contact: Department Head
Talent and modeling agency for film, television, radio, theater,
and fashion promotions.

Fort Worth Productions
P.O. Box 125
Fort Worth, TX 76101
(817) 336-0777
Accepts resumes by mail only.
Contact: Mitchell Johnson
Independent television production company, providing program-
ming for network syndicators, public broadcasting, and cable.

277

Goodnight Audio
11260 Goodnight Lane
Dallas, TX 75229
(214) 241-5182
Studio Manager: Debb Rooney
Complete 24-track recording studio.

Kidd, Richard, Productions
5610 Maple Ave.
Dallas, TX 75235
(214) 638-5433
Contact: Barbara Ratliff
Full-service production company for film, video, and A/V presentations.

Magnum Audio-Visual
1333 Maryland Dr.
Irving, TX 75061
(214) 554-0533
Contact: Sharon Stone
Industrial shows, audio, and video production work.

Omega Audio & Productions
7027 Twin Hills, Suite #5
Dallas, TX 75231
(214) 891-9585
Senior Engineer: Steve Lowney
Complete remote audio multi-track recording service for records, film, and video.

Southwest Teleproductions
2649 Tarna Dr.
Dallas, TX 75229
(214) 243-5719
Contact: J.P. Shives or Lee Harrison for operations positions and Suzanne Morris for administrative
Production and post-production services for 35mm and 16mm film and videotape.

Stokes Group,The
5642 Dyer St.
Dallas, TX 75206
(214) 363-0161
C.E.O.: Bill Stokes
Full service film, video, computer animation, and audio production company.

Video Post and Transfer
2727 Inwood Rd.
Dallas, TX 75235
(214) 350-2676
Send resumes by mail only.

Personnel: Betty Lajoie
Complete video post-production services, including film-to-tape transfer, graphics, animation, and special effects.

Zimmersmith
6311 N. O'Connor Rd., Suite 113
Dallas Communications Complex, Bldg. #3
Irving, TX 75039
(214) 869-4611
Production Coordinator: Vickie Meyer
Full-service music production company.

"Models are born, not made"

On an average day, 30 phone calls and 15 letters are directed to George Dawson, talent coordinator for the Kim Dawson Agency, Inc. Here's what he tells eager applicants who want to break into the area's growing fashion, film, and talent industries:

Send several color photographs along with your measurements, height, phone number, and address where you can be reached. "Most people think you have to pay for expensive portfolio photographs, and that's not the case," Dawson says.

Out of 50 or 60 inquiries, he may find one person who has the potential to make it in the highly competitive Dallas market. Many people don't meet one necessary requirement—height. A women must be 5 feet, 8 inches, to 5 feet, 11 inches and a man should be between 5 feet, 11 inches, and 6 feet, 2 inches.

Dawson interviews promising candidates. If he thinks they have potential, he advises them to get a series of quality pictures taken. If those turn out well, the person is signed with the agency and assisted in putting together a "composite" (photo sheet) and portfolio.

"The first year can be rough financially for new models," Dawson says. "They should be prepared to moonlight during the first six months to a year because few novices make a livable income."

People who sign with the agency can take modeling and grooming classes, but it's not a requirement. "We never tell a person they will be a model after taking a certain number of courses," he says. "Models are usually born, not made." ∎

Food/Beverage Producers and Distributors

You may also want to look at the section on **Restaurants.**

For information about the food industry and related fields, contact the following professional organizations.

PROFESSIONAL ORGANIZATIONS:

American Institute of Food Distribution
28-12 Broadway
Fairlawn, NJ 07410
(201) 791-5570

Association of Food Industries
P.O. Box 776
5 Ravine Dr.
Matawan, NJ 07747
(908) 583-8188

Distilled Spirits Council
1250 I St., NW
Washington, DC 20005
(202) 628-3544

Food Marketing Institute
800 Connecticut Ave., NW
Washington, DC 20006
(202) 452-8444

National Association of Beverage Importers—Wine—Spirits—Beer
1025 Vermont Ave.
Washington DC 20005
(202) 638-1617

National Association for Specialty Food Trade
8 W. 40th St.
New York, NY 10018
(212) 921-1690

National Food Distributors Association
401 N. Michigan Ave.
Chicago, IL 60611
(312) 644-6610

National Food Processors Association
1401 New York Ave.

Washington, DC 20005
(202) 639-5900

National Frozen Foods Association
P.O. Box 6069, 4755 Linglestown Rd.
Harrisburg, PA 17112
(717) 657-8601

National Soft Drink Association
1101 16th St., NW
Washington, DC 20036

Wine & Spirits Wholesalers of America
1025 15th St., NW
Washington, DC 20005

PROFESSIONAL PUBLICATIONS:

Beverage World
Fancy Food
Food and Beverage Marketing
Food Industry Newsletter
Food Management
Food and Wine
Foodservice Product News
Forecast for Home Economics
Grocery Marketing
Institutional Distribution
Progressive Grocer
Quick Frozen Foods
Wines and Vines

DIRECTORIES:

Directory of the Canning, Freezing, Preserving Industry (Edward
    C. Judge & Sons, Westminster, MD)
Frozen Food Fact Book & Directory (National Frozen Food Asso-
    ciation, Harrisburg, PA)
Impact Yearbook: A Directory of the Wine and Spirits Industry (M.
    Shanken Communications, New York, NY)
Modern Brewery Age Blue Book (Business Journals, Norwalk, CT)
National Beverage Marketing Directory (Beverage Marketing
    Corp., New York, NY)
Texas Retail Grocers Association Directory (Texas Retail Grocers
    Association, Austin, TX)

EMPLOYERS:

Albertson's
1100 Executive Dr. West, Suite 100

Richardson, TX 75083
(214) 238-7231
Contact: Human Resources Department
Grocery and drug store chain.

American Produce & Vegetable Co.
4721 Simonton Rd.
Dallas, TX 75244
(214) 233-5750
Personnel: Brenda Alcala
Distributes canned and fresh food to hotels, caterers, restaurants, and airlines.

Arrow Industries
2625 Belt Line Rd.
Carrollton, TX 75006
(214) 416-6500
Contact: Personnel Department
Packages dry food products.

Borden
5327 S. Lamar St.
Dallas, TX 75215
(214) 565-0332
Personnel Manager: Judy Roberts
Produces milk, ice cream, and dairy products.

Cabell's Dairy
4017 Commerce St.
Dallas, TX 75226
(214) 234-6761
Personnel Manager: Gary McNeil
Produces and distributes dairy products.

Campbell Taggert
6211 Lemmon Ave.
Dallas, TX 75209
(214) 358-9211
Manager of Personnel Administration: Ellen Einsohn
Produces white breads, earth grains, and sweet goods.

Coca-Cola Bottling Co. of North Texas
3400 Fossil Creek Blvd.
Fort Worth, TX 76137
(817) 232-8600
Contact: Personnel Department
Bottlers of soft drink beverages.

Continental Grain Co.
2301 Terminal Rd.
Fort Worth, TX 76106
(817) 624-4171

General Manager: Roger Sellers
Buys and sells grains.

Coors Distributing Co.
2550 McMillan Pkwy. S.
Fort Worth, TX 76137
(817) 838-1600
Contact: Personnel Director
Beer distributor.

Dean, Jimmy, Meat Co.
10430 Shady Trail
Dallas, TX 75220
(214) 350-6755
Contact: Personnel
Produces sausage and prepared meats.

Decker Food Co.
3200 W. Kingsley Rd.
Garland, TX 75041
(214) 278-6192
Human Resources Director: Vicki Minden
Processes bacon, sausage, boiled ham, and smoked and cured
pork.

Deli Express
2005 108th St., Suite 504
Grand Prairie, TX 75053
(214) 647-8198
Contact: Personnel Department
Produces and distributes wholesale sandwiches, snacks, and
Mexican food.

Dr Pepper/7UP Cos.
8144 Walnut Hill Lane
Dallas, TX 75231
(214) 360-7000
Contact: Personnel Department
Soft drink beverage bottlers.

Frito-Lay
National Headquarters
7701 Legacy Dr.
Plano, TX 75024-4099
(214) 334-7000
Contact: Professional Placement
Produces and markets snack products.

Glazer's Wholesale Distributors
10750 Denton Dr.
Dallas, TX 75220
(214) 357-1245

Contact: Department Head
Wholesale wine and liquor distributor.

H & M / Design Foods
3709 E. First St.
Fort Worth, TX 76111
(817) 831-0981
Personnel Manager: Sharon Mullarkey
Produces meats for institutional and commercial customers.

Hormel, George A., & Co.
4114 Mint Way
Dallas, TX 75224
(214) 784-9055
Contact: Personnel Office at (507) 437-5611
Processes and distributes fresh and canned meat products, frozen
and prepared foods, and institutional food.

ITT Continental Baking Co.
9000 Denton Dr.
Dallas, TX 75235
(214) 358-0232
Contact: Personnel Department
Produces and distributes bread and bakery items.

Keebler Co.
3900 Meecham Blvd.
Halton City, TX 76117
Metro (817) 577-2933
Personnel: Al Godoy
Distributes cookie, cracker, and snack products.

Keith, Ben E., Co.
601 E. 7th St.
Fort Worth, TX 76102
Metro (817) 429-8488
Contact: Department Head
Beer distributor and wholesaler of frozen foods and produce.

Kroger Food Co.
1901 Gateway Dr.
Irving, TX 75038
(214) 580-3000
Contact: Human Resources Department
Major food retailer and operator of food processing, dairies,
bakeries, and egg-producing facilities.

Miller Brewing Co.
7001 South Frwy.
Fort Worth, TX 76134
(817) 551-3300

Personnel Manager: Dominick Feragotti
Produces, bottles, and distributes beer and malt beverages.

Mrs Baird's Bakeries
Dallas Office
5230 E. Mockingbird Lane
Dallas, TX 75205
(214) 526-7201
Contact: Personnel Department
Produces bread and baked goods.

Mrs Baird's Bakeries
Fort Worth Office
7301 South Frwy.
Fort Worth, TX 76134
(817) 293-6230
Contact: Personnel Department
Same as Dallas.

Owens Country Sausage
1403 Lookout Dr.
Richardson, TX 75082
(214) 235-7181
Vice President: Lindsey Borden
Produces sausage and pork products.

Pepsi-Cola Bottling Group
4532 Hwy. 67
Mesquite, TX 75150
(214) 324-8500
Bottles soft drink beverages.

Pilgrim's Pride Corp.
2411 Ferris St.
Dallas, TX 75226
(214) 421-7625
Personnel: Claudia Stamp
Poultry wholesaler.

Quaker Oats Co.
13745 Jupiter Rd.
Dallas, TX 75238
(214) 340-0370
Personnel Manager: Jim Lamberson
Distributor for foods, pet foods, and specialty chemicals.

Rainbow Baking Co.
3500 Manor Way
Dallas, TX 75235
(214) 357-1754
Personnel: Sandie Wilkerson
Produces bread and bakery products.

How to Get a Job

Rodriguez Festive Foods
899 N. Houston St.
Fort Worth, TX 76106
(817) 429-1980
Personnel Manager
Produces Mexican food products.

Southland Corp.
2711 N. Haskell Ave.
Dallas, TX 75204
(214) 828-7107
Contact: Personnel Department
Corporate headquarters for 7-Eleven convenience stores and dairy products producer.

Supreme Beef Co.
5219 Second Ave.
Dallas, TX 75210
(214) 428-1761
Personnel Safety Director: Gayla Hensley
Beef processing plant.

Sysco Food Systems
14330 Gillis Rd.
Dallas, TX 75244
(214) 233-9700
Personnel Director: Rick Nolan
Institutional food distributor.

Tom Thumb Food and Drug
14303 Inwood Rd.
Dallas, TX 75244
(214) 661-9700
Employment Training Manager: Marsha Crawford
Operates regional chain of supermarkets, drug stores, wholesale grocery distribution, and meat packing, including Tom Thumb Page Food & Drug Centers.

Vandervoort Dairy Foods
900 S. Main St.
Fort Worth, TX 76104
(817) 332-7551
Contact: Texas Employment Commission for production positions, and send resumes for management positions
Dairy foods processor.

White Swan
1515 Big Town Blvd.
Mesquite, TX 75149
(214) 388-7700
Contact: Personnel Department
Institutional food distributor.

286

Willow Distribution
2601 Cockrell Ave.
Dallas, TX 75315
(214) 426-5636
Contact: Department Head
Beer distributor.

Winn-Dixie Texas
5500 South Frwy.
Fort Worth, TX 76115
(817) 921-1100
Contact: Department Head
Grocery store chain and dairy products producer.

Furniture and Fixtures Manufacturers

For networking in the furniture and fixtures industry and related fields, check out this professional organization listed in Chapter 5.

PROFESSIONAL ORGANIZATIONS:

International Furnishings and Design Association

To help you learn more about the furniture industry, you can contact:

American Furniture Manufacturers Association
918 16th St., NW
Washington, DC 20006

National Home Furnishings Association
P.O. Box 2396
High Point, NC 27261

PROFESSIONAL PUBLICATIONS:

HFD - Retail Home Furnishings
Home Improvements Center
Home Furnishings Review
Textile Products and Processes
Textile World

DIRECTORIES:

Furniture Manufacturers Directory (American Business Directories, Omaha, NE)

Who's Who in Furniture Distribution (National Wholesale Furniture Association, High Point, NC)

EMPLOYERS:

Duro Metal Manufacturing Co.
410 Hilburn St.
Dallas, TX 75217
(214) 391-3181
Plant Manager: Frank Ramirez
Office Manager: Pricilla Siegel
Executive V.P. for Sales Positions: Chuck Siegel
Manufactures bed frames, mirror supports, bed rails, and trundle beds.

Inca Metal Products Corp.
501 E. Purnell St.
Lewisville, TX 75067
(214) 436-5581
Contact: Department Head
Manufactures workbenches, shop desks, and industrial shelving.

Levolor Corp.
1750 Monetary Lane
Carrollton, TX 75006
(214) 323-4510
Personnel Director: Cathy Dillard
Manufactures window coverings.

Massould Furniture Manufacturing Co.
8208 Moberly Lane
Dallas, TX 75227
(214) 388-8655
Plant Manager: Dwain Seabolt
Manufactures household furniture, including sofas, loveseats, and chairs.

Pillowtex Corp.
4111 Mint Way
Dallas, TX 75237
(214) 333-3225
Contact: Personnel Department
Manufactures bedding, pillows, mattress pads, and comforters.

Simmons Co.
1625 Diplomat Dr.
Carrollton, TX 75006
(214) 241-9100
Contact: Personnel Department
Manufactures mattresses and box springs.

Smith System Manufacturing Co.
1714 E. 14th St.
Plano, TX 75074
(214) 424-6591
Plant Manager: Ron Smith
Manufactures furniture for schools and offices.

Southland Bedding Co.
1207 W. Crosby Rd.
Carrollton, TX 75006
(214) 242-7666
Owner: Larry Bannister
Manufactures bedding.

Universal Display & Fixtures
613 Easy St.
Garland, TX 75042
(214) 276-8335
Personnel Manager: Todd Hudson
Manufactures wire and tubular products.

Vecta Contract
1800 S. Great Southwest Pkwy.
Grand Prairie, TX 75051
(214) 641-2860
Personnel Manager: Betty Creamer
Manufactures contemporary office furniture.

Government

For networking in **government** and related fields, check out these professional organizations listed in Chapter 5:

PROFESSIONAL ORGANIZATIONS:

American Planning Association
Texas Society of Professional Surveyors
Urban Management Assistants of North Texas

For additional information, you can contact:

American Federation of Government Employees
80 F St., NW
Washington, DC 20001
(202) 737-8700

American Society for Public Administration
1120 G St., NW
Washington, DC 20005
(202) 393-7878

Civil Service Employees Association
P.O. Box 125, Capital Station
143 Washington Ave.
Albany, NY 12210
(518) 434-0191

National Association of Government Employees
2011 Crystal Dr., #206
Arlington, VA 22202
(703) 979-0290

PROFESSIONAL PUBLICATIONS:

AFSCME Leader
The Beacon
Federal Times
FedNews
The Municipal Forum
Public Employee Newsletter
Public Management

DIRECTORIES:

Braddock's Federal-State-Local Government Directory (Braddock
Communications, Alexandria, VA)

Directory of Texas City Officials (Texas Municipal League, Austin, TX)

Legislative Directory (North Central Texas Council of Government, Arlington, TX)

Texas Legislative Handbook (Legislative Associates, Dallas, TX)

EMPLOYERS, CITY GOVERNMENT:

Addison, Town of
16801 Westgrove Dr.
Addison, TX 75248
(214) 450-2817
Jobline: (214) 450-2815
Personnel Assistant: Marilyn LeBlanc

Arlington, City of
501 Main St.
Arlington, TX 76010
Metro (817) 265-3311
Employment Specialist: Leonard Jefferson

Balch Springs, City of
3117 Hickory Tree Rd.
Balch Springs, TX 75180
(214) 557-6070
Contact: Personnel

Bedford, City of
2000 Forest Ridge Dr.
Bedford, TX 76021
Metro (817) 952-2100
Contact: Personnel Department

Burleson, City of
141 W. Renfro St.
Burleson, TX 76028
(817) 295-1113
Personnel: Ginger Allen

Carrollton, City of
1945 Jackson Rd.
Carrollton, TX 75006
(214) 466-3000
Jobline (214) 466-3376
Contact: Personnel Department

Cedar Hill, City of
502 Cedar St.
Cedar Hill, TX 75104
(214) 291-5100
Director of Community Services: Greg Porter

Cockrell Hill, City of
4125 W. Clarendon Dr.
Cockrell Hill, TX 75211
(214) 330-6333
City Secretary: Elizabeth White

Colleyville, City of
5400 Bransford Rd.
Colleyville, TX 76034
Metro (817) 577-7575
Contact: Department Head

Colony, The, City of
5151 N. Colony Blvd.
The Colony, TX 75056
(214) 370-5667
Personnel Director: Margaret Burkett

Dallas, City of
1500 Marilla St., 6A North
Dallas, TX 75201
(214) 670-3552
Jobline: (214) 670-5908
Contact: Personnel Department

DeSoto, City of
211 E. Pleasant Run Rd.
DeSoto, TX 75115
(214) 230-9600
Contact: Personnel Department

Duncanville, City of
203 E. Wheatland Rd.
Duncanville, TX 75116
(214) 780-5006
Personnel Administrator: Greg Weaver

Euless, City of
201 N. Ector Dr.
Euless, TX 76039
(817) 685-1400
Contact: Personnel Department

Everman, City of
212 N. Race St.
Everman, TX 76140
(817) 293-0525
City Manager: David Honeycutt

Farmers Branch, City of
13000 William Dodson Pkwy.
Farmers Branch, TX 75234

(214) 247-3131
Personnel Specialist: Sondra Coldwell

Forest Hill, City of
6800 Forest Hill Dr.
Forest Hill, TX 76140
(817) 293-3695
Contact: Department Head

Fort Worth, City of
1000 Throckmorton St.
Fort Worth, TX 76102
(817) 871-8900
Temporary Services Coordinator: Barbara Reyna

Garland, City of
203 N. 5th St.
Garland, TX 75040
(214) 205-2000
Jobline (214) 205-2349
Contact: Personnel Department

Grand Prairie, City of
326 W. Main St.
Grand Prairie, TX 75050
(214) 660-8190
Contact: Personnel Department

Grapevine, City of
413 S. Main St.
Grapevine, TX 76051
Metro (817) 481-0300
Contact: Personnel Department

Haltom City, City of
5024 Broadway Ave.
Haltom City, TX 76117
J(817) 834-7341
Personnel Assistant: Ruby Leath

Highland Park, Town of
4700 Drexel Dr.
Dallas, TX 75205
(214) 521-4161
Contact: Personnel Department

Hurst, City of
1505 Precinct Line Rd.
Hurst, TX 76054
(817) 788-7000
Personnel Manager: Doris Elston

Irving, City of
825 W. Irving Blvd.
Irving, TX 75061
(214) 721-2532
Contact: Personnel Department

Lake Worth, City of
6720 Telephone Rd.
Lake Worth, TX 76135
(817) 237-1211
Personnel: Dorothy Praily

Lancaster, City of
211 N. Henry St.
Lancaster, TX 75146
(214) 227-2111
Assistant City Manager: Evelyn Kelly

Mansfield, City of
1305 E. Broad St.
Mansfield, TX 76063
(817) 473-9371
Personnel Officer: Barbara Parker

Mesquite, City of
1515 N. Galloway Ave.
Mesquite, TX 75149
(214) 216-6218
Personnel: Karen Skidmore

North Richland Hills, City of
7301 NE Loop 820
North Richland Hills, TX 76180
(817) 581-5500
Personnel Director: Ron McKinney

Plano, City of
1520 Ave. K
Plano, TX 75074
(214) 424-6531
Joblines: Professional (214) 578-7116; and Maintenance
(214) 578-7117
Contact: Personnel Department

Richardson, City of
411 W. Arapaho Rd.
Richardson, TX 75080
(214) 238-4150
Jobline: (214) 238-4151
Contact: Personnel Department

Richland Hills, City of
3200 Diana Dr.
Richland Hills, TX 76118
(817) 595-6600
City Secretary: Terri Willis

Saginaw, City of
333 W. McLeroy Blvd.
Saginaw, TX 76179
(817) 232-4640
Payroll Supervisor: Sharon Rogers

Seagoville, City of
702 N. Hwy. 175
Seagoville, TX 75159
(214) 287-2050
Personnel Director: Cindy Brown

University Park, City of
3800 University Blvd.
Dallas, TX 75205
(214) 363-1644
Personnel Director: Louanne Best

Watauga, City of
7101 Whitley Rd.
Watauga, TX 76148
(817) 281-8047
City Receptionist: Sandy Toney

EMPLOYERS, COUNTY GOVERNMENT:

Dallas County
1500 Marilla
Dallas, TX 75201
(214) 670-3552
Contact: Personnel Department

Tarrant County
100 E. Weatherford St.
Fort Worth, TX 76196
(817) 884-1188
Personnel Director: Gerald Wright

EMPLOYERS, STATE OF TEXAS:

Fort Worth State School
5000 Campus Dr.
Fort Worth, TX 76119
(817) 534-4831
Assistant Personnel Director: Francis Sherbert

Human Services
Regional Office
631 106th St.
Arlington, TX 76011
Metro (817) 640-5090
Contact: Personnel Office

Parks & Wildlife
Fort Worth Office
5400 Airport Frwy., Suite E
Fort Worth, TX 76117
(817) 831-3128
Contact: Office Manager

Public Health
Region 5 Office
2561 Matlock Rd.
Arlington, TX 76015
Metro (817) 261-2911
Contact: Personnel Department

Public Safety
Region 1
350 W. Interstate 30
Garland, TX 75043
(214) 226-7611
Contact: Personnel Department

Public Safety
Fort Worth District Office
624 NE Loop 820
Hurst, TX 76053
(817) 284-1490

Rehabilitation Commission
Regional Office
3005 Alta Mere Dr.
Fort Worth, TX 76116
(817) 731-7343
Human Resource Officer: Jesus Quiroga

Texas Department of Transportation
Dallas District Office
9700 E. R. L. Thornton Frwy.
Dallas, TX 75228
(214) 320-6100
District Human Resources Officer: Stephen D. Thomas

Texas Department of Transportation, Highway Division
Fort Worth District Office
2501 SW Loop 820
Fort Worth, TX 76133

(817) 292-6510
Contact: Personnel Department

Texas Employment Commission
Administrative Office
8300 John W. Carpenter Frwy.
Irving, TX 75247
(214) 631-6050
Contact: Personnel Office

EMPLOYERS, UNITED STATES GOVERNMENT:

Agriculture Department
Food & Nutrition Division
1100 Commerce St., Room 5C 30
Dallas, TX 75242
(214) 767-0224
Personnel Specialists: Lupe Gomez, Cindy Guy, or Alex Annan

Agriculture Department
Fruit and Vegetable Division
819 Taylor St., Room 8B08
Fort Worth, TX 76102
(817) 633-1211
Director: Bryon White

Army Corps of Engineers
Fort Worth District Office
819 Taylor St., Room 4A18
Fort Worth, TX 76102
(817) 334-2208
Contact: Shirley Reece, Chief of Recruitment and Placement Division.

Carswell Air Force Base
301 SPTG/ DPCS
Carswell Air Force Base, TX 76127
(817) 782-7044
Contact: Chief of Civilian Personnel or Texas Employment Commission

Defense, Department of
106 Decker Ct., Suite 300
Irving, TX 75062-2795
(214) 650-4878
Contact: Personnel RCP-3

Education, Department of
Regional Office
1200 Main Tower Bldg., Room 2125
Dallas, TX 75202

(214) 767-3651
Personnel Director: Pauline Torres

Environmental Protection Agency
Regional Office
1445 Ross Ave.
Dallas, TX 75202
(214) 655-6444
Contact: Personnel Director

Federal Bureau of Investigation
Dallas Office
1801 N. Lamar St., Suite 300
Dallas, TX 75202
(214) 720-2200
Applicant Coordinator: Stanley Chapman

General Services Administration
Personnel Division
819 Taylor St., 7CPT
Fort Worth, TX 76102
(817) 334-2361
Contact: Personnel Department

Health & Human Services, Dept. of
Dallas Office
1200 Main Tower, Suite 930
Dallas, TX 75202
(214) 767-3126
Jobline: (214) 767-4930
Contact: Staffing Specialist

Housing & Urban Development, Dept. of
Fort Worth Office
1600 Throckmorton St.
Fort Worth, TX 76102
(817) 885-5541
Personnel Officer: James G. Garcia, Jr.

Internal Revenue Service
Dallas Office
IRS Personnel
1100 Commerce St., Room 11A20
Dallas, TX 75242
(214) 742-2440
Staffing Specialist: Rose Riley

Interstate Commerce Commission
Fort Worth Office
411 W. 7th St., Suite 510
Fort Worth, TX 76102

(817) 334-3101
Contact: Mail resume to office

Justice, Department of
Dallas Office, Anti-trust Division
1100 Commerce St., Room 8C6
Dallas, TX 75242
(214) 767-8051
Office Service Specialist: Lucy Lumbreras

Justice, Department of
Fort Worth Office
801 Cherry St., Suite 1700
Fort Worth, TX 76102-6897
(817) 334-3291
Personnel Officer: Janie Esclavon

Labor, Department of
Office of Information
525 Griffin St.
Dallas, TX 75202
(214) 767-6812
Contact: Personnel Department

Labor, Department of
Fort Worth Office, Room 7A08
819 Taylor St.
Fort Worth, TX 76102
(817) 581-7303
Contact: Dallas Labor Department office

Personnel Management, Office of
1100 Commerce St., Room 6B12
Dallas, TX 75242
(214) 767-8235
Jobline: (214) 767-8035
Contact: Write for job listings

Postal Service
Main Post Office-Dallas
951 W. Bethel Rd.
Coppell, TX 75099
(214) 393-6780
Contact: Personnel Department

Postal Service
Main Post Office-Fort Worth
4600 Mark IV Pkwy.
Fort Worth, TX 76161
(817) 625-3366
Contact: Personnel Department

Small Business Administration
Regional Office
8625 King George Dr., Building C
Dallas, TX 75235
(214) 767-7649
Contact: Personnel

Transportation, Department of
Southwest Regional Office
DOT, Federal Aviation Administration
4400 Blue Mound Rd.
Fort Worth, TX 76193
(817) 624-5838
Contact: Recruitment Section

Treasury, Department of
Dallas Office
1200 Main St., Room 2550
Dallas, TX 75202
(214) 767-2250
Management Analyst: Sharon Rhine

Veterans Administration
Dallas Office
1114 Commerce St., Suite 218
Dallas, TX 75242
Contact: Office of Personnel Management

Health Care

Also check out the section on **Human Services.**

For networking in the health care industry, check out the following professional organizations listed in Chapter 5:

PROFESSIONAL ORGANIZATIONS:

American Association of Medical Assistants
American Association for Respiratory Care
Christian Medical and Dental Society
Dallas County Chiropractic Society
Dallas County Dental Society
Dallas Dietetic Association
Dallas Group Psychotherapy Society
Dallas Metropolitan Black Nurses Association
Dallas Psychological Association
Fort Worth District Dental Society
North Texas Optometric Society

For additional information, you can contact:

American Dental Association
211 E. Chicago Ave.
Chicago, IL 60611
(312) 440-2500

American Health Care Association
1201 L St., NW
Washington, DC 20005
(202) 842-4444

American Hospital Association
840 N. Lake Shore Dr.
Chicago, IL 60611
(312) 280-6000

American Medical Association
515 N. State St.
Chicago, IL 60610
(312) 464-5000

American Public Health Association
1015 15th St., NW
Washington, DC 20005
(202) 789-5600

Federation of American Health Systems
1111 19th St., NW

Washington, DC 20036
(202) 833-3090

PROFESSIONAL PUBLICATIONS:

ADA News
AHA News
American Journal of Medicine
American Journal of Nursing
American Journal of Public Health
HMO Practice
Hospital & Health Services Administration
Hospitals
Modern Healthcare
Nations Health
Nursing Outlook

DIRECTORIES:

AHA Guide to the Health Care Field (American Hospital Association, Chicago, IL)
Directory of Hospital Personnel (Medical Device Register, Stamford, CT)
Medical & Health Information Directory (Gale Research Co., Detroit, MI)
Saunders Health Care Directory (W.B. Saunders, Philadelphia, PA)

EMPLOYERS:

All Saints Episcopal Hospital
1400 Eighth Ave.
Fort Worth, TX 76104
(817) 926-2544
Contact: Personnel Department

Alliance Health Providers
1400 S. Main St., Suite 414
Fort Worth, TX 76104
(817) 332-4537
Contact: Lovie Pollinger

Arlington Memorial Hospital
800 W. Randol Mill Rd.
Arlington, TX 76012
Metro (817) 265-5581
Personnel Director: Aleyne Brochet

Baylor Medical Center at Garland
2300 Marie Curie Dr.

Garland, TX 75042
(214) 487-5000
Contact: Personnel Office

Baylor University Medical Center
3500 Gaston Ave.
Dallas, TX 75246
(214) 820-1111
Assistant Personnel Director: Beverly Bradshaw

CIGNA Healthplan
600 E. Las Colinas Blvd.
Irving, TX 75039
(214) 401-5347
Contact: Human Resources

Cook's Fort Worth Children's Medical Center
801 Seventh Ave.
Fort Worth, TX 76104
(817) 885-4000
Personnel Director: David Blackwell

Corphealth Inc.
1300 Summit Ave.
Fort Worth, TX 76102
(817) 654-2440
Contact: Patrick Gotcher

Dallas/Fort Worth Medical Center
2709 Hospital Blvd.
Grand Prairie, TX 75051
Metro (214) 647-1141
Employee Coordinator: Linda Cox

Dallas VA Medical Center
4500 S. Lancaster Rd.
Dallas, TX 75216
(214) 376-5451
Staffing Specialist: Kim Fenton

Fort Worth Osteopathic Medical Center
1000 Montgomery St.
Fort Worth, TX 76107
(817) 735-3535
Contact: Personnel Office

Garland Community Hospital
2696 W. Walnut
Garland, TX 75042
(214) 276-7116
Personnel Director: Ed Winkelmeyer

Grapevine Medical Center
1650 W. College St.
Grapevine, TX 76051
Metro (817) 481-1588
Jobline: (817) 329-2677

HCA Medical Center of Plano
3901 W. 15th St.
Plano, TX 75075
(214) 519-1174
Contact: Personnel Department

HCA Medical Plaza Hospital
900 Eighth Ave.
Fort Worth, TX 76104
(817) 336-2100
Jobline: 1. Professional, Certified or Licensed (817) 347-5793
2. All other (817) 347-5763
Human Resources Director: Sarah Spinharney

HCA South Arlington Medical Center
3301 Matlock Rd.
Arlington, TX 76015
Metro (817) 467-7486
Contact: Personnel Department

Harris Hospital-H.E.B.
1600 Hospital Pkwy.
Bedford, TX 76022
Metro (817) 355-7950
Contact: Personnel Department

Harris Methodist Fort Worth
1301 Pennsylvania Ave.
Fort Worth, TX 76104
(817) 882-2000
Employment Supervisor: Harvey Raymond

Harris Methodist Health Plan
1300 Summit , Suite 300
Fort Worth, TX 76102
(817) 878-5831
Contact Human Resources

Humana Hospital—Medical City Dallas
7777 Forest Lane
Dallas, TX 75230
(214) 661-7000
Contact: Personnel Department

Irving Community Hospital
1901 N. MacArthur Blvd.

Irving, TX 75061
(214) 579-8100
Recruitment Manager: Linda Bryan

Kaiser Foundation Health Plan of Texas
12720 Hillcrest Rd.
Dallas, TX 75230
(214) 458-5000
Contact: Human Resources

Medical Care International
5080 Spectrum Ave., Suite 300 W.
Dallas, TX 75248
(214) 581-2600
Director of Employee Benefits: Connie Pritchett

Medical Control
9649 Webbs Chapel Rd.
Dallas, TX 75220
(214) 352-2666
Contact: J. Ward Hunt

Mesquite Community Hospital
3500 Hwy. I 30
Mesquite, TX 75150
(214) 270-3300
Personnel: Cindy Selph

Methodist Medical Center
1441 N. Beckley
Dallas, TX 75265
(214) 944-8181
Contact: Personnel Department

Metlife Healthcare Network of Texas
1320 Greenway, Suite 400
Irving TX 75038
(214) 751-0777

Network for Physical Therapy
P.O. Box 515837
Dallas TX 75251
(214) 991-7191
Contact: Alan Morris

Northeast Community Hospital
1301 Airport Frwy.
Bedford, TX 76021
(817) 283-6700
Contact: Personnel Office

North Texas Healthcare Network
5501 N. MacArthur Blvd.
Irving, TX 75038
(214) 751-0047
Contact: Charles R. Coil

Parkland Memorial Hospital
5201 Harry Hines Blvd.
Dallas, TX 75235
(214) 590-8000
Contact: Personnel Department

Planned Behavioral Health Care
9535 Forest Lane
Dallas, TX 75243
(214) 680-0400
Contact: Joyce Ramay

Presbyterian Hospital of Dallas
8200 Walnut Hill Lane
Dallas, TX 75231
(214) 696-7863
Contact: Personnel Department

ProAmerica Managed Care
714 Main St.
Fort Worth, TX 76102
(817) 523-3669
Contact: Nancy Connaway

Provider Networks of America
4100 International Plaza, #180
Fort Worth, TX 76109
(800) 462-7554
Contact: Allen Rafeh

PruCare of North Texas
4100 Alpha Rd.
Dallas, TX 75244
(214) 991-0014
Contact: Human Resources

R.H.D. Memorial Medical Center
7 Medical Pkwy.
Farmers Branch, TX 75381
(214) 247-1000
Contact: Personnel Department

Richardson Medical Center
401 W. Campbell Rd.
Richardson, TX 75080

Metro (214) 231-1441
Contact: Personnel Department

St. Joseph Hospital
1401 S. Main St.
Fort Worth, TX 76104
(817) 336-9371
Contact: Personnel Department

St. Paul Medical Center
5909 Harry Hines Blvd.
Dallas, TX 75235
(214) 879-1000
Nurse Recruiter: Carey Morris
Allied Recruiter: Mary Hunt

Sanus Texas Health Plan
4500 Fuller Dr.
Irving, TX 75038
(214) 791-3900
Contact: Department Heads

Smith, John Peter, Hospital
1500 S. Main St.
Fort Worth, TX 76104
(817) 921-3431
Contact: Personnel Department

Southwestern Aetna Health Plan
2750 Lakeside Blvd., Suite 500
Richardson, TX 75082
(214) 470-7832

Texas Scottish Rite Hospital
2222 Welborn St.
Dallas, TX 75219
(214) 521-3168
Director of Human Resources: Denise Montazeri

Timberlawn Psychiatric Hospital
4600 Samuell Blvd.
Dallas, TX 75228
(214) 381-7181
Recruitment Director: Sheryl Howard

Travelers Health Network of Texas
2250 Lakeside Blvd., Suite 330
Richardson, TX 75082
(214) 263-8899
Contact: Human Resources

Trinity Health Network
1612 Summit Ave.
Fort Worth, TX 76102
(817) 336-1044
Contact: Larry Olive

USA Healthnet of Texas
400 E. Las Colinas Blvd., Suite 450
Irving, TX 75 039
(214) 869-6900
Contact: Human Resources

Vencor Fort Worth Hospital
1802 Hwy. 157 North
Mansfield, TX 76063
(817) 473-6101
Executive Secretary: Michele Shero

Hotels/Motels/Conventions

You might also want to look at the section on **Restaurants.**

For information about the hospitality industry and related fields, you can contact these professional organizations.

PROFESSIONAL ORGANIZATIONS:

American Hotel & Motel Association
1201 New York Ave., NW, Suite 600
Washington, DC 20005-3931
(202) 289-3100

Hotel Sales & Marketing Association International
1300 L St., NW
Washington, DC 20005
(202) 789-0089

International Association of Exposition Managers
1 College Park
Indianapolis, IN 46268
(317) 871-7272

International Special Events Society
8335 Allison Point Trail, Suite 1100
Indianapolis, IN 46250
(800) 688-4737

Meeting Planners International Infomart
1950 Stemmons Freeway
Dallas, TX 75207
(214) 712-7700

PROFESSIONAL PUBLICATIONS:

Hotel & Motel Management
Lodging Magazine
Meeting Manager
Meeting News
Meetings & Conventions

DIRECTORIES:

Directory of Hotel and Motel Systems (American Hotel Association, Directory Corporation, Washington, DC)
Hotel and Motel Red Book (American Hotel and Motel Association, Washington, DC)

How to Get a Job

Meetings and Conventions Directory Issue (Murdock Magazines, New York, NY)
Membership Directory (Meeting Planners International, Dallas, TX)
Successful Meetings Sourcebook (Bill Communications, New York, NY)
Who's Who in Exposition Management (International Association of Exposition Managers, Indianapolis, IN)

EMPLOYERS:

Adolphus Hotel
1321 Commerce St.
Dallas, TX 75202
(214) 742-8200
Personnel Director: Karen Ranker

Clarion Hotel
1241 W. Mockingbird Lane
Dallas, TX 75247
(214) 630-7000
Contact: Human Resources

Crescent Court Hotel
400 Crescent Court
Dallas, TX 75201
(214) 871-3200
Contact: Personnel Department

Dallas/Fort Worth Airport Marriott
8440 Freeport Pkwy.
Irving, TX 75063
(214) 929-8800
Human Resources Director: Kitty Meyers

Dallas Grand Hotel
1914 Commerce St.
Dallas, TX 75201
(214) 747-7000
Contact: Personnel Department

Dallas Marriott Park Central
7750 LBJ Frwy.
Dallas, TX 75251
(817) 233-4421
Contact: Human Resources

Dallas Marriott Quorum
14901 Dallas Pkwy.
Dallas, TX 75240
(214) 661-2800
Director of Human Resources: Bob O'Brien

DMC Exposition
1605 N. Stemmons Frwy.
Dallas, TX 75235
(214)744-3131

Doubletree at Lincoln Center
5410 LBJ Frwy.
Dallas, TX 75240
(214) 934-8400
Contact: Human Resources

Embassy Suites Hotel
3880 W. Northwest Hwy.
Dallas, TX 75220
(214) 357-4500
Director of Human Resources: Kassy Tanner

Fairmont Hotel
1717 N. Akard St.
Dallas, TX 75201
(214) 720-2020
Personnel Director: Ray Hassan

Four Seasons Hotel and Resort
4150 N. MacArthur Blvd.
Irving, TX 75038
(214) 717-0700
Human Resources Manager: Brenda Ruben

Grand Kempinski Dallas, The
15201 Dallas Pkwy.
Dallas, TX 75248
(214) 386-6000
Contact: Personnel Department

Green Oaks Inn/Conference Center
6901 West Frwy.
Fort Worth, TX 76116
(817) 738-7311
Personnel Director: Karin Naron

Harvey Hotel-DFW Airport
4545 W. John Carpenter Frwy.
Irving, TX 75063
(214) 929-4500
Personnel Manager: Olivia Monograss

Hyatt Regency Dallas
300 Reunion Blvd.
Dallas, TX 75207
(214) 651-1234
Employment Manager: Cheryl Chabot

Hyatt Regency DFW
P.O. Box 619014
International Pkwy.
DFW Airport, TX 75261
(214) 453-8400
Employment Manager: Donna Golden

Loews Anatole Hotel
2201 N. Stemmons Frwy.
Dallas, TX 75207
(214) 748-1200
Director of Personnel: Carole Kohn

Mansion on Turtle Creek Hotel, The
2821 Turtle Creek Blvd.
Dallas, TX 75219
(214) 559-2100
Contact: Human Resources

Plaza of the Americas Hotel
650 N. Pearl St.
Dallas, TX 75201
(214) 979-9000
Human Resources Director: Linda Wissen

Radisson Suite Hotel
700 E. Ave. H
Arlington, TX 76011
Metro (817) 640-0440
Contact: Department Head

Sheraton Inn Mockingbird West
1893 W. Mockingbird Lane
Dallas, TX 75235
(214) 634-8850
Assistant General Manager: Reaz Chaudhry

Sheraton Park Central Hotel
12720 Merit Dr.
Dallas, TX 75251
(214) 385-3000
Director of Human Resources: Sheila Jackson

Show Management
3100 Carlisle St.
Dallas TX 75201
(214) 871-9514

Stouffer Dallas Hotel
2222 Stemmons Frwy.
Dallas, TX 75207

(214) 631-2222
Personnel Assistant: Laurie Strum

TWI International Exhibition Services
9103 Vista Creek Dr.
Dallas, TX 75219
(214) 748-5044

Westin Hotel Galleria, The
13340 Dallas Pkwy.
Dallas, TX 75240
(214) 934-9494
Personnel Director: Patty Evans

Worthington Hotel
200 Main St.
Fort Worth, TX 76102
(817) 870-1000
Contact: Personnel

**Big rewards in
hospitality business**

The hotel business offers people unparalleled opportunities, says a managing director of a large Dallas hotel. Often, executives work their way up from the bottom as he did.

While still in high school, this manager began busing tables and working as a waiter and bartender. He didn't intend to stay in the business after college graduation until he realized that he could get a better job at a hotel than in another field.

He moved swiftly through the ranks from catering director to food and beverage manager and finally to general manager of one of the largest hotels in the Southwest.

He advises aspiring hotel managers to get a degree in business and be willing to start in a less glamorous position to establish a solid understanding of the operation.

"The hotel business is more of a lifestyle than a career because of the odd hours of working on holidays and weekends," he says. "But the rewards are great for people who prove their abilities." ■

Human Services

Also check out the section on **Health Care.**

For more information, you can contact:

PROFESSIONAL ORGANIZATIONS:

Center for Human Services
5530 Wisconsin Ave.
Chevy Chase, MD 20815

National Association of Social Workers
750 1st St., NE
Washington, DC 20002
(202) 408-8600

Volunteers of America
3813 N. Causeway Blvd.
Metairie, LA 70002
(504) 836-5225

PROFESSIONAL PUBLICATIONS:

Children and Youth Services
The Nonprofit Times
Society

DIRECTORIES:

Directory of Agencies (National Association of Social Workers, Washington, DC)
Directory of Community Resources for Fort Worth and Tarrant County (United Way, Fort Worth, TX)
Directory of Hotlines and Crisis Intervention Centers (Covenant House, New York, NY)
Directory of Services (Community Council of Greater Dallas)
National Directory of Children and Youth Services (Marion Peterson, Longmont, CO)
National Directory of Private Social Agencies (Croner Publications, Queens Village, NY)

EMPLOYERS:

American Cancer Society
Area V Office
8900 John Carpenter Frwy.
Dallas, TX 75247
(214) 631-3850

Contact: Personnel Department
Charitable organization that provides counseling, cancer screening, public and professional education, and conducts research.

American Cancer Society
Texas Division
2501 Parkview, Suite 100
Fort Worth, TX 76102
(817) 335-1500
Contact: Department Head
Parallels Dallas office.

American Heart Association
National Center Office
7320 Greenville Ave.
Dallas, TX 75231
(214) 373-6300
Contact: Personnel Department
Volunteer health association for science, research, and education.

American Red Cross
Dallas County Chapter
2300 McKinney Ave.
Dallas, TX 75201
(214) 871-2175
Contact: Human Resources Department
Services provided for military families, 24-hour disaster assistance, and community volunteer programs.

American Red Cross
Tarrant County Chapter
1515 Sylvania Ave.
Fort Worth, TX 76111
(817) 335-9137
Contact: Personnel Department
Provides first-aid classes, disaster training programs, community volunteer service, military family assistance, and transportation for the elderly.

Arthritis Foundation
3145 McCart Ave.
Fort Worth, TX 76110
(817) 926-7733
Executive Director: Marty Cook
Public education and special help for arthritis victims.

Association for Retarded Citizens
National Headquarters
P.O. Box 1047
Arlington, TX 76004
Metro (817) 261-6003
Contact: Personnel Department

Information and referral services for mentally retarded and their families. Also includes respite care, citizen advocacy, and continuing education for mentally retarded adults.

Boy Scouts of America
National Office
1325 Walnut Hill Lane
Irving, TX 75015
(214) 580-2122
Contact: Employment Office
Headquarters for national organization that sponsors education and character-building programs for boys seven years old through high school.

Boys' and Girls' Club of Greater Dallas
4816 Worth St.
Dallas, TX 75246
(214) 821-2950
Controller: Craig Price
Physical, educational, and vocational guidance program for boys and girls between the ages of 6 and 18.

Buckner Baptist Benevolences
5200 S. Buckner Blvd.
Dallas, TX 75227
(214) 328-3141
Contact: Department Head
Baptist General Convention of Texas supports adoption services, Buckner's Children's Home, Ryburn Home For Aging, and Mary E. Trew Home for Aging.

Catholic Charities Diocese of Dallas
3845 Oak Lawn Ave.
Dallas, TX 75219
(214) 526-2772
Administrator: Sharon Hoskin
Manages the Catholic Counseling Service, Marillac Social Center, St. Joseph Youth Center, St. Joseph Residence, and migration and refugee services.

Catholic Charities Diocese of Fort Worth
1300 S. Lake St.
Fort Worth, TX 76104
(817) 926-1231
Contact: Department Head
Programs for underprivileged families, counseling, and foster care. Also manages St. Theresa's Home.

Community Council of Greater Dallas
2121 Main St., Suite 500
Dallas, TX 75201
(214) 741-5851

Financial Officer: Vicki White
Organization for public and non-profit voluntary service agencies.
Council provides information and referral to social services,
publishes a directory, conducts surveys, and provides management assistance and planning.

Dallas County Mental Health and Mental Retardation Center
1341 W. Mockingbird Lane, Suite 1000 E
Dallas, TX 75247
(214) 637-4600
Contact: Personnel Department
Comprehensive community mental health and mental retardation
program with hospital, day treatment, and outpatient services.

Fort Worth State School
5000 Campus Dr.
Fort Worth, TX 76119
Metro (817) 429-0810
Personnel: Francis Sherbert
Residential campus and non-residential programs for mentally
retarded.

Girl Scout Council
4411 Skillman Ave.
Dallas, TX 75206
(214) 823-1342
Assistant Executive Director: Sue Duran
Worldwide organization for girls between the ages of 5 and 17.

Gladney, Edna, Center
2300 Hemphill St.
Fort Worth, TX 76110
Metro (817) 429-1461
Director of Maternity Services: Elaine Brown
Unwed mother services and adoption agency.

Goodwill Industries of Dallas
2800 N. Hampton Rd.
Dallas, TX 75212
(214) 638-2800
Personnel Manager: Joy Jones
Rehabilitation services for handicapped adults. Operates stores
with donated and repaired merchandise. Has job placement and
vocational testing departments.

Jewish Federation of Greater Dallas
7800 Northaven Rd., Suite A
Dallas, TX 75230
(214) 369-3313
Contact: Personnel Director
Plans and coordinates health, recreation, and social services for

the Dallas Jewish community, including the Dallas Home For Jewish Aged, Jewish Community Center of Dallas, and Jewish Family Services.

Jewish Federation of Fort Worth and Tarrant County
6801 Dan Danciger Rd.
Fort Worth, TX 76133
(817) 292-3081
Director of Counseling: Michele Adler
Provides professional social work and counseling services in the areas of marriage and family counseling, individual counseling, vocational counseling, information and referrals.

March of Dimes, Birth Defects Foundation
North Texas Chapter
5720 LBJ Frwy., Suite 180
Dallas, TX 75240
Metro (214) 988-7126
Director of Operations: Richard Stout
Provides public health education, conducts fund-raising campaigns, and provides services for polio patients.

Mothers Against Drunk Driving
National Headquarters
511 E. John Carpenter Frwy.
Dallas, TX 75062
Personnel Manager: Debbie Owing
Provides education for responsible drinking.

Multiple Sclerosis Association
Tarrant County
617 Seventh Ave., Suite 405
Fort Worth, TX 76104
(817) 877-1222
Executive Director: Carole Sue Wheeler
Counseling, support groups, group aquatic exercises, neurological exercises, and education.

Multiple Sclerosis Society
North Texas Chapter
8214 Westchester Dr.
Dallas, TX 75225
(214) 373-1400
Administrative Assistant: Diane Jochum
Sponsors education programs, supports research, and provides patient services and counseling.

National Kidney Foundation of Texas
13500 Midway Rd., Suite 101
Dallas, TX 75244
(214) 934-8057
Executive Director: Marlin Roberts

Provides education about kidney disease, supports research, and sponsors organ donor program.

Sickle Cell Anemia Association of Texas
2914 E. Rosedale
Fort Worth, TX 76105
(817) 534-5997
Office Manager: Linda Green
Screening, counseling, and educational programs.

Tarrant County Mental Health & Mental Retardation Services
1319 Summit Ave.
Fort Worth, TX 76102
(817) 884-1258
Contact: Personnel Department
Provides treatment, training, and social services for mental health patients in Tarrant County, including programs for the elderly, alcohol center, family services, diagnosis service, sheltered workshops, and industrial training for the retarded.

United Way of Metropolitan Dallas
901 Ross Ave.
Dallas, TX 75202
(214) 978-0000
V.P. of Human Resources: Calvin Smith
Voluntary non-profit organization providing support to local, state, and national health agencies, family agencies, and character-building organizations. Conducts annual fund-raising campaign. Coordinates allocations of contributed funds.

United Way of Metropolitan Tarrant County
210 E. Ninth St.
Fort Worth, TX 76102
(817) 878-0000
Contact: Department Head
Parallels Dallas division.

YMCA-Dallas Metropolitan Offices
601 N. Akard St.
Dallas, TX 75201
(214) 880-9622
V.P. of Human Resources and Training: Vera Mackie
Recreational and social activities for all ages and sexes at 23 area branches.

YMCA-Tarrant County Offices
540 Lamar St.
Fort Worth, TX 76102
(817) 335-6147
Contact: Personnel or individual branches

Offers similar programs as Dallas YMCA at 11 Tarrant County centers.

YWCA-Metropolitan Dallas
4621 Ross Ave.
Dallas, TX 75204
(214) 821-9595
Contact: Department Head
Provides social and recreational activities, licensed day care, and year-round special programs at seven branches.

YWCA-Tarrant County
512 W. Fourth St.
Fort Worth, TX 76102
(817) 332-6191
Contact: Personnel Department
Provides residential and support services for women, child care, Y-Teens, and handicapped programs.

Employment programs for older workers

Job-hunting techniques that work for younger people aren't always as effective for individuals over the age of 50, says Wayne Snyder, a retired volunteer for the AARP. The good-ol'-boy network begins breaking down for senior citizens as their friends retire.

It's especially hard on people who didn't plan on working past a certain age and thought they could live off savings, Social Security benefits, or pensions. Everyone thinks, this won't happen to me, but inflation and health costs can wipe out savings.

The following organizations run programs to help older workers gain employment.

The **AARP** provides a 25-hour course in career change and employment search designed especially for the mature worker. The content is appropriate for executive as well as administrative people. The cost is $35.

American Association of Retired Persons (AARP)
8144 Walnut Hill Lane, Suite 700
Dallas, TX 75231
(214) 361-3060

Forty Plus is a self-help peer support group for unemployed professionals over age 40. Program offers a mentor system, weekly guest speakers, mock interviews, and use of office facilities. Fee is $750 plus monthly dues.

Forty Plus of Dallas
301 E. Carillon Tower
13140 Coit Rd., Suite 300
Dallas, TX 75240
(214) 783-2300

IATREIA/Outpath Job Search Club is a professionally managed program which meets weekly on Thursday evenings. This is a cost-effective group program conducted by professional career counselors. New groups begin each month.

IATREIA/Outpath
1152 Country Club Lane
Fort Worth, TX 76112
(817) 654-9600
Contact: Rob Rainey

Prime Timers, a Dallas-based contract and temporary help firm, specializes in assisting workers over the age of 40. With six locations throughout the Metroplex, they have become a reliable source of dependable, mature workers for area companies of all sizes.

Prime Timers
5550 LBJ Frwy.
Dallas, TX 75242
(214) 386-8040
Contact: R. Jay Freeman ■

Insurance

For networking in insurance and related fields, check out the following professional organizations listed in Chapter 5:

PROFESSIONAL ORGANIZATIONS:

Dallas Association of Life Underwriters
Independent Insurance Agents of Dallas
Insurance Women of Dallas
Insurance Women of Fort Worth

For additional information, you can contact:

Amercian Council of Life Insurance
1001 Pennsylvania Ave., NW
Washington, DC 20004-2599
(202) 624-2000

American Insurance Association
1130 Connecticut Ave., NW
Washington, DC 20036
(202) 828-7100

National Association of Life Underwriters
1922 F St., NW
Washington, DC 20006
(202) 331-6000

Society of Certified Insurance Counselors
P.O. Box 27027
Austin, TX 78755-1027
(512) 345-7932

PROFESSIONAL PUBLICATIONS:

Best's Review
Business Insurance
Independent Agent
Insurance Advocate
The Insurance Agent
Insurance Times
National Underwriter
Underwriter's Report

DIRECTORIES:

Best's Directory of Insurance Agencies (A.M. Best Co., Oldwick, NY)

Best's Insurance Reports (A.M. Best Co., Oldwick, NY)
Insurance Almanac (Underwriter Publishing Co., Englewood, NJ)
Texas Insurance Directory (Insurance Field Co., Louisville, KY)
Underwriters Handbook (National Underwriter Company, Cincinnati, OH)

EMPLOYERS:

Aetna Life & Casualty
2350 Lakeside Blvd.
Richardson, TX 75082
(214) 470-7000
Commercial Division: Donna Waller

Alexander & Alexander of Texas
Dallas Office
717 N. Harwood St., 19th Floor
Dallas, TX 75201
Metro (214) 263-1366
Human Resource Director: Meryl Frank

Alexander & Alexander of Texas
Fort Worth Office
6100 Western Place, Suite 1000
Fort Worth, TX 76107
Metro (817) 429-3653
Personnel Administrator: Laure Yancy

Allianz Life Insurance Co. of North America
P.O. Box 500
Dallas, TX 75221
(214) 978-7004
Contact: Human Resources

Allstate Insurance Co.
8711 Freeport Pkwy.
Irving, TX 75063
Metro (214) 915-5000
Human Resources Manager: Bill Ayo

American Life & Accident Insurance Co.
2909 N. Buckner Blvd.
Dallas, TX 75228
(214) 321-9700
Personnel Director: Chris Gaddis

Associates Insurance Group
250 E. John Carpenter Frwy.
Irving, TX 75062
(214) 541-3800
Contact: Human Resources Department

Auto Club Insurance Agency
4425 N. Central Expwy.
Dallas, TX 75205
(214) 526-7911
Personnel: Melanie Osborn

Blue Cross-Blue Shield of Texas
901 S. Central Expwy.
Richardson, TX 75080
Metro (214) 669-5364
Contact: Employment Department

Chubb Group of Insurance Companies
717 N. Harwood St., Suite 300
Dallas, TX 75201
(214) 754-0777
Human Resources Manager: Janice Wilsford

Combined Insurance Co. of America
1345 Riverbend, Suite 200
Dallas, TX 75247
(214) 905-3466
Contact: Personnel Department

Commercial Union Insurance Co.
9229 LBJ Frwy., Suite 200
Dallas, TX 75243-3405
(214) 783-6100
Recruiting Director: Ruby Jones

Corrigan Jordan Insurance Agency
4301 Westside, Suite 200
Dallas, TX 75209
(214) 528-3210
Office Manager: Jo Enzone

Employers Insurance of Texas
1301 Young St.
Dallas, TX 75202
(214) 760-6100
Contact: Human Resources

Fireman's Fund Insurance Co.
1999 Bryan St.
Dallas, TX 75201
(214) 220-4000
Recruiter: Jeanine Cremers

Great Southern Life Insurance Co.
500 N. Akard St.
Dallas, TX 75201

(214) 954-8100
Contact: Personnel Department

Group Life & Health Insurance Co.
901 S. Central Expwy.
Richardson, TX 75080
(214) 669-6900
Contact: Personnel Department

ITT Hatrford Insurance Group
5001 LBJ Frwy.
Dallas, TX 75244
(214) 980-1900
Human Resource: Jackie Robbins

Jackson National Life Insurance Co. of Texas
P.O. Box 515769
Dallas, TX 75251-5769
(214) 991-9193
Regional Vice President: Amanda Stevens

Kirby Head-Teas Insurance
One Summit Ave., Suite 400
Fort Worth, TX 76102
(817) 336-2721
Partner: Clovis Putnam

Life Insurance Co. of the Southwest
1300 W. Mockingbird Lane
Dallas, TX 75247
(214) 638-7100
Personnel: Kelly Gates

Lone Star Life Insurance Co.
4201 Spring Valley Rd.
Dallas, TX 75244
(214) 702-6400
Personnel: Rod Heninger

Millers Insurance Group
300 Burnett St.
Fort Worth, TX 76103
(817) 332-7761
Supervisor of Personnel Services: Nancy Underhill

Mutual of Omaha Insurance Co.
6263 Harry Hines Blvd.
Dallas, TX 75235
(214) 630-4100
Personnel Department

National Financial Life Insurance
403 S. Akard St.
Dallas, TX 75202
(214) 670-9700
Manager of Personnel and Payroll: Dot Pryer

National Foundation Life
777 Main St., Suite 900
Fort Worth, TX 76102
(817) 878-3300
Manager of Human Resources: Paula Hunter

National Health Insurance Co.
P.O. Box 619999
D/FW Airport, TX 75261
Metro (817) 640-1900
Personnel Assistant: Sandra Harris

Penny, J.C., Life Insurance
2700 W. Plano Pkwy.
Plano, TX 75075
(214) 881-6513
Personnel Department

Philadelphia Life Insurance Co.
(800) 525-7662
Human Resources Recruiter: Chris Babler

Republic Insurance
2727 Turtle Creek Blvd.
Dallas, TX 75219
(214) 559-1271
Director of Employee Relations: Larry Westerfield

Rigg, William, Co.
309 W. Seventh St., Suite 200
Fort Worth, TX 76102
Metro (817) 429-0040
Controller: James Couch

Southwestern Life Insurance Co.
500 N. Akard St., 6th Floor
Dallas, TX 75201
Metro (214) 954-7703
Contact Personnel Department

States General Life Insurance Co.
115 W. Seventh St., Suite 1205
Fort Worth, TX 76102
(817) 338-4395
Secretary/Treasurer: Don Morris

Texas Credit Union League and Affiliates
4455 LBJ Frwy., Suite 917
Farmers Branch, TX 75244
(214) 980-5111
Recruiter: Perry Nelson

Transport Insurance Co.
4100 Harry Hines Blvd.
Dallas, TX 75219
(214) 526-3876
Human Resources Associate: Eva Mayberry

Transport Life Insurance Co.
714 Main St., 20th Floor
Fort Worth, TX 76102
Metro (817) 429-1620
Vice President Human Resources: Jack Kocks

Travelers Insurance Co.
2270 Lakeside Blvd.
Richardson, TX 75082
(214) 470-8000
Jobline: (214) 470-8920
Contact: Personnel Department

Trinity Universal Insurance
10000 N. Central Expy
Dallas, TX 75231
(214) 360-8000
Manager of Human Resources: Lisa King

Union Bankers Insurance Co.
500 N. Akard
Dallas, TX 75201
(214) 939-0821
Director of Employee Relations: Brad Beam

United American Insurance
2909 N. Buckner Blvd.
Dallas, TX 75228
(214) 328-2841
Contact: Personnel Department

US Life Corporation
1380 River Bend Dr.
Dallas, TX 75247
(214) 631-2422
Manager of Human Resource Administration: Jan Creel

Wausau Insurance Co.
105 Decker Ct., Suite 600
Irving, TX 75062-2211

Metro (214) 650-1955
Human Resource Manager: Valerie Lee

Law Firms

For networking in law and related fields, check out the following
professional organizations listed in Chapter 5:

PROFESSIONAL ORGANIZATIONS:

Dallas Association of Black Women Attorneys
Dallas Association of Law Librarians
Dallas Association of Legal Secretaries
Dallas Association of Young Lawyers
Dallas Bar Association
Dallas Business League
Dallas Women Lawyers Association
Fort Worth/Tarrant County Young Lawyers Association
Tarrant County Bar Association
Tarrant County Women's Bar Association

For more information about the legal profession, you can contact
the following organizations:

American Bar Association
750 N. Lake Shore Dr.
Chicago, IL 60611
(312) 988-5000

Association of Trial Lawyers of America
1050 31st St., NW
Washington, DC 20007
(202) 965-3500

National Bar Association (minority attorneys)
1225 11th St., NW
Washington, DC 20001
(202) 842-3900

National Paralegal Association
6186 Honey Hollow Rd.
Solebury, PA
(215) 297-8333

PROFESSIONAL PUBLICATIONS:

ABA Journal
American Lawyer

Banking Law Journal
Criminal Law Bulletin
Lawyers' Weekly
The Paralegal
Texas Lawman
Trial

DIRECTORIES:

ABA Directory (American Bar Association, Chicago, IL)
Directory of Local Paralegal Clubs (National Paralegal Association, Solebury, PA)
Martindale-Hubbell Law Directory (Martindale-Hubbell, Summit, NJ)

EMPLOYERS:

Akin, Gump, Strauss, Hauer & Feld
4100 First City Center
1700 Pacific Ave., Suite 4100
Dallas, TX 75201
(214) 969-2800
Contact: Personnel Department

Arter, Hadden, Johnson and Bromberg
1717 Main St., Suite 4100
Dallas, TX 75201
(214) 761-2100
Contact: Bill Lott

Barlow & Garsek
3815 Lisbon St.
Fort Worth, TX 76107
(817) 731-4500
Office Manager for support positions: Marsha Stewart

Brown, Herman, Scott, Dean & Miles
203 Fort Worth Club Building
306 W. Seventh St.
Fort Worth, TX 76102
(817) 332-1391
Contact: Partners for attorney positions
Office Administrator: Debra Bales for support positions

Canty & Hanger
801 Cheery St.
Fort Worth,TX 76102
(817) 877-2800
Contact: Partners for attorney positions
Managing Partner: Allan Howeth

Carrington, Coleman, Sloman & Blumenthal
200 Crescent Court, Suite 1500
Dallas, TX 75201
(214) 855-3000
Personnel Director: Candy Dickey

Cowles & Thompson
4000 NCNB Plaza
901 Main St., Suite 4000
Dallas, TX 75202
(214) 670-1100
Recruiting Coordinator: Dwayne Hermes
Personnel Director: Shirly Sinks

Decker, Jones, McMackim, McClain, Hall & Bates
2400 City Center Tower II
301 Commerce St.
Fort Worth, TX 76102
Metro (817) 429-2740
Office Administrator: Jerry Prader

Dushman & Friedman
2620 Airport Frwy.
Fort Worth, TX 76111
(817) 834-8851
Office Manager: Larry Forderhause

Gandy, Michener, Swindle & Whitaker
3500 City Center, Tower II
Fort Worth, TX 76102
Metro (817) 429-6268
Managing Partner: John Michener

Gardere & Wynne, L.L.P.
1601 Elm, Suite 3000
Dallas, TX 75201
(214) 999-3000
Director of Recruitment: Llene Jones

Godwin, Carlton
3300 NCNB Plaza
901 Main St. , Suite 3300
Dallas, TX 75202
(214) 939-4400
Personnel Director: Linda Phillips

Harris, Finley & Bogle
777 Main, Suite 3100
Fort Worth, TX 76102
(817) 335-5050
Partner: Roland Johnson

Haynes & Boone
3100 NCNB Plaza
901 Main St., Suite 3100
Dallas, TX 75202
(214) 651-5000
Office Manager: Dee Lee

Hughes & Luce
2800 Momentum Place
1717 Main St., Suite 2800
Dallas, TX 75201
(214) 939-5500
Personnel Director: Denni Washington

Jackson & Walker
6000 NCNB Plaza
901 Main St., Suite 6000
Dallas, TX 75202
(214) 953-6000
Personnel Coordinator: Gail Horne

Jenkins & Gilchrist
1445 Ross Ave., Suite 3200
Dallas, TX 75202
(214) 855-4500
Personnel Director: Larry Cox

Johnson & Gibbs
100 Founders Square
900 Jackson St.
Dallas, TX 75202
(214) 977-9000
Recruiting Administrator: Lynn Kurtz

Jones, Day, Reavis & Pogue
2001 Ross Ave., Suite 2300
Dallas, TX 75201
(214) 220-3939
Recruiting Coordinator: Jerrie Hawley
Office Administrator: Marge Johnson

Kelly, Hart & Hallman
2500 First City Bank Tower
201 Main St., Suite 2500
Fort Worth, TX 76102
Metro (817) 429-2500
Personnel Director: Donna Gilley

Law, Snakard & Gambill
3200 Bank One Tower
Fort Worth, TX 76102

Metro (817) 429-2991
Recruiting Coordinator: Sarah Jubela

Locke Purnell Rain Harrell
2200 Ross Ave., Suite 2200
Dallas, TX 75201
(214) 740-8000
Recruiting Coordinator: Joruth Oden
Office Staff: Mark Hounce

Mankoff & Hill
3878 Oaklawn Ave., 4th Floor
Dallas, TX 75219
(214) 523-3700
Director of Human Resources: Jeannie Newell

Murphey, Moore & Bell
1300 S. University Dr., Suite 500
Fort Worth, TX 76107
(817) 336-4456
Managing Partner: Franklin Moore

Ross and Hartley
500 E. Border St., Suite 517
Arlington, TX 76010
Metro (817) 261-7711
Firm Administrator: Linda Douglas

Shannon, Gracey, Ratliff & Miller, L.L.P.
2200 Texas Commerce Tower
201 Main St.
Fort Worth, TX 76102
(817) 336-9333
Partner: John Bonds

Simon, Anisman, Doby & Wilson
303 W. Tenth St., Suite 400
Fort Worth, TX 76102
Metro (817) 429-3245
Personnel Manager: Suzy Stark

Strasburger & Price
901 Main St., Suite 4300
Dallas, TX 75202
(214) 651-4300

Thompson, Coe, Cousins & Irons
200 Crescent Ct., 11th Floor
Dallas, TX 75201-1840
(214) 871-8288
Partner: Jon Pettersen

Vial, Hamilton, Koch & Knox
1717 Main St., Suite 4400
Dallas, TX 75201
(214) 712-4400
Attorney: Stephen Baskind

Winstead, Sechrest & Minick
5400 Renaissance Tower
1201 Elm St.
Dallas, TX 75270
(214) 745-5406

Worsham, Forsythe, Samples & Wooldridge
2001 Bryan St., Suite 3200
Dallas TX 75201
(214) 979-3000
Office Administrator: Frances Mendoza

Management Consultants

For information about management consulting and related fields, you can contact:

PROFESSIONAL ORGANIZATIONS:

ACME—The Association of Management Consulting Firms
521 5th Ave., 35th Floor
New York, NY 10175
(212) 697-9693

Institute of Management Consultants
521 5th Ave., 35th Floor
New York, NY 10175
(212) 697-8262

Society of Professional Consultants
51 Sawyer Rd., Suite 150
Waltham, MA 02154
(617) 894-2547

PROFESSIONAL PUBLICATIONS:

ACME Newsletter
Academy of Management Review
Consultant News
Harvard Business Review
Journal of Management
Management Review

DIRECTORIES:

ACME Directory (ACME-Association of Management Consultants, New York, NY)
Association of Management Consulting Firms–Directory of Members (Council of Consulting Organizations, New York, NY)
Consultants & Consulting Organizations (Gale Research, Detroit, MI)
Directory of Management Consultants (Kennedy Publications, Fitzwilliam, NH)
Dun's Consultants Directory (Dun & Bradstreet Corp., Parsippany, NJ)
IMC Directory (Institute of Management Consultants, New York, NY)
Management Consulting (Harvard Business School Press, Cambridge, MA)

EMPLOYERS:

Alexander Consulting Group
4099 McEwen Rd.
Dallas, TX 75240
(214) 448-0700

Appleton, D., Co.
222 W. Las Colinas Blvd., Suite 1141
Irving , TX 75039
(214) 869-1066

Bigby Havis and Lifson
12201 Merit Dr.
Dallas, TX 75251
(214) 233-6055

Blackmarr, B. R., & Associates
2515 McKinney Ave., Suite 1700
Dallas, TX 75201
(214) 922- 9030

Booz, Allen & Hamilton
901 Main St., Suite 6500
Dallas, TX 75202
(214) 746-6500
Recruiting: Marshall Anderson

Communispond Inc.
12750 Merit Dr.
Dallas, TX 75251
(214) 385-0385

Coopers & Lybrand
1999 Bryan St.
Dallas TX 75201
(214) 754-5000

Corbin, Carolyn, Inc.
4012 Candlenut Lane
Dallas, TX 75244
(214) 484-2985

Drake Beam Morin
5005 LBJ Frwy.
Dallas TX 75240
(214) 788-5302
Group Vice President: China Gorman

Hay Management Consultants
12801 N. Central Expwy.

How to Get a Job

Dallas, TX 75201
(214) 934-6800

Hogan & Associates
16479 Dallas Pkwy.
Dallas TX 75248
(214) 931-7597

Mercer, William, Inc.
2200 Ross Ave.
Dallas, TX 76106
(214) 220-3500

Mok-Bledsoe International
14455 Webbs Chapel Rd., Suite 102
Dallas, TX 75234
(214) 484-4444
President: Larry Bledsoe

RCM Corp.
1140 Fort Worth Club Tower
Fort Worth, TX 76102
(817) 335-9951
Owner: John W. Ratliff
Specialty: Mergers and acquisitions.

R. H. R. International Company
17766 Preston, Rd., Suite 100
Dallas, TX 75252
(214) 380-9212

Taylor Management Systems
9242 Markville Dr., Suite B
Dallas, TX 75243
(214) 701-2600
President: David Taylor
Small business consulting.

Towers Perrin
12377 Merit Dr., Suite 1200
Dallas, TX 75251
(214) 701-2600
Personnel Manager: Liz Malloy

Wyatt Company
2121 San Jacinto St., Suite 2400
Dallas, TX 75201
(214) 978-3400

Manufacturers

Also check out the sections on **Auto/Truck Equipment, Furniture**, and **Metal Products.**

To learn more about manufacturing, you can contact:

PROFESSIONAL ORGANIZATION:

National Association of Manufacturers
1331 Pennsylvania Ave.
Washington, DC 20004
(202) 637-3000

PROFESSIONAL PUBLICATIONS:

Assembly Engineering
Design News
Iron Age
Manufacturing Engineering
Manufacturing Systems
Manufacturing Week

DIRECTORIES:

Directory of Texas Manufacturers (Bureau of Business Research,
    Austin, TX)
Thomas Register of Manufacturers (Thomas Publishing, New
    York, NY)
US Industrial Directory (Cahners Publications, Stamford, CT)

EMPLOYERS:

American Permanent Ware Co.
729 Third Ave.
Dallas, TX 75226
(214) 421-7366
Personnel Manager: Barbara Asbury
Restaurant equipment.

Atlas Match Corp.
1801 S. Airport Circle
Euless, TX 76040
Metro (817) 267-1500
Assistant Controller: Regina Clark
Advertising matchbooks.

Baker Hughes Mining Tools
1600 S. Great Southwest Pkwy.

Grand Prairie, TX 75051
Metro (214) 988-3322
Manager of Human Resources: Pat Morris
Rock drilling bits.

Beckett Co.
2521 Willowbrook Rd.
Dallas, TX 75220
(214) 357-6421
Chairman CEO: Wingate Sung
Waterpumps for drinking fountains and air conditioners.

Brinkman Corp.
4215 McEwen Rd.
Dallas, TX 75244
(214) 387-4939
Personnel Director: Sandra Scott
Metal detectors, meat smokers, spotlights, flashlights, and radar detectors.

Cook Machinery Co.
4301 S. Fitzhugh Ave.
Dallas, TX 75210
(214) 421-2135
Contact: Department Head
Commercial laundry equipment.

Crane, Susan
8107 Chancellor Row
Dallas, TX 75247
(214) 631-6490
Human Resources: Janice Barlow
Manufactures display materials and gift wrappings.

Dahlgren Manufacturing Co.
1725 Sandy Lake Rd.
Carrollton, TX 75006
(214) 245-0035
Contact: Wayne Rich
Dampening systems and printing press equipment.

Dallas Lighthouse for The Blind
4245 Office Pkwy
Dallas, TX 75204
(214) 821-2375
Personnel Department: Dohn Taylor
Household items, commissary items, and refurbish laser cartridges for the government.

Dallas Woodcraft/Division of Bomar Manufacturing
2829 Sea Harbour Rd.
Dallas, TX 75212

(214) 638-2270
General Manager: Robert Adams
Picture frames.

Esco Elevators
4720 Esco Dr.
Fort Worth, TX 76140
Metro (817) 478-4251
Hydraulic passenger and freight elevators.

Fojtasek Companies
2101 Union Bower Rd.
Irving, TX 75061
(214) 438-4787
Plant: Georgia Delatorri
Office: Shirley Crutcher
Aluminum extrusions, shapes, forms, windows, and patio doors.

Forney International
3405 Wiley Post Rd.
Carrollton, TX 75006
(214) 233-1871
Contact: Human Resources
Manufactures industrial boiler burners and process control systems.

Fruehauf Corp.
4132 Irving Blvd
Dallas, TX 76247
(214) 263-2266
Contact: Personnel Department
Semi-trailers.

Gifford-Hill American
1003 Meyers Rd.
Grand Prairie, TX 75050
Metro (214) 263-1990
Personnel Assistant: Billie Amick
Concrete pressure pipe and pipe fittings.

Halliburton Energy Services
2601 Belt Line Rd.
Carrollton, TX 75006
(214) 418-3000
Valves and controls used in oil and gas, marine, and other large industries.

Hobart Corp.
4407 Alpha Rd.
Farmers Branch, TX 75244
(214) 233-7781

Contact: Department Head
Food equipment.

Hogan, Ben, Co.
2912 W. Pafford St.
Fort Worth, TX 76110
(817) 921-2661
Contact: Personnel Department
Golf clubs, golf balls, and golf apparel.

Johnson Controls
1111 S. Shiloh Rd.
Garland, TX 75042
(214) 494-2461
Personnel Assistant: Suzanne Richardson
Auto, marine, and commercial storage batteries.

Justin Industries
2821 W. Seventh St.
Fort Worth, TX 76107
(817) 336-5125
Contact: Personnel Department
Diversified products, including Acme brick, Justin and Nocona
boots, ceramic cooling towers, and concrete products.

LTV Energy Products, Oil States Industries Division
7701 S. Cooper St.
Arlington, TX 76017
(817) 468-1400
Contact: Personnel Department
Rubber molded products and drilling equipment.

Lasko Metal Products
1700 Mecham Blvd.
Fort Worth, TX 76106
(817) 625-6381
Contact: Texas Employment Commission
Plastic electric fans.

MPI
1301 Cold Springs Rd.
Fort Worth, TX 76113
(817) 347-7200
Personnel: Gary Tallaut
Carpet underlay.

Overhead Door Corp.
6750 LBJ Frwy., Suite 1200
Dallas, TX 75240
(214) 233-6611
Manufactures overhead and garage doors.

PVI Industries
3209 Galvez St.
Fort Worth, TX 76111
Metro (817) 429-1313
Human Resources Manager: Tom Lynch
Commercial, institutional, and industrial water heaters and heat
exchangers.

Publishers Equipment Corp.
16660 Dallas Pkwy., Suite 1100
Dallas, TX 75248
(214) 931-2312
Contact: Roger Baier at (815) 874-8877
Newspaper printing presses.

Redman Industries
2550 Walnut Hill Lane, Suite 200
Dallas, TX 75229
(214) 353-3600
Personnel: Carolyn Miller
Mobile homes.

Rochester Gauges of Texas
11616 Harry Hines Blvd.
Dallas, TX 75229
(214) 241-2161
Personnel Administrator: Sam Sims
Industrial gauges.

Samsill Corp.
4301 Mansfield Hwy.
Fort Worth, TX 76119
(817) 535-0203
Contact: Personnel
Office products.

Sargent-Sowell
1185 108th St.
Grand Prairie, TX 75050
(214) 647-1525
Street signs.

Snapper Power Equipment
5000 South Frwy.
Fort Worth, TX 76115
(817) 921-3611
Personnel Director: Maggie Grinstead
Garden and lawn equipment.

Snow Corp.
3817 Rutledge St.
Fort Worth, TX 76107

(817) 732-5554
Comptroller: Monty Rockwell
Plastic process machinery and molded plastic products.

Southwestern Petroleum Corp.
534 N. Main St.
Fort Worth, TX 76101
(817) 332-2336
Contact: Personnel Department
Building products, roofing materials, and lubricants.

Telsco Industries
3301 W. Kingsley Rd.
Garland, TX 75041
(214) 278-6131
Contact: Texas Employment Commission
Lawn sprinklers and compression systems.

Texas Industries
7610 N. Stemmons Frwy.
Dallas, TX 75247
Toll Free (214) 842-5773
Contact: Personnel Department
Cement, concrete products, and related materials.

Texstar
802 Ave. J East
Grand Prairie, TX 75050
Metro (214) 647-1366
Vice President of Industrial Relations: Debra Carson
Plastics manufacturer.

Trane Co.
13821 Diplomat Dr.
Dallas, TX 75234
(214) 406-6000
Contact: Department Head
Air-conditioning equipment for buildings, buses, trucks, and mass
transit vehicles.

Triangle Pacific Corp.
16803 Dallas Pkwy.
Dallas, TX 75248
(214) 931-3000
Personnel Assistant: Sally Kinkade
Cabinets and hardwood floors.

Universal Manufacturing Co.
900 S. Cedar Ridge Rd.
Duncanville, TX 75137
(214) 298-0531

Contact: Department Head
Metal enclosures for electrical wiring.

Media: Print

Also see the section on **Book Publishers**

For networking in the magazine and newspaper publishing business, check out the following professional organizations listed in Chapter 5:

PROFESSIONAL ORGANIZATIONS:

Dallas Professional Photographers Association
Network of Hispanic Communicators
Newspaper Advertising Sales Association
Press Club of Dallas
Women in Communications

For additional information, you can contact:

Magazine Publishers Association
919 Third Ave., 22nd Floor
New York, NY 10022
(212) 872-3700

National Newspaper Association
1627 K St., NW, #400
Washington, DC 20006
(202) 466-7200

Newspaper Association of America
11600 Sunrise Valley Dr.
Reston, VA 22091-1412
(703) 648-1000

Suburban Newspapers of America
401 N. Michigan Ave.
Chicago, IL 60611
(312) 644-6610

PROFESSIONAL PUBLICATIONS:

Columbia Journalism Review
Editor & Publisher Market Guide
Folio
Publishers Auxiliary
Suburban Publisher

The Writer
Writer's Digest

DIRECTORIES:

Editor & Publisher International Yearbook (Editor & Publisher, New York, NY)
Hispanic Media and Markets Directory (Standard Rate & Data Service, Wilmette, IL)
Magazine Industry Marketplace (R.R. Bowker, Inc., New York, NY)
Media Review Digest (Pierian Press, Ann Arbor, MI)
National Directory of Magazines (Oxbridge Communications, New York, NY)
SNA Membership Directory (Suburban Newspapers of America, Chicago, IL)

EMPLOYERS:

Adweek/Southwest
2909 Cole Ave., Suite 220
Dallas, TX 75204
(214) 871-9550
Editor: Kathy Thacker
Weekly trade publication for the advertising, marketing, and public relations industries.

Arlington Star Telegram
1111 W. Abram St.
Arlington, TX 76010
Metro (817) 261-1191
Contact: Fort Worth Star-Telegram personnel office, (817) 390-7459
Community newspaper published twice weekly.

Associated Press
4851 LBJ Frwy., Suite 300
Dallas, TX 75244
(214) 991-2100
Contact: John Bolt
Wire service.

Aura of Fort Worth
2917 Morton
Fort Worth, TX 76107
(817) 336-7453
Editor: John Paschal
Publisher: Le Nelle Campbell
Bimonthly city lifestyle magazine.

Carrollton Chronicle
Box 110938
Carrollton, TX 75011
(214) 446-0303
Executive Editor: Wayne Esperson
Weekly newspaper.

D/FW People
400 Fuller-Wiser Rd., Suite 125
Euless, TX 76039
Metro (817) 540-4666
General Manager: Janie Ross
Weekly newspaper.

Dallas Business Journal
4131 N. Central Expwy., Suite 310
Dallas, TX 75204
Metro (214) 988-7106
Contact: Department Head
Weekly business newspaper.

Dallas/Fort Worth Suburban Newspapers
1000 Ave. H East
Arlington, TX 76011
Metro (817) 695-0500
Editor: Banks Disham
Chain of community newspapers owned by the Belo Corporation
that publishes the Arlington Daily News, Garland Daily News,
Grand Prairie Daily News, Irving Daily News, Mesquite Daily
News, Mid-Cities Daily News, and Richardson Daily News.

Dallas Morning News
P.O. Box 655237
Dallas, TX 75265
(214) 977-8222
Contact: Personnel Department
Major daily newspaper with a morning edition.

Dallas Observer
3211 Irving Blvd., Suite 110
Dallas, TX 75247
(214) 637-2072
Weekly entertainment and features publication.

Duncanville Suburban
606 Oriole Blvd.
Duncanville, TX 75116
(214) 298-4211
Personnel Manager: Cathy Ramsy
Weekly newspaper.

El Sol De Texas
4260 Spring Valley Rd.
Dallas, TX 75244
(214) 386-9120
Contact: Jaime Montano
Weekly Spanish-language newspaper with news about Dallas,
Fort Worth, and Latin countries.

Farmers Branch Times
1712 Belt Line Rd.
Carrollton, TX 75006
(214) 446-0303
Executive Editor: Wayne Epperson
Weekly newspaper.

Fort Worth Star-Telegram
400 W. Seventh St.
Fort Worth, TX 76101
Metro (817) 429-2655
Contact: Jerry W. Graves, Personnel Manager
Fort Worth's major daily newspaper with morning and evening
editions.

Grapevine Sun
322 S. Main St.
Grapevine, TX 76051
(214) 434-2300
Personnel Director: Carol Puckett
Newspaper published twice weekly.

Lancaster News
330 W. Pleasant Run Rd.
Lancaster, TX 75146
(214) 227-6033
Publisher: Linda Ball
Weekly newspaper.

Lewisville Daily Leader
Professional Building, Suite 100
Lakeland Plaza
Lewisville, TX 75067
(214) 436-3566
Editor: Wayne Epperson
Newspaper published five times a week.

Lewisville News
131 W. Main St.
Lewisville, TX 75067
(214) 436-5551
Contact: Editor
Newspaper published three times a week.

Metrocrest News
1720 Josey Lane, Suite 100
Carrollton, TX 75006
(214) 418-9999
Personnel Director: Phyllis Masalkoski
Weekly newspaper.

Park Cities News
8115 Preston Rd., Suite 120
Dallas, TX 75225
(214) 369-7570
Publisher: Marj Waters
Weekly newspaper.

Park Cities People
8115 Preston Rd., Suite 120
Dallas, TX 75225
(214) 739-2244
Publisher and Editor: Jim Goodson
Weekly newspaper.

Plano Daily Star-Courier
801 E. Plano Parkway
Plano, TX 75074
(214) 424-6565
Editor: Wayne Epperson
Daily newspaper.

Texas Lawyer
1 Ferris Plaza
400 S. Record St., Suite 1400
Dallas, TX 75202
(214) 744-9300
Publisher/Editor: Mark Obbie
Weekly publication for the legal profession.

Travelhost Magazine
10701 N. Stemmons Frwy.
Dallas, TX 75220
(214) 691-1163
Office Manager: Nancy E. Chaussee
Weekly tourist magazine.

United Press International
750 N. Saint Paul
Dallas, TX 75201
(214) 880-0444
Personnel Coordinator: Christa Clark at main office in Fairfax,
VA, (703) 359-6262
Wire service.

How to Get a Job

Wall Street Journal
1233 Regal Row
Dallas, TX 75247
(214) 631-7250
Personnel Manager: Lisa Charles in South Brunswick, New
Jersey (609) 520-4137
Publishing office for the Southwest edition of this leading financial newspaper, published Monday through Friday.

Trials of the trailing spouse

Most relocating people feel uprooted and really miss the support systems they have developed in their former cities. Spouses who are out of work because their mates have been transferred often need special assistance in "plugging into" the D/FW area as well as assistance in finding a new job.

The staff at IATREIA/Outpath, who have extensive experience in assisting people to accomplish both goals simultaneously, offer the following advise: Talk to the people you already know in your former city. Ask friends, colleagues at work and in professional organizations, fellow church members, school and fraternity alums who they know in D/FW. Follow up with a note, phone call, or luncheon invitation. Any one of these referrals can turn out to be your entree into an excellent network of people with like interests. ■

Metal Products

Also check the section on **Manufacturers.**

Major trade publications read by metal products manufacturers include:

PROFESSIONAL PUBLICATIONS:

Assembly Engineering
Design News
Die Casting Engineer
Iron Age
Manufacturing Systems
Metal Center News
U. S. Glass, Metal, and Glazing Magazine

DIRECTORY:

Dun's Industrial Guide: The Metalworking Directory (Dun's
    Marketing Services, Mountain Lakes, NJ)

EMPLOYERS:

Anchor Crane & Hoist Service Co.
2020 E. Grauwyler Rd.
Irving, TX 75061
(214) 438-5100
Contact: Department Head
Manufactures overhead cranes and hoists.

Barker & Bratton Steel
10733 Newkirk St.
Dallas, TX 75220
(214) 556-1951
Contact: J.W. Bratton for shop positions and David Bratton for
office positions
Steel fabricators.

Business Records Corp.
1111 W. Mockingbird, Suite 1400
Dallas, TX 75247
(214) 905-2590
Contact: Personnel Department
Manufactures voting equipment.

Commercial Metals Co.
7800 Stemmons Frwy.
Dallas, TX 75247

(214) 689-4300
Corporate Personnel Director: Jesse Barnes
Secondary metals processing, steel manufacturing, and trading.

General Aluminum Corp.
1001 W. Crosby Rd.
Carrollton, TX 75006
(214) 242-5271
Professional positions: Hal Giddens; Industrial and office personnel: Linda Boustos
Manufactures aluminum windows and sliding glass doors.

Glitsch Inc.
4900 Singleton Blvd.
Dallas, TX 75212
(214) 631-3841
Employee Relations: Peggy White
Heavy metal fabricator that manufactures metal plates, petroleum refinery processing equipment, and pollution control devices.

Hensley, G. H., Co.
2108 Joe Field Rd.
Dallas, TX 75229
(214) 241-2321
Personnel Manager: Tom McKormick
Steel foundry, producing steel castings and construction equipment parts.

Keystone Consolidated Industries
5430 LBJ Frwy., Suite 1740
Dallas, TX 75240
(214) 458-0028
Contact: Personnel Manager
Manufactures wire products and locks.

M&M Manufacturing Co.
200 Adolph St.
Fort Worth, TX 76107
(817) 336-2311
Shop Supervisor: Don Colley
Manufactures air-conditioning ducts and pipes and sheet metal products.

Martin Sprocket & Gear
3600 McCart St.
Fort Worth, TX 76101
Metro (817) 654-4505
Contact: Personnel Department
Manufactures mechanical power transmissions and bulk materials-handling equipment.

Mesco Metal Buildings Corp.
Hwy. 114 and 400 N. Kimball Rd.
Southlake, TX 76092
Metro (817) 481-2501
Contact: Department Heads
Manufactures metal building systems.

North Texas Steel Co.
412 W. Bolt St.
Fort Worth, TX 76110
Metro (817) 654-3328
Controller: Bill Fudge
Fabricated structural steel.

RSR Corp.
1111 W. Mockingbird Lane
Dallas, TX 75247
(214) 631-6070
Industrial Relations Manager: William C. White
Secondary lead smelter.

Skotty Aluminum Products Co.
2100 E. Union Bower Rd.
Irving, TX 75061
(214) 445-0040
Office Manager: Shirly Crutcher
Manufactures aluminum windows.

Temtex Industries
3010 LBJ Frwy., Suite 650
Dallas, TX 75234
(214) 484-1845
Vice President of Finance: Roger Stibers
Manufactures fabricated metal and structural clay products.

Texas Steel Co.
3901 Hemphill St.
Fort Worth, TX 76110
(817) 923-4611
Industrial Relations Manager: Wendall Pender
Manufactures steel castings for machinery parts.

Thornton Industries
2700 W. Pafford St.
Fort Worth, TX 76110
(817) 926-3321
Contact: Department Head
Structural steel fabricators.

Trinity Industries
501 Maple Ave.
Dallas, TX 75235

How to Get a Job

(214) 631-4420
Human Resources: Bobbie Carol
Produces fabricated structural steel and steel platework.

Trinity Industries
2548 NE 28th St.
Fort Worth, TX 76111
Metro (817) 429-3453
Contact: Personnel Department
Steel fabricators.

West, Vic, Steel
404 E. Dallas Rd.
Grapevine, TX 76051
Metro (817) 481-3521
Contact: Department Head
Metal building components.

Museums and Art Galleries

To learn more about careers in museums and art galleries, you can contact:

PROFESSIONAL ORGANIZATIONS:

American Association of Museums
1225 I St., NW
Washington, DC 20005
(202) 289-1818

American Federation of Arts
41 E. 65th St.
New York, NY 10021
(212) 988-7700

National Assembly of Local Art Agencies
927 15th St., NW, 12th Floor
Washington, DC 20005
(202) 371-2830

National Assembly of State Arts Agencies
1010 Vermont Ave., NW
Washington, DC 20005
(202) 347-6352

PROFESSIONAL PUBLICATIONS:

ART COM
Art Forum
Art World
Aviso
Connections Monthly
Museum News
NASAA News

DIRECTORIES:

Artsource Texas (Dallas Public Library, Dallas, TX)
Directory for the Arts (Center for Arts Information, New York, NY)
NASAA Directory (National Assembly of State Arts Agencies, Washington, DC)
Official Museum Directory (American Association of Museums, Washington, DC)
Texas Museum Directory (Texas Historical Commission, Austin, TX)

353

EMPLOYERS:

Amon Carter Museum
3501 Camp Bowie Blvd.
Fort Worth, TX 76107
(817) 738-1933
Personnel Services Coordinator: Kathy Goodale
Western art collection with special exhibits.

Biblical Arts Center
7500 Park Lane
Dallas, TX 75225
(214) 691-4661
Director: Ronnie Roesy
Religious-theme exhibits.

Dallas Fire Fighters Museum
3801 Parry Ave.
Dallas, TX 75226
(214) 821-1500
Director: James L. Clay
Display of antique fire trucks and fire fighting equipment in
historic setting.

Dallas Museum of Art
1717 N. Harwood St.
Dallas, TX 75201
(214) 922-1200
Personnel Director: Scott Gensemer
Dallas' largest fine arts museum, with Old Masters, modern, pre-
Columbian, and American art.

Fort Worth Museum of Science & History
1501 Montgomery St.
Fort Worth, TX 76107
Metro (817) 654-1356
Contact: Department Head
Hall of Texas history exhibit, planetarium, and Omni Theater.

Kimbell Art Museum
3333 Camp Bowie Blvd.
Fort Worth, TX 76107
Metro (817) 654-1034
Associate Director for Administration: Barbara White
Fort Worth's largest fine arts museum, with extensive permanent
collection and special exhibits.

Meadows Museum
Owen Fine Arts Center
SMU Campus
Dallas, TX 75275
(214) 768-2516

Director: Samuel K. Heath
Spanish drawings and prints and paintings.

Modern Art Museum of Fort Worth
1309 Montgomery St.
Fort Worth, TX 76107
(817) 738-9215
Contact: Personnel Department
Modern art museum, with special exhibits.

Old City Park
1717 Gano St.
Dallas, TX 75215
(214) 421-5141
Director: Mr. Daniel R. Baldwin
Historical buildings and exhibits located in park near downtown Dallas.

Richardson, Sid, Collection of Western Art
309 Main St.
Fort Worth, TX 76102
(817) 332-6554
Director: Jan Brenneman
Western art.

Science Place
Fair Park
1318 2nd Ave.
Dallas, TX 75210
(214) 428-7200
Contact: Personnel Department
Museum with permanent and special science and energy exhibits and planetarium shows.

Paper/Packaging/Allied Products

For more information about the paper industry, you can contact:

PROFESSIONAL ORGANIZATIONS:

American Paper Institute
260 Madison Ave.
New York, NY 10016

Paper Industry Management Association
2400 E. Oakton St.
Arlington Hts., IL 60005
(708) 956-0250

Technical Association of the Pulp and Paper Industry
Technology Park, Box 105113
Atlanta, GA 30348

PROFESSIONAL PUBLICATIONS:

Good Packaging Magazine
Packaging
Paper Trade Journal
Pulp and Paper
Pulp and Paper Week
TAPPI Journal
World Wood

DIRECTORIES:

American Papermaker—Mill and Personnel Issue (MacClean/
   Hunter Publishing, Atlanta, GA)
Lockwood-Post's Directory of the Pulp, Paper and Allied Trades
   (Miller Freeman, New York, NY)
Secondary Wood Products Manufacturers Directory (Miller
   Freeman, New York, NY)
TAPPI Directory (Technical Association of the Pulp and Paper
   Industry, Atlanta, GA)

EMPLOYERS:

American Excelsior Co.
900 Ave. H East
Arlington, TX 76011
Metro (817) 640-2161
Branch Manager: Bob Landon
Manufactures protective shipping pads, fabricated polyurethane
foam, and related products.

Arrow Industries
2625 Belt Line Rd.
Carrollton, TX 75006
(214) 416-6500
Contact: Personnel Department
Manufactures paper plates and packaged dry food products.

Bates Container
6433 Davis Blvd.
North Richland Hills, TX 76180
Metro (817) 498-3200
Personnel Manager: Sally Hackfeld
Manufactures corrugated board.

Campbell Paper Co.
5300 W. Vickery Blvd.
Fort Worth, TX 76107
Metro (817) 738-2194
President: Jerry Whittacker
Distributor of paper for food service, retail, janitorial supplies,
and computers.

Champion International Corp.
1901 Windsor Place
Fort Worth, TX 76110
(817) 926-6661
Contact: Texas Employment Commission
Manufactures milk cartons.

Clampitt Paper Co.
2101 Franklin Dr.
Fort Worth, TX 76106
Metro (817) 625-1695
Contact: Roger Hale or Steve Romaine
Paper distribution company.

Container Corp. of America
6701 South Frwy.
Fort Worth, TX 76134
(817) 568-3420
Personnel: Bess Miller
World's largest producer of paperboard packaging, including
folding cartons, sanitary food containers, and sales promotional
products.

Dixico
1300 Polk St.
Dallas, TX 75224
(214) 943-0740
Human Resource Manager: Peggy Reeves
Manufactures snack food packaging.

Kimberly-Clark Corp.
545 E. John W. Carpenter Frwy.
Irving, TX 75062
(214) 830-1483
Human Resources: Barbara Kimps
World headquarters for producer of household, personal care,
business, and health care paper products.

Olmsted-Kirk Paper Co.
2420 Butler St.
Dallas, TX 75235
(214) 637-2220
Personnel Director: Tom Harmon
Wholesale paper distributor for specialty products and industrial
papers. Operates graphic arts and retail centers. Branch offices in
Fort Worth, Waco, Houston, and Austin.

Packaging Corp. of America
1001 113th St.
Arlington, TX 76011
Metro (817) 640-1888
Contact: Personnel Department
Manufactures corrugated containers and disposable tableware.

Princeton Packaging
14240 Proton Rd.
Dallas TX 75244
(214) 387-0700
Director of Human Resources: T.M. Foran
Manufactures flexible packaging products.

Rock-Tenn Co.
1120 E. Clarendon Dr.
Dallas, TX 75203
(214) 941-3400
Personnel: Kent Southerland
Manufactures paperboard and paperboard packing products.

Stone Container Corp.
2302 W. Marshall Dr.
Grand Prairie, TX 75051
Metro (214) 647-1333
Personnel Administrator: Marj Hanke or contact department
head.
Manufactures corrugated boxes.

Westvaco Corp.
10700 Harry Hines Blvd.
Dallas, TX 75220
(214) 352-9791
Personnel: Rebecca Logan
Manufactures envelopes.

Printers

For networking in printing and related fields, you can check out the following professional organization listed in Chapter 5:

PROFESSIONAL ORGANIZATIONS:

Printing Industries Association of Texas

For more information, you can contact:

National Association of Printers and Lithographers
780 Palisade Ave.
Teaneck, NJ 07666
(201) 342-0700

Printing Industries of America
100 Daingerfield Rd.
Alexandria, VA 22314
(703) 519-8100

Technical Association of the Graphic Arts
P.O. Box 9887
Rochester, NY 14614
(716) 272-0557

PROFESSIONAL PUBLICATIONS:

American Printer
Graphic Arts Monthly
Print
Printing News

DIRECTORIES:

Design Firms Directory (Wefler and Associates, Evanston, IL)
Graphic Arts Monthly Buyer's Guide/Directory Issue (Cahners
    Publishing, New York, NY)
Graphic Arts Green Book (A.F. Lewis & Co., Hinsdale, IL)
Printing Trades Blue Book (A.F. Lewis & Co., New York, NY)

EMPLOYERS:

Allied Printing Co.
501 N. Good-Latimer Expwy.
Dallas, TX 75204
(214) 827-5151
Contact: Department Head
Printing and publishing company.

American Signature Graphics
6320 Denton Dr.
Dallas, TX 75235
(214) 358-1371
Contact: Department Head
Prints periodicals.

Anchor Press
820 N. Main St.
Fort Worth, TX 76106
(817) 335-4861
Office Manager: Mark Vahala
Commercial printing.

Blanks Color Imaging
2343 N. Beckley Ave.
Dallas, TX 75208
(214) 741-3905
Personnel Manager: Elaine Grant
Four-color separations, flexo-separations, stripping, photopolymer plates.

Branch-Smith
120 St. Louis Ave.
Fort Worth, TX 76104
(817) 332-6306
Contact: Department Head
Advertising, printing, and publishing of trade magazines.

Buchanan Printing Co.
2330 Jett St.
Farmer's Branch, TX 75234
(214) 241-3311
Contact: Department Head
Commercial printing.

Colotone Press
990 S. St. Paul St.
Dallas, TX 75201
(214) 741-7751
Plant Manager: Joe Singleton
Commercial printing.

Deluxe Check Printers
9125 Viscount Row
Dallas, TX 75247
(214) 631-7780
Personnel Manager: Lisa Shinn
Check printing company.

Evans Press
5133 Northeast Pkwy.

Fort Worth, TX 76106
(817) 626-1901
Plant Manager: Willie McCranie
Prints college handbooks, information manuals, and business
catalogs

Horticulture Printers
3638 Executive Blvd.
Mesquite, TX 75149
(214) 289-0705
Vice President: Vera Rhodes
Commercial and horticultural printing.

Printing Center of Texas
701 E. Fifth St.
Fort Worth, TX 76102
Metro (817) 429-2320
Contact: Personnel Department
Prints books, newspapers, circulars, and college catalogs.

Retail Graphics Printing Co.
8000 Ambassador Row
Dallas, TX 75247
(214) 630-9900
Personnel: Margrett Kemp
Newspaper insert printing.

Riverside Press
4901 Woodall St.
Dallas, TX 75247
(214) 631-1150
Contact: Personnel Department
Commercial printing.

VIP Printing
2800 112th St.
Grand Prairie, TX 75050
Metro (214) 647-8888
Personnel: Lori Fabic
Commercial printing.

Williamson Printing Corp.
6700 Denton Dr.
Dallas, TX 75235
(214) 352-1122
Vice President - Personnel: Tony LaLumia
Commercial printing

Real Estate

You may also want to look at the section on **Contractors/ Construction.**

For information about real estate and related fields, contact the following professional organizations.

PROFESSIONAL ORGANIZATIONS:

American Association of Certified Appraisers
800 Compton Rd.
Cincinnati, OH 45231
(513) 729-1400

American Society of Appraisers
535 Herndon Pkwy., #150
Herndon, VA 22070
(703) 478-2228

Building Owners & Managers Association International
1201 New York Ave., NW
Washington, DC 20006
(202) 408-2662

National Association of Realtors
430 N. Michigan Ave.
Chicago, IL 60611
(312) 329-8200

PROFESSIONAL PUBLICATIONS:

Banker & Tradesman
National Real Estate Investor
Real Estate News
Realty & Building
Southwest Real Estate News

DIRECTORIES:

American Real Estate Guide (LL&IL Publishing, Marhasset, NY)
American Society of Real Estate Counselors Directory (ASREC, Chicago, IL)
Construction Users Guide & Directory (Associated Builders & Contractors, Burlington, MA)
Directory of Certified Residential Brokers (Retail National Marketing Institute, Chicago, IL)
National Roster of Realtors (Stanats Communications, Cedar Rapids, IA)

EMPLOYERS:

BEI Real Estate Services
5310 Harvest Hill Rd., Suite 222
Dallas, TX 75230
(214) 385-8333
Personnel Director: Jean Higgens

Blackland Properties
P.O. Box 2129
Dallas, TX 75221
(214) 954-0099
Contact: Mail resume to Personnel Department

Bramalea Texas
901 Main St., Suite 5000
Dallas, TX 75202
(214) 761-6200
Personnel: Cheri Mastor

C. B. Commercial Real Estate
5400 LBJ Frwy., Suite 1100
Dallas, TX 75240
(214) 458-4800
Sales Manager: Jana Tharp

Century 21 South Central States
420 Decker Rd., Suite 200
Irving, TX 75062
(214) 541-0221
Contact: Department Head

Crow, Trammell, Co.
3500 Trammell Crow Center
2001 Ross Ave.
Dallas, TX 75201
(214) 979-6400
Contact: Staff Recruiter

Cushman & Wakefield of Texas
5430 LBJ Frwy., Suite 1400
Dallas, TX 75240
(214) 770-2500
Contact: Department Head or Branch Manager

Dickerson, Hank, & Co.
8333 Douglas Ave., Suite 1300
Dallas, TX 75225
(214) 691-5300
Contact: Personnel Manager

ERA Real Estate
Southwest Regional Headquarters
1431 Greenway Dr., Suite 230
Irving, TX 75038
Metro # (214) 751-0597
Contact: Office managers at ERA offices

Folsom Companies
16475 Dallas Pkwy., Suite 800
Dallas, TX 75248
(214) 931-7400
Contact: Department Head

Fox & Jacobs/Centex
3333 Lee Pkwy.
Dallas, TX 75219
(214) 559-6500
Coordinator: Jane Mongiafico

General Homes Corp.
14800 Quorum, Suite 370
Dallas, TX 75240
(214) 392-9200
Office Manager: Pam Bagget

Halliday, Ebby, Realtors
4455 Sigma Rd.
Dallas, TX 75244
(214) 980-6600
Personnel Director: Mary Stout

JPI Realty
600 E. Las Colinas Blvd., Suite 1800
Irving, TX 75039
(214) 541-1122
Contact: Department Head

Lehndorff Management USA
2501 Cedar Springs Rd., Suite 525
Dallas, TX 75201
(214) 855-5800
Contact: Employment

Lincoln Property Co.
3300 Lincoln Plaza
500 N. Akard St.
Dallas, TX 75201
(214) 740-3300
Employee Benefits Manager: Steve Fallon

Miller, Henry S., Real Estate Co.
5485 Beltline Rd., Suite 300

Dallas, TX 75240
(214) 239-8000
Personnel: Robert DuBois

Nasher, Raymond D., Co.
8950 N. Central Expwy., Suite 400
Dallas, TX 75231
(214) 369-1234
Contact: Personnel Department

Paragon Group
7557 Rambler Rd., Suite 1200
Dallas, TX 75231
(214) 891-2000
Contact: Department Head

Prentiss Properties
1717 Main St., Suite 5000
Dallas, TX 75201
(214) 761-1440
Personnel: Richard Bartel or Joyce Wadsworth

Pulte Home Corp. of Texas
1431 Greenway Dr., Suite 700
Irving, TX 75038
Metro (817) 581-0177
Contact: Personnel Department

Swearingan Co.
3811 Turtlecreek Blvd., Suite 1400
Dallas, TX 75219
(214) 443-2700
Contact: Employee Benefits Coordinator

Trendmaker Homes
5720 LBJ Frwy., Suite 610
Dallas, TX 75240
(214) 458-9909
Personnel Director: Thelma Wallace

Vantage Companies
2911 Turtle Creek Blvd.
Dallas, TX 75219
(214) 559-9702
Contact: Human Resources at (214) 689-2350

Woodbine Development Corp.
1445 Ross at Field
Dallas, TX 75202
Metro (214) 263-2724
Contact: Personnel

Recreation/Sports/Fitness

For networking in recreation/sports/fitness and related fields, check out this professional organization listed in Chapter 5:

PROFESSIONAL ORGANIZATIONS:

Texas Recreation & Park Society

For additional information, you can contact:

Aerobics & Fitness Association of America
15250 Ventura Blvd., Suite 200
Sherman Oaks, CA 91403
(818) 905-0040

National Association of Sporting Goods Wholesalers
P. O. Box 11344
Chicago, IL 60611
(312) 565-0233

National Collegiate Athletic Association
6201 College Blvd.
Overland Park, KS 66211
(913) 339-1906

National Recreation & Parks Association
2775 S. Quincy St., Suite 300
Arlington, VA 22206-2204
(703) 820-4940

National Sporting Goods Association
1699 Wall St.
Mt. Prospect IL 60056
(703) 439-4000

PROFESSIONAL PUBLICATIONS:

American Fitness
NCAA News
Parks & Recreation
Sporting Goods Dealer
Sporting Goods Trade
Sporting Goods Wholesaler
Team Lineup

DIRECTORIES:

Health Clubs Directory (American Business Directories, Omaha, NE)

NCAA Directory (NCAA, Overland Park, KS)

New American Guide to Athletics, Sports, and Recreation (New American Library, New York, NY)

Salesman's Guide to Sporting Goods Buyers (Salesman's Guides, New York, NY)

Sporting Goods Directory (Sporting Goods Dealer, St. Louis, MO)

Sports Administration Guide & Directory (National Sports Marketing Bureau, New York, NY)

Sports Marketplace (Sportsguide, Princeton, NJ)

EMPLOYERS:

Aerobics Activity Center
12100 Preston Rd.
Dallas, TX 75230
(214) 233-4832
Contact: Sheri Pearce
Fitness center.

Bent Tree Country Club
5201 Westgrove Dr.
Dallas, TX 75248
(214) 931-7326
Contact: Personnel
Private country club.

Brookhaven Country Club
3333 Golfing Green Dr.
Farmers Branch, TX 75234
(214) 243-6151
Personnel Director: Deborah Travis
Private country club.

Colonial Country Club
3735 Country Club Circle
Fort Worth, TX 76109
(817) 927-4200
Personnel Director: Colleen Lautensack
Private country club.

Cosmopolitan Lady
1320 Tennis Dr.
Bedford, TX 76201
(817) 282-8600
Contact: Personnel Director
Fitness center.

Dallas Country Club
4100 Beverly Dr.
Dallas, TX 75205
(214) 521-2151
Contact: Rosemary Burke
Private country club.

Dallas Cowboys
1 Cowboy Pkwy.
Irving, TX 75063
(214) 556-9900
Mail resume to department head.

Dallas Mavericks
777 Sports St.
Dallas, TX 75207
(214) 748-1808
Contact: Department Head
Headquarters for professional basketball team.

Dallas Sidekicks
777 Sports St.
Dallas, TX 75207
(214) 653-0200
Contact: Department Head
Headquarters for professional soccer team.

Exchange Athletic Club
700 N. Harwood St., Lock Box 11
Dallas, TX 75201
(214) 953-1144
Operations Manager: Brian Kimberly
Fitness center.

North Dallas Athletic Club
13701 N. Dallas Pkwy.
Dallas, TX 75240
(214) 458-2582
Club Director: Mike Chandler
Fitness center.

Las Colinas Country Club
4900 N. O'Connor Rd.
Irving, TX 75062
(214) 541-1141
Manager: Don Rucker
Private country club.

Premier Club
5910 N. Central Expwy.
Dallas, TX 75206
(214) 891-6600

Contact: Department Head
Fitness center.

President's Health and Racquetball Clubs
13714 Gamma Rd., Suite 100
Dallas, TX 75244
(214) 239-7190
Contact: Department Head
Fitness center.

Prestonwood Country Club
15909 Preston Rd.
Dallas, TX 75248
(214) 239-7111
General Manager: Tonie Tony
Private country club.

Ridglea Country Club
3700 Bernie Anderson Ave.
Fort Worth, TX 76116
(817) 732-8111
Contact: Department Head
Private country club.

Riverbend Sports Club
2201 E. Loop 820 North
Fort Worth, TX 76118
(817) 589-0940
Contact: Business Office
Fitness center.

Texas Rangers
1250 Copeland Rd., Suite 1100
Arlington, TX 76011
(817) 273-5222
Contact: Department Head
Headquarters for professional baseball team.

University Club of Dallas/Galleria
13350 Dallas Pkwy., Suite 4000
Dallas, TX 75240
(214) 239-0050
Contact: Department Head
Private club with fitness center.

Willow Bend Polo & Hunt Club
5845 W. Park Blvd.
Plano, TX 75093
(214) 248-6298
General Manager: Robert Payne
Private polo club.

Woodhaven Country Club
913 Country Club Lane
Fort Worth, TX 76112
(817) 457-5150
Comptroller: Judy Benson
Private country club.

YMCA/Metropolitan Branch
Dallas headquarters
601 N. Akard St.
Dallas, TX 75201
(214) 880-9622
V.P. Human Resources: Zera Mackie
Fitness center and special programs.

YMCA/Metropolitan Branch
Fort Worth headquarters
540 Lamar St.
Fort Worth, TX 76102
(817) 335-6147
Personnel Director: Patsy Green
Fitness center and special programs.

Restaurant Chains

For networking in the restaurant industry and related fields, check out the following organization listed in Chapter 5:

PROFESSIONAL ORGANIZATIONS:

Dallas Restaurant Association

For more information, you can contact:

Chefs de Cuisine Association of America
830 Eighth St.
New York, NY 10019
(212) 262-0404

National Restaurant Association
1200 17th St., NW
Washington, DC 20036
(202) 331-5900

PROFESSIONAL PUBLICATIONS:

Beverage Media
Food and Beverage Marketing
Food Industry Newsletter
Food Management
Food and Wine
Foodservice Product News
Nation's Restaurant News
Restaurant Business
Restaurant Hospitality
Restaurants & Institutions
Signature Magazine

DIRECTORIES:

Directory of Chain Restaurant Operators (Chain Store Guide, New York, NY)
Directory of Food Service Distributors (Information Services, New York, NY)
Restaurant Hospitality: Restaurant Industry Hospitality Issue (Penton Publishing, Cleveland, OH)
Restaurants & Institutions: 400 Issue, July (Cahners Publishing, Des Plaines, IL)

EMPLOYERS:

Bennigan's
12404 Park Central Dr.
Dallas, TX 75251
(214) 404-5912
Contact: Tammy Skaife for corporate positions, and Human
Resources at (214) 404-5000 for management positions.

Burger King Corp.
12404 Park Central Dr., Suite 250
Plano, TX 75251
(214) 934-7969
Contact: Personnel Department

Chili's
6820 LBJ Frwy.
Dallas, TX 75240
(214) 980-9917
Contact: Human Resources Department

Denny's Restaurant
Regional Office
801 E. Ave. H, Suite 104
Arlington, TX 76011
Metro (817) 640-0731
Contact: Personnel Department

Domino's Pizza
Regional Office
1 Galleria Tower
13355 Noel Rd., Suite 455
Dallas, TX 75240
(214) 392-3030
Contact: Personnel Department

El Chico Corp.
12200 Stemmons Frwy., Suite 100
Dallas, TX 75234
(214) 241-5500
Contact: Director of Recruiting

Grandy's
Corporate Office
997 Grandy's Lane
Lewisville, TX 75067
(214) 317-8000
Contact: Recruiting Department

Jack-In-The-Box Drive-Thru
Administrative Office
3010 LBJ Frwy., Suite 1000

Dallas, TX 75234
(214) 247-8622
Personnel Director: Mary Dixon

Kentucky Fried Chicken
District Office
5605 N. MacArthur, Suite 650
Irving, TX 75038
(214) 751-8300
Contact: Personnel Department

Long John Silver's Seafood Shoppes
Southwest Divisional Office
3030 LBJ Frwy., Suite 1140
Dallas, TX 75234
(214) 247-9801
Contact: Personnel

McDonald's
Regional Office
511 E. John W. Carpenter Frwy., Suite 375
Irving, TX 75062
(214) 869-1888
Contact: Personnel Department

Pancho's Mexican Buffet
3500 Noble St.
Fort Worth, TX 76111
(817) 831-0081
V.P. of Human Resources: David Dixon

Pizza Hut
Texas Division
6606 LBJ Frwy, Suite 170
Dallas, TX 75240
(817) 357-6363
Contact: Personnel Department

Pizza Inn
International Headquarters
5050 Quorum Dr., Suite 500
Dallas, TX 75240
(214) 701-9955
Personnel Department: Candi Farley

Prufrock Restaurants
8115 Preston Rd., Lock Box 7
Dallas, TX 75225
(214) 363-9514
V.P. of Human Resources: Rosemary Maellaro

Pulido Associates
4924 Old Benbrook Rd.
Fort Worth, TX 76116
(817) 731-4241
General Manager: John Rodriguez

S&A Restaurant Corp.
12404 Park Central Dr.
Dallas, TX 75251
Metro (214) 404-5000
Contact: Tammy Skaife for corporate positions, or **Human Resources** at (214) 404-5000 for management positions.

Sky Chefs
524 E. Lamar Blvd.
Arlington, TX 76011-3999
Metro (817) 792-2123
Contact: Human Resources Department

TGI Friday's
14665 Midway Rd.
Addison, TX 75244
(214) 450-5400
Corporate Recruiter: Randy Smith

Wyatt Cafeterias
P.O. Box 38388
Dallas, TX 75238
(214) 349-0060
Human Resources Regional Manager: Faye Figgers

Jobs for younger workers

Younger workers who are looking for summer or part-time work face a common dilemma: how do you get a job when you haven't had much work experience?

Special employment programs assist youths in overcoming this problem. College placement services are also good sources for job leads. You can also check with employers in the restaurant, hotel, recreation, and entertainment fields, who traditionally hire younger workers.

Six Flags Over Texas is the area's largest employer of youths. More than 2,400 seasonal staff members are hired to work full-time during the summer and on weekends during the spring and fall. The best time to apply is in January when the theme park begins hiring for the new season. You can apply later in the year, too.

The secret is to get a jump on everyone else and not wait until the last day of school to begin looking for a summer job. You want the odds to be in your favor, considering that the number of applicants always outnumbers the openings. Contact the Personnel Department regarding specific opportunities at **(817) 640-8900 ext. 444.** ■

Retailers/Wholesalers

For information about retailing and wholesaling, check out the following professional organizations listed in Chapter 5:

PROFESSIONAL ORGANIZATIONS:

Dallas Business League
Fort Worth Florist's Association
New Car Dealers Association of Metropolitan Dallas
Sales and Marketing Executives of Fort Worth
Southwest Home Furnishings Association

For additional information, you can contact:

American Pharmaceutical Association
2215 Constitution Ave., NW
Washington DC, 20037
(202) 628-4410

Manufacturers' Agents National Association
23016 Mill Creek Rd.
Laguna Hills, CA 92653
(714) 859-4040

National Association of Chain Drug Stores
413 N. Lee St.
Box 1417-D49
Alexandria, VA 22314
(703) 549-3001

National Association of Convenience Stores
1605 King St.
Alexandria, VA 22314
(703) 684-3600

National Association of Retail Druggists
205 Daingerfield Rd.
Alexandria, VA 22314
(703) 683-8200

National Association of Wholesaler Distributors
1725 K St., NW

Washington, DC 20006
(202) 872-0885

National Grocers Association
1825 Samuel Morse Dr.
Reston, VA 22090
(703) 437-5300

National Retail Federation
100 W. 31st. St.
New York, NY 10001
(212) 244-8780

National Retail Hardware Association
5822 W. 74th St.
Indianapolis, IN 46278
(317) 290-0338

PROFESSIONAL PUBLICATIONS:

Chain Store Age
DIY Retailing
Merchandiser
National Grocer
Pharmacy Weekly
Stores
Women's Wear Daily

DIRECTORIES:

Chain Drug Stores Membership Directory (National Assoc. of Chain Drug Stores, Alexandria, VA)
Convenience Stores Membership Directory (National Assoc. of Convenience Stores, Alexandria, VA)
Fairchild's Financial Manual of Retail Stores (Fairchild Books, New York, NY)
Nationwide Directory-Mass Market Merchandisers (Salesman's Guides, New York, NY)
Sheldon's Department Stores (PS & H Inc., Fairview, NJ)

EMPLOYERS:

Ace Hardware Stores
Southwest Distribution Center
2257 Commerce Dr.
Arlington, TX 76011
(817) 649-5118
Contact: Human Resources Department
Dealer-owned hardware cooperative.

Arendale, Ted, Ford
Arendale Ford
201 E. Division St.
Arlington, TX 76011
Metro (817) 261-4261
Contact: Department Head
Automobile dealership.

Army Air Force Exchange Service
3911 S. Walton Walker Blvd.
Dallas, TX 75236
(214) 312-2278
Contact: Headquarters for retail and food services located in army
and air force bases throughout the world.

Barber's Book Stores
215 W. Eighth St.
Fort Worth, TX 76102
(817) 335-5469
Owner: Brian Perkins
Fort Worth's oldest bookstore.

B Dalton Bookseller
738 North Park Center
Dallas, TX 75225
(214) 265-8246
Contact: individual store manager
National chain of bookstores.

BeautiControl Cosmetics
2121 Midway Rd.
Carrollton, TX 75006
(214) 458-0601
Vice President of Human Resources : Sandra England
Direct sales cosmetics manufacturer.

Bedroom Shop
2012 W. Pioneer Pkwy.
Arlington, TX 76013
Metro (817) 261-2244
Personnel: Jim Coone
Retailer of mattresses, box springs, and bedding accessories.

Bookstop
5400 E. Mockingbird Lane, Suite 103
Dallas, TX 75206
(214) 828-4210
Contact: Store Manager
Discount bookstore.

Cokesbury
19200 Preston Rd.

Dallas, TX 75252
(214) 964-5777
Manager: Sam Albright
Christian bookstore.

Color Tile
515 Houston St.
Fort Worth, TX 76102
(817) 870-9400
Vice President Human Resources: Dick Andrews
Retail home improvement outlet.

Contempo Casuals
715 NorthPark Center
Dallas, TX 75225
(214) 739-4106
Contact: Personnel
Women's apparel.

Davis, Don, Oldsmobile
1901 N. Collins St.
Arlington, TX 76010
Metro (817) 461-1000
Contact: Department Head
Automobile dealership.

Dillard Department Stores
4501 N. Beach St.
Fort Worth, TX 76137
(817) 831-5111
Personnel Manager: Stephanie Ashbaugh
Retail department store.

Eagle Lincoln Mercury
6116 Lemmon Ave.
Dallas, TX 75209
(214) 357-0461
Contact: Department Head
Automobile dealership.

Eckerd Drugs
4409 Action St.
Garland, TX 75042
(214) 272-0411
Human Resource Manager: Bill Hofrichter
Large specialty store with pharmacy and photo finish services,
cosmetics, drugs, and general merchandise.

Foley's
1100 Main St.,
Houston, TX 77002
(713) 651-7038.

Contact store manager for hourly positions.
Contact: Houston headquarters for managerial positions
Department store chain.

Fox Photo
70 N. E. Loop 410, Suite 1100
San Antonio, TX 78216.
Contact photo lab manager for hourly positions.
Contact San Antonio headquarters for managerial positions
Photo lab chain.

Friendly Chevrolet/Geo
5601 Lemmon Ave.
Dallas, TX 75209
(214) 526-8811
Contact: Department Head
Automobile dealership.

Hillard, Charlie
5000 Bryant Irvin
Fort Worth, TX 76132
(817) 730-5000
Contact: Department Head
Automobile dealership.

Home Interiors & Gifts
4550 Spring Valley Rd.
Dallas, TX 75244
(214) 386-1000
Personnel Manager: George Burton
Decorative accessories sold through home demonstrations.

Horchow Collection
5800 E. Campus Circle Dr., Suite 101
Irvin, TX 75063
(214) 714-3100
Contact: Personnel Department
Mail order clothing and furniture.

K-Mart Corp.
199 Planters Rd.
Sunnyvale, TX 75182
Metro (214) 226-0295
Contact: Personnel Department
General discount merchandiser.

Macy's
13375 Noel Rd.
Dallas, TX 75240
(214) 851-3300
Contact: Personnel Department
General retail store.

Mary Kay Cosmetics
8787 Stemmons Frwy.
Dallas, TX 75247
(214) 630-8787
Contact: Personnel Department
International headquarters for cosmetics sold through home demonstrations.

McDavid, David, Pontiac
3700 W. Airport Frwy.
Irving, TX 75062
(214) 790-6000
Contact: Department Head
Automobile dealership.

Mervyn's Department Stores
Mervyn's Distribution Center
1600 E. Plano Pkwy.
Plano, TX 75074
(214) 578-9536
Contact: Personnel Department
Softgoods department store.

Michaels/MJ Designs
9015 Sterling St.
Irving, TX 75063
(214) 929-8595
Personnel Director: Bolinda Neal
Arts, crafts, and framing store.

Miller Business Systems
2230 Avenue J
Arlington, TX 76006-5866
Metro (817) 640-1541
Contact: Human Resources Department
Office supplies and furniture.

Montgomery Ward & Co.
2700 E. Pioneer Pkwy.
Arlington, TX 76010
(817) 633-1100
Contact: Personnel Department
National mass market retail chain.

Neiman Marcus
1618 Main St.
Dallas, TX 75201
(214) 741-6911
Contact: Executive Personnel Departments
Major national chain with several area locations.

Parra, Frank, Chevrolet
1000 E. Airport Frwy.
Irving, TX 75062
(214) 721-4300
Contact: Department Head
Automobile dealership.

Pearle Vision
2534 Royal Lane
Dallas, TX 75229
(214) 277-5000
Contact: Deborah Flaherty for management positions; contact
Belinda Summers for hourly positions
Retail eyewear.

Penney, J. C., Co.
6501 Legacy Drive
Plano, TX 75024
(214) 431-1000
Contact: Personnel Department
National headquarters for retail merchandise sales and service
stores, with several area locations.

Pier 1 Imports
P.O. Box 961020
Fort Worth, TX 76161-0020
(817) 878-8000
Vice President of Human Resources: Ronni Rosen
Imported merchandise with several area stores.

Radio Shack
500 One Tandy Center
Fort Worth, TX 76102
(817) 390-3011
V.P. of Human Resources: George Berger
National headquarters for retailer of electronic equipment and
computers.

Sears, Roebuck & Co.
13131 Preston Rd.
Dallas, TX 75240
(214) 458-3415
Contact: Jenny Kerr or call the "Job Machine" at (214) 716-7919.
One of world's largest retailers and catalog merchandisers, with
subsidiaries in insurance and real estate. Several area locations.

Sherwin-Williams Co.
10440 E. Northwest Hwy.
Dallas, TX 75238
(214) 553-2979
Personnel Director: Con Barthell
Retail and wholesale paint, wallpaper, and floor covering.

Sound Warehouse
10911 Petal St.
Dallas, TX 75238
(214) 343-4700
Contact: Department Head
One of area's largest record and tape chains.

Sunbelt Nursery Group
6500 West Frwy., Suite 600
Fort Worth, TX 76116
(817) 738-8111
Personnel Director: Becky Hendrick
Retail garden centers and nurseries.

Tandycrafts
1400 Everman Pkwy.
Fort Worth, TX 76140
(817) 551-9600
Contact: Patsy Brantley
Home office for leather crafts, Christian books, and cargo furniture.

Target Stores
555 Republic Dr., Suite 500
Plano, TX 75074
(214) 422-7400
Regional Personnel Director: Dave Biron
Discount stores.

Taylors Bookstores
Corporate Office
10495 Olympic Dr., Suite 100
Dallas, TX 75220
(214) 357-1700
Vice President of Operations: Howard Maher
Large bookstore with several area locations.

Tom Thumb Food and Pharmacy
General Offices
14303 Inwood Rd.
Dallas, TX 75244
(214) 661-9700
Contact: Marlyn Smith for management positions.
Contact Human Resources Department for warehouse and office positions
Drug store and grocery chain.

Tuesday Morning
14621 Inwood Rd.
Dallas, TX 75244
(214) 387-3562

Human resources: Debra Steenrod
Discount linens, towels, and other household merchandise.

Vandergriff Chevrolet Co.
901 E. Division St.
Arlington, TX 76011
Metro (817) 860-7171
President: Victor Vandergriff
Automobile dealership.

Waldenbooks
1084 Prestonwood Town Center
5301 Belt Line Rd.
Dallas, TX 75240
Contact: individual store manager
National bookstore chain.

Wilson, James K.
Service Center
2503 Butler St.
Dallas, TX 75235
(214) 905-9945
Contact: Store Manager or corporate office at 222 Lasalle St.,
15th Floor, Chicago, IL 60601
Men's and women's clothing store chain.

Zale Corp.
Employment Center: P.O. Box 152777
Irving, TX 75015-2777
(214) 580-4172
Staffing Manager: Joan Shaw
Retail jewelry chain.

Stock Brokers/Investment Bankers

You may also want to look at the sections on **Accounting** and **Banking**.

For information about finance and related fields, you can contact:

PROFESSIONAL ORGANIZATIONS:

Financial Analysts Federation
5 Boar's Head Lane
P.O. Box 3668
Charlottesville, VA 22903
(804) 977-6600

International Association for Financial Planning
2 Concourse Pkwy., Suite 800
Atlanta, GA 30328
(404) 395-1605

Investment Counsel Association of America
20 Exchange Pl.
New York, NY 10005
(212) 344-0999

National Association of Securities Dealers
1750 K St., NW
Washington, DC 20006
(202) 728-8000

National Venture Capital Association
1655 N. Fort Myer Dr., #700
Arlington, VA 22209
(703) 351-5267

Securities Industry Association
120 Broadway
New York, NY 10271
(212) 608-1500

Security Traders Association
1 World Trade Center, #4511
New York, NY 10048
(212) 524-0484

PROFESSIONAL PUBLICATIONS:

Business Credit
CFO
Commodity Perspective

Corporate Finance
Dun's Business Month
Finance
Financial Analysts Journal
Financial Executive
Financial World
Institutional Investor
Investment Dealers Digest
Market Chronicle
Mergers & Acquisitions
Registered Representative
Securities Week
Traders Magazine
Wall St. Transcript

DIRECTORIES:

Corporate Finance Sourcebook (National Register, Wilmette, IL)
Directory of Registered Investment Advisors (Money Market
    Directories, Charlottesville, VA)
ERISA Red Book of Pension Funds (Duns Marketing Services,
    Mountain Lakes, NJ)
F.A.F. Membership Directory (Financial Analysts Federation,
    Charlottesville, VA)
Investment & Securities Directory (American Business Directo-
    ries, Omaha, NE)
Money Market Directory (Money Market Directories, Inc.,
    Charlottesville, VA)
Securities Dealers of North America (Standard and Poor's, New
    York, NY)
S.I.A. Yearbook (Securities Industry Association, New York, NY)
S.T.A. Traders Annual (Securities Traders Association, New
    York, NY)
Who's Who in the Securities Industry (Economist Publishing Co.,
    New York, NY)

EMPLOYERS:

Bear, Stearns & Co.
1601 Elm St., 40th Floor
Dallas, TX 75201
(214) 754-8300
Office Manager: Paula Castonguay

Cullum & Sandow
1601 Elm St., Suite 4343
Dallas, TX 75201
(214) 754-0111
CEO: Richard Sandow

Dean Witter Reynolds
2300 Lincoln Plaza
500 N. Akard St.
Dallas, TX 75201
(214) 740-2000
Assistant Branch Manager: Jolie Caldwell

Donaldson, Lufkin & Jenrette Securities Corp.
2200 Ross Ave., Suite 2900
Dallas, TX 75201
(214) 979-4000
Contact: Branch Manager Rhodes Bobbitt for sales positions and
Office Manager Helen Cohn for support staff positions

Edwards, A.G., & Sons
1201 Main St., Suite 100
Dallas, TX 75202-3995
(214) 741-7911
Assistant Branch Manager: Elizabeth Rivera

Eppler, Guerin & Turner
1445 Ross Ave., Suite 2300
Dallas, TX 75202
(214) 880-9000
Personnel Director: Laura Mellor

First Southwest Co.
1700 Pacific Ave., Suite 500
Dallas, TX 75201
(214) 953-4000
Executive Vice President: Daniel Son

IDS Financial Services
801 E. Campbell Rd., Suite 150
Richardson, TX 75081
(214) 437-9311
Contact: Leann Dickson

Paine Webber
Thanksgiving Square
1601 Elm St., Suite 2000
Dallas, TX 75201
(214) 978-6000
Branch Manager

Prudential Securities
10440 N. Central Expwy., Suite 1600
Dallas, TX 75231
(214) 373-2700
Branch Manager: Michael McClain

Rauscher Pierce Refsnes
Plaza of the Americas, Suite 2500
RPR North Tower, L.B. 331
Dallas, TX 75201
(214) 978-0111
Employment Specialist: Kerry Shaughnessy

Rotan Mosle
1201 Elm St., Suite 2600
Dallas, TX 75270
(214) 651-6000
Administrative Manager: Pat Rawson

Smith, Barney, Shearson
1999 Bryan St., Suite 2600
Dallas, TX 75201
(214) 979-7000
Operations Manager: Joann Wilkison

Southwest Securities
1201 Elm St., Suite 4300
Dallas, TX 75270
(214) 651-1800
Contact: Personnel Administrator

Vest, H.D., Financial Services
433 E. Las Colinas Blvd., 3rd Floor
Irving, TX 75039
(214) 556-1651
Contact: Department Head

Weber Investment Corporation
1525 Elm St., Suite 1800
Dallas, TX 75201
(214) 954-9472
President: Terry Rader

Telecommunications

Also check sections on **Computers** and **Electronics**.

To learn more about the telecommunications field, you can contact:

PROFESSIONAL ORGANIZATIONS:

Association of Local Telecommunications Services
1200 19 th St.
Washington, DC 20036
(202) 833-1306

Competitive Telecommunications Association
1140 Connecticut Ave., NW
Washington, DC 20036
(202) 296-6650

Electronics Industry Association
2001 Pennsylvania Ave., NW
Washington, DC 20006
(202) 457-4900

Institute of Electrical & Electronics Engineers (IEEE)
345 W. 47th St.
New York, NY 10017
(212) 705-7900

National Association of Telecommunications Officers & Advisors
C/O National League of Cities
1301 Pennsylvania Ave., NW
Washington, DC 20004
(202) 626-3160

North American Telecommunications Association
2000 M St., NW
Washington, DC 20036
(202) 296-9800

Telecommunications Association
701 N. Haven Ave.
Ontario, CA 91764
(909) 945-1122

Telecommunications Industry Association
2001 Pennsylvania Ave., NW
Washington, DC 20006
(202) 457-4912

PROFESSIONAL PUBLICATIONS:

Communications Week
Data Pro Reports on Telecommunications
Electronics News
New Connections
Technology Review
Telecommunications
Telecommunications Reports
Telecommunications Week
Telephony

DIRECTORIES:

American Electronics Association Directory (American Electronics Association, Santa Clara, CA)
Corporate Technology Directory (Corporate Technology Association, Washington, DC)
Directory & Buyers Guide (Telephony, Chicago, IL)
EIA Trade Directory & Membership Guide (Electronics Industry Association, Washington, DC)
Guide to High Technology Companies (Corporate Technology Information Services, Woburn, MA)
Telecommunications Sourcebook (North American Telecommunications Association, Washington, DC)
Who's Who in Electronics (Harris Publications, Twinsburg, OH)

EMPLOYERS:

ADC Teling Development Center
1651 N. Glenville Ave.
Richardson, TX 75081
(214) 680-6900
Financial Administration: Regina Smith
Manufactures high-speed digital switches for telecommunications systems.

BNR
1150 Arapaho Rd.
Richardson, TX 75081
(214) 997-4500
Contact: Staffing Department
Designs digital switching systems.

DSC
1000 Coit Rd.
Plano, TX 75075
(214) 519-3000
Contact: Personnel Department
Designs, manufactures, installs, and repairs telecommunications and switching systems.

Electrospace Systems
1301 E. Collins Blvd.
Richardson, TX 75083
(214) 470-2000
Contact: Personnel Department
Designs, manufactures, installs, and repairs telecommunications and switching systems.

Ericsson North America
730 International Pwky.
Richardson, TX 75081
(214) 669-9900
Human Resources Assistant: Sue Wallace
Manufactures telecommunications equipment.

Intervoice
17811 Waterview
Dallas, TX 75252
(214) 669-3988
Senior Personnel Administrator: Kathy Hackney
Manufactures voice automation systems.

NEC America
1555 W. Walnut Hill Lane
Irving, TX 75038
(214) 580-9100
Human Resources Manager: Linda Johnson
Manufactures telecommunications equipment.

Netcom
13719 Omega
Dallas, TX 75244
(214) 991-9677
Sales Manager: Eric Symula
Sells and services telecommunications and computer equipment.

Northern Telecom
2221 Lakeside Blvd.
Richardson, TX 75082
(214) 234-5300
Contact: Human Resources Department
Sales office for telecommunications company that offers a complete line of digital switching and transmissions systems.

Rockwell International Corp.
3200 E. Renner
Richardson, TX 75082
(214) 996-5434
Contact: Staffing Department
Manufactures electronics and communications systems for commercial and defense applications.

Rolm Co.
15303 Dallas Pkwy., Suite 1100
Dallas, TX 75248
(214) 980-0098
Contact: Personnel Department
Sells and services telecommunications equipment.

Travel/Transportation/Shipping

For information about the travel and shipping industries, contact the following organizations:

PROFESSIONAL ORGANIZATIONS:

American Society of Travel Agents
1101 King St.
Alexandria, VA 22314
(703) 739-2782

American Trucking Association
1200 Mill Rd.
Alexandria, VA 22314
(703) 838-0230

Association of American Railroads
50 F St., SW
Washington, DC 20024
(202) 554-8050

Association of Retail Travel Agents
1745 Jefferson Davis Hwy., Suite 300
Arlington, VA 22202
(703) 413-2222

Travel Industry Association of America
1133 21 St, NW
Lafayette Center
Washington, DC 20036
(202) 293-1433

U.S. Tour Operators Association
211 E. 51st St.
New York, NY 10022
(212) 944-5727

PROFESSIONAL PUBLICATIONS:

Air Travel Journal
ASTA Travel News

Fleet Owner
The Professional Broker
Tours & Resorts
Traffic Management
Travel Agent
Trux

DIRECTORIES:

Aviation Directory (E.A. Brennan Co., Garden Grove, CA)
Membership Directory (Aviation Distributors & Manufacturers
   Association, Philadelphia, PA)
Moody's Transportation Manual (Moody's Investor Service, New
   York, NY)
Travel Industry Personnel Directory (Fairchild Publications, New
   York, NY)
Worldwide Travel Information Contact Book (Gale Research,
   Detroit, MI)

EMPLOYERS:

ABF Freight System
6814 Harry Hines Blvd.
Dallas, TX 75235
(214) 350-8901
Contact: Personnel
Common freight carrier.

American Airlines
P.O. Box 619616
DFW airport, TX 75261
Metro (817) 963-1234
Contact: Personnel Department
Passenger and air freight services.

American Express Travel Co.
5080 Spectrum Dr., Suite 608 W
Dallas, TX 75248
(214) 991-8500
Personnel Supervisor: Lori Larson
Travel agency.

Amtrak, National Railway Passenger Corp.
400 S. Houston St.
Dallas, TX 75202
(214) 653-1101
Contact: Main office at 210 S. Canal St., Chicago, IL 60606
Passenger rail service.

Avis Rent A Car
1 W. N. International Pkwy.

Dallas/Fort Worth Airport, TX 75261
Metro (214) 574-4110
Operations Manager: Suzanne McCormack
Automobile rentals.

Budget Rent-A-Car Systems
3350 Boyington
Carrollton, TX 75006
(214) 404-7600
Contact: Personnel Department
Automobile and truck rentals.

Burlington Northern Railroad Co.
3000 Continental Plaza
777 Main St.
Fort Worth, TX 76102
(817) 878-2000
Contact: Mail resume to Human Resources Department
Freight transporter.

Carlson Travel Company
1112 E. Copeland Rd.
Arlington, TX 76011
Metro (817) 461-9551
Office Manager: Christy Zackery
Corporate travel services.

Central Freight Lines
5200 E. Loop 820 South
Fort Worth, TX 76119
(817) 478-8211
Contact: Assistant General Manager
Common freight carrier.

Cooper, Jack, Co.
2909 E. Abram St.
Arlington, TX 76010
Metro (817) 640-0829
Office Manager: Cheri Wilson
Automobile transporter.

Dallas/Fort Worth International Airport
Dallas/Fort Worth Airport, TX 75261
(214) 574-6031
Contact: Personnel Department
Major international airport.

DART
1401 Pacific
Dallas, TX 75202
(214) 749-3259

Contact: Personnel
Regional transportation authority.

Delta Air Lines
District Marketing Office
8700 N. Stemmons Frwy., Suite 212
Dallas, TX 75247
(214) 879-6000
Contact: Personnel or headquarters in Atlanta, GA, (404) 715-2501
Passenger and air freight services.

Frozen Food Express Industries
1145 Empire Central Place
Dallas, TX 75247
(214) 630-8090
Contact: Personnel Department
Transporter of general commodities sold in grocery, discount, and department stores.

Greyhound Lines
P.O. Box 660362
Dallas, TX 75266
(800) 231-2222
Contact: Recruiting Department
Regional division of a national bus line.

Hertz Rent A Car
8505 Freeport Pkwy., Suite 300
Irving, TX 75063
Metro (214) 453-0370
Employee Relations Manager: Robert Salmon
Automobile renting and leasing.

Kerrville Bus Company
710 E. Davis St.
Grand Prairie, TX 75050
(214) 263-0294
Transportation Supervisor: Ray Gardner
Chartered buses.

Southwest Airlines
2702 Love Field Dr.
Dallas, TX 75235
(214) 904-4803
Contact: Personnel Department
Headquarters for interstate airline.

State Taxicab Co.
3538 Singleton Blvd
Dallas, TX 75212
(214) 630-9595

Contact: Department Head
Taxi company.

Sunbelt Motivation & Travel
909 E. Las Colinas Blvd., Suite 200
Irving, TX 75039
(214) 401-0210
Personnel Manager: D'ann Hardy
Travel service.

T-Fort Worth Transportation Authority
2304 Pine St.
Fort Worth, TX 76102
(817) 871-6220
Personnel Supervisor: Ruth Lyon
Fort Worth's public transportation service.

TNT Bestway
11430 Newkirk
Dallas, TX 75229
(214) 247-2426
Contact: Terminal Manager
Common freight carrier.

Interested in becoming a flight attendant?

Kim Rouse from the "People" Department at **Southwest Airlines** says that exciting opportunities are available at Southwest with the competition being very intense. "Southwest flight attendants ensure that customers' safety and comfort are first and foremost, while also making flights more fun and memorable."

Flight attendant requirements include proper education, good people skills, availability to relocate, and an ability to work as a team player, as well as other listed criteria. Training includes a 5-6 week training period, then assignment to one of Southwest's bases in Dallas, Houston, or Phoenix.

The Southwest job hotline is **(214) 904-4803**

Utilities

For additional information about public utilities you can contact:

American Public Gas Association
11094 D Suite 102 Lee Hwy
Fairfax, VA 22030
(703) 352-3890

American Public Power Association
2301 M St., NW
Washington, DC 20037
(202) 467-2900

United States Telephone Association
900 19th St., NW
Washington, DC 20006
(202) 835-3100

PROFESSIONAL PUBLICATIONS:

Electric Light & Power
Electrical World
Powerline
Public Power
Public Utilities
Telephone Engineering & Management

DIRECTORIES:

APGA Directory of Municipal Gas Systems (Amer. Public Gas Assoc., Vienna, VA)
Brown's Directory of North American & International Gas Companies (Edgel Communications, Cleveland, OH)
Electrical World Directory of Electrical Utilities (McGraw-Hill, New York, NY)
Moody's Public Utility Manual (Moody's Investor Service, New York, NY)

EMPLOYERS:

AT&T
5501 LBJ Frwy., 10th Floor
Dallas, TX 75240
(214) 308-5542
Supplier of communication
services and equipment.

AT&T
2501 Parkview Dr., Suite 200
Fort Worth, TX 76102
(817) 870-4420
Contact: Dallas Office
Supplier of communication
services and equipment.

GTE Directories Corp.
2200 W. Airfield Dr.
D/FW International Airport,
TX 75261
(214) 453-7000
Telephone directories and
listings.

GTE Corp.
600 Hidden Ridge
Irving, TX 75038
Metro (214) 718-5000
Contact: Human Resources
National headquarters.

Lone Star Gas Co.
Dallas Office
1817 Wood St., Room 105 W
Dallas, TX 75201
(214) 741-3711
Contact: Senior Employment
Representative Scott Brock
for managerial positions and
Employment Representative
Pam Hixon for support
positions
Headquarters for one of the
largest natural gas companies.

Lone Star Gas Go.
Fort Worth Office
908 Monroe St.
Fort Worth, TX 76102
(817) 336-8381
Personnel Manager: H.
Shukers

Southwestern Bell Tele-phone
Dallas Office
308 S. Akard St., Room 101
Dallas, TX 75202
(214) 461-3174
Contact: Employment Office

Southwestern Bell Telephone
Fort Worth Office
1116 Houston St., Room 105
Fort Worth, TX 76102
(817) 884-0408
Contact: Employment Office

Southwestern Electric Service
1717 Main St., Suite 3300
Dallas, TX 75201
(903) 741-3125
Contact: Personnel Office in
Jacksonville, TX
(214) 586-9851

Texas-New Mexico Power
4100 International Plaza
820 Hulen Tower II
Fort Worth, TX 76109
(817) 731-0099
Employment Coordinator:
Susan Overcash
Electrical utility.

Tri-County Electric Cooperative
600 Northwest Pkwy.
Azle, TX 76020
(817) 444-3201
Office Manager: Tom Weems
Headquarters for electric co-op.

TU Electric
115 W. Seventh St.
Fort Worth, TX 76102
(817) 336-9411
Contact: Dallas Office
Electric service.

TU Electric
400 N. Olive Rd.
Dallas, TX 75201
(214) 812-8633
Contact: Employment Office
Electric service.

US Sprint Communications
1520 E. Rochelle Blvd.
Irving, TX 75039
(214) 506-1000
Staffing Manager: Todd
Young
Long distance carrier.

Employers Index

A

ABB Impel Corp, 262
Abbott Laboratories, 235
ABF Freight System, 392
Ace Hardware Stores, 376
ADC Teling Development Center, 389
Addison, Town of, 291
Adolphus Hotel, 310
Adweek/Southwest, 344
Aerobics Activity Center, 367
Aerospace Optics, 187
Aerospace Technologies, 187
Aetna Life & Casualty, 323
Agriculture Department, 297
AIC Analysts Corp., 222
Airborn Connectors, 251
Akin, Gump, Strauss, Hauer & Feld, 329
AKM Distributing Co., 235
Albertson's, 281
Alcon Laboratories, 235
Alexander & Alexander of Texas, 323
Alexander Consulting Group, 335
All Saints Episcopal Hospital, 302
All Saints Episcopal School, 241
Alliance Health Providers, 302
Allianz Life Insurance Co. of North America, 323
Allied Printing Co., 359
Allstate Insurance Co., 323
Amber University, 246
Amdahl Corp., 226
American Airlines, 392
American Airlines Employees Federal Credit Union, 204
American Cancer Society, 314, 315
American Cyanamid Co., 218
American Eurocopter, 187
American Excelsior Co., 356
American Express Travel Co., 392
American Federal Bank, 204
American Heart Association, 315
American Life & Accident Insurance Co., 323
American Medical Electronics, 251
American Permanent Ware Co., 337
American Produce & Vegetable Co., 282
American Red Cross, 315
American Signature Graphics, 360
Amon Carter Museum, 354
Amstrad, 226
Amtrak, 392

Anchor Crane & Hoist Co., 349
Anchor Press, 360
Andersen, Arthur, & Co., 175
Anderson Fischel Thompson, 180
APAC-Texas, 231
Apple Computers, 226
Appleton, D., Co., 335
Arch Petroleum Co., 255
Arendale, Ted, Ford, 377
Arjo Engineers, 262
Arlington, City of, 291
Arlington Memorial Hospital, 302
Arlington School District, 238
Arlington Star Telegram, 344
Army Air Force Exchange Service, 377
Army Corps of Engineers, 297
Arrow Industries, 282, 357
Arter, Hadden, Johnson and Bromberg, 329
Arthritis Foundation, 315
Ashland Chemical, 219
Associated Air Center, 187
Associated Press, 344
Associates Insurance Group, 323
Association for Retarded Citizens, 315
AT&T, 396
AT&T Information Systems, 251
Atlantic Richfield Company, 255
Atlas Match Corp., 337
Atlas Powder Co., 219
Aura of Fort Worth, 344
Austin Industries, 231
Auto Club Insurance Agency, 324
Avis Rent A Car, 392
AVW Audio Visual, 277
Aztec Manufacturing Co., 255

B

B Dalton Bookseller, 377
Bailey Vaught Robertson & Co., 175
Baker Hughes Mining Tools, 337
Balch Springs, City of, 291
Bank of America, 204
Bank of Commerce, 204
Bank of North Texas, 205
Bank One Texas, 205
Barber's Book Stores, 377
Barker & Bratton Steel, 349
Barlow & Garsek, 329
Bates Container, 357
Baylor College of Dentistry, 246

M

N

Employers Index

North Texas Healthcare Network, 306
North Texas Steel Co., 351
Northeast Community Hospital, 305
Northern Telecom, 390
NorthPark National Bank, 206
NRM and Edisto Resources, 258

O

Oak Hill Academy, 244
Oakridge School, 244
Old City Park, 355
Olmsted-Kirk Paper Co., 358
Omega Audio & Productions, 278
OmniPlan, 198
ORYX Energy Co., 258
Overhead Door Corp., 340
Overton Bank & Trust, 206
Owens Country Sausage, 285
Owens Highland Academy, 244

P

Pacific Enterprises, 258
Packaging Corp. of America, 358
Page Southerland Page, 198
Paine Webber, 386
Pancho's Mexican Buffet, 373
Pantego Christian Academy, 244
Paragon Group, 365
Park Cities News, 347
Park Cities People, 347
Parker/Croston Partnership, 198
Parkland Memorial Hospital, 306
Parks & Wildlife, 296
Parra, Frank, Chevrolet, 381
Pearle Vision, 381
Peerless Manufacturing Co., 259
Penney, J. C., Co., 381
Penny, J.C., Life Insurance, 326
Pepsi-Cola Bottling Group, 285
Personnel Management, Office of, 299
Petro Hunt Corp., 259
Philadelphia Life Insurance Co., 326
Pier 1 Imports, 381
Pilgrim's Pride Corp., 285
Pillowtex Corp., 288
Pizza Hut, 373
Pizza Inn, 373
Planned Behavioral Health Care, 306
Plano, City of, 294
Plano Daily Star-Courier, 347
Plano School District, 241
Plastics Manufacturing Co., 220
Plaza of the Americas Hotel, 312

Plumber, Allen & Associates, 266
Plummer, Allen, & Associates, 275
Point Communications, 183
Poly-America, 220
Postal Service, 299
PR/Texas, 183
Premier Club, 368
Prentice Hall School Division, 209
Prentiss Properties, 365
Presbyterian Hospital of Dallas, 306
President's Health and Racquetball Clubs, 369
Prestonwood Country Club, 369
Price Waterhouse, 177
Princeton Packaging, 358
Printing Center of Texas, 361
ProAmerica Managed Care, 306
Progressive, 189
Prophecy Corp., 193
Provider Networks of America, 306
PruCare of North Texas, 306
Prudential Securities, 386
Prufrock Restaurants, 373
Public Health, 296
Public Safety, 296
Publishers Equipment Corp., 341
Pulido Associates, 374
Pulte Home Corp. of Texas, 365
Puskar Gibbon Chapin, 183
Putoma Corp., 189
PVI Industries, 341

Q

Quaker Oats Co., 285
Quest Medical, 236

R

R. H. R. International Company, 336
R.H.D. Memorial Medical Center, 306
Radio Shack, 381
Radio Stations, 211-217
Radisson Suite Hotel, 312
Rady and Associates, 266
Rainbow Baking Co., 285
Rauscher Pierce Refsnes, 387
RCM Corp., 336
Recognition Equipment, 252
Redman Industries, 233, 341
Rees Associates, 199
Regian Associates, 183
Rehabilitation Commission, 296
Republic Insurance, 326
Resistol Hats, 194
Retail Graphics Printing Co., 361

405

General Index

W,Y

Want Ads, 67-68, 89, 90
"Watering Holes" for Networking, 107
Wholesalers: *see Retailers/
Wholesalers*

Women:
  career resources, 26-27, 112-115,
  127
  resource books for, 15
Youth Employment Resources, 185,
  374